Robert DiYanni is Director of International Services for The College Board. Dr. DiYanni, who holds a B.A. from Rutgers University and a Ph.D. from the City University of New York, has taught English and Humanities at a variety of institutions, including NYU, CUNY, and Harvard. An Adjunct Professor of English and Humanities at New York University, he has written and edited more than thirty-five books, mostly for college students of writing, literature, and humanities.

Fifty Great Essays

Fifty Great Essays

Third Edition

Edited by

Robert DiYanni
New York University

PENGUIN ACADEMICS

New York   San Francisco   Boston
London   Toronto   Sydney   Tokyo   Singapore   Madrid
Mexico City   Munich   Paris   Cape Town   Hong Kong   Montreal

Senior Vice President and Publisher: Joseph Opiela
Senior Sponsoring Editor: Virginia L. Blanford
Senior Marketing Manager: Sandra McGuire
Production Manager: Savoula Amanatidis
Project Coordination and Text Design: Elm Street Publishing Services, Inc.
Electronic Page Makeup: Integra Software Services, Pvt. Ltd.
Cover Design Manager: Wendy Ann Fredericks
Cover Photo: © Christian J. Matuschek / www.foto-lounge.de
Manufacturing Buyer: Roy Pickering, Jr.
Printer and Binder: R. R. Donnelley and Sons Company—Harrisonburg
Cover Printer: Phoenix Color Corporation

For permission to use copyrighted material, grateful acknowledgment is made to the
copyright holders on pp. 385–388, which are hereby made part of this copyright page.

Library of Congress Cataloging-in-Publication Data
Fifty great essays / edited by Robert DiYanni.—3rd ed.
    p. cm. — (Penguin academics)
  Includes index.
  ISBN 0-205-53353-1 (alk. paper)
  1. College readers. 2. English language—Rhetoric—Problems, exercises, etc.
 3. Report writing—Problems, exercises, etc. 4. Essays. I. Title: 50 great essays.
II. DiYanni, Robert III. Series.

  PE1417.O56 2008
  808'.0427—dc22

Please visit our website at www.ablongman.com.

For more information about the Penguin Academics series, please contact us by mail
at Longman Publishers, attn. Marketing Department, 1185 Avenue of the Americas
25th Floor, New York, NY 10036, or by e-mail at www.ablongman.com.

ISBN-10: 0-205-53353-1
ISBN-13: 978-0-205-53353-4

  4 5 6 7 8 9 10—DOH—10 09

For Eric Wimmers
Cherished Colleague and Friend

Contents

Preface xiii

INTRODUCTION: READING AND WRITING *1*

GLORIA ANZALDÚA,
  How to Tame a Wild Tongue 31

FRANCIS BACON,
  Of Studies 44

DAVE BARRY,
  Road Warrior 47

ROLAND BARTHES,
  Toys 51

SUSAN BROWNMILLER,
  Femininity 54

JUDITH ORTIZ COFER,
  Casa: A Partial Remembrance of a Puerto Rican Childhood 60

K. C. COLE,
  Calculated Risks 67

BERNARD COOPER,
  Burl's 77

CHARLES DARWIN,
  Natural Selection 88

JOAN DIDION,
  Marrying Absurd 101

ANNIE DILLARD,
  Living Like Weasels 106

FREDERICK DOUGLASS,
   Learning to Read and Write   112

BRIAN DOYLE,
   Joyas Voladoras   119

W. E. B. DUBOIS,
   Of Our Spiritual Striving   123

GRETEL EHRLICH,
   About Men   132

RALPH ELLISON,
   Living with Music   136

RICHARD FEYNMAN,
   The Value of Science   146

BENJAMIN FRANKLIN,
   Arriving at Perfection   154

JOHN LEWIS GADDIS,
   The Landscape of History   159

ELLEN GOODMAN,
   The Company Man   173

MARY GORDON,
   More than Just a Shrine—Ellis Island   176

WILLIAM HAZLITT,
   On the Pleasure of Hating   182

MICHAEL HOGAN,
   The Colonel   193

LANGSTON HUGHES,
   Salvation   199

PICO IYER,
   Nowhere Man   203

MARTIN LUTHER KING, JR.,
   Letter from Birmingham Jail   207

MAXINE HONG KINGSTON,
   On Discovery   224

CHARLES LAMB,
    A Bachelor's Complaint   227

CHANG-RAE LEE,
    Coming Home Again   234

ABRAHAM LINCOLN,
    The Gettysburg Address   245

NICCOLÒ MACHIAVELLI,
    The Morals of the Prince   247

JAMES MCBRIDE,
    Shul   256

N. SCOTT MOMADAY,
    The Way to Rainy Mountain   272

MICHEL DE MONTAIGNE,
    Of Smells   279

NUALA O'FAOLAIN,
    Are You Somebody?   282

GEORGE ORWELL,
    Shooting an Elephant   286

CYNTHIA OZICK,
    The Din in the Head   294

NEIL POSTMAN,
    The Medium Is the Metaphor   299

SCOTT RUSSELL SANDERS,
    Under the Influence   311

SUSAN SONTAG,
    A Woman's Beauty: Put-Down or Power Source?   325

ELIZABETH CADY STANTON,
    Declaration of Sentiments and Resolutions   329

BRENT STAPLES,
    Just Walk on By: Black Men and Public Space   333

JONATHAN SWIFT,
    A Modest Proposal   338

AMY TAN,
  Mother Tongue   347

HENRY DAVID THOREAU,
  Why I Went to the Woods   354

JAMES THURBER,
  University Days   361

SOJOURNER TRUTH,
  And Ain't I a Woman?   368

E. B. WHITE,
  Once More to the Lake   370

MARY WOLLSTONECRAFT,
  A Vindication of the Rights of Woman   377

VIRGINIA WOOLF,
  The Death of the Moth   381

Credits   385

Index   389

Preface

Fifty Great Essays is one volume of a three-book series designed to provide college students and teachers with an outstanding collection of essays for use in university writing courses. The other volumes are *One Hundred Great Essays* and *Twenty-Five Great Essays*. All three volumes are based upon the conviction that reading and writing are reciprocal acts that should be married rather than divorced. Because reading and writing stimulate and reinforce one another, it is best that they be allied rather than separated. In learning to read and respond critically both to their own writing and to the writing of others, students mature as writers themselves.

Fifty Great Essays offers a compendium of the best essays written during the past four hundred years. Readers will find here essays by the great early practitioners of the genre, Montaigne and Bacon, as well as numerous examples from the centuries that follow, both classic and contemporary. Taken together, the essayists whose work is anthologized here offer an abundance of nonfiction that takes the form of autobiographical and polemical essays, observations and speculations, reminiscences and sketches, meditations and expostulations, celebrations and attacks. Overall, the selections balance and blend the flamboyant and innovative with the restrained and classically lucid.

Each of the essays in *Fifty Great Essays* can be considered "great," but is not necessarily great in the same way. Montaigne's greatness as an essayist is not Franklin's, nor is Bacon's essay writing matched equivalently by Swift's. And Orwell's greatness, inspired by a political animus, differs dramatically from that of E. B. White, whose inspiration and emphasis derive less from grand social issues than from personal observation and experience. Yet however much these essayists and essays differ, two aspects of greatness they share are readability and teachability. Whether classic, modern, or contemporary, and whatever their styles, subjects, and rhetorical strategies, these fifty essays are worth reading and teaching. They have served students and teachers of reading and writing well for many years.

The second edition of *Fifty Great Essays* deviates only slightly from the first two editions. The introduction to reading and writing essays and the format for the collection of great essays remain the same. The changes occur in the anthology of essays, with thirteen essays from the second edition being replaced by thirteen new selections. The new essays are provided with the same apparatus—author biography, essay headnote, and questions—just as the selections carried over from the second edition.

This collection should be of great value to university instructors who are teaching writing courses both introductory and advanced. They will find here an abundance of outstanding writing to serve as models for their students–models of style and structure, models of thought and feeling expressed in, with, and through carefully wrought language.

Students will find in this valuable collection a source of ideas and models for their own writing. They will also discover here writers who will serve as inspiration and influence as they develop their own styles and voices. In studying these essays as models of good writing, students will profit from analyzing not so much what these writers say, but as how they say what they do.

Writers, too, can benefit from reading the essays collected here and studying the craftsmanship they embody. Montaigne's ease and elegance, and his quirky individuality, while not easily imitated, provide an example of how the familiar material of everyday life can be artfully blended with the exploration of ideas. Bacon's pithy prose exemplifies ideas expressed with aphoristic acuteness. And while these early stars of the constellation of essayists may shine more brightly than others, writers who read with care the contemporary pieces collected here will learn new tricks of the trade and discover unexpected surprises and pleasures.

The heart and soul of *Fifty Great Essays* are fifty outstanding essays that span seven centuries. The essays provide a rich sampling of styles and voices across a wide spectrum of topics. They range in length and complexity—some more accessible, others more challenging—all worth reading. These fifty essays provide excellent opportunities for readers to meet new writers and to become reacquainted with writers and essays they already know. General readers—both those who have completed their formal education and those still in college—will find in these excellent essays promises and provocations, ideas to respond to and wrestle with, and sometimes argue against.

The Introduction to *Fifty Great Essays* provides an historical overview of the essay from antiquity to the present. It traces developments in the ways writers used essays to entertain readers as well as to inform and persuade them, and it describes the wide range of interests that writers of essays have pursued over the centuries. The Introduction also includes discussion of various types of essays and the pleasures that readers find in them.

Guidelines for reading essays are identified and exemplified with a close reading of a contemporary essay—Annie Dillard's "Living Like Weasels." Readers are provided with a series of guiding questions, commentary about the essay's style and voice, as well as its structure and ideas. The guidelines for reading essays are supplemented by guidelines for writing them. A discussion of the qualities of good writing is complemented by an approach to the writing process, which includes consideration of three major phases or stages—planning, drafting, and revising.

In addition to a set of general essay writing guidelines, the Introduction provides an approach to writing about reading, with a sample from the text of Susan Sontag's essay "A Woman's Beauty: Put-Down or Power Source?" The approach to writing about Sontag's essay takes the form of strategies for blending critical reading and writing, including annotating, freewriting, using a double-column notebook, and writing a summary. A further set of guidelines linking reading with writing focuses on observing details, making connections, drawing inferences, and formulating an interpretation. Throughout the discussion of writing and the sample demonstration, the emphasis is on analysis, reflection, and deliberation—on considering what the essayist is saying, what the reader thinks of it, and why.

Students should be interested in the Introduction's advice about how to read essays critically and thoughtfully. Other readers may be interested in the historical overview of the essay's development. And all readers can practice their reading skills by reading Susan Sontag's essay "A Woman's Beauty: Put-Down or Power Source?" along with the commentary that explains and explores the writer's ideas.

Each essay in *Fifty Great Essays* is preceded by a headnote, which includes a biographical sketch along with an overview of the essay's key ideas. The biographical information provides context, while the commentary provides a starting point for consideration of the writer's ideas and values. A brief set of questions for thinking and writing follows each essay. All in all, *Fifty Great Essays* should provide readers with many hours of reading pleasure and numerous ideas and models for writing.

Patient and persistent work with *Fifty Great Essays* in the classroom and out will help users understand the qualities of good writing and discover ways to emulate it. With the guided practice in critical reading and essay writing that *Fifty Great Essays* provides, students will increase both their competence and their confidence as perceptive readers and as cogent and able writers. Through repeated acts of attention to their own writing and to the writing of others, students can be expected to acquire a sense of the original meaning of "essay": a foray into thought, an attempt to discover an idea, work out its implications, and express it with distinctiveness. Readers and users of *Fifty Great Essays* should come to see the essay as a way of enriching their experience and their thinking while discovering effective ways to share them with others.

ROBERT DiYANNI
New York University

Fifty Great
Essays

Introduction:
Reading and
Writing Essays

History and Context

The essay has a long and distinguished history. Its roots go back to Greco-Roman antiquity. Forerunners of the essay include the Greek writer Plutarch (46–120), whose *Parallel Lives* of noble Greeks and Romans influenced the art of biography, and who also wrote essays in his *Moralia*. The early Roman writer Seneca, a philosopher, dramatist, and orator, also wrote essays in the grand manner of classical oratory, on topics that include "Asthma" and "Noise." These two early western writers of essays are complemented by a pair of Japanese writers: Sei Shonagon, a court lady who lived and wrote in the tenth century, and Yoshida Kenko (1283–1350), a poet and Buddhist monk, whose brief, fragmentary essays echo the quick brushstrokes of Zen painting.

In one sense, the modern essay begins with Michel de Montaigne in France and with Francis Bacon in England. Both writers published books of essays at the end of the sixteenth century. Montaigne's first two books of essays came out together in 1580 and Bacon's first collection in 1597. Each followed with additional volumes, Montaigne in 1588, Bacon in 1612 and 1625. With each later volume, both writers revised and expanded essays previously published in the earlier volumes as well as adding new ones. Both writers also wrote longer and more elaborate essays from one collection to the next.

Generally recognized as the father of the essay, Michel de Montaigne called his works "essais," French for attempts. In his essays, Montaigne explored his thinking on a wide variety of subjects, including virtue and vice, customs and behavior, children and cannibals. Although Montaigne's first essays began as reflections about his reading and made liberal use of quoted passages, his later essays relied much less on external sources for impetus and inspiration.

The power of Montaigne's essays derives largely from their personal tone, their improvisatory nature, and their display of an energetic and inquiring mind. In his essays, Montaigne talks about himself and the world as he experienced it. He repeatedly tests his opinions and presents an encyclopedia of information that sets him thinking. Amidst an essay's varied details, Montaigne reveals himself, telling us what he likes, thinks, and believes. The openness and flexibility of his essay form make its direction unpredictable, its argument arranged less as a logical structure than as a meandering exploration of its subject. But what is most revealing about Montaigne's essays is that they reveal his mind in the act of thinking. The self-revelatory circling around his subject constitutes the essential subject of the essays. Ironically, in reading him we learn not only about Montaigne but about ourselves.

Another Renaissance writer credited with an influential role in the development of the essay is Francis Bacon—statesman, philosopher, scientist, and essayist. Unlike Montaigne, who retired from active political life early to read, reflect, and write in his private library tower, Bacon remained politically active and intellectually prominent until the last few years of his life. His life and work exhibit a curious interplay between ancient and modern forms of thought. Coupled with a modernity that valued experiment and individual experience was a respect for the authority of tradition. Bacon's scientific and literary writings both display this uneasy alliance of tradition and innovation.

Bacon's essays differ from Montaigne's in striking ways. First, most of Bacon's essays are short. Second, his essays are much less personal than Montaigne's. And third, many of Bacon's essays offer advice in how to live. Their admonitory intent differs from Montaigne's more exploratory temper.

Eighteenth-century America included a profusion of essayists writing in a variety of nonfictional forms. Thomas Paine wrote essays of political persuasion in the periodical *The Crisis*. J. Hector St. John de Crèvecoeur wrote his essayistic *Letters from an American Farmer*. And Benjamin Franklin compiled his *Autobiography* and his *Poor Richard's Almanack*, which is a loosely stitched collection of aphorisms, including "haste makes waste," "a stitch in time saves nine," and "Fish and visitors stink after three days."

During the eighteenth century, more and more writers produced essays, along with their work in other genres. Among them are Samuel Johnson (1709–1784), whose philosophical and moral periodical essays appeared regularly in his own *Rambler*, *Idler*, and *Adventurer*. The gravity and sobriety of Johnson's essays were complemented by the more lighthearted and satirical vein mined by Joseph Addison (1672–1719), and Richard Steele (1672–1729), whose essays in their *Tatler* and *Spectator* periodicals, which they jointly wrote and published, were avidly awaited when they appeared, as often as three times a week. Jonathan Swift (1667–1745), best known for his satire, *Gulliver's Travels*, also wrote a number of essays, including what is perhaps the most famous satirical essay ever written (and the essay with one of the longest titles): "A Modest Proposal for Preventing the Children of the Poor People in Ireland from being a Burden to their Parents or Country; and for making them beneficial to their Publick."

The nineteenth century saw the rise of the essay less as moralistic and satirical than as entertaining and even a bit eccentric. Among the most notable practitioners were Charles Lamb (1775–1834), whose *Essays of Elia* and *More Essays of Elia* are constructed to read less like random assortments than as books centered on characters, and whose stories form a loose plot. Among these essays is his "A Bachelor's Complaint," in which Lamb, himself a lifelong bachelor, takes up a list of grievances he holds against his married friends and acquaintances. Complementing the playful essays of Charles Lamb during this time are the passionate and highly opinionated essays of William Hazlitt (1778–1830), a friend of the English Romantic poets William Wordsworth and Samuel Taylor Coleridge. Hazlitt's "On the Pleasure of Hating" is written with his customary "gusto," a characteristic he brought to his writing from his life and one in synch with the Romantic poets' emphasis on the importance of feeling.

Nineteenth-century American essayists include the powerful twosome of Ralph Waldo Emerson and Henry David Thoreau. Emerson's essays grew out of his public lectures. He was at home in the form and wrote a large number of essays in a highly aphoristic style that contained nuggets of wisdom served up in striking images and memorably pithy expressions. A few quotable examples include "hitch your wagon to a star," "trust thyself," and "give all to love." Much of Emerson's writing focused on nature, which he envisioned as a divine moral guide to life.

Thoreau, a friend and protégé of Emerson, was another New Englander who limned the natural world in prose. Like Emerson, Thoreau wrote essays on a variety of topics, but mostly about nature. Thoreau's most famous essay, however, is political—his "On the Duty of Civil Disobedience," in which he argues that each individual human being has not only the right but the obligation to break the law when the law is unjust or immoral. Thoreau's "Civil Disobedience," a much cited essay, has also been an influential one, affecting the stances of peaceful non-violent political resistance taken up by both Mahatma Gandhi and Martin Luther King, Jr. But it is Thoreau's *Walden* that contains his most beautifully crafted essays in his most artfully composed book. Who can forget the matchless prose of sentences such as "If a man cannot keep pace with his companions, perhaps he hears the sound of a different drummer. Let him step to the music which he hears, however measured or far away."

If in one sense the Renaissance can be considered the beginnings of the modern essay, in another, the modern essay is synonymous with the twentieth-century essay, a period in which the essay developed into a literary genre that began to rival fiction and poetry in importance. George Orwell (1903–1950), best known for his satirical *Animal Farm* and *1984*, is equally eminent for the four thick volumes of essays and letters he produced. Orwell's "A Hanging" and "Shooting an Elephant" are modern classics of the genre, as is his "Politics and the English Language," perhaps the best-known essay on language in English. Another English writer better known for her work as a novelist, Virginia Woolf (1882–1941), like Orwell, left a splendid set of essay volumes, including her "Common Reader" series, in which she presents her views on a wide range of authors and works of literature in a relaxed, casual style. "The Death of a Moth" is deservedly among her most highly regarded essays.

On the twentieth-century American scene E. B. White (1899–1985) stands out as a modern master of the genre. White, too, is best known for his fiction, in his case the books he wrote for children, all gems with the diamond among them the ever-popular *Charlotte's Web*. White published many of his essays in *The New Yorker* and a number of others in *Harper's* magazine. "Once More to the Lake," his best known and oft reprinted essay, is also among his most beautifully written, and some would argue, among his most enduring contributions to literature.

Along with White, who rarely wrote about social issues per se, there is James Baldwin (1924–1987), who wrote almost exclusively about race, particularly about race relations in America and about his place in society as a black man and a writer. In fact, Baldwin's consistent theme is identity, his identity as a black writer, who became an expatriate, living in Paris, in part to discover what it meant for him to be an American. A third modern American essayist is James Thurber, a humorist who published satirical cartoons, humorous stories, and parables, as well as journalism. His "The Secret Life of Walter Mitty" and "The Catbird Seat" are two comic story masterpieces. His *My Life and Hard Times* is a classic of American autobiography, and his *Is Sex Necessary?* a spoof on pop psychology.

At the beginning of the twenty-first century, the essay is continuing to thrive. Essayists of all stripes and persuasions continue to publish in magazines and anthologies and in books of collected essays. The annual series, *The Best American Essays*, has recently celebrated its twentieth anniversary. Other annual series of essays have joined it, notably *The Anchor Essay Annual*. These essay volumes are joined by others that are not part of any annual series, but which, nevertheless, come out with great frequency and regularity. The essay, in short, is alive and well in the new millennium.

Pleasures of the Essay

But why has the essay been so well regarded for such a long time? What attracts readers to essays? And what attracts writers to the form? Why has the essay endured?

One answer lies in the wide variety the genre affords. There are essays for everybody, essay voices and visions and styles to suit every taste, to satisfy every kind of intellectual craving. There is variety of subject—of topic—from matters of immediate and practical concern to those of apparently purely theoretical interest; from essays of somber gravity to those in a lighter more playful vein; from easy essays on familiar topics to complex and challenging ones on subjects outside the bounds of most readers' knowledge and experience.

An essay can be about anything. And essayists have written about every topic under the sun, from their own lives and experience to what they have read and observed in the world, to their speculations and imaginings. All of these are available, for example, in Montaigne's little essay, "Of Smells." In fact, to list just a handful of the more than one hundred essays Montaigne alone wrote is to convey a sense of the essay's bewildering variety. In addition to "Of Smells," Montaigne wrote "Of Friendship," "Of Sadness," "Of Idleness," "Of Liars," "Of Constancy," "Of Solitude," "Of Sleep," "Of Fear," "Of Age," "Of Prayers," "Of Conscience," "How We Cry and Laugh for the Same Thing," "Of Moderation," "Of Thumbs," "Of Cannibals," "Of Names," "Of Virtue," "Of Anger," "Of Vanity," "Of Cruelty," "Of Cripples," "Of Glory," "Of Presumption," "Of Books," "How Our Mind Hinders Itself," "That Our Desire Is Increased By Difficulty," "Of the Inconsistency of Our Actions," "Of the Love of Fathers for Their Children," and "That to Philosophize Is to Learn to Die." A similarly wide-ranging list of topics could be culled from Bacon's essays, expressing an equally strong interest in the human condition.

For all his essayistic variety, Montaigne did not write much about nature. Many others, however, have written about the natural world, including Ralph Waldo Emerson in "Nature," N. Scott Momaday in "The Way to Rainy Mountain," Annie Dillard in "Living Like Weasels," Mark Twain in "Reading the River," and Virginia Woolf in "The Death of the Moth." In each of these essays the writer describes an encounter with nature and explores his or her relationship to it.

When not writing about themselves or about nature, and when not speculating on one or another aspect of the human condition, essayists often write about the social world. Joan Didion's "Marrying Absurd" is about Las Vegas weddings; James Thurber's "University Days," about college; and Pico Iyer's "Nowhere Man," about living in multiple places and being a member of no single social group.

Identity, in fact, is a frequent topic among contemporary essayists, with writers exploring their roots and their relationships in essays that touch on race and gender, and on broad social and cultural values. James Baldwin explores what it means to be a black man in a white world. Frederick Douglass writes about his struggle for literacy as a black slave; Judith Ortiz Cofer writes about her dual cultural and linguistic identity; Martin Luther King, Jr., writes about racial prejudice and injustice, and what must be done to establish and ensure racial equality, and why; and Jamaica Kincaid writes about finding and valuing her Caribbean Antiguan identity under the seductive influence of British colonial culture.

Issues of gender are equally important for essayists. Gretel Ehrlich writes about what it means to be a cowboy who cares for animals as an integral part of his life, and of how cowboys, if they are to be good at what they do, need as much maternalism as machismo, if not a good deal more. Maxine Hong Kingston writes about the power and place of gender in traditional China by telling the story of a man, Tang Ao, who visits the land of women, was captured, and was transformed into a woman. Another strong woman who appears in an essay is N. Scott Momaday's Kiowa Indian grandmother, who reflects the cultural values of her tribe and its Native American tradition.

Besides a wide variety of topic and a broad spectrum of human concerns, including gender, race, culture, and identity, essays appeal, too, because of their style, the craftsmanship and beauty with which they are written. And just as there are many essay subjects, so also are there many styles. There are as many styles, in fact, as essayists, for each essayist of distinction develops his or her own style, finding a voice and tone appropriate to the topic, audience, and situation that occasioned the writing of each essay.

E. B. White's "Once More to the Lake" is written in a style at once easy and elegant, familiar and formal, in a splendid blend of language that is as easy on the ear as it is on the eye. For the sheer beauty of language, it begs to be read aloud. George Orwell's "Shooting an Elephant" is less lyrical but no less memorable, written in a style that seems to be no style at all—as clear as a windowpane. Amy Tan's "Mother Tongue" is written in a mixture of styles, an indication that she speaks more than one brand of English, as she describes the worlds of English both she and her Chinese mother inhabit. Langston Hughes uses a simple and direct style in his "Salvation," which tells the story of his religious "anti-conversion." Martin Luther King, Jr., writes in a style that appeals to thinking people, as he develops his own arguments and rebuts the arguments of others about the right of African Americans to protest against racial injustice.

Types of Essays

The word "essay" comes from the French "essai" (essay), which derives from the French verb "essayer"—to try or attempt. The word "essay" suggests less a formal and systematic approach to a topic than a casual, even random one. In this sense, an essay differs from other prose forms such as the magazine article, whose purpose is usually to inform or persuade, and the review, which evaluates a book or performance. Essays, to be sure, may also evaluate, and they often inform as well as persuade. But their manner of going about offering information, making a case, and providing an evaluation differs from those less variable genres.

The essay can be compared with the short story in that some essays, like short stories, include narrative. But the short story is fiction, the essay fact. And fiction works largely by implication, the essay mostly by expository discursiveness. Essays explain what stories imply. This is not to say that essayists don't make use of fictional techniques and strategies. They do so often, particularly in personal or familiar essays, which include narration and description.

The essay can also be linked with poetry, particularly with the more discursive poems that explain as well as image ideas that tell straightforwardly rather than hint or suggest in a more oblique manner. Essayists, on the other hand, typically say what's on their mind fairly directly. They explain what they are thinking. Poets more often write about one thing in terms of another (they write about love, for example, in terms of war). And they prefer implication to explication, which is more characteristic of the essay writer.

Kinds of essays include, broadly, personal essays and formal essays. Personal essays are those in which the writer is amply evident—front and center. Employing the personal pronoun "I," personal essays include opinions and perspectives explicitly presented as the writer's own in a personal, even idiosyncratic, manner. Formal essays, by contrast, typically avoid the pronoun "I," and they omit personal details. Formal essays include expository essays, analytical essays, and argumentative, or persuasive, essays. Expository essays explain ideas and scenarios, using standard patterns of organization, including comparison and contrast, classification, and cause and effect. Analytical essays offer an analysis and interpretation of a text or performance, typically breaking that text or performance into parts or aspects, and presenting both an evaluative judgment and the evidence on which it is based. Argumentative, or persuasive, essays advance a thesis or claim and present evidence that is organized as part of a logical demonstration, utilizing the modes of deductive and inductive reasoning, and including support for the argumentative claim in the form of reasons, examples, and data as evidence.

Most essays, even the most personal ones, are composites and blends. They may tell personal stories rich in descriptive detail to provide evidence to support an idea or claim to persuasion. They may use traditional patterns of expository organization such as comparison and contrast in the cause of developing a logical argument. And they may include information and explanation along with personal experience and argumentation. More often than not, the most interesting and memorable of essays mix and match what are typically thought of as distinct essay types and the conventions associated with them. Contemporary essayists, in particular, cross borders and mix modes, as they write essays that break the rules in a quest to be engaging, persuasive, and interesting.

Reading Essays

Reading essays is a lot like reading other forms of literature. It requires careful attention to language—to the words on the page and to what's "written between the lines." Reading essays involves essentially four interrelated mental acts: observing, connecting, inferring, and concluding. Good readers attend to the details of language and structure of the essays they read. They note not only the information that writers of essays provide, but also how that information is presented, how any stories are told, how arguments are made, and evidence presented. Good readers of essays look for connections among the details they observe—details of image and structure, argument and evidence. And good readers draw inferences based on those connected observations, inferences that prepare them to make an interpretive conclusion from their inferences.

Good readers are also engaged by what they read. They respond with questions that echo in their minds as they read. They make their reading an active engagement with the essay text, an involvement that continues after their actual reading of the words on the page has been completed.

Reading in this manner—observing, connecting, inferring, concluding, and questioning—alerts readers to nuances, to things rendered but not explained or elaborated by the writer. Active, deliberative reading of this sort involves both intellectual comprehension and emotional apprehension, a consideration of the feelings essays generate as well as the thinking they stimulate. This reading process requires that readers make sense of gaps in texts; that they recognize linguistic, literary, and cultural conventions; that they generalize on the basis of textual details; that they bring their values to bear on the essays they read; and that they do all these things concurrently and simultaneously.

Reading Annie Dillard's "Living Like Weasels"

We can illustrate this kind of active, engaged reading by looking at the opening paragraphs of Annie Dillard's "Living Like Weasels," an essay printed in full on pages 106–111.

> A weasel is wild. Who knows what he thinks? He sleeps in his underground den, his tail draped over his nose. Sometimes he lives in his den for two days without leaving. Outside, he stalks rabbits, mice, muskrats, and birds, killing more bodies than he can eat warm, and often dragging the carcasses home. Obedient to instinct, he bites his prey at the neck, either splitting the jugular vein at the throat or crunching the brain at the base of the skull, and he does not let go. One naturalist refused to kill a weasel who was socketed into his hand deeply as a rattlesnake. The man could in no way pry the tiny weasel off, and he had to walk half a mile to water, the weasel dangling from his palm, and soak him off like a stubborn label.

First, a few questions. What strikes us most about this passage? What do we notice on first reading it? What observations would we most like to make about it? What questions do we have? What feelings does the text inspire? What expectations do we have about where the essayist is taking us?

Next, some observations. The first sentence is abrupt. It announces forcefully the key point that a weasel is wild. But what does it imply? What do we understand by the word "wild"? How wild? In what way is the weasel wild? The second sentence is a question, one that invites us to consider what a weasel thinks about. (Or perhaps it suggests that we shouldn't bother because we simply cannot know.) "Who knows what he thinks?" How we take this sentence depends on how we hear it, which in turn, affects how we say it. Here's one way: Who knows what he *thinks?* Here's another: Who knows *what* he thinks? And still another: Who *knows* what he thinks? Whichever way we prefer, we recognize the possibility of alternative emphases and thus, alternative ways of understanding what the writer is saying and suggesting about weasels.

Dillard's next two sentences provide information—that weasels sleep in dens where they can remain for up to two days at a time. There's nothing really surprising here. But what about that other little bit of information—*how* the weasel sleeps: with his tail draped over his nose. Whether factual or fanciful, that draped tail is a lovely surprise, a gratuitous image offered to engage and entertain as well as inform.

The fifth and sixth sentences of the opening paragraph reveal the weasel as hunter—stalking prey, killing it, dragging it to his den, where he eats it and then, presumably, sleeps. When we are told that the weasel is obedient to instinct and are shown exactly how he kills—by splitting the jugular vein or by crunching his victim's brain—we remember the opening sentence: "A weasel is wild." And we begin to understand in a new way just what this means. Although we "understood" before, on first encountering the sentence, that vague and general knowledge is now particularized. We have since acquired specific information that we can understand intellectually and respond to emotionally. Now, we know more fully what it means to say that a weasel is "wild."

It is here, in the middle of the paragraph, that we perhaps register our strongest emotional response. How do we respond to Dillard's details about the weasel's method of killing its victims? Are we amazed? Engaged? Appalled? Or what? That question about response is directed at our experience of the essay. We can also ask a technical question: Does Dillard need that degree of detail? Suppose she had diluted it or perhaps even omitted such concrete details entirely. Or conversely, suppose that she had provided an even fuller rendition of the killing. How would such alternatives have affected our response?

Dillard's opening paragraph concludes with an anecdote about a naturalist bitten by the tenacious weasel. The anecdote makes a point, to be sure. But it does more. The image impresses itself on our minds in language worth noting: the verb "socketed"; the comparison with the rattlesnake; the image of the stubborn label. To make sense of Dillard's opening paragraph, even a preliminary kind of sense, is to make such observations and to wonder about their significance. And it is to wonder, too, where the essay is heading, where the writer is taking us. What *do* we expect at this point? Why?

Once we read the second paragraph of Dillard's essay, we can consider how it affects our understanding of and response to the first. How does it follow from the opening paragraph? What does it do rhetorically? That is, what effect does it have on us, and how does it advance Dillard's point about the wildness of the weasel?

Here is Dillard's next paragraph:

> And once, says Ernest Thompson Seton—once, a man shot an eagle out of the sky. He examined the eagle and found the dry skull of a weasel fixed by the jaws to his throat. The supposition is that the eagle had pounced on the weasel and the weasel swiveled and bit as instinct taught him, tooth to neck, and nearly won. I would like to have seen that eagle from the air a few weeks or months before he was shot: was the whole weasel still attached to his feathered throat, a fur pendant? Or did the eagle eat what he could reach, gutting the living weasel with his talons before his breast, bending his beak, cleaning the beautiful airborne bones?

Our questions at the beginning of this second paragraph of Dillard's essay necessarily invite our responses, both intellectual and emotional. In asking what strikes us about the details or the language of this paragraph, we move from subjective responses to objective considerations. On the basis of the details we notice and relate, we form inferences. We move backward, in a way, from our initial response to a set of observations about the essay's rhetoric. We might observe, for example, that the second paragraph begins with an image very much like the one at the end of the opening paragraph. The tenacious weasel holds on fiercely, in one instance to a man's hand, and in another, to an eagle's throat. And we might register the justness of this pair of images, the more striking image of the eagle following and intensifying the first image of the weasel socketed to a man's hand. We might also observe that the second paragraph begins with statements—with declarative sentences—and ends with questions. We might notice, further, that it includes a reference to another written text (did we notice that this occurs in the opening paragraph as well?). And, finally, that the writer speaks personally, using the personal pronoun "I," revealing her desire to have seen the amazing thing she had only read about.

In addition, we should note Dillard's profusion of precise, vivid, strong verbs, which contribute to the power of her prose. We should note, too, the image of the eagle gutting the living weasel, bending his beak and cleaning the weasel's bones of its flesh—an image brought forward and elaborated from the previous sentence, where it exists as a pair of adjectives and corresponding nouns: "his feathered throat, a fur pendant." Dillard actually brings the dormant image to life in that string of participles: *gutting, living, bending, cleaning.*

The repeated words in this second paragraph create a litany of eagle and weasel, their rhyming sound echoed again in *"eat," "reach," "beak,"* and *"cleaning."* We should notice, as well, the alliterative b's of the final sentence: "his talons *b*efore his *b*reast, *b*ending his *b*eak, cleaning the *b*eautiful air*b*orne *b*ones." And further, we might see how the paragraph's monosyllabic diction is counterpointed against both the polysyllabic name of the naturalist, Ernest Thompson Seton, and the continual yoking and re-yoking of the animals, eagle and weasel always coming together. To hear the remarkable sound play of Dillard's prose, including its subtle yet muscular rhythms, we must read it aloud.

We can make some observations about the overall structure of Dillard's complete essay. We have described how the first two paragraphs present facts about weasels, especially about their wildness and their tenaciousness. This introductory section of the essay is followed by a section, paragraphs 3–7, that depicts Dillard's encounter with a weasel and their exchange of glances. The middle paragraphs of that section—4 through 6—set the scene, while paragraphs 3 and 7 frame this section, with an emphasis on Dillard's and the weasel's repeated locked glances. Paragraph 5 is of particular interest in its mix of details that contrast wilderness and civilization. They exist, surprisingly, side-by-side, one within the other: beer cans coexist with muskrat holes; turtle eggs sit in motorcycle tracks; a highway runs alongside a duck pond.

Dillard's next large section of the essay, paragraphs 8–13, provides a crescendo and a climax. Dillard describes the weasel in detail, emphasizing the shock of their locked looks and the shattering of the spell. She also laments her unsuccessful attempt to re-forge the link with the weasel after the spell had been broken. The section ends with Dillard and her readers pondering the mysterious encounter she experienced.

In her concluding section, paragraphs 14–17, Dillard speculates about the meaning of her encounter with the weasel. She contemplates living like a weasel—what it means, why it appeals to her. She explores the implications of what a weasel's life is like, and how its life relates to the life of human beings like her own. She concludes with an image from the opening: an eagle carrying something that is clinging fiercely to it, not letting go, holding on into and beyond death. The image brings the essay full circle—but with the important difference that we, Dillard's readers, have taken the weasel's place.

We are now poised to consider the ideas, the meaning, of "Living Like Weasels," though, clearly, it is necessary to read the essay in its entirety at least once for the following remarks to be completely comprehensible.

What begins as an expository essay that outlines facts about the wildness and tenacity of weasels turns into a meditation on the value of wildness and the necessity of tenacity in human life. By the end of the essay, Dillard has made the weasel a symbol and a model of how human beings might, even should, live. And her tone changes from the factual declaration of the essay's introductory section to speculative wonder, and finally to admonition. Dillard encourages her readers to identify their one necessity, and then, like the weasel, to latch on to it and never let it go.

Dillard also suggests that there is between human and animal the possibility of communication, of understanding. She opts for a mystical communion between woman and weasel, by necessity a brief communion, one beyond the power of words to describe. The experience for Dillard stuns her into stillness and momentarily stops time. In linking her mind even briefly with the weasel, Dillard undergoes an extraordinary transforming experience. But it's an experience that, as much as she wishes it to continue, she cannot prolong because her own consciousness, the distinctive human quality of her thinking mind, which enables her to appreciate the experience in the first place, prevents her, finally, from staying at one with an animal.

There seems to be, thus, in Dillard's essay, a pull in two directions. On one hand, there is the suggestion that human beings can link themselves with the animal world, and like the weasel, live in necessity instinctively. On the other hand sits an opposing idea: that human beings cannot stay linked with the weasel or any animal, primarily because our minds prohibit it. We are creatures for whom remembering is necessary, vital. The mindlessness of the weasel, thus, can never be ours, for we are mindful creatures, not mindless ones. Our living as we should is necessarily different from the weasel's living as it should. And although we can certainly learn from the weasel's tenacity and purity of living, we can follow it only so far on the way to wildness.

Writing Essays

Reading actively and with critical judgment is a necessary adjunct to writing well. In reading carefully and critically, we learn about suggestiveness, about allusion, about economy, about richness. We learn about rhetorical and stylistic possibilities for our own essay writing.

The Qualities of Good Writing

But what constitutes good writing, the kind of writing expected of students in college courses, the kind expected of professional employees on the job? Writing, essentially, that is characterized by the following qualities: (1) clarity; (2) coherence; (3) logical organization; (4) accuracy and correctness; (5) sufficiency; and (6) style.

Good writing is *clear* writing. Readers can follow and understand it easily. This is harder to accomplish than it sounds because what is clear to the writer may not be clear to the reader. Writers need to remember that the entire context of their thinking is not readily apparent to their readers. Readers can determine what a writer is saying only from the words on the page.

Good writing is *coherent* writing. Coherence refers to how a writer's sentences "hang together," how those sentences relate to one another sensibly and logically. We can think of coherence, first, though not exclusively, as a quality of paragraphs. Good writing allows readers to determine the focus and point of every paragraph, and to determine, further, the relation of one paragraph to another. This aspect of coherence reveals a writer's inescapable concern with essay organization overall.

Good writing is carefully *organized* writing. A well-written essay has a discernible beginning, middle, and ending (a clearly identifiable introduction, body, and conclusion). Each of these three main parts of an essay need not be baldly announced, but each should be readily discernible by a careful reader. But the organization of an essay requires more than including these three broad aspects. Of particular importance is how the essay unfolds, how its information and evidence are deployed, how each aspect of the writer's idea leads into the next, how the paragraphs that make up the middle, or body, of an essay exhibit a logical structure.

Good writing is also *accurate* and *correct* both in terms of information included, and in terms of its language. Grammatical accuracy is essential. So is accurate spelling and punctuation. These elements of good writing can be assisted through the use of grammar and spell-check features of word processing programs, through the use of a good dictionary, and through keeping a good handbook, such as *The Scribner Handbook for Writers*, nearby.

Good writing is also *sufficient* to the scope of its subject and the limits of its topic. Short essays may be adequate to discussing highly focused aspects of a topic, while broader and more inclusive topics require longer, more detailed writing. Sufficiency, of course, is a relative concept. But it is important for a writer to include enough evidence to support an idea persuasively, enough examples to illustrate a concept clearly, a sufficient number of reasons to support a claim in developing an argument.

Good writing, finally, has a sense of *style*. Every writer needs to develop his or her own way with words. Paradoxically, one of the best ways to do this is to observe and imitate the style of other writers. Good writers attend to how other successful writers structure their essays, shape their sentences, and select their words. One of the reasons to develop skillful habits of reading is to glean, from that attentiveness, strategies and techniques for good writing.

An Overview of the Writing Process

These six qualities of good writing require patience, persistence, and practice. Good writing can't be rushed. It requires planning, drafting, and revising.

Planning

In the planning stage of the writing process, it is important to take notes and to make notes. Taking notes involves mostly marking or copying passages, which you might use in your essay. It also involves summarizing and paraphrasing what you read—putting it into your own words. Making notes refers to the act of thinking about what you have marked, copied, summarized, or paraphrased. Writing out notes about what you think about your reading, beginning to formulate your own thinking about it, is an active and reflective process that provides an important step toward drafting your essay.

Planning your essay requires making notes to yourself in other ways as well. You can make lists of observations from your reading or lists of aspects or elements of your topic to consider in your essay draft. You can jot down questions, and you can do some freewriting to jumpstart your thinking. These and other preliminary planning strategies are necessary for all but the most informal of writing projects. Time spent on them pays off later during the drafting stage.

Drafting

A draft is a first take, one that provides an overview of your essay, including some kind of beginning and ending, and much of the body or middle, with its examples and evidence to support and develop your ideas. First drafts of essays are often called "rough" drafts, and for good reason. The preliminary draft is not meant to be worried into final form. The first draft is not intended to be a finished product, fit for public display. It is, rather, an attempt the writer makes to see where the topic is going, and whether there are sufficient examples and evidence to support the idea. The idea too, may very well require adjustment and revision, more often than not.

In drafting an essay, it is important to consider your purpose. Are you writing to provide information? To convey an experience? To amuse and entertain? To present an idea for your readers' consideration? To persuade your readers to see something your way? Being clear about your purpose will help with decisions about other aspects of writing your essay, including how to begin and end, as well as choices of language and tone.

Your draft should also make a good start toward providing the supporting evidence necessary for making your ideas persuasive. In marshalling evidence for your ideas from your reading of primary sources, such as works of literature (including the essays in this book), and from secondary sources written about the primary sources, keep the following guidelines in mind:

1. Be fair-minded. Be careful not to oversimplify or distort either a primary or secondary source.
2. Be cautious. Qualify your claims. Limit your assertions to what you can comfortably demonstrate.
3. Be logical. See that the various elements of your argument fit together and that you don't contradict yourself.
4. Be accurate. Present facts, details, and quotations with care.
5. Be confident. Believe in your ideas and present them with conviction.

After writing a draft of an essay, put it aside for a while—ideally for at least a day or two. When you return to it, assess whether what you are saying still makes sense, whether you have provided enough examples to clarify your ideas and presented sufficient evidence to make them persuasive. Read the draft critically, asking yourself what is convincing and what is not, what makes sense and what doesn't. Consider whether the draft centers on a single idea and stays on track.

If the first draft accomplishes these things, you can begin thinking about how to tighten its organization and refine its style. If, on the other hand, the draft contains frequent changes of direction, confusions of thought, multiple unrelated ideas, incoherent paragraphs, and more, you will need to decide what to salvage and what to discard. You will need to return to the planning stage—though now with a clearer sense of your essay's possibilities, and begin the process of drafting your essay again—a second attempt in a second draft. This scenario, by the way, is not uncommon. It simply represents the way first efforts often begin: in some degree of confusion that is eventually dispelled. This common scenario, moreover, argues for leaving enough time to do a second (and, if necessary, a third) draft.

Revising

Revision is not something that occurs only once, at the end of the writing process. Redrafting your essay to consider the ordering of paragraphs and the use of examples is itself a significant act of revision. So, too, is doing additional reading and even rereading some materials to reconsider your original idea. Revision occurs throughout the entire arc of the writing process. It requires you to reconsider your writing and your thinking not once, but several times. This reconsideration is made on three levels: conceptual, organizational, and stylistic.

Conceptual revision involves reconsidering your ideas. As you write your first and subsequent drafts, your understanding of the topic may change. While accumulating evidence in support of your idea, you may find evidence that subverts or challenges it. And you might decide, if not to change your idea dramatically, at least to qualify it to account for this contradictory or complicating evidence. On the other hand, as you write your various drafts, you might find yourself thinking of additional ways to develop and strengthen your idea, to support it with additional evidence, examples, and reasons.

Organizational or structural revision involves asking yourself whether your essay's arrangement best presents your line of thinking. You might ask yourself questions such as these: Is the organizational framework readily discernible? Does it make sense? Have you written an introduction that identifies your topic and clarifies your intent? Have you organized your supporting details in a sensible and logical manner? Does your conclusion follow from your discussion, and does it bring your essay to a satisfying close? However you choose to end your essay, your conclusion should answer the question "So what?" for the reader. Even though you may have presented details, reasons, and examples to support your idea, your readers will still expect you to explain their significance, and in ways that they themselves will want to see as interesting and valuable.

Stylistic revision concerns smaller-scale details, such as matters of syntax or word order, of diction or word choice, of tone, imagery, and rhythm. Even though you may think about some of these things a bit in early drafts, it is better to defer critical attention to them until your final draft, largely because such microscopic stylistic considerations may undergo significant alteration as you rethink and reorganize your essay. You might find, for example, that a paragraph you worked on carefully for style in a first draft is no longer important or relevant, and thus disappears from the final draft.

Focus on aspects of style that may require revision with the following questions:

1. Are your sentences concise and clear?
2. Can you eliminate words that are not doing their job?
3. Is your tone consistent? (For example, you need to avoid shifts from a formal to an informal or colloquial tone.)
4. Is your level of language appropriate for the subject of your essay?
5. Are there any grammatical errors? Any mistakes in spelling or punctuation? And, finally, before letting an essay go public, be sure to proofread it to check for typos and other unintended mistakes.

Writing from Reading—An Example

In order to write essays about what you read, it is always useful to work through some preliminary, informal writing en route to preparing a more formal piece, whether a short summary or a longer, full-fledged essay.

Earlier, some types of preliminary writing were mentioned. Here they will be illustrated with a short excerpt from Susan Sontag's essay, "A Woman's Beauty" (pp. 325–328).

We begin with annotation.

Annotations are brief notes you write about a text while reading it. You can underline and circle words and phrases that strike you as important. You can highlight passages. You can make marginal comments that reflect your understanding of and attitude toward the text. Your annotations might also include arrows that link related points, question marks that indicate possible confusion, and exclamation marks to express surprise or agreement.

Annotations can be single words or brief phrases; they can be written as statements or as questions. And depending on how extensively you annotate a text, your annotations may form a secondary text that reminds you of the one you are reading and analyzing. Annotations used this way serve as an abbreviated guide to what the text says and what you think about it.

As you read the following passage, notice the various types of annotations, and, if you like, add additional annotations of your own.

Here, first, for convenience, is an excerpt from Sontag's essay.

Excerpt from Susan Sontag's
A Woman's Beauty: Put-Down or Power Source?

Is beauty really essential? Seems exaggerated. Society defines norms of beauty. Women are pushed into _overconcern_ with their appearance. Contrast: men _do_ well; women _look_ good.

To be called beautiful is thought to name something essential to women's character and concerns. (In contrast to men—whose essence is to be strong, or effective, or competent.) It does not take someone in the throes of advanced feminist awareness to perceive that the way women are taught to be involved with beauty encourages narcissism, reinforces dependence and immaturity. Everybody (women and men) knows that. For it is "everybody," a whole society, that has identified being feminine with caring about how one looks. (In contrast to being masculine—which is identified with caring about <u>what one *is* and *does*</u> and only secondarily, if at all, about how one looks.) [. . .]

It is not, of course, the desire to be beautiful that is wrong but the obligation to be—or to try. What is accepted by most women as a flattering idealization of their sex is a way of <u>making women feel inferior</u> to what they actually are—or normally grow to be. For the ideal of beauty is administered as a form of <u>self-oppression</u>. Women are taught to see their bodies in parts, and to evaluate each part separately. <u>Breasts</u>, feet, <u>hips</u>, waistline, neck, eyes, nose, <u>complexion</u>, hair, and so on—each in turn is submitted to an anxious, fretful, often despairing scrutiny. Even if some pass muster, some will always be found wanting. [. . .]

In <u>men, good looks is a whole</u>, something taken in at a glance. It does not need to be confirmed by giving measurements of different regions of the body; nobody encourages a man to dissect his appearance, feature by feature. As for <u>perfection</u>, that is considered trivial—almost unmanly.

Contrast: <u>desire</u> for beauty versus <u>obligation</u> to be beautiful. Sontag politicizes the issue—beauty as means of oppression. Women + beauty = body parts.

Doesn't author exaggerate here about perfection? Nice distinction here on beauty and the sexes.

Freewriting

Your initial impressions of a text, which you can record with annotations, will often lead you to further thoughts about it. You can begin developing these thoughts with freewriting. As with annotating, in freewriting you record ideas, reactions, or feelings about a text without arranging them in any special order. Freewriting is free-form writing. You simply write down what you think about the passage, without worrying about logical organization. The point is to get your ideas down on paper and not to censor or judge them prematurely. Freewriting, in fact, provides a way to pursue an idea and develop your thinking to see where it may lead.

Both annotation and freewriting precede the more intricate and deliberative work of analysis, interpretation, and evaluation. Annotation and freewriting also provide a convenient way to prepare for writing essays and reports. These two informal techniques work well together; the brief, quickly noted annotations complement the more leisurely paced, longer elaborations of freewriting.

Here is an example of freewriting about the Susan Sontag essay excerpt annotated earlier. Notice how the freewriting includes questions that stimulate reflection on the passage.

Example of Freewriting

Interesting questions. Women do seem to think more about their looks than men do. But since it's men women wish to please by looking good, men may be responsible (some? much?) for women's obsession with appearance. How far have women bought into the beauty myth? How much are they responsible for obsessing about beauty? How about money and profit? And at whose expense?

Why don't men *need* to be beautiful? To please parents—employers? To attract a mate? To be considered "normal"? Sontag says beauty is irrelevant for men—men judged by different standards—strength, competence, effectiveness. She doesn't mention power, money, status—leaves out intelligence and moral qualities—kindness, decency, generosity? How important?

Distinction between *desiring* to be beautiful (perhaps to be desired or admired) and *needing* to be. Nothing wrong with women wanting to be attractive, to look good. Problem is when desire becomes *obligation*— a waste of women's talents—minimizes them, keeps them subservient.

Parts and whole—are women concerned with *parts* of their bodies—certain parts? Their overall appearance? Their sense of self? Silicone breast implants? Face lifts? (But men have nose jobs, pec implants.) Men are concerned with *some parts* of their bodies more than others—like women? Or not?

What about the words for good-looking women— and men? Beautiful women, but handsome men. Foxy

```
lady—gorgeous woman (guy?) attractive girl. And what
of men? Handsome, good-looking. Pretty boy? Hunk—
derogatory for men. A real "he-man."
```

Double-Column Notebook

Still another way to develop your thinking about what you read is to make entries in a double-column notebook. To create a double-column notebook, simply divide a page in half. One half is for summarizing and interpreting what you read. Use this side to record your understanding of the text. Use the other side to respond to what you read, to think about implications, and to relate it to knowledge gleaned elsewhere.

The advantage of a double-column notebook is that it encourages you to be an active reader, to think about your reading, and to make connections with your other reading and with your experience. You can use the double-column notebook to think further about your earlier reactions and thoughts recorded in your annotations and freewriting.

Here are, first, a generic look at how a double-column notebook page appears, and then an example based on the Sontag essay excerpt.

Double-Column Notebook Page

Summary	*Comments*
Summarize the text.	Respond to your summary.
Interpret the author's ideas.	Reflect on the author's ideas.
Explain the ideas succinctly.	Consider your agreement or disagreement.
Identify important details.	Raise questions about those details.
Relate details to central idea.	Relate main idea to reading & experience.

The following sample page details how a double-column notebook page might look based on Sontag's essay excerpt. But it's not an attempt to comment on every aspect of her essay.

Double-Column Notebook
for Sontag Essay Excerpt

Summary

Sontag argues that women's beauty is more dangerous than beneficial. Their beauty and their concern with it hurt women by distracting them from more important things, such as intellectual pursuits and political opportunities.

Sontag claims that women are seen as superficial and frivolous because they occupy much of their time with attempting to improve their appearance.

She criticizes a society that relegates women to a form of second-class citizenship in which beauty counts less than brains, and in which obsessing about appearance instead of devoting time and energy to power and status allow women to be dismissed as superficial and decorative.

She sets the standards and ideals for women's beauty over and against those for men, and she finds the standards for men's appearance more sensible, reasonable, and meaningful.

Comments

Sontag's agenda here seems genuine. She values women as intelligent people with a contribution to make to society. She seems genuinely angry by their being forced to be overly concerned with their appearance.

Sontag implies that women are damned if they do and damned if they don't. Women have to look their best in a world that expects nothing less of them. If women neglect their looks they are criticized for it; if they labor to be beautiful, they are equally criticized. It's a no-win situation for them.

In blaming society for women's beauty dilemma, is she really blaming men? Isn't it men who continue to rule the world and set the standards and expectations? Or is she blaming the consumerism and commercialism that dominate contemporary culture?

Writing a Summary

A summary is a compressed version of a text in which you explain the author's meaning in your own words. You summarize a text when you need to give your readers the gist of what it says. A summary should present the author's text accurately and represent his or her views fairly. You build your summary on the observations, connections, and inferences you make while reading. Although there is no rule for how long or short a summary should be, a summary of a text is always shorter than the text itself.

Writing a summary requires careful reading, in part to ensure that you thoroughly understand what you are reading. Writing a summary helps you respond to what you read by requiring careful analysis and consideration of its details.

Writing a summary requires essentially two kinds of skills: identifying the idea of the text you are summarizing, and recognizing the evidence that supports that idea. One strategy for writing a summary is to find the key points that support the main idea. You can do this by looking for clusters of sentences or groups of paragraphs that convey the writer's meaning. Because paragraphs work together, you cannot simply summarize each paragraph independently. You may need to summarize a cluster of paragraphs to convey the idea of a text effectively. It all depends on the length and complexity of the text you are summarizing and on how it is organized.

Here is an example of the process applied to the essay excerpt by Sontag.

Sample Notes toward Summary

General idea of passage: Women are seen as superficial and trivial, concerned with surface beauty rather than with deeper qualities of character. Women are viewed as beautiful objects, valued for how they look rather than for who they are and what they have achieved.
Key supporting points:

- Women's preoccupation with their beauty is a sign of their self-absorption.
- Women's concern for beauty is a form of enslavement to appearances.

- Men are less concerned with appearances, especially with perfecting their appearance.
- Women are objectified in connection with parts of their bodies.
- Women are deemed inconsequential and frivolous.

To create a smooth summary from these key-supporting points, it is necessary to expand and elaborate on them a bit. It is also necessary to put them in a logical order, and to create introductory and concluding sentences for the summary paragraph. Transitions also need to be provided.

Here is an example of such a summary. This one avoids direct quotation from Sontag's text, though quoting her essay is certainly permissible in a summary. Opinions and judgmental words and phrases are avoided, and the writer and text are identified in the opening sentence.

Sample Summary

Sontag Essay Excerpt

In her essay "A Woman's Beauty: Put-Down or Power Source?" Susan Sontag explains how women's need to appear beautiful trivializes them, making them sound superficial and identifying them as creatures preoccupied with how they look rather than with who they are and what they have achieved. Sontag suggests that women's preoccupation with physical beauty is a sign of their self-absorption and triviality. Through being taught to see themselves as mere body parts, women become both objectified and ridden with anxiety that their parts may not measure up. Unlike women, men are viewed as a whole rather than for their parts. Their looks are considered as part of an over-all package, one that includes not only the appearance they present, but their knowledge, intelligence, and status. Unlike women, who lack power, men are perceived as more serious, more confident, and more powerful than the women who anxiously labor to be beautiful in order to please them.

Going Further

Once you have gotten far enough to be comfortable with the writer's idea so that you can summarize it accurately, you are ready to return to the text to look for additional evidence to develop and expand your summary into a full-fledged essay. Earlier a process for accomplishing this revisionary reading was described. Now we will add some notes which, coupled with the summary, can prepare for the writing of a more elaborate essay about Sontag's perspective on women's beauty. The notes can help you expand your summary.

There are four basic steps in this process: observing details of the text, connecting or relating them, making inferences based on those connections, and drawing a conclusion about the text's meaning and significance. This four-stage process allows for the accumulation of the evidence needed to support a textual interpretation that could be formulated in an essay about it.

Observing Details

The kinds of observations you make about text depend on the kind of text you are reading. Here are some observations about Sontag's essay excerpt:

- Sontag focuses throughout on surface beauty—on appearance.
- She distinguishes between beauty in women and in men.
- She sees women's obsession with beauty as dangerous.
- She describes men as strong and competent.
- She italicizes certain key words.
- She places certain sentences in parentheses.
- She puts some words in quotation marks.
- She punctuates heavily with dashes.

Look back at the passage. Make your own observations about the ideas in Sontag's comments; select one sentence in each paragraph that crystallizes her thought. Make a few observations about Sontag's sentences: their type, length, and form. Notice how she begins and ends her paragraphs. Observe what evidence she provides to support her views.

Connecting Details

It is not enough, however, simply to observe details about a text. You must also connect them; relate them to one another. To make a connection is to see one thing in relation to another. You may notice that some details reinforce others, or that the writer repeats certain words or ideas. Perhaps she sets up a contrast, as Sontag does between men's and women's attitudes toward beauty.

While you are noticing aspects of a text, you can also begin making connections among its details. Your goal is to see how the connected details help you make sense of the text as a whole. One way to do this is to group information in lists or in outline form. This involves setting up categories or headings for related kinds of details. In the Sontag passage, for example, you could create heads for details about men and about women. Or you could group observations about style under one head and observations about ideas under another. Notice, for example, how the list of observations made earlier can be divided exactly in this manner, with the first four items concerning Sontag's ideas and the last four her style.

Making observations about a text and establishing connections among them form the basis of analysis. From that basis you begin to consider the significance of what you observe and proceed to develop an interpretation of the text overall. Breaking the interpretive process down in this manner enables you to understand what it involves and should prepare you to practice it on other occasions.

Making Inferences

An inference is a statement based on what has been observed. You infer a writer's idea or point of view, for instance, from the examples and evidence he or she provides. Inferences drive the interpretive process. They push readers beyond making observations and toward explaining their significance. Without inferences there can be no interpretation based on textual evidence.

There is nothing mysterious about the process of making inferences. We do it all the time in our everyday lives, from inferring what someone feels when they complain about something we have done (or failed to do) to inferring the significance of a situation based upon visual observation, as when we see someone with a large ring of keys opening rooms in an academic building early in the morning.

The same is true of making inferences about a text. The inferences we make in reading represent our way of "reading between the lines" by discovering what is implied rather than explicitly stated. The freewriting sample about the Sontag essay excerpt contains inferences. Here are a few additional inferences a reader could draw from the Sontag passage:

- Sontag thinks that the double standard by which women are judged for their beauty and men for other qualities is wrong (paragraph 1).
- She implies that few women can meet the high standards for beauty that society imposes (paragraph 2).
- She seems to approve of the way masculine beauty is considered as a sum of each feature of a man's overall appearance (paragraph 3).
- She implies that women would be better off regarded as whole beings as well.

Sontag does not say any of these things outright. But readers can infer them based on what she does say explicitly. Remember that an inference can be right or wrong, and thus different readers might debate the reliability of these or other inferences we might make about Sontag's essay excerpt. The important thing is not to be afraid to make inferences because of uncertainty about their accuracy. Critical reading and writing involve thinking, and thinking involves making inferences. It is this kind of inferential thinking, moreover, that is essential to good reading and good writing.

Arriving at an Interpretation

The step from making inferences to arriving at an interpretation is not an overly large one. An interpretation is a way of explaining the meaning of a text; it represents your way of understanding the text expressed as an idea. In formulating an interpretation of the Sontag essay, you might write something like the following:

> Sontag examines the meaning of beauty in the lives of women, seeing women's beauty, to echo her title, as more of a "put-down" than a source of power. Although she recognizes that beautiful women can use their attractive appearance to their advantage, she argues that the very beauty that gives beautiful women a social advantage, simultaneously detracts from the overall estimation and regard which others have of them.

This interpretation can be debated, and it can be, indeed needs to be, further elaborated and explained. But the interpretation is based on the inferences made while reading the text, and upon the observations and connections among them that provided the foundation for those inferences. In arriving at this or any interpretation, it is necessary to look back at the text's details to reconsider your initial observations, as well as to review the connections and inferences based upon them. Your inferences must be defensible, that is supportable, either by textual evidence or by logical reasoning.

In looking back at the Sontag passage, you might notice something you overlooked earlier. You might notice, for example, that Sontag mentions society's responsibility for foisting certain ideals of beauty upon women. In thinking about the implications of that observation, you might make other inferences, which may lead you to an interpretive emphasis that differs from your previous understanding of her text. You might decide that the central issue for Sontag is society's role and responsibility in forcing such an ideal of beauty upon women. In that case, you would probably select your evidence from the essay differently to support this new focus of your interpretation.

In writing a full-fledged interpretive essay based on Sontag's piece, or in writing your own essay on the subject of beauty—whether or not you restrict it to "women's beauty"—you would go through the same process described here. The only difference is that the essay you develop would be long enough to provide a full explanation of your ideas and sufficient evidence to make your ideas worthy of a reader's consideration, and that it be long and detailed enough either to fulfill the demands of an assignment to which it might be a response, or to satisfy you as its writer that you have said what you wanted to with enough evidence to make it convincing to others.

Gloria Anzaldúa (1942–2004) grew up in the Rio Grande Valley of south Texas, a rural area near the Mexican border that was home to many Chicanos. She graduated from Pan American University in Austin, taught high school, and later found her way to San Francisco, where she became an outspoken member of the feminist movement. A lesbian and a woman of mixed cultural heritage, she has described herself as the "new mestiza," straddling many personal and cultural influences. In addition to several children's stories, Anzaldúa has published two highly influential books in the field of cultural studies: Borderlands/La Frontera: The New Mestiza *(1987), which mixes prose and poetry, narrative and polemic, and* Making Face, Making Soul/Haciendo Caras: Creative and Critical Perspectives by Women of Color, *co-edited with Cherie Moraga.*

Gloria Anzaldúa

How to Tame a Wild Tongue

In "How to Tame a Wild Tongue," from her book *Borderlands/La Frontera*, Gloria Anzaldúa addresses intertwined issues of language, culture, identity, and power. Her essay is radical in idea, organization, and style. Anzaldúa's idea includes suggestions about the need for a broader view of what constitutes both "English" and "Spanish." She argues for the usefulness of a Chicano Spanish, which deviates in many ways from the Spanish brought from Europe to Mexico and to Central and South America. She also argues for the value of a border-crossing Tex-Mex blend of Spanish and English in a kind of "Spanglish."

The structure of Anzaldúa's essay follows less the logical and systematic development of a single idea than a network of related ideas, each developed within a chunked unit of her essay, and each with its own topical heading. Anzaldúa's style is noteworthy for the border-crossing fusion of the forms of language she describes, as she argues that language is bound up inextricably with ethnic personal identity.

"We're going to have to control your tongue," the dentist says, pulling out all the metal from my mouth. Silver bits plop and tinkle into the basin. My mouth is a motherlode.

The dentist is cleaning out my roots. I get a whiff of the stench when I gasp. "I can't cap that tooth yet, you're still draining," he says.

"We're going to have to do something about your tongue," I hear the anger rising in his voice. My tongue keeps pushing out the wads of cotton, pushing back the drills, the long thin needles. "I've never seen anything as strong or as stubborn," he says. And I think, how do you tame a wild tongue, train it to be quiet, how do you bridle and saddle it? How do you make it lie down?

Who is to say that robbing a people of its language is less violent than war?

RAY GWYN SMITH[1]

I remember being caught speaking Spanish at recess—that was good for three licks on the knuckles with a sharp ruler. I remember being sent to the corner of the classroom for "talking back" to the Anglo teacher when all I was trying to do was tell her how to pronounce my name. "If you want to be American, speak 'American.' If you don't like it, go back to Mexico where you belong."

"I want you to speak English. *Pa'hallar buen trabajo tienes que saber hablar el inglés bien. Qué vale toda tu educación si todavía hablas inglés con un 'accent',*" my mother would say, mortified that I spoke English like a Mexican. At Pan American University, I and all Chicano students were required to take two speech classes. Their purpose: to get rid of our accents.

Attacks on one's form of expression with the intent to censor are a violation of the First Amendment. *El Anglo con cara de inocente nos arrancó la lengua.* Wild tongues can't be tamed, they can only be cut out.

Overcoming the Tradition of Silence

> Ahogadas, escupimos el oscuro.
> Peleando con nuestra propia sombra
> el silencio nos sepulta.

En boca cerrada no entran moscas. "Flies don't enter a closed mouth" is a saying I kept hearing when I was a child. *Ser habladora* was to be a gossip and a liar, to talk too much. *Muchachitas bien criadas*, well-bred girls don't answer back. *Es una falta de respeto* to talk back to one's mother or father. I remember one of the sins I'd recite to the priest in the confession box the few times I went to confession: talking back to my mother, *hablar pa' 'tras, repelar. Hocicona, repelona, chismosa,* having a big mouth, questioning, carrying tales are all signs of being *mal criada*. In my culture they are all words that are derogatory if applied to women—I've never heard them applied to men.

---

[1]Ray Gwyn Smith, *Moorland Is Cold Country*, unpublished book.

The first time I heard two women, a Puerto Rican and a Cuban, say the word *"nosotras,"* I was shocked. I had not known the word existed. Chicanas use *nosotros* whether we're male or female. We are robbed of our female being by the masculine plural. Language is a male discourse.

> And our tongues have become
> dry   the wilderness has
> dried out our tongues   and
> we have forgotten speech.
>
> IRENA KLEPFISZ[2]

Even our own people, other Spanish speakers *nos quieren poner candados en la boca.* They would hold us back with their bag of *reglas de academia.*

> Oyé como ladra:
> el lenguaje de la frontera
>
> Quien tiene boca se equivoca.
>
> MEXICAN SAYING

"Pocho, cultural traitor, you're speaking the oppressor's language by speaking English, you're ruining the Spanish language," I have been accused by various Latinos and Latinas. Chicano Spanish is considered by the purist and by most Latinos deficient, a mutilation of Spanish.

But Chicano Spanish is a border tongue which developed naturally. Change, *evolución, enriquecimiento de palabras nuevas por invención o adopción* have created variants of Chicano Spanish, *un nuevo lenguaje. Un lenguaje que corresponde a un modo de vivir.* Chicano Spanish is not incorrect, it is a living language.

For a people who are neither Spanish nor live in a country in which Spanish is the first language; for a people who live in a country in which English is the reigning tongue but who are not Anglo; for a people who cannot entirely identify with either standard (formal, Castilian) Spanish nor standard English, what recourse is left to them but to create their own language? A language which they can connect their identity to, one

---

[2]Irena Klepfisz, *"Di rayze aheym/*The Journey Home," in *The Tribe of Dina: A Jewish Women's Anthology,* Melanie Kaye/Kantrowitz and Irena Klepfisz, eds. (Montpelier, VT: Sinister Wisdom Books, 1986), 49.

capable of communicating the realities and values true to themselves—a language with terms that are neither *español ni inglés*, but both. We speak a patois, a forked tongue, a variation of two languages.

Chicano Spanish sprang out of the Chicanos' need to identify ourselves as a distinct people. We needed a language with which we could communicate with ourselves, a secret language. For some of us, language is a homeland closer than the Southwest—for many Chicanos today live in the Midwest and the East. And because we are a complex, heterogeneous people, we speak many languages. Some of the languages we speak are

1. Standard English
2. Working class and slang English
3. Standard Spanish
4. Standard Mexican Spanish
5. North Mexican Spanish dialect
6. Chicano Spanish (Texas, New Mexico, Arizona, and California have regional variations)
7. Tex-Mex
8. *Pachuco* (called *caló*)

My "home" tongues are the languages I speak with my sister and brothers, with my friends. They are the last five listed, with 6 and 7 being closest to my heart. From school, the media, and job situations, I've picked up standard and working class English. From Mamagrande Locha and from reading Spanish and Mexican literature, I've picked up Standard Spanish and Standard Mexican Spanish. From *los recién llegados*, Mexican immigrants, and *braceros*, I learned the North Mexican dialect. With Mexicans I'll try to speak either Standard Mexican Spanish or the North Mexican dialect. From my parents and Chicanos living in the Valley, I picked up Chicano Texas Spanish, and I speak it with my mom, younger brother (who married a Mexican and who rarely mixes Spanish with English), aunts, and older relatives.

With Chicanas from *Nuevo México* or *Arizona* I will speak Chicano Spanish a little, but often they don't understand what I'm saying. With most California Chicanas I speak entirely in English (unless I forget). When I first moved to San Francisco, I'd rattle off something in Spanish, unintentionally embarrassing them. Often it is only with another Chicana *tejano* that I can talk freely.

Words distorted by English are known as anglicisms or *pochismos*. The *pocho* is an anglicized Mexican or American of Mexican origin who speaks Spanish with an accent characteristic of North Americans and who distorts and reconstructs the language according to the influence of English.[3] Tex-Mex, or Spanglish, comes most naturally to me. I may switch back and forth from English to Spanish in the same sentence or in the same word. With my sister and my brother Nune and with Chicano *tejano* contemporaries I speak in Tex-Mex.

From kids and people my own age I picked up *Pachuco*. *Pachuco* (the language of the zoot suiters) is a language of rebellion, both against Standard Spanish and Standard English. It is a secret language. Adults of the culture and outsiders cannot understand it. It is made up of slang words from both English and Spanish. *Ruca* means girl or woman, *vato* means guy or dude, *chale* means no, *simón* means yes, *churro* is sure, talk is *periquiar*, *pigionear* means petting, *que gacho* means how nerdy, *ponte águila* means watch out, death is called *la pelona*. Through lack of practice and not having others who can speak it, I've lost most of the *Pachuco* tongue.

Chicano Spanish

Chicanos, after 250 years of Spanish/Anglo colonization, have developed significant differences in the Spanish we speak. We collapse two adjacent vowels into a single syllable and sometimes shift the stress in certain words such as *maíz/maiz, cohete/cuete*. We leave out certain consonants when they appear between vowels: *lado/lao, mojado/mojao*. Chicanos from South Texas pronounce *f* as *j* as in *jue (fue)*. Chicanos use "archaisms," words that are no longer in the Spanish language, words that have been evolved out. We say *semos, truje, haiga, ansina*, and *naiden*. We retain the "archaic" *j*, as in *jalar*, that derives from an

---

[3]R. C. Ortega, *Dialectología Del Barrio*, trans. Hortencia S. Alwan (Los Angeles, CA: R. C. Ortega Publisher & Bookseller, 1977), 132.

earlier *h* (the French *halar* or the Germanic *halon*, which was lost to standard Spanish in the sixteenth century), but which is still found in several regional dialects such as the one spoken in South Texas. (Due to geography, Chicanos from the Valley of South Texas were cut off linguistically from other Spanish speakers. We tend to use words that the Spaniards brought over from Medieval Spain. The majority of the Spanish colonizers in Mexico and the Southwest came from Extremadura—Hernán Cortés was one of them—and Andalucía. Andalucians pronounce *ll* like a *y*, and their *d*'s tend to be absorbed by adjacent vowels: *tirado* becomes *tirao*. They brought *el lenguaje popular, dialectos y regionalismos.*[4])

Chicanos and other Spanish speakers also shift *ll* to *y* and *z* to *s*.[5] We leave out initial syllables, saying *tar* for *estar*, *toy* for *estoy*, *hora* for *ahora* (*cubanos* and *puertorriqueños* also leave out initial letters of some words). We also leave out the final syllable such as *pa* for *para*. The intervocalic *y*, the *ll* as in *tortilla*, *ella*, *botella*, gets replaced by *tortia* or *tortiya*, *ea*, *botea*. We add an additional syllable at the beginning of certain words: *atocar* for *tocar*, *agastar* for *gastar*. Sometimes we'll say *lavaste las vacijas*, other times *lavates* (substituting the *ates* verb endings for the *aste*).

We used anglicisms, words borrowed from English: *bola* from ball, *carpeta* from carpet, *máchina de lavar* (instead of *lavadora*) from washing machine. Tex-Mex argot, created by adding a Spanish sound at the beginning or end of an English word, such as *cookiar* for cook, *watchar* for watch, *parkiar* for park, and *rapiar* for rape, is the result of the pressures on Spanish speakers to adapt to English.

We don't use the word *vosotros/as* or its accompanying verb form. We don't say *claro* (to mean *yes*), *imaginate*, or *me emociona*, unless we picked up Spanish from Latinas, out of a book, or in a classroom. Other Spanish-speaking groups are going through the same, or similar, development in their Spanish.

---

[4]Eduardo Hernandéz-Chávez, Andrew D. Cohen, and Anthony F. Beltramo, El Lenguaje de los Chicanos: *Regional and Social Characteristics of Language Used By Mexican Americans* (Arlington, VA: Center for Applied Linguistics, 1975), 39.

[5]Hernandéz-Chávez, xvii.

Linguistic Terrorism

> *Deslenguadas. Somos los del español deficiente.* We are your linguistic nightmare, your linguistic aberration, your linguistic *mestisaje*, the subject of your *burla*. Because we speak with tongues of fire we are culturally crucified. Racially, culturally, and linguistically *somos huérfanos*—we speak an orphan tongue.

Chicanas who grew up speaking Chicano Spanish have internalized the belief that we speak poor Spanish. It is illegitimate, a bastard language. And because we internalize how our language has been used against us by the dominant culture, we use our language differences against each other.

Chicana feminists often skirt around each other with suspicion and hesitation. For the longest time I couldn't figure it out. Then it dawned on me. To be close to another Chicana is like looking into the mirror. We are afraid of what we'll see there. *Pena.* Shame. Low estimation of self. In childhood we are told that our language is wrong. Repeated attacks on our native tongue diminish our sense of self. The attacks continue throughout our lives.

Chicanas feel uncomfortable talking in Spanish to Latinas, afraid of their censure. Their language was not outlawed in their countries. They had a whole lifetime of being immersed in their native tongue; generations, centuries in which Spanish was a first language, taught in school, heard on radio and TV, and read in the newspaper.

If a person, Chicana or Latina, has a low estimation of my native tongue, she also has a low estimation of me. Often with *mexicanas y latinas* we'll speak English as a neutral language. Even among Chicanas we tend to speak English at parties or conferences. Yet, at the same time, we're afraid the other will think we're *agringadas* because we don't speak Chicano Spanish. We oppress each other trying to out-Chicano each other, vying to be the "real" Chicanas, to speak like Chicanos. There is no one Chicano language just as there is no one Chicano experience. A monolingual Chicana whose first language is English or Spanish is just as much a Chicana as one who speaks several variants of Spanish. A Chicana from Michigan or Chicago or Detroit is just as much a Chicana as one from the Southwest. Chicano Spanish is as diverse linguistically as it is regionally.

By the end of this century, Spanish speakers will comprise the biggest minority group in the United States, a country where students in high schools and colleges are encouraged to take French classes because French is considered more "cultured." But for a language to remain alive it must be used.[6] By the end of this century English, and not Spanish, will be the mother tongue of most Chicanos and Latinos.

So, if you want to really hurt me, talk badly about my language. Ethnic identity is twin skin to linguistic identity—I am my language. Until I can take pride in my language, I cannot take pride in myself. Until I can accept as legitimate Chicano Texas Spanish, Tex-Mex, and all the other languages I speak, I cannot accept the legitimacy of myself. Until I am free to write bilingually and to switch codes without having always to translate, while I still have to speak English or Spanish when I would rather speak Spanglish, and as long as I have to accommodate the English speakers rather than having them accommodate me, my tongue will be illegitimate.

I will no longer be made to feel ashamed of existing. I will have my voice: Indian, Spanish, white. I will have my serpent's tongue—my woman's voice, my sexual voice, my poet's voice. I will overcome the tradition of silence.

> My fingers
> move sly against your palm
> Like women everywhere, we speak in code.
> MELANIE KAYE/KANTROWITZ[7]

"Vistas," corridos, y comida:

My Native Tongue

In the 1960s, I read my first Chicano novel. It was *City of Night* by John Rechy, a gay Texan, son of a Scottish father and a Mexican mother. For days I walked around in stunned amazement that a Chicano could write and could get published. When I read *I Am Joaquín*[8] I was surprised

---

[6]Irena Klepfisz, "Secular Jewish Identity: Yidishkayt in America," in *The Tribe of Dina*, Kaye/Kantrowitz and Klepfisz, eds., 43.

[7]Melanie Kaye/Kantrowitz, "Sign," in *We Speak In Code: Poems and Other Writings* (Pittsburgh, PA: Motheroot Publications, Inc., 1980), 85.

[8]Rodolfo Gonzales, *I Am Joaquín/Yo Soy Joaquín* (New York, NY: Bantam Books, 1972). It was first published in 1967.

to see a bilingual book by a Chicano in print. When I saw poetry written in Tex-Mex for the first time, a feeling of pure joy flashed through me. I felt like we really existed as a people. In 1971, when I started teaching High School English to Chicano students, I tried to supplement the required texts with works by Chicanos, only to be reprimanded and forbidden to do so by the principal. He claimed that I was supposed to teach "American" and English literature. At the risk of being fired, I swore my students to secrecy and slipped in Chicano short stories, poems, a play. In graduate school, while working toward a Ph.D., I had to "argue" with one adviser after the other, semester after semester, before I was allowed to make Chicano literature an area of focus.

Even before I read books by Chicanos or Mexicans, it was the Mexican movies I saw at the drive-in—the Thursday night special of $1.00 a carload—that gave me a sense of belonging. *"Vámonos a las vistas,"* my mother would call out and we'd all—grandmother, brothers, sister, and cousins—squeeze into the car. We'd wolf down cheese and bologna white bread sandwiches while watching Pedro Infante in melodramatic tearjerkers like *Nosotros los pobres,* the first "real" Mexican movie (that was not an imitation of European movies). I remember seeing *Cuando los hijos se van* and surmising that all Mexican movies played up the love a mother has for her children and what ungrateful sons and daughters suffer when they are not devoted to their mothers. I remember the singing-type "westerns" of Jorge Negrete and Miquel Aceves Mejía. When watching Mexican movies, I felt a sense of homecoming as well as alienation. People who were to amount to something didn't go to Mexican movies, or *bailes,* or tune their radios to *bolero,* *rancherita,* and *corrido* music.

The whole time I was growing up, there was *norteño* music sometimes called North Mexican border music, or Tex-Mex music, or Chicano music, or *cantina* (bar) music. I grew up listening to *conjuntos,* three- or four-piece bands made up of folk musicians playing guitar, *bajo sexto,* drums, and button accordion, which Chicanos had borrowed from the German immigrants who had come to Central Texas and Mexico to farm and build breweries. In the Rio Grande Valley, Steve Jordan and Little Joe Hernández were popular, and Flaco Jiménez was the accordion king. The rhythms of Tex-Mex music are those of the polka, also adapted from the Germans, who in turn had borrowed the polka from the Czechs and Bohemians.

I remember the hot, sultry evenings when *corridos*—songs of love and death on the Texas-Mexican borderlands—reverberated out of cheap amplifiers from the local *cantinas* and wafted in through my bedroom window.

Corridos first became widely used along the South Texas/Mexican border during the early conflict between Chicanos and Anglos. The *corridos* are usually about Mexican heroes who do valiant deeds against the Anglo oppressors. Pancho Villa's song, "*La cucaracha*," is the most famous one. *Corridos* of John F. Kennedy and his death are still very popular in the Valley. Older Chicanos remember Lydia Mendoza, one of the great border *corrido* singers who was called *la Gloria de Tejas*. Her "*El tango negro*," sung during the Great Depression, made her a singer of the people. The ever-present *corridos* narrated one hundred years of border history, bringing news of events as well as entertaining. These folk musicians and folk songs are our chief cultural mythmakers, and they made our hard lives seem bearable.

I grew up feeling ambivalent about our music. Country-western and rock-and-roll had more status. In the fifties and sixties, for the slightly educated and *agringado* Chicanos, there existed a sense of shame at being caught listening to our music. Yet I couldn't stop my feet from thumping to the music, could not stop humming the words, nor hide from myself the exhilaration I felt when I heard it.

There are more subtle ways that we internalize identification, especially in the forms of images and emotions. For me food and certain smells are tied to my identity, to my homeland. Woodsmoke curling up to an immense blue sky; woodsmoke perfuming my grandmother's clothes, her skin. The stench of cow manure and the yellow patches on the ground; the crack of a .22 rifle and the reek of cordite. Homemade white cheese sizzling in a pan, melting inside a folded *tortilla*. My sister Hilda's hot, spicy *menudo*, *chile colorado* making it deep red, pieces of *panza* and hominy floating on top. My brother Carito barbequing *fajitas* in the backyard. Even now and 3,000 miles away, I can see my mother spicing the ground beef, pork, and venison with *chile*. My mouth salivates at the thought of the hot steaming *tamales* I would be eating if I were home.

Si le preguntas a mi mamá, "¿Qué eres?"

> Identity is the essential core of who
> we are as individuals, the conscious
> experience of the self inside.
>
> *GERSHEN KAUFMAN*[9]

Nosotros los Chicanos straddle the borderlands. On one side of us, we are constantly exposed to the Spanish of the Mexicans, on the other side we hear the Anglos' incessant clamoring so that we forget our language. Among ourselves we don't say *nosotros los americanos, o nosotros los españoles, o nosotros los hispanos.* We say *nosotros los mexicanos* (by *mexicanos* we do not mean citizens of Mexico; we do not mean a national identity, but a racial one). We distinguish between *mexicanos del otro lado* and *mexicanos de este lado.* Deep in our hearts we believe that being Mexican has nothing to do with which country one lives in. Being Mexican is a state of soul—not one of mind, not one of citizenship. Neither eagle nor serpent, but both. And like the ocean, neither animal respects borders.

> *Dime con quien and as y te diré quien eres.*
> (Tell me who your friends are and I'll tell you who you are.)
>
> *MEXICAN SAYING*

Si le preguntas a mi mamá, "¿Qué eres?" te dirá, "Soy mexicana." My brothers and sister say the same. I sometimes will answer *"soy mexicana"* and at others will say *"soy Chicana" o "soy tejana."* But I identified as *"Raza"* before I ever identified as *"mexicana"* or *"Chicana."*

As a culture, we call ourselves Spanish when referring to ourselves as a linguistic group and when copping out. It is then that we forget our predominant Indian genes. We are 70–80 percent Indian.[10] We call ourselves Hispanic[11] or Spanish-American or Latin American or Latin when linking ourselves to other Spanish-speaking peoples of the

---

[9]Kaufman, 68.

[10]Chávez, 88–90.

[11]"Hispanic" is derived from *Hispanis* (*España*, a name given to the Iberian Peninsula in ancient times when it was part of the Roman Empire) and is a term designated by the U.S. government to make it easier to handle us on paper.

Western hemisphere and when copping out. We call ourselves Mexican-American[12] to signify we are neither Mexican nor American, but more the noun "American" than the adjective "Mexican" (and when copping out).

Chicanos and other people of color suffer economically for not acculturating. This voluntary (yet forced) alienation makes for psychological conflict, a kind of dual identity—we don't identify with the Anglo-American cultural values and we don't totally identify with the Mexican cultural values. We are a synergy of two cultures with various degrees of Mexicanness or Angloness. I have so internalized the borderland conflict that sometimes I feel like one cancels out the other and we are zero, nothing, no one. *A veces no soy nada ni nadie. Pero hasta cuando no lo soy, lo soy.*

When not copping out, when we know we are more than nothing, we call ourselves Mexican, referring to race and ancestry; *mestizo* when affirming both our Indian and Spanish (but we hardly ever own our Black) ancestry; Chicano when referring to a politically aware people born and/or raised in the United States; *Raza* when referring to Chicanos; *tejanos* when we are Chicanos from Texas.

Chicanos did not know we were a people until 1965 when Cesar Chavez and the farmworkers united and *I Am Joaquín* was published and *la Raza Unida* party was formed in Texas. With that recognition, we became a distinct people. Something momentous happened to the Chicano soul—we became aware of our reality and acquired a name and a language (Chicano Spanish) that reflected that reality. Now that we had a name, some of the fragmented pieces began to fall together—who we were, what we were, how we had evolved. We began to get glimpses of what we might eventually become.

Yet the struggle of identities continues, the struggle of borders is our reality still. One day the inner struggle will cease and a true integration take place. In the meantime, *tenémos que hacer la lucha. ¿Quién está protegiendo los ranchos de mi gente? ¿Quién está tratando de cerrar la fisura entre la india y el blanco en nuestra sangre? El Chicano, si, el Chicano que anda como un landrón en su propia casa.*

---

[12]The Treaty of Guadalupe Hidalgo created the Mexican-American in 1848.

Los Chicanos, how patient we seem, how very patient. There is the quiet of the Indian about us.[13] We know how to survive. When other races have given up their tongue we've kept ours. We know what it is to live under the hammer blow of the dominant *norteamericano* culture. But more than we count the blows, we count the days the weeks the years the centuries the aeons until the white laws and commerce and customs will rot in the deserts they've created, lie bleached. *Humildes* yet proud, *quietos* yet wild, *nosotros los mexicanos-Chicanos* will walk by the crumbling ashes as we go about our business. Stubborn, persevering, impenetrable as stone, yet possessing a malleability that renders us unbreakable, we, the *mestizas* and *mestizos*, will remain.

Possibilities for Writing

1. Anzaldúa focuses here not only on language but on other aspects of culture as well, including music and movies. How do these various examples contribute to her overall argument?

2. After the introductory paragraphs, the essay is divided into four separately headed sections. What points does Anzaldúa make in each section? What links can you find among the sections? For you, does she succeed in making a coherent argument?

3. Think about your own use of language—at home, at school, at work, among friends, with strangers, in formal and informal situations. When do you feel most comfortable and when least comfortable? How do you account for your feelings? Are they in any way related to the point Anzaldúa is making?

---

[13]Anglos, in order to alleviate their guilt for dispossessing the Chicano, stressed the Spanish part of us and perpetrated the myth of the Spanish Southwest. We have accepted the fiction that we are Hispanic, that is Spanish, in order to accommodate ourselves to the dominant culture and its abhorrence of Indians. Chávez, 88–91.

Francis Bacon (1561–1626) was born in London to parents who were members of the court of Queen Elizabeth I. He attended Trinity College, entered the practice of law in his late teens, and became a member of the House of Commons at the age of 23. His career flourished under King James I, but later scandals ended his life as a politician. A philosopher/scientist by nature and one of the most admired thinkers of his day, Bacon was a founder of the modern empirical tradition based on closely observing the physical world, conducting controlled experiments, and interpreting results rationally to discover the workings of the universe. Of his many published works, he is best remembered today for his Essays *(collected from 1597 until after his death), brief meditations noted for their wit and insight.*

Francis Bacon
Of Studies

In his classic essay, "Of Studies," Francis Bacon explains how and why study—knowledge—is important. Along with Michel de Montaigne, who published his first essays less than twenty years before Francis Bacon published his first collection in 1597, Bacon is concidered the father of the English essay (with Montaigne the father of the French essay). Bacon's essays differ from Montaigne's in being more compact and more formal. Where Montaigne conceived of the essay as an opportunity to explore a subject through mental association and a casual ramble of the mind, Bacon envisioned the essay as an opportunity to offer advice. The title of his essay collection: "Essays or Counsels: Civil and Moral," suggests that didactic intent.

In "Of Studies," Bacon lays out the value of knowledge in practical terms. Bacon considers to what use studies might be put. He is less interested in their theoretical promise than in their practical utility—a proclivity more English, perhaps, than French. Bacon's writing in "Of Studies" is direct and pointed. It avoids the meandering find-your-way free form of Montaigne's essays. From his opening sentence Bacon gets directly to the point: "Studies serve for delight, for ornament, and for ability." He then elaborates on how studies are useful in these three ways. And he wastes no words in detailing the uses of "studies" for a Renaissance gentleman.

One of the attractions of Bacon's essay is his skillful use of parallel sentence structure, as exemplified in the opening sentence and throughout "Of Studies." This stylistic technique lends clarity and order to the writing, as in "crafty men condemn studies, simple men admire them, and wise men use them," which in its straightforward assertiveness exhibits confidence and elegance in addition to clarity and emphasis.

Studies serve for delight, for ornament, and for ability. Their chief use for delight is in privateness and retiring; for ornament, is in discourse;

and for ability, is in the judgment and disposition of business. For expert men can execute, and perhaps judge of particulars, one by one; but the general counsels, and the plots and marshaling of affairs, come best from those that are learned. To spend too much time in studies is sloth; to use them too much for ornament is affectation; to make judgment wholly by their rules is the humor of a scholar. They perfect nature, and are perfected by experience; for natural abilities are like natural plants, that need pruning by study; and studies themselves do give forth directions too much at large, except they be bounded in by experience. Crafty men contemn studies, simple men admire them, and wise men use them, for they teach not their own use; but that is a wisdom without them, and above them, won by observation. Read not to contradict and confute, nor to believe and take for granted, nor to find talk and discourse, but to weigh and consider. Some books are to be tasted, others to be swallowed, and some few to be chewed and digested; that is, some books are to be read only in parts; others to be read, but not curiously and some few to be read wholly, and with diligence and attention. Some books also may be read by deputy and extracts made of them by others, but that would be only in the less important arguments and the meaner sort of books; else distilled books are like common distilled waters, flashy things. Reading maketh a full man, conference a ready man, and writing an exact man. And therefore, if a man write little, he had need have a great memory; if he confer little, he had need have a present wit and if he read little, he had need have much cunning, to seem to know that he doth not. Histories make men wise; poets, witty, the mathematics, subtle; natural philosophy, deep; moral, grave; logic and rhetoric, able to contend. *Abeunt studia in mores*, Nay, there is no stond or impediment in the wit but may be wrought out by fit studies, like as diseases of the body may have appropriate exercises. Bowling is good for the stone and reins, shooting for the lungs and breast, gentle walking for the stomach, riding for the head, and the like. So if a man's wit be wandering, let him study the mathematics; for in demonstrations, if his wit be called away never so little, he must begin again. If his wit be not apt to distinguish or find differences, let him study the schoolmen, for they are *cumini sectores*. If he be not apt to beat over matters and to call up one thing to prove and illustrate another, let him study the lawyer's cases. So every defect of the mind may have a special receipt.

Possibilities for Writing

1. Bacon's essay was composed some four hundred years ago in a society that was in many ways very different from ours today. Write an analysis of "Of Studies" in which you summarize the main points Bacon makes and then go on to explore the extent to which his remarks continue to seem relevant. As you reread "Of Studies" and make preliminary notes, you will need to find ways to "translate" much of his vocabulary into its modern equivalent.

2. Bacon's brief essay contains many aphorisms, concise statements of a general principle or truth—for example, "Read not to contradict and confute, nor to believe and take for granted, nor to find talk and discourse, but to weigh and consider." Take one of these, put it into your own words, and use it as the starting point for an essay of your own. Elaborate on the statement with examples and further details that come from your own experience or imagination.

3. Changing Bacon's focus a bit, write an essay for modern audiences titled "On Reading." In it consider different types of reading, purposes for reading, benefits of reading, difficulties involved in reading, and so forth. Your essay may be quite personal, focusing on your own experiences as a reader, or, like Bacon's, more formal.

Dave Barry (b. 1947), a native of Armonk, New York, graduated from Haverford College. After ten years of working as a newspaper reporter and later as a business writing consultant, he began turning out a freelance humor column in 1980. He is now on the staff of the Miami Herald, *and his popular column is syndicated in more than one hundred fifty papers around the country. Barry has published many collections of these columns, which often find irony and humor in the everyday circumstances of middle-class Americans; among his most recent collections are* Big Trouble *(1999) and* Dave Barry Is Not Taking This Sitting Down *(2000). Barry was awarded a Pulitzer Prize for commentary in 1988.*

Dave Barry
Road Warrior

In "Road Warrior," the humor columnist Dave Barry writes about the recently diagnosed quality of "road rage" that is said to afflict America's motorists. "Road rage" refers to the pent-up and explosively released anger and hostility that drivers feel and express in an era of increasing automobile traffic congestion and ever increasing delays. Social analysts attribute driver "road rage" not only to all the additional cars and drivers clogging the roads, but also to a decline in civility that seems to many to afflict American society today.

Barry pokes fun at the drivers who flout the rules of the road, and in criticizing their misbehavior, he works himself up into a kind of rage, indicated by his use of CAPITAL LETTERS. In venting a bit over road rage, Barry segues into describing what he calls "Parking Lot Rage" and "Shopping Cart Rage," two forms of anger that push Barry's discussion of road rage into comic territory.

Barry has some fun as he describes the frustration that drivers feel when, looking for a parking space, they see someone sitting in a car, apparently ready to pull out, without finally doing so. They just sit there, leading, as Barry suggests, to "Parking Lot Rage." He also describes the congestion of shopping carts in supermarket aisles, which leads to still another kind of rage that Barry describes while offering up criticism of both the proliferation of product choices confronting supermarket patrons, and the automated telephone service—which leads to yet another kind of "rage." Barry's humor both describes these various reasons for anger and simultaneously defuses that anger.

If you do much driving on our nation's highways, you've probably noticed that, more and more often, bullets are coming through your windshield. This is a common sign of Road Rage, which the opinion-makers in the news media have decided is a serious problem, currently ranking just behind global warming and several points ahead of Asia.

How widespread is Road Rage? To answer that question, researchers for the National Institute of Traffic Safety recently did a study in which they drove on the interstate highway system in a specially equipped observation van. By the third day, they were deliberately running other motorists off the road.

"These people are MORONS!" was their official report.

That is the main cause of Road Rage: the realization that many of your fellow motorists have the same brain structure as a cashew. The most common example, of course, is the motorists who feel a need to drive in the left-hand, or "passing," lane, even though they are going slower than everybody else. Nobody knows why these motorists do this. Maybe they belong to some kind of religious cult that believes the right lane is sacred and must never come in direct contact with tires. Maybe one time, years ago, these motorists happened to be driving in the left lane when their favorite song came on the radio, so they've driven over there ever since, in hopes that the radio will play that song again.

But whatever makes these people drive this way, there's nothing you can do about it. You can honk at them, but it will have no effect. People have been honking at them for years: It's a normal part of their environment. They've decided that, for some mysterious reason, wherever they drive, there is honking. They choose not to ponder this mystery any further, lest they overburden their cashews.

I am very familiar with this problem, because I live and drive in Miami, which proudly bills itself as The Inappropriate-Lane-Driving Capital Of The World, a place where the left lane is thought of not so much as a thoroughfare as a public recreational area, where motorists feel free to stop, hold family reunions, barbecue pigs, play volleyball, etc. Compounding this problem is another common type of Miami motorist, the aggressive young male whose car has a sound system so powerful that the driver must go faster than the speed of sound at all times, because otherwise the nuclear bass notes emanating from his rear speakers will catch up to him and cause his head to explode.

So the tiny minority of us Miami drivers who actually qualify as normal find ourselves constantly being trapped behind people drifting along on the interstate at the speed of diseased livestock, while at the same time we are being tailgated and occasionally bumped from behind by testosterone-deranged youths who got their driver training from watching the space-fighter battle scenes in *Star Wars*. And of course nobody EVER signals or yields, and people are CONSTANTLY cutting us off, and AFTER A WHILE WE START TO FEEL SOME RAGE, OK? YOU GOT A PROBLEM WITH THAT, MISTER NEWS MEDIA OPINION-MAKER??

In addition to Road Rage, I frequently experience Parking Lot Rage, which occurs when I pull into a crowded supermarket parking lot, and I see people get into their car, clearly ready to leave, so I stop my car and wait for them to vacate the spot, and . . . nothing happens! They just stay there! WHAT THE HELL ARE THEY DOING IN THERE??!! COOKING DINNER???

When I finally get into the supermarket, I often experience Shopping Cart Rage. This is caused by the people—and you just KNOW these are the same people who always drive in the left-hand lane—who routinely manage, by careful placement, to block the entire aisle with a single shopping cart. If we really want to keep illegal immigrants from entering the United States, we should employ Miami residents armed with shopping carts; we'd only need about two dozen to block the entire Mexican border.

What makes the supermarket congestion even worse is that shoppers are taking longer and longer to decide what to buy, because every product in America now comes in an insane number of styles and sizes. For example, I recently went to the supermarket to get orange juice. For just *one brand* of orange juice, Tropicana, I had to decide whether I wanted Original, HomeStyle, Pulp Plus, Double Vitamin C, Grovestand, Calcium, or Old-Fashioned; I also had to decide whether I wanted the 16-ounce, 32-ounce, 64-ounce, 96-ounce, or six-pack size. This is WAY too many product choices. It caused me to experience Way Too Many Product Choices Rage. I would have called Tropicana and complained, but I probably would have wound up experiencing Automated Phone Answering System Rage (". . . For questions about Pulp Plus in the 32-ounce size, press 23. For questions about Pulp Plus in the 64-ounce size, press 24. For questions about . . .").

My point is that there are many causes for rage in our modern world, and if we're going to avoid unnecessary violence, we all need to "keep our cool." So let's try to be more considerate, OK? Otherwise I will kill you.

Possibilities for Writing

1. Barry's point, he writes, is that "there are many causes for rage in our modern world, and if we're going to avoid unnecessary violence, we all need to 'keep our cool.' " Use this idea as the basis for a more serious essay on the topic of controlling conflict and violence.

2. Write a comic essay about other sorts of behavior that can spark irritation or "rage." Don't be afraid to use exaggeration, as Barry does, but do so in ways that readers will find amusing rather than offensive.

3. Scan some newspapers or magazines for another recent social trend, being reported in the media. Examine this trend from your own perspective and using your own examples—either comically, as Barry does, or more seriously.

---

*Roland Barthes (1915–1980) was born in France and studied French literature
and classics at the University of Paris. After teaching in universities in
Bucharest, Romania, and Alexandria, Egypt, he joined the National Center for
Scientific Research, where he pursued research studies in sociology and
language. As a leader of France's new critics, Barthes drew on the insights of
Karl Marx and Sigmund Freud as well as on the work of the influential linguist
Ferdinand de Saussure to expand the science of semiology, the study of signs
and symbols underlying all aspects of human culture. His many works include*
Elements of Semiology, Empire of Signs, A Lover's Discourse, The Pleasure of
the Text, *and* Mythologies, *from which "Toys" has been taken.*

Roland Barthes

Toys

In "Toys," Barthes meditates on the cultural significance of French toys, seeing
them as a "microcosm" of the adult world. Barthes analyzes the social
implications of French toys, arguing that it is no accident that toys reflect the
"myths and techniques" of modern life. Toys, according to Barthes, epitomize
what is socially important and culturally validated by the country in which they
are produced and purchased.

A second area Barthes investigates concerns the forms and materials from
which French toys are made. He considers the extent to which certain kinds of
toys are imitative of actual life—girl's dolls that take in and eliminate water
being one example. He contrasts such imitative toys with simple toys such as
wooden blocks, which allow children to be more creative in their play.

French toys: one could not find a better illustration of the fact that the
adult Frenchman sees the child as another self. All the toys one commonly sees are essentially a microcosm of the adult world; they are all
reduced copies of human objects, as if in the eyes of the public the child
was, all told, nothing but a smaller man, a homunculus to whom must
be supplied objects of his own size.

Invented forms are very rare: a few sets of blocks, which appeal
to the spirit of do-it-yourself, are the only ones which offer dynamic
forms. As for the others, French toys *always mean something*, and this
something is always entirely socialized, constituted by the myths or the
techniques of modern adult life: the Army, Broadcasting, the Post
Office, Medicine (miniature instrument-cases, operating theatres for
dolls), School, Hair-Styling (driers for permanent-waving), the Air

Force (Parachutists), Transport (trains, Citroëns, Vedettes, Vespas, petrol-stations), Science (Martian toys).

The fact that French toys *literally* prefigure the world of adult functions obviously cannot but prepare the child to accept them all, by constituting for him, even before he can think about it, the alibi of a Nature which has at all times created soldiers, postmen and Vespas. Toys here reveal the list of all the things the adult does not find unusual: war, bureaucracy, ugliness, Martians, etc. It is not so much, in fact, the imitation which is the sign of an abdication, as its literalness: French toys are like a Jivaro head, in which one recognizes, shrunken to the size of an apple, the wrinkles and hair of an adult. There exist, for instance, dolls which urinate; they have an oesophagus, one gives them a bottle, they wet their nappies; soon, no doubt, milk will turn to water in their stomachs. This is meant to prepare the little girl for the causality of house-keeping, to 'condition' her to her future role as mother. However, faced with this world of faithful and complicated objects, the child can only identify himself as owner, as user, never as creator; he does not invent the world, he uses it: there are, prepared for him, actions without adventure, without wonder, without joy. He is turned into a little stay-at-home householder who does not even have to invent the mainsprings of adult causality; they are supplied to him ready-made: he has only to help himself, he is never allowed to discover anything from start to finish. The merest set of blocks, provided it is not too refined, implies a very different learning of the world: then, the child does not in any way create meaningful objects, it matters little to him whether they have an adult name; the actions he performs are not those of a user but those of a demiurge. He creates forms which walk, which roll, he creates life, not property: objects now act by themselves, they are no longer an inert and complicated material in the palm of his hand. But such toys are rather rare: French toys are usually based on imitation, they are meant to produce children who are users, not creators.

The bourgeois status of toys can be recognized not only in their forms, which are all functional, but also in their substances. Current toys are made of a graceless material, the product of chemistry, not of nature. Many are now moulded from complicated mixtures; the plastic material of which they are made has an appearance at once gross and hygienic, it destroys all the pleasure, the sweetness, the humanity of touch. A sign which fills one with consternation is the gradual disappearance of wood,

in spite of its being an ideal material because of its firmness and its softness, and the natural warmth of its touch. Wood removes, from all the
forms which it supports, the wounding quality of angles which are too
sharp, the chemical coldness of metal. When the child handles it and
knocks it, it neither vibrates nor grates, it has a sound at once muffled
and sharp. It is a familiar and poetic substance, which does not sever the
child from close contact with the tree, the table, the floor. Wood does not
wound or break down; it does not shatter, it wears out, it can last a long
time, live with the child, alter little by little the relations between the
object and the hand. If it dies, it is in dwindling, not in swelling out like
those mechanical toys which disappear behind the hernia of a broken
spring. Wood makes essential objects, objects for all time. Yet there
hardly remain any of these wooden toys from the Vosges, these fretwork
farms with their animals, which were only possible, it is true, in the days
of the craftsman. Henceforth, toys are chemical in substance and colour;
their very material introduces one to a coenaesthesis of use, not pleasure.
These toys die in fact very quickly, and once dead, they have no posthu-
mous life for the child.

Possibilities for Writing

1. Barthes suggests that French toys "always mean something."
   Consider the examples he provides and identify just how and
   what they signify about French society and culture at the time
   the essay was written.
2. To what extent do you agree with Barthes that toys can stifle as
   well as stimulate creativity? What sorts of toys limit the imagination of children, and what kinds of toys help them develop their
   imaginative capacity? Why?
3. Write an essay in which you explore and analyze contemporary
   American toys and the extent to which they convey implications
   about American cultural and social life today. Or write an essay
   in which you analyze another aspect of American popular culture, such as fast food, wrestling, casino gambling, or video
   games, to explain how and what they reveal about American
   social and cultural life.

Susan Brownmiller (b. 1935), one of the founders of the contemporary feminist movement, grew up in Brooklyn and attended Cornell University and the Jefferson School of Social Sciences. For several years a newspaper reporter and network news writer, she was instrumental in organizing, in 1968, the New York Radical Feminists. Her concern with women's issues led to her first book, the widely discussed Against Our Will: Men, Women, and Rape *(1975), which posited the then controversial notion that rape was not a sexual act but an act of power. This was followed by* Femininity *(1984), in which Brownmiller considered female stereotypes and the pressures on women to conform to them, and* Waverly Place *(1989), a novel focusing on an abusive marriage. Brownmiller is still active in the women's movement and a frequent contributor to a variety of periodicals.*

Susan Brownmiller
Femininity

In "Femininity," an introductory essay that prefaces her book of that title, Susan Brownmiller defines what femininity is by identifying its aspects, analyzing its qualities, and considering the limitations that society has imposed upon females. In the process, Brownmiller invokes her own experience as a woman and a writer. Her prefatory essay, however, though including stories from her life as support for her views, is less about herself than about the larger issues of femininity and feminism set in the context of culture and history.

Brownmiller examines not just what femininity is, but what it means—its associated implications and connotations. She considers what it means to be feminine in a masculine world. She asks questions about the differences between women and men—differences that transcend stereotypical notions, biological realities, and social expectations. Throughout her essay, Brownmiller breaks down and through simplistic assumptions about femininity. In considering the relation of the feminine to the masculine, Brownmiller defines the distinctiveness of femininity and explains the sources of its power.

We had a game in our house called "setting the table" and I was Mother's helper. Forks to the left of the plate, knives and spoons to the right. Placing the cutlery neatly, as I recall, was one of my first duties, and the event was alive with meaning. When a knife or a fork dropped on the floor, that meant a man was unexpectedly coming to dinner. A falling spoon announced the surprise arrival of a female guest. No matter that these visitors never arrived on cue, I had learned a rule of gender identification. Men were straight-edged, sharply pronged and formidable, women were softly curved and held the food in a rounded well. It made perfect sense, like the division of pink and blue that I saw in babies, an orderly way of viewing the world. Daddy, who was gone all day at work and who loved to putter at home with his pipe tobacco and tool chest, was knife and fork. Mommy and Grandma, with their ample proportions and pots and pans, were grownup soup spoons, large and capacious. And I was a teaspoon, small and slender, easy to hold and just right for pudding, my favorite dessert.

Being good at what was expected of me was one of my earliest projects, for not only was I rewarded, as most children are, for doing things right, but excellence gave pride and stability to my childhood existence. Girls were different from boys, and the expression of that difference seemed mine to make clear. Did my loving, anxious mother, who dressed me in white organdy pinafores and Mary Janes and who cried hot tears when I got them dirty, give me my first instruction? Of course. Did my doting aunts and uncles with their gifts of pretty dolls and miniature tea sets add to my education? Of course. But even without the appropriate toys and clothes, lessons in the art of being feminine lay all around me and I absorbed them all: the fairy tales that were read to me at night, the brightly colored advertisements I pored over in magazines before I learned to decipher the words, the movies I saw, the comic books I hoarded, the radio soap operas I happily followed whenever I had to stay in bed with a cold. I loved being a little girl, or rather I loved being a fairy princess, for that was who I thought I was.

As I passed through a stormy adolescence to a stormy maturity, femininity increasingly became an exasperation, a brilliant, subtle esthetic that was bafflingly inconsistent at the same time that it was minutely, demandingly concrete, a rigid code of appearance and behavior defined by do's and don't-do's that went against my rebellious grain. Femininity was a challenge thrown down to the female sex, a challenge no proud, self-respecting young woman could afford to ignore, particularly one with enormous ambition that she nursed in secret, alternately feeding or starving its inchoate life in tremendous confusion.

"Don't lose your femininity" and "Isn't it remarkable how she manages to retain her femininity?" had terrifying implications. They spoke of a bottom-line failure so irreversible that nothing else mattered. The pinball machine has registered "tilt," the game had been called. Disqualification was marked on the forehead of a woman whose femininity was lost. No records would be entered in her name, for she had destroyed her birthright in her wretched, ungainly effort to imitate a man. She walked in limbo, this hapless creature, and it occurred to me that one day I might see her when I looked in the mirror. If the danger was so palpable that warning notices were freely posted, wasn't it possible that the small bundle of resentments I carried around in secret might spill out and place the mark on my own forehead? Whatever quarrels with femininity I had I kept to myself; whatever handicaps femininity imposed, they were mine to deal with alone, for there was no women's movement to ask the tough questions, or to brazenly disregard the rules.

Femininity, in essence, is a romantic sentiment, a nostalgic tradition of imposed limitations. Even as it hurries forward in the 1980s, putting on lipstick and high heels to appear well dressed, it trips on the ruffled petticoats and hoop-skirts of an era gone by. Invariably and necessarily, femininity is something that women had more of in the past, not only in the historic past of prior generations, but in each woman's personal past as well—in the virginal innocence that is replaced by knowledge, in the dewy cheek that is coarsened by age, in the "inherent nature" that a woman seems to misplace so forgetfully whenever she steps out of bounds. Why should this be so? The XX chromosomal message has not been scrambled, the estrogen-dominated hormonal balance is generally as biology intended, the reproductive organs, whatever use one has made of them, are usually in place, the breasts of whatever size are most often where they should be. But clearly, biological femaleness is not enough.

Femininity always demands more. It must constantly reassure its audience by a willing demonstration of difference, even when one does not exist in nature, or it must seize and embrace a natural variation and compose a rhapsodic symphony upon the notes. Suppose one doesn't care to, has other things on her mind, is clumsy or tone-deaf despite the best instruction and training? To fall at the feminine difference is to appear not to care about men, and to risk the loss of their attention and approval. To be insufficiently feminine is viewed as a failure in core sexual identity, or as a failure to care sufficiently about oneself, for a woman found wanting will be appraised (and will appraise herself) as mannish or neutered or simply unattractive, as men have defined these terms.

We are talking, admittedly, about an exquisite esthetic. Enormous pleasure can be extracted from feminine pursuits as a creative outlet or purely as relaxation; indeed, indulgence for the sake of fun, or art, or attention, is among femininity's great joys. But the chief attraction (and the central paradox, as well) is the competitive edge that femininity seems to promise in the unending struggle to survive, and perhaps to triumph. The world smiles favorably on the feminine woman: it extends little courtesies and minor privilege. Yet the nature of this competitive edge is ironic, at best, for one works at femininity by accepting restrictions, by limiting one's sights, by choosing an indirect route, by scattering concentration and not giving one's all as a man would to his own, certifiably masculine, interests. It does not require a great leap of imagination for a woman to understand the feminine principle as a grand collection of compromises, large and small, that she simply must make in order to render herself a successful woman. If she has difficulty in satisfying femininity's demands, if its illusions go against her grain, or if she is criticized for her shortcomings and imperfections, the more she will see femininity as a desperate strategy of appeasement, a strategy she may not have the wish or the courage to abandon, for failure looms in either direction.

It is fashionable in some quarters to describe the feminine and masculine principles as polar ends of the human continuum and to sagely profess that both polarities exist in all people. Sun and moon, yin and yang, soft and hard, active and passive, etcetera, may indeed be opposites, but a linear continuum does not illuminate the problem. (Femininity, in all its contrivances, is a very active endeavor.) What, then, is the basic distinction? The masculine principle is better understood as a driving ethos of superiority designed to inspire straightforward, confident success, while the feminine principle is composed of vulnerability, the need for protection, the formalities of compliance and the avoidance of conflict—in short, an appeal of dependence and good will that gives the masculine principle its romantic validity and its admiring applause.

Femininity pleases men because it makes them appear more masculine by contrast; and, in truth, conferring an extra portion of unearned gender distinction on men, an unchallenged space in which to breathe freely and feel stronger, wiser, more competent, is femininity's special gift. One could say that masculinity is often an effort to please women, but masculinity is known to please by displays of mastery and competence while femininity pleases by suggesting that these concerns, except in small matters, are beyond its intent. Whimsy, unpredictability and patterns of thinking and behavior that are dominated by emotion, such as tearful expressions of sentiment and fear, are thought to be feminine precisely because they lie outside the established route to success.

If in the beginnings of history the feminine woman was defined by her physical dependency, her inability for reasons of reproductive biology to triumph over the forces of nature that were the tests of masculine strength and power, today she reflects both an economic and emotional dependency that is still considered "natural," romantic and attractive. After an unsettling fifteen years in which many basic assumptions about the sexes were challenged, the economic disparity did not disappear. Large numbers of women—those with small children, those left high and dry after a mid-life divorce—need financial support. But even those who earn their own living share a universal need for connectedness (call it love, if you wish). As unprecedented numbers of men abandon their sexual interest in women, others, sensing opportunity, choose to demonstrate their interest through variety and a change in partners. A sociological fact of the 1980s is that female competition for two scarce resources—men and jobs—is especially fierce.

So it is not surprising that we are currently witnessing a renewed interest in femininity and an unabashed indulgence in feminine pursuits. Femininity serves to reassure men that women need them and care about them enormously. By incorporating the decorative and the frivolous into its definition of style, femininity functions as an effective antidote to the unrelieved seriousness, the pressure of making one's way in a harsh, difficult world. In its mandate to avoid direct confrontation and to smooth over the fissures of conflict, femininity operates as a value system of niceness, a code of thoughtfulness and sensitivity that in modern society is sadly in short supply.

There is no reason to deny that indulgence in the art of feminine illusion can be reassuring to a woman, if she happens to be good at it. As sexuality undergoes some dizzying revisions, evidence that one is a woman "at heart" (the inquisitor's question) is not without worth. Since an answer of sorts may be furnished by piling on additional documentation, affirmation can arise from such identifiable but trivial feminine activities as buying a new eyeliner, experimenting with the latest shade of nail color, or bursting into tears at the outcome of a popular romance novel. Is there anything destructive in this? Time and cost factors, a deflection of energy and an absorption in fakery spring quickly to mind, and they need to be balanced, as in a ledger book, against the affirming advantage.

Possibilities for Writing

1. How is Brownmiller defining "femininity" here? In what ways does she suggest that contemporary culture values femininity? In the twenty plus years since this essay was written, to what extent have notions of femininity changed? Is femininity still valued in the same way?

2. As you were growing up, what images of gender difference were you presented with? How did you learn to distinguish between "feminine" and "masculine"? Looking back from your present perspective, how accurate or fair do these distinctions seem?

3. Analyze some current media images for their portrayal of gender roles. You may wish to look at recent television series, films, advertisements, contemporary music, and the like. Make sure that the examples you choose are clearly related.

Judith Ortiz Cofer *(b. 1952) spent her childhood in the small Puerto Rican town where she was born and in Paterson, New Jersey, where her family lived for most of each year, from the time she was three. She attended Catholic schools in Paterson and holds degrees from the University of Georgia and Florida Atlantic University. She has published several volumes of poetry, including* Reaching for the Mainland *(1996), and her 1989 novel* The Line of the Sun *was nominated for a Pulitzer Prize. Cofer has also published two autobiographical works:* Silent Dancing: A Partial Remembrance of a Puerto Rican Childhood *(1990) and* The Latin Deli: Prose and Poetry *(1993). Her most recent books are* Woman in Front of the Sun: On Becoming a Writer *(2000) and* The Meaning of Consuelo *(2003). She currently teaches creative writing at the University of Georgia.*

Judith Ortiz Cofer

Casa: A Partial Remembrance of a Puerto Rican Childhood

In "Casa: A Partial Remembrance of a Puerto Rican Childhood," Judith Ortiz Cofer describes the bonds that obtain among a community of women—three generations of a family headed by the matriarch, Mamá, the author's grandmother. In celebrating the intertwined lives of these women of her family, Cofer simultaneously celebrates the power of storytelling. Weaving these two strands of her essay together—family and stories—Cofer conveys some important ideas about women and their relations with men along with important ideas about culture and its significance for identity.

Cofer's "Casa" is about living in and moving between two worlds—the warm world of her Puerto Rican tropical home and the cold new world of New York and Paterson, New Jersey. Cofer alludes to this dual existence early on and explains its significance later in her essay, referring to herself as an outsider who spoke English with a Spanish accent and Spanish with an English accent. And although this dual linguistic identity made her stand out in both groups, Cofer benefits from her double linguistic and cultural heritage. It allows her to shift back and forth readily between two very different worlds, with their different sets of cultural values.

At three or four o'clock in the afternoon, the hour of *café con leche*, the women of my family gathered in Mamá's living room to speak of important things and retell familiar stories meant to be overheard by us young girls, their daughters. In Mamá's house (everyone called my grandmother

Mamá) was a large parlor built by my grandfather to his wife's exact specifications so that it was always cool, facing away from the sun. The doorway was on the side of the house so no one could walk directly into her living room. First they had to take a little stroll through and around her beautiful garden where prize-winning orchids grew in the trunk of an ancient tree she had hollowed out for that purpose. This room was furnished with several mahogany rocking chairs, acquired at the births of her children, and one intricately carved rocker that had passed down to Mamá at the death of her own mother.

It was on these rockers that my mother, her sisters, and my grandmother sat on these afternoons of my childhood to tell their stories, teaching each other, and my cousin and me, what it was like to be a woman, more specifically, a Puerto Rican woman. They talked about life on the island, and life in *Los Nueva Yores*, their way of referring to the United States from New York City to California: the other place, not home, all the same. They told real-life stories though, as I later learned, always embellishing them with a little or a lot of dramatic detail. And they told *cuentos*, the morality and cautionary tales told by the women in our family for generations: stories that became a part of my subconscious as I grew up in two worlds, the tropical island and the cold city, and that would later surface in my dreams and in my poetry.

One of these tales was about the woman who was left at the altar. Mamá liked to tell that one with histrionic intensity. I remember the rise and fall of her voice, the sighs, and her constantly gesturing hands, like two birds swooping through her words. This particular story usually would come up in a conversation as a result of someone mentioning a forthcoming engagement or wedding. The first time I remember hearing it, I was sitting on the floor at Mamá's feet, pretending to read a comic book. I may have been eleven or twelve years old, at that difficult age when a girl was no longer a child who could be ordered to leave the room if the women wanted freedom to take their talk into forbidden zones, nor really old enough to be considered a part of their conclave. I could only sit quietly, pretending to be in another world, while absorbing it all in a sort of unspoken agreement of my status as silent auditor. On this day, Mamá had taken my long, tangled mane of hair into her ever-busy hands. Without looking down at me and with no interruption of her flow of words, she began braiding my hair, working at it with the quickness and determination that characterized all her actions. My mother was watching us impassively from her rocker across the room. On her lips played a little ironic smile. I would never sit still for *her* ministrations, but even then, I instinctively knew that she did not possess Mamá's matriarchal power to command and keep everyone's attention. This was never more evident than in the spell she cast when telling a story.

"It is not like it used to be when I was a girl," Mamá announced. "Then, a man could leave a girl standing at the church altar with a bouquet of fresh flowers in her hands and disappear off the face of the earth. No way to track him down if he was from another town. He could be a married man, with maybe even two or three families all over the island. There was no way to know. And there were men who did this. Hombres with the devil in their flesh who would come to a pueblo, like this one, take a job at one of the haciendas, never meaning to stay, only to have a good time and to seduce the women."

The whole time she was speaking, Mamá would be weaving my hair into a flat plait that required pulling apart the two sections of hair with little jerks that made my eyes water; but knowing how grandmother detested whining and *boba* (sissy) tears, as she called them, I just sat up as straight and stiff as I did at La Escuela San Jose, where the nuns enforced good posture with a flexible plastic ruler they bounced off of slumped shoulders and heads. As Mamá's story progressed, I noticed how my young Aunt Laura lowered her eyes, refusing to meet Mamá's meaningful gaze. Laura was seventeen, in her last year of high school, and already engaged to a boy from another town who had staked his claim with a tiny diamond ring, then left for Los Nueva Yores to make his fortune. They were planning to get married in a year. Mamá had expressed serious doubts that the wedding would ever take place. In Mamá's eyes, a man set free without a legal contract was a man lost. She believed that marriage was not something men desired, but simply the price they had to pay for the privilege of children and, of course, for what no decent (synonymous with "smart") woman would give away for free.

"María La Loca was only seventeen when *it* happened to her." I listened closely at the mention of this name. María was a town character, a fat middle-aged woman who lived with her old mother on the outskirts of town. She was to be seen around the pueblo delivering the meat pies the two women made for a living. The most peculiar thing about María, in my eyes, was that she walked and moved like a little girl though she had the thick body and wrinkled face of an old woman. She would swing her hips in an exaggerated, clownish way, and sometimes even hop and skip up to someone's house. She spoke to no one. Even if you asked her a question, she would just look at you and smile, showing her yellow teeth. But I had heard that if you got close enough, you could hear her humming a tune without words. The kids yelled out nasty things at her calling her *La Loca*, and the men who hang out at the bodega playing dominoes sometimes whistled mockingly as she passed by with her funny, outlandish walk. But María seemed impervious to it all, carrying her basket of *pasteles* like a grotesque Little Red Riding Hood through the forest.

María La Loca interested me, as did all the eccentrics and crazies of our pueblo. Their weirdness was a measuring stick I used in my serious quest for a definition of normal. As a Navy brat shuttling between New Jersey and the pueblo, I was constantly made to feel like an oddball by my peers, who made fun of my two-way accent: a Spanish accent when I spoke English, and when I spoke Spanish I was told that I sounded like a *Gringa*. Being the outsider had already turned my brother and me into cultural chameleons. We developed early on the ability to blend into a crowd, to sit and read quietly in a fifth story apartment building for days and days when it was too bitterly cold to play outside, or, set free, to run wild in Mamá's realm, where she took charge of our lives, releasing Mother for a while from the intense fear for our safety that our father's absences instilled in her. In order to keep us from harm when Father was away, Mother kept us under strict surveillance. She even walked us to and from Public School No. 11, which we attended during the months we lived in Paterson, New Jersey, our home base in the states. Mamá freed all three of us like pigeons from a cage. I saw her as my liberator and my model. Her stories were parables from which to glean the *Truth*.

"María La Loca was once a beautiful girl. Everyone thought she would marry the Méndez boy." As everyone knew, Rogelio Méndez was the richest man in town. "But," Mamá continued, knitting my hair with the same intensity she was putting into her story, "this *macho* made a fool out of her and ruined her life." She paused for the effect of her use of the word "Macho," which at that time had not yet become a popular epithet for an unliberated man. This word had for us the crude and comical connotation of "male of the species," stud; a *macho* was what you put in a pen to increase your stock.

I peeked over my comic book at my mother. She too was under Mamá's spell, smiling conspiratorially at this little swipe at men. She was safe from Mamá's contempt in this area. Married at an early age, an unspotted lamb, she had been accepted by a good family of strict Spaniards whose name was old and respected, though their fortune had been lost long before my birth. In a rocker Papá had painted sky blue sat Mamá's oldest child, Aunt Nena. Mother of three children, stepmother of two more, she was a quiet woman who liked books but had married an ignorant and abusive widower whose main interest in life was accumulating wealth. He too was in the mainland working on his dream of returning home rich and triumphant to buy the *finca* of his dreams. She was waiting for him to send for her. She would leave her children with Mamá for several years while the two of them slaved away in factories. He would one day be a rich man, and she a sadder woman. Even now her life-light was dimming. She spoke little, an aberration in Mamá's house, and she read avidly, as if storing up spiritual food for the long winters that awaited her in Los Nueva Yores without her family. But even Aunt Nena came alive to Mamá's words, rocking gently, her hands over a thick book in her lap.

Her daughter, my cousin Sara, played jacks by herself on the tile porch outside the room where we sat. She was a year older than I. We shared a bed and all our family's secrets. Collaborators in search of answers, Sara and I discussed everything we heard the women say, trying to fit it all together like a puzzle that, once assembled, would reveal life's mysteries to us. Though she and I still enjoyed taking part in boys' games—chase, volleyball, and even *vaqueros*, the island version of cowboys and Indians involving cap-gun battles and violent shoot-outs under the mango tree in Mamá's backyard—we loved best the quiet hours in the afternoon when the men were still at work, and the boys had gone to play serious baseball at the park. Then Mamá's house belonged only to us women. The aroma of coffee perking in the kitchen, the mesmerizing creaks and groans of the rockers, and the women telling their lives in *cuentos* are forever woven into the fabric of my imagination, braided like my hair that day I felt my grandmother's hands teaching me about strength, her voice convincing me of the power of storytelling.

That day Mamá told how the beautiful María had fallen prey to a man whose name was never the same in subsequent versions of the story;

it was Juan one time, José, Rafael, Diego, another. We understood that neither the name nor any of the *facts* were important, only that a woman had allowed love to defeat her. Mamá put each of us in María's place by describing her wedding dress in loving detail: how she looked like a princess in her lace as she waited at the altar. Then, as Mamá approached the tragic denouement of her story, I was distracted by the sound of my aunt Laura's violent rocking. She seemed on the verge of tears. She knew the fable was intended for her. That week she was going to have her wedding gown fitted, though no firm date had been set for the marriage. Mamá ignored Laura's obvious discomfort, digging out a ribbon from the sewing basket she kept by her rocker while describing María's long illness, "a fever that would not break for days." She spoke of a mother's despair: "that woman climbed the church steps on her knees every morning, wore only black as a *promesa* to the Holy Virgin in exchange for her daughter's health." By the time María returned from her honeymoon with death, she was ravished, no longer young or sane. "As you can see, she is almost as old as her mother already," Mamá lamented while tying the ribbon to the ends of my hair, pulling it back with such force that I just knew I would never be able to close my eyes completely again.

"That María's getting crazier every day." Mamá's voice would take a lighter tone now, expressing satisfaction, either for the perfection of my braid, or for a story well told—it was hard to tell. "You know that tune María is always humming?" Carried away by her enthusiasm, I tried to nod, but Mamá still had me pinned between her knees.

"Well, that's the wedding march." Surprising us all, Mamá sang out, "Da, da, dara . . . da, da, dara." Then lifting me off the floor by my skinny shoulders, she would lead me around the room in an impromptu waltz—another session ending with the laughter of women, all of us caught up in the infectious joke of our lives.

Possibilities for Writing

1. The longest and most elaborate example Cofer uses is that of María La Loca. Explain the significance of this example, and identify and explain the significance of another example that Cofer includes.

2. Cofer uses a number of Spanish words and phrases in "Casa," some of which she translates and others of which she leaves

untranslated. What is the effect of these Spanish words and phrases? What would be gained or lost if they had been omitted?

3. Use the following quotation as a springboard to write about identity as a theme in "Casa": "It was on these rockers that my mother, her sisters, and my grandmother sat on these afternoons of my childhood to tell their stories, teaching each other, and my cousin and me, what it was like to be a woman, more specifically, a Puerto Rican woman."

K. C. Cole (b. 1946), a science writer for the Los Angeles Times, *was born in Detroit, Michigan, and was educated at Columbia University, from which she received her B.A. She has taught science at the University of California and the University of Wisconsin. Cole began doing science writing in the 1970s and has written for publications that include* Smithsonian, Omni, *and* Discover *magazines. Her books include* Visions *(1978),* Sympathetic Vibrations *(1984),* The Universe and the Teacup: The Mathematics of Truth and Beauty *(1998), and* The Hole in the Universe *(2001).*

K. C. Cole
Calculated Risks

In "Calculated Risks," from her book *The Universe and the Teacup: The Mathematics of Truth and Beauty* (1998), K. C. Cole explains why people take some risks and not others, and how their risk assessment analysis typically lacks a sound mathematical or scientific basis. Using a clear, direct style of writing, and providing numerous examples from everyday experience, Cole is able to explain complex ideas lucidly and engagingly.

Throughout "Calculated Risks," Cole shows how irrational people's behavior choices often are and how little real analysis typically precedes them. She explains how personal risks differ from societal ones and why certain kinds of risks are more widely publicized than others.

Newsweek magazine plunged American women into a state of near panic some years ago when it announced that the chance of a college-educated thirty-five-year-old woman finding a husband was less than her chance of being killed by a terrorist. Although Susan Faludi made mincemeat of this so-called statistic in her book *Backlash*, the notion that we can precisely quantify risk has a strong hold on the Western psyche. Scientists, statisticians, and policy makers attach numbers to the risk of getting breast cancer or AIDS, to flying and food additives, to getting hit by lightning or falling in the bathtub.

Yet despite (or perhaps because of) all the numbers floating around, most people are quite properly confused about risk. I know people who live happily on the San Andreas Fault and yet are afraid to ride the New York subways (and vice versa). I've known smokers who can't stand to be in the same room with a fatty steak, and women afraid of the side effects of birth control pills who have unprotected sex with strangers. Risk assessment is rarely based on purely rational considerations—even if people could agree on what those considerations were. We worry about negligible quantities of Alar in apples, yet shrug off the much higher probability of dying from smoking. We worry about flying, but not driving. We worry about getting brain cancer from cellular phones, although the link is quite tenuous. In fact, it's easy to make a statistical argument—albeit a fallacious one—that cellular phones prevent cancer, because the proportion of people with brain tumors is smaller among cell phone users than among the general population.[1]

Even simple pleasures such as eating and breathing have become suspect. Love has always been risky, and AIDS has made intimacy more perilous than ever. On the other hand, not having relationships may be riskier still. According to at least one study, the average male faces three times the threat of early death associated with not being married as he does from cancer.

Of course, risk isn't all bad. Without knowingly taking risks, no one would ever walk out the door, much less go to school, drive a car, have a baby, submit a proposal for a research grant, fall in love, or swim in the ocean. It's hard to have any fun, accomplish anything productive, or experience life without taking on risks—sometimes substantial ones. Life, after all, is a fatal disease, and the mortality rate for humans, at the end of the day, is 100 percent.

Yet, people are notoriously bad at risk assessment. I couldn't get over this feeling watching the aftermath of the crash of TWA Flight 800 and the horror it spread about flying, with the long lines at airports, the increased security measures, the stories about grieving families day after day in the newspaper, the ongoing attempt to figure out why and who and what could be done to prevent such a tragedy from happening again.

Meanwhile, tens of thousands of children die every day around the world from common causes such as malnutrition and disease. That's roughly the same as a hundred exploding jumbo jets full of children every single day. People who care more about the victims of Flight 800 aren't callous or ignorant. It's just the way our minds work. Certain kinds of tragedies make an impact; others don't. Our perceptual apparatus is

---

[1]John Allen Paulos was the first person I know of to make this calculation; it is probably related to the fact that people who use cellular phones are on average richer, and therefore healthier, than people who don't.

geared toward threats that are exotic, personal, erratic, and dramatic. This doesn't mean we're ignorant; just human.

This skewed perception of risk has serious social consequences, however. We aim our resources at phantoms, while real hazards are ignored. Parents, for example, tend to rate drug abuse and abduction by strangers as the greatest threats to their children. Yet hundreds of times more children die each year from choking, burns, falls, drowning, and other accidents that public safety efforts generally ignore.

We spend millions to fight international terrorism and wear combat fatigues for a morning walk to protect against Lyme disease. At the same time, "we see several very major problems that have received relatively little attention," write Bernard Cohen and I-Sing Lee in *Health Physics*. The physicists suggest—not entirely tongue in cheek—that resources might be far more efficiently spent on programs such as government-organized computer dating services. "Favorable publicity on the advantages of marriage might be encouraged."

It's as if we incarcerated every petty criminal with zeal, while inviting mass murderers into our bedrooms. If we wanted to put the money on the real killers, we'd go after suicide, not asbestos.

Even in terms of simple dollars, our policies don't make any sense. It's well known, for example, that prenatal care for pregnant women saves enormous amounts of money—in terms of care infants need in the first year of life—and costs a pittance. Yet millions of low-income women don't get it.

Numbers are clearly not enough to make sense of risk assessment. Context counts, too. Take cancer statistics. It's always frightening to hear that cancer is on the rise. However, at least one reason for the increase is simply that people are living longer—long enough to get the disease.

Certain conclusions we draw from statistics are downright silly. Physicist Hal Lewis writes in *Technological Risk* that per mile traveled a person is more likely to be killed by a car as a pedestrian than as a driver or passenger. Should we conclude that driving is safer than walking and therefore that all pedestrians should be forced into cars?

Charles Dickens made a point about the absurdity of misunderstanding numbers associated with risk by refusing to ride the train. One day late in December, the story goes, Dickens announced that he couldn't travel by train any more that year, "on the grounds that the average annual quota of railroad accidents in Britain had not been filled and therefore further disasters were obviously imminent."

Purely numerical comparisons also may be socially unacceptable. When the state of Oregon decided to rank its medical services according to benefit-cost ratios, some results had to be thrown out—despite their statistical validity. Treatment for thumb sucking, crooked teeth, and headaches, for example, came out on the priorities list ahead of therapy for cystic fibrosis and AIDS.

What you consider risky, after all, depends somewhat on the circumstances of your life and lifestyle. People who don't have enough to eat don't worry about apples contaminated with Alar. People who face daily violence at their front door don't worry about hijackings on flights to the Bahamas. Attitudes toward risk evolve in cultural contexts and are influenced by everything from psychology to ethics to beliefs about personal responsibility.

In addition to context, another factor needed to see through the maze of conflicting messages about risk is human psychology. For example, imminent risks strike much more fear in our hearts than distant ones; it's much harder to get a teenager than an older person to take long-term dangers like smoking seriously.

Smoking is also a habit people believe they can control, which makes the risk far more acceptable. (People seem to get more upset about the effects of passive smoking than smoking itself—at least in part because smokers get to choose, and breathers don't.)

As a general principle, people tend to grossly exaggerate the risk of any danger perceived to be beyond their control, while shrugging off risks they think they can manage. Thus, we go skiing and skydiving, but fear asbestos. We resent and fear the idea that anonymous chemical companies are putting additives into our food; yet the additives we load onto our own food—salt, sugar, butter—are millions of times more dangerous.

This is one reason that airline accidents seem so unacceptable—because strapped into our seats in the cabin, what happens is completely beyond our control. In a poll taken soon after the TWA Flight 800 crash, an overwhelming majority of people said they'd be willing to pay up to fifty dollars more for a round-trip ticket if it increased airline safety. Yet the same people resist moves to improve automobile safety, for example, especially if it costs money.

The idea that we can control what happens also influences who we blame when things go wrong. Most people don't like to pay the costs for treating people injured by cigarettes or riding motorcycles because we think they brought these things on themselves. Some people also hold these attitudes toward victims of AIDS, or mental illness, because they think the illness results from lack of character or personal morals.

In another curious perceptual twist, risks associated with losing something and gaining something appear to be calculated in our minds according to quite different scales. In a now-classic series of studies, Stanford psychologist Amos Tversky and colleague Daniel Kahneman concluded that most people will bend over backward to avoid small risks, even if that means sacrificing great potential rewards. "The threat of a loss has a greater impact on a decision than the possibility of an equivalent gain," they concluded.

In one of their tests, Tversky and Kahneman asked physicians to choose between two strategies for combating a rare disease, expected to kill 600 people. Strategy A promised to save 200 people (the rest would die), while Strategy B offered a one-third probability that everyone would be saved, and a two-thirds probability that no one would be saved. Betting on a sure thing, the physicians choose A. But presented with the identical choice, stated differently, they choose B. The difference in language was simply this: Instead of stating that Strategy A would guarantee 200 out of 600 saved lives, it stated that Strategy A would mean 400 sure deaths.

People will risk a lot to prevent a loss, in other words, but risk very little for possible gain. Running into a burning house to save a pet or fighting back when a mugger asks for your wallet are both high-risk gambles that people take repeatedly in order to hang on to something they care about. The same people might not risk the hassle of, say, fastening a seat belt in a car even though the potential gain might be much higher.

The bird in the hand always seems more attractive than the two in the bush. Even if holding on to the one in your hand comes at a higher risk and the two in the bush are gold-plated.

The reverse situation comes into play when we judge risks of commission versus risks of omission. A risk that you assume by actually doing something seems far more risky than a risk you take by not doing something, even though the risk of doing nothing may be greater.

Deaths from natural causes, like cancer, are more readily acceptable than deaths from accidents or murder. That's probably one reason it's so much easier to accept thousands of starving children than the death of one in a drive-by shooting. The former is an act of omission—a failure to step in and help, send food or medicine. The latter is the commission of a crime—somebody pulled the trigger.

In the same way, the Food and Drug Administration is far more likely to withhold a drug that might help a great number of people if it threatens to harm a few; better to hurt a lot of people by failing to do something than act with the deliberate knowledge that some people will be hurt. Or as the doctors' credo puts it: First do no harm.

For obvious reasons, dramatic or exotic risks seem far more dangerous than more familiar ones. Plane crashes and AIDS are risks associated with ambulances and flashing lights, sex and drugs. While red dye #2 strikes terror in our hearts, that great glob of butter melting into our baked potato is accepted as an old friend. "A woman drives down the street with her child romping around in the front seat," says John Allen Paulos. "Then they arrive at the shopping mall, and she grabs the child's hand so hard it hurts, because she's afraid he'll be kidnapped."

Children who are kidnapped are far more likely to be whisked away by relatives than strangers, just as most people are murdered by people they know.

Familiar risks creep up on us like age and are often difficult to see until it's too late to take action. Mathematician Sam C. Saunders of Washington State University reminds us that a frog placed in hot water will struggle to escape, but the same frog placed in cool water that's slowly warmed up will sit peacefully until it's cooked. "One cannot anticipate what one does not perceive," he says, which is why gradual accumulations of risk due to lifestyle choices (like smoking or eating) are so often ignored. We're in hot water, but it's gotten hot so slowly that no one notices.

To bring home his point, Saunders asks us to imagine that cigarettes are not harmful—with the exception of an occasional one that has been packed with explosives instead of tobacco. These dynamite-stuffed cigarettes look just like normal ones. There's only one hidden away in every 18,250 packs—not a grave risk, you might say. The only catch is, if you smoke one of those explosive cigarettes, it might blow your head off.

The mathematician speculates, I think correctly, that given such a situation, cigarettes would surely be banned outright. After all, if 30 million packs of cigarettes are sold each day, an average of 1,600 people a day would die in gruesome explosions. Yet the number of deaths is the same to be expected from normal smoking. "The total expected loss of life or health to smokers using dynamite-loaded (but otherwise harmless) cigarettes over forty years would not be as great as with ordinary filtered cigarettes," says Saunders.

We can accept getting cooked like a frog, in other words, but not getting blown up like a firecracker.

It won't come as a great surprise to anyone that ego also plays a role in the way we assess risks. Psychological self-protection leads us to draw consistently wrong conclusions. In general, we overestimate the risks of bad things happening to others, while vastly underrating the possibility that they will happen to ourselves. Indeed, the lengths people go to minimize their own perceived risks can be downright "ingenious," according to Rutgers psychologist Neil Weinstein. For example, people asked about the risk of finding radon in their houses always rate their risk as "low" or "average," never "high." "If you ask them why," says Weinstein, "they take anything and twist it around in a way that reassures them. Some say their risk is low because the house is new; others, because the house is old. Some will say their risk is low because their house is at the top of a hill; others, because it's at the bottom of a hill."

Whatever the evidence to the contrary, we think: "It won't happen to me." Weinstein and others speculate that this has something to do with preservation of self-esteem. We don't like to see ourselves as vulnerable. We like to think we've got some magical edge over the others. Ego gets involved especially in cases where being vulnerable to risk implies personal failure—for example, the risk of depression, suicide, alcoholism, drug addiction. "If you admit you're at risk," says Weinstein, "you're admitting that you can't handle stress. You're not as strong as the next person."

Average people, studies have shown, believe that they will enjoy longer lives, healthier lives, and longer marriages than the "average" person. Despite the obvious fact that they themselves are, well, average people, too. According to a recent poll, 3 out of 4 baby boomers (those born between 1946 and 1964) think they look younger than their peers, and 4 out of 5 say they have fewer wrinkles than other people their age—a statistical impossibility.

Kahneman and Tversky studied this phenomenon as well and found that people think they'll beat the odds because they're special. This is no doubt a necessary psychological defense mechanism, or no one would ever get married again without thinking seriously about the potential for divorce. A clear view of personal vulnerability, however, could go a long way toward preventing activities like drunken driving. But then again, most people think they are better than average drivers—even when intoxicated.

We also seem to believe it won't happen to us if it hasn't happened yet. That is, we extrapolate from the past to the future. "I've been taking that highway at eighty miles per hour for ten years and I haven't crashed yet," we tell ourselves. This is rather like reasoning that flipping a coin ten times that comes up heads guarantees that heads will continue to come up indefinitely.

Curiously, one advertising campaign against drunken driving that was quite successful featured the faces of children killed by drunken drivers. These children looked real to us. We could identify with them. In the same way as we could identify with the people on TWA Flight 800. It's much easier to empathize with someone who has a name and a face than a statistic.

That explains in part why we go to great expense to rescue children who fall down mine shafts, but not children dying from preventable diseases. Economists call this the "rule of rescue." If you know that someone is in danger and you know that you can help, you have a moral obligation to do so. If you don't know about it, however, you have no obligation. Columnist Roger Simon speculates that's one reason the National Rifle Association lobbied successfully to eliminate the program at the Centers for Disease Control that keeps track of gun deaths. If we don't have to face what's happening, we won't feel obligated to do anything about it.

Even without the complication of all these psychological factors, however, calculating risks can be tricky because not everything is known about every situation. "We have to concede that a single neglected or unrecognized risk can invalidate all the reliability calculations, which are based on known risk," writes Ivar Ekeland. There is always a risk, in other words, that the risk assessment itself is wrong.

Genetic screening, like tests for HIV infection, has a certain probability of being wrong. If your results come back positive, how much should you worry? If they come back negative, how safe should you feel?

The more factors involved, the more complicated the risk assessment becomes. When you get to truly complex systems like nationwide telephone networks and power grids, worldwide computer networks and hugely complex machines like space shuttles, the risk of disaster becomes infinitely harder to pin down. No one knows when a minor glitch will set off a chain reaction of events that will culminate in disaster. Potential risks in complex systems, in other words, are subject to the same kinds of exponential amplification discussed in the previous chapter.

Needless to say, the way a society assesses risk is very different from the way an individual views the same choices. Whether or not you wish to ride a motorcycle is your own business. Whether society pays the bills for the thousands of people maimed by cycle accidents, however, is everybody's business. Any one of us might view our own survival on a transatlantic flight as more important than the needs of the nation's children. Governments, one presumes, ought to have a somewhat different agenda.

But how far does society want to go in strictly numerical accounting? It certainly hasn't helped much in the all-important issue of health care, where an ounce of prevention has been proven again and again to be worth many pounds of cures. Most experts agree that we should be spending much more money preventing common diseases and accidents, especially in children. But no one wants to take health dollars away from precarious newborns or the elderly—where most of it goes. These are decisions that ultimately will not be made by numbers alone. Calculating risk only helps us to see more clearly what exactly is going on.

According to anthropologist Melvin Konner, author of *Why the Reckless Survive*, our poor judgment about potential risks may well be the legacy of evolution. Early peoples lived at constant risk from predators, disease, accidents. They died young. And in evolutionary terms, "winning" means not longevity, but merely sticking around long enough to pass on your genes to the next generation. Taking risk was therefore a "winning" strategy, especially if it meant a chance to mate before dying. Besides, decisions had to be made quickly. If going for a meal of ripe berries meant risking an attack from a saber-toothed tiger, you dove for the berries. For a half-starved cave dweller, this was a relatively simple choice. Perhaps our brains are simply not wired, speculates Konner, for the careful calculations presented by the risks of modern life.

Indeed, some of our optimistic biases toward personal risk may still serve important psychological purposes. In times of stress and danger, they help us to put one foot in front of the other; they help us to get on with our lives, and out the door.

In the end, Konner, the cautious professor, ruminates somewhat wistfully about his risk-taking friends—who smoke, and ride motorcycles, and drive with their seat belts fastened behind them. Beside them, he feels "safe and virtuous," yet somehow uneasy. "I sometimes think," he muses, "that the more reckless among us may have something to teach the careful about the sort of immortality that comes from living fully every day."

Possibilities for Writing

1. Select any three of K. C. Cole's examples and explain why you do or do not agree with what she says about people's behavior (your own included) with respect to each.

2. Identify two analogies or uses of exaggeration (or two instances where she uses analogy and exaggeration together) and discuss the point of the analogy/exaggeration and the extent to which you think it is effective.

3. Write a personal essay explaining your own attitudes toward taking risks. Illustrate your essay with examples from your own experience in deciding to engage in or to avoid particular kinds of behaviors. You may use examples from Cole's essay or provide others.

***Bernard Cooper** (b. 1951) grew up in Hollywood, California, and received a B.F.A and an M.F.A from the California Institute of the Arts. Winner of the PEN/Ernest Hemingway award and the O. Henry Prize, Cooper has published two highly praised collections of short stories,* A Year of Rhymes *(1993) and* Guess Again *(2000). He is also the author of two volumes of autobiographical essays, in he which focuses on coming to terms with his homosexuality and with the onset of AIDS:* Maps to Anywhere *(1990) and* Truth Serum *(1996). He currently teaches creative writing at Antioch College in Los Angeles and is an art critic for the* Los Angeles Times.

Bernard Cooper

Burl's

In "Burl's," Bernard Cooper explores the theme of sexual identity through telling a series of interconnected boyhood stories about his growing awareness of sexual feelings. Cooper describes four scenes: a restaurant scene that segues into an uncanny experience outside; a scene inside his parents' walk-in closet; a scene that involves a classroom, a gymnastics studio, and a pet store; and, finally, a return to the restaurant scene that opens the essay. The circular structure of Cooper's essay and the carefully linked details among the scenes give the essay a strong sense of unity and coherence.

Cooper's essay presents a young boy's understanding through the lens and from the perspective of his adult self. Cooper is careful not to reveal too much too soon about the boy's gradual realization of the complications and variousness of sexual identity. He is also resourceful in conveying the young boy's confused sense of how the world is ordered.

I

I loved the restaurant's name, a compact curve of a word. Its sign, five big letters rimmed in neon, hovered above the roof. I almost never saw the sign with its neon lit; my parents took me there for early summer dinners, and even by the time we left—father cleaning his teeth with a toothpick, mother carrying steak bones in a doggie bag—the sky was still bright. Heat rippled off the cars parked along Hollywood Boulevard, the asphalt gummy from hours of sun.

With its sleek architecture, chrome appliances, and arctic temperature, Burl's offered a refuge from the street. We usually sat at one of the booths in front of the plate-glass windows. During our dinner, people came to a halt before the news-vending machine on the corner and burrowed in their pockets and purses for change.

The waitresses at Burl's wore brown uniforms edged in checked gingham. From their breast pockets frothed white lace handkerchiefs. In between reconnaissance missions to the table, they busied themselves behind the counter and shouted "Tuna to travel" or "Scorch that patty" to a harried short-order cook who manned the grill. Miniature pitchers of cream and individual pats of butter were extracted from an industrial refrigerator. Coca-Cola shot from a glinting spigot. Waitresses dodged and bumped one another, frantic as atoms.

My parents usually lingered after the meal, nursing cups of coffee while I played with the beads of condensation on my glass of ice water, tasted Tabasco sauce, or twisted pieces of my paper napkin into mangled animals. One evening, annoyed with my restlessness, my father gave me a dime and asked me to buy him a *Herald Examiner* from the vending machine in front of the restaurant.

Shouldering open the heavy glass door, I was seared by a sudden gust of heat. Traffic roared past me and stirred the air. Walking toward the newspaper machine, I held the dime so tightly it seemed to melt in my palm. Duty made me feel large and important. I inserted the dime and opened the box, yanking a *Herald* from the spring contraption that held it as tight as a mousetrap. When I turned around, paper in hand, I saw two women walking toward me.

Their high heels clicked on the sun-baked pavement. They were tall, broad-shouldered women who moved with a mixture of haste and defiance. They'd teased their hair into nearly identical black beehives. Dangling earrings flashed in the sun, brilliant as prisms. Each of them wore the kind of clinging, strapless outfit my mother referred to as a cocktail dress. The silky fabric—one dress was purple, the other pink—accentuated their breasts and hips and rippled with insolent highlights. The dresses exposed their bare arms, the slope of their shoulders, and the smooth, powdered plane of flesh where their cleavage began.

I owned at the time a book called *Things for Boys and Girls to Do*. There were pages to color, intricate mazes, and connect-the-dots. But another type of puzzle came to mind as I watched those women walking toward me: What's Wrong With This Picture? Say the drawing of a dining room looked normal at first glance; on closer inspection, a chair was missing its leg and the man who sat atop it wore half a pair of glasses.

The women had Adam's apples.

The closer they came, the shallower my breathing was. I blocked the sidewalk, an incredulous child stalled in their path. When they saw me staring, they shifted their purses and linked their arms. There was something sisterly and conspiratorial about their sudden closeness. Though their mouths didn't move, I thought they might have been communicating without moving their lips, so telepathic did they seem as they joined arms and pressed together, synchronizing their heavy steps. The pages of the *Herald* fluttered in the wind. I felt them against my arm, light as batted lashes.

The woman in pink shot me a haughty glance and yet she seemed pleased that I'd taken notice, hungry to be admired by a man, or even an awestruck eight-year-old boy. She tried to stifle a grin, her red lipstick more voluptuous than the lips it painted. Rouge deepened her cheekbones. Eye shadow dusted her lids, a clumsy abundance of blue. Her face was like a page in *Things for Boys and Girls to Do*, colored by a kid who went outside the lines.

At close range, I saw that her wig was slightly askew. I was certain it was a wig because my mother owned several; three Styrofoam heads lined a shelf in my mother's closet; upon them were perched a Page-Boy, an Empress, and a Baby-Doll, all in shades of auburn. The woman in the pink dress wore her wig like a crown of glory.

But it was the woman in the purple dress who passed nearest me, and I saw that her jaw was heavily powdered, a half-successful attempt to disguise the telltale shadow of a beard. Just as I noticed this, her heel caught on a crack in the pavement and she reeled on her stilettos. It was then that I witnessed a rift in her composure, a window through which I could glimpse the shades of maleness that her dress and wig and makeup obscured. She shifted her shoulders and threw out her hands like a surfer riding a curl. The instant she regained her balance, she smoothed her dress, patted her hair, and sauntered onward.

Any woman might be a man. The fact of it clanged through the chambers of my brain. In broad day, in the midst of traffic, with my parents drinking coffee a few feet away, I felt as if everything I understood, everything I had taken for granted up to that moment—the curve of the earth, the heat of the sun, the reliability of my own eyes—had been squeezed out of me. Who were those men? Did they help each other get inside those dresses? How many other people and things were not what they seemed? From the back, the impostors looked like women once again, slinky and curvaceous, purple and pink. I watched them disappear into the distance, their disguises so convincing that other people on the street seemed to take no notice, and for a moment I wondered if I had imagined the whole encounter, a visitation by two unlikely muses.

Frozen in the middle of the sidewalk, I caught my reflection in the window of Burl's, a silhouette floating between his parents. They faced one another across a table. Once the solid embodiments of woman and man, pedestrians and traffic appeared to pass through them.

II

There were some mornings, seconds before my eyes opened and my senses gathered into consciousness, that the child I was seemed to hover above the bed, and I couldn't tell what form my waking would take— the body of a boy or the body of a girl. Finally stirring, I'd blink against the early light and greet each incarnation as a male with mild surprise. My sex, in other words, didn't seem to be an absolute fact so much as a pleasant, recurring accident.

By the age of eight, I'd experienced this groggy phenomenon several times. Those ethereal moments above my bed made waking up in the tangled blankets, a boy steeped in body heat, all the more astonishing. That this might be an unusual experience never occurred to me; it was one among a flood of sensations I could neither name nor ignore.

And so, shocked as I was when those transvestites passed me in front of Burl's, they confirmed something about which I already had an inkling: the hazy border between the sexes. My father, after all, raised his pinky when he drank from a teacup, and my mother looked as faded and plain as my father until she fixed her hair and painted her face.

Like most children, I once thought it possible to divide the world into male and female columns. Blue/Pink. Rooster/Hens. Trousers/ Skirts. Such divisions were easy, not to mention comforting, for they simplified matter into compatible pairs. But there also existed a vast range of things that didn't fit neatly into either camp: clocks, milk, telephones, grass. There were nights I fell into a fitful sleep while trying to sex the world correctly.

Nothing typified the realms of male and female as clearly as my parents' walk-in closets. Home alone for any length of time, I always found my way inside them. I could stare at my parents' clothes for hours, grateful for the stillness and silence, haunting the very heart of their privacy.

The overhead light in my father's closet was a bare bulb. Whenever I groped for the chain in the dark, it wagged back and forth and resisted my grasp. Once the light clicked on, I saw dozens of ties hanging like stalactites. A monogrammed silk bathrobe sagged from a hook, a gift my father had received on a long-ago birthday and, thinking it fussy, rarely wore. Shirts were cramped together along the length of an alu-minum pole, their starched sleeves sticking out as if in a half-hearted gesture of greeting. The medicinal odor of mothballs permeated the boxer shorts that were folded and stacked in a built-in drawer. Immaculate under-wear was proof of a tenderness my mother couldn't otherwise express; she may not have touched my father often, but she laundered his boxers with infinite care. Even back then, I suspected that a sense of duty was the final erotic link between them.

Sitting in a neat row on the closet floor were my father's boots and slippers and dress shoes. I'd try on his wingtips and clomp around, slip-ping out of them with every step. My wary, unnatural stride made me all the more desperate to effect some authority. I'd whisper orders to imag-ined lackeys and take my invisible wife in my arms. But no matter how much I wanted them to fit, those shoes were as cold and hard as marble.

My mother's shoes were just as uncomfortable, but a lot more fun. From a brightly colored array of pumps and slingbacks, I'd pick a pair with the glee and deliberation of someone choosing a chocolate. Whatever embarrassment I felt was overwhelmed by the exhilaration of being taller in a pair of high heels. Things will look like this someday, I said to myself, gazing out from my new and improved vantage point as if from a crow's nest. Calves elongated, arms akimbo, I gauged each step so that I didn't fall over and moved with what might have passed for grace had someone seen me, a possibility I scrupulously avoided by locking the door.

Back and forth I went. The longer I wore a pair of heels, the better my balance. In the periphery of my vision, the shelf of wigs looked like a throng of kindly bystanders. Light streamed down from a high window, causing crystal bottles to glitter, the air ripe with perfume.

A makeup mirror above the dressing table invited my self-absorption. Sound was muffled. Time slowed. It seemed as if nothing bad could happen as long as I stayed within those walls.

Though I'd never been discovered in my mother's closet, my parents knew that I was drawn toward girlish things—dolls and jump rope and jewelry—as well as to the games and preoccupations that were expected of a boy. I'm not sure now if it was my effeminacy itself that bothered them as much as my ability to slide back and forth, without the slightest warning, between male and female mannerisms. After I'd finished building the model of an F-17 bomber, say, I'd sit back to examine my handiwork, pursing my lips in concentration and crossing my legs at the knee.

III

One day my mother caught me standing in the middle of my bedroom doing an imitation of Mary Injijikian, a dark, overeager Armenian girl with whom I believed myself to be in love, not only because she was pretty but because I wanted to be like her. Collector of effortless A's, Mary seemed to know all the answers in class. Before the teacher had even finished asking a question, Mary would let out a little grunt and practically levitate out of her seat, as if her hand were filled with helium. "Could we please hear from someone else today besides Miss Injijikian," the teacher would say. *Miss Injijikian.* Those were the words I was repeating over and over to myself when my mother caught me. To utter them was rhythmic, delicious, and under their spell I raised my hand and wiggled like Mary. I heard a cough and spun around. My mother froze in the doorway. She clutched the folded sheets to her stomach and turned without saying a word. My sudden flush of shame confused me. Weren't boys supposed to swoon over girls? Hadn't I seen babbling, heartsick men in a dozen movies?

Shortly after the Injijikian incident, my parents decided to send me to gymnastics class at the Los Angeles Athletic Club, a brick relic of a building on Olive Street. One of the oldest establishments of its kind in Los Angeles, the club prohibited women from the premises. My parents didn't have to say it aloud: they hoped a fraternal atmosphere would toughen me up and tilt me toward the male side of my nature.

My father drove me downtown so I could sign up for the class, meet the instructor, and get a tour of the place. On the way there, he reminisced about sports. Since he'd grown up in a rough Philadelphia neighborhood, sports consisted of kick-the-can or rolling a hoop down the street with a stick. The more he talked about his physical prowess, the more convinced I became that my daydreams and shyness were a disappointment to him.

The hushed lobby of the athletic club was paneled in dark wood. A few solitary figures were hidden in wing chairs. My father and I introduced ourselves to a man at the front desk who seemed unimpressed by our presence. His aloofness unnerved me, which wasn't hard considering that no matter how my parents put it, I knew their sending me here was a form of disapproval, a way of banishing the part of me they didn't care to know.

A call went out over the intercom for someone to show us around. While we waited, I noticed that the sand in the standing ashtrays had been raked into perfect furrows. The glossy leaves of the potted plants looked as if they'd been polished by hand. The place seemed more like a well-tended hotel than an athletic club. Finally, a stoop-shouldered old man hobbled toward us, his head shrouded in a cloud of white hair. He wore a T-shirt that said "Instructor"; his arms were so wrinkled and anemic, I thought I might have misread it. While we followed him to the elevator, I readjusted my expectations, which had involved fantasies of a hulking drill sergeant barking orders at a flock of scrawny boys.

The instructor, mumbling to himself and never turning around to see if we were behind him, showed us where the gymnastics class took place. I'm certain the building was big, but the size of the room must be exaggerated by a trick of memory, because when I envision it, I picture a vast and windowless warehouse. Mats covered the wooden floor. Here and there, in remote and lonely pools of light, stood a pommel horse, a balance beam, and parallel bars. Tiers of bleachers rose into darkness. Unlike the cloistered air of a closet, the room seemed incomplete without a crowd.

Next we visited the dressing room, empty except for a naked middle-aged man. He sat on a narrow bench and clipped his formidable toenails. Moles dotted his back. He glistened like a fish.

We continued to follow the instructor down an aisle lined with numbered lockers. At the far end, steam billowed from the doorway that led to the showers. Fresh towels stacked on a nearby table made me think of my mother; I knew she liked to have me at home with her—I was often her only companion—and I resented her complicity in the plan to send me here.

The tour ended when the instructor gave me a sign-up sheet. Only a few names preceded mine. They were signatures, or so I imagined, of other soft and wayward sons.

IV

When the day of the first gymnastics class arrived, my mother gave me money and a gym bag and sent me to the corner of Hollywood and Western to wait for a bus. The sun was bright, the traffic heavy. While I sat there, an argument raged inside my head, the familiar, battering debate between the wish to be like other boys and the wish to be like myself. Why shouldn't I simply get up and go back home, where I'd be left alone to read and think? On the other hand, wouldn't life be easier if I liked athletics, or learned to like them?

No sooner did I steel my resolve to get on the bus than I thought of something better: I could spend the morning wandering through Woolworth's, then tell my parents I'd gone to the class. But would my lie stand up to scrutiny? As I practiced describing phantom gymnastics, I became aware of a car circling the block. It was a large car in whose shaded interior I could barely make out the driver, but I thought it might be the man who owned the local pet store. I'd often gone there on the pretext of looking at the cocker spaniel puppies huddled together in their pen, but I really went to gawk at the owner, whose tan chest, in the V of his shirt, was the place I most wanted to rest my head. Every time the man moved, counting stock or writing a receipt, his shirt parted, my mouth went dry, and I smelled the musk of sawdust and dogs.

I found myself hoping that the driver was the man who ran the pet store. I was thrilled by the unlikely possibility that the sight of me, slumped on a bus bench in my T-shirt and shorts, had caused such a man to circle the block. Up to that point in my life, lovemaking hovered somewhere in the future, an impulse a boy might aspire to but didn't indulge. And there I was, sitting on a bus bench in the middle of the city, dreaming I could seduce an adult. I showered the owner of the pet store with kisses and, as aquariums bubbled, birds sang, and mice raced in a wire wheel, slipped my hand beneath his shirt. The roar of traffic brought me to my senses. I breathed deeply and blinked against the sun. I crossed my legs at the knee in order to hide an erection. My fantasy left me both drained and changed. The continent of sex had drifted closer.

The car made another round. This time the driver leaned across the passenger seat and peered at me through the window. He was a complete stranger, whose gaze filled me with fear. It wasn't the surprise of not recognizing him that frightened me, it was what I did recognize—the unmistakable shame in his expression, and the weary temptation that drove him in circles. Before the car behind him honked, he mouthed "hello" and cocked his head. What now, he seemed to be asking. A bold, unbearable question.

I bolted to my feet, slung the gym bag over my shoulder, and hurried toward home. Now and then I turned around to make sure he wasn't trailing me, both relieved and disappointed when I didn't see his car. Even after I became convinced that he wasn't at my back—my sudden flight had scared him off—I kept turning around to see what was making me so nervous, as if I might spot the source of my discomfort somewhere on the street. I walked faster and faster, trying to outrace myself. Eventually, the bus I was supposed to have taken roared past. Turning the corner, I watched it bob eastward.

Closing the kitchen door behind me, I vowed never to leave home again. I was resolute in this decision without fully understanding why, or what it was I hoped to avoid; I was only aware of the need to hide and a vague notion, fading fast, that my trouble had something to do with sex. Already the mechanism of self-deception was at work. By the time my mother rushed into the kitchen to see why I'd returned so early, the thrill I'd felt while waiting for the bus had given way to indignation.

I poured out the story of the man circling the block and protested, with perhaps too great a passion, my own innocence. "I was just sitting there," I said again and again. I was so determined to deflect suspicion away from myself, and to justify my missing the class, that I portrayed the man as a grizzled pervert who drunkenly veered from lane to lane as he followed me halfway home.

My mother cinched her housecoat. She seemed moved and shocked by what I told her, if a bit incredulous, which prompted me to be more dramatic. "It wouldn't be safe," I insisted, "for me to wait at the bus stop again."

No matter how overwrought my story, I knew my mother wouldn't question it, wouldn't bring the subject up again; sex of any kind, especially sex between a man and a boy, was simply not discussed in our house. The gymnastics class, my parents agreed, was something I could do another time.

And so I spent the remainder of that summer at home with my mother, stirring cake batter, holding the dustpan, helping her fold the sheets. For a while I was proud of myself for engineering a reprieve from the athletic club. But as the days wore on, I began to see that my mother had wanted me with her all along, and forcing that to happen wasn't such a feat. Soon a sense of compromise set in; by expressing disgust for the man in the car. I'd expressed disgust for an aspect of myself. Now I had all the time in the world to sit around and contemplate my desire for men. The days grew long and stifling and hot, an endless sentence of self-examination.

Only trips to the pet store offered any respite. Every time I went there, I was too electrified with longing to think about longing in the abstract. The bell tinkled above the door, animals stirred within their cages, and the handsome owner glanced up from his work.

V

I handed my father the *Herald*. He opened the paper and disappeared behind it. My mother stirred her coffee and sighed. She gazed at the sweltering passersby and probably thought herself lucky. I slid into the vinyl booth and took my place beside my parents.

For a moment, I considered asking them about what had happened on the street, but they would have reacted with censure and alarm, and I sensed there was more to the story than they'd ever be willing to tell me. Men in dresses were only the tip of the iceberg. Who knew what other wonders existed—a boy, for example, who wanted to kiss a man— an exception the world did its best to keep hidden.

It would be years before I heard the word "transvestite," so I struggled to find a word for what I'd seen. "He-she" came to mind, as lilting as "Injijikian." "Burl's" would have been perfect, like "boys" and "girls" spliced together, but I can't claim to have thought of this back then.

I must have looked stricken as I tried to figure it all out, because my mother put down her coffee cup and asked if I was O.K. She stopped just short of feeling my forehead. I assured her I was fine, but something within me had shifted, had given way to a heady doubt. When the waitress came and slapped down our check—"Thank You," it read, "Dine out more often"—I wondered if her lofty hairdo or the breasts on which her nametag quaked were real. Wax carnations bloomed at every table.

Phony wood paneled the walls. Plastic food sat in a display case: fried eggs, a hamburger sandwich, a sundae topped with a garish cherry.

Possibilities for Writing

1. Cooper writes that, as a child, he thought it "possible to divide the world into male and female columns" but that, even so, he found many things that "didn't fit neatly into either camp." Examine the imagery he uses throughout this essay to suggest distinctions between male and female and also the blurring of lines between the two.

2. Cooper is quite explicit here about his burgeoning sense of homosexuality at a fairly young age. What purposes do you think he might have for writing this essay? How do you respond? What makes you feel the way you do?

3. Think about your own childhood in terms of how you tried to understand the mysteries of the larger world of adults and your place there as you began growing up. Write an essay in which you focus on some of these experiences; like Cooper, be sure to link your scenes so as to give your essay unity and coherence.

Charles Darwin (1809–1882) was born in Shrewsbury, England, and studied both medicine and religion before turning his attention full-time to his first love, natural history. From 1831 to 1836, he served as official naturalist on an ocean voyage exploring the coast of South America, and his studies there, along with the many specimens he shipped back to England, led him to develop the theory of organic evolution based on natural selection that still predominates in scientific thinking today. His seminal Origin of Species *(1859) outlined his theory with abundant supporting detail and was followed by subsequent works in which he refined and elaborated on the theory, including* The Descent of Man *(1871). He is considered one of the most original thinkers in history.*

Charles Darwin
Natural Selection

In the following excerpt from "Natural Selection," a chapter from *The Origin of Species*, Charles Darwin explains the concept of natural selection and provides scientific evidence for its existence and its ramifications. According to Darwin, natural selection is the process by which the evolution of species occurs. He lays out his theory of evolution by natural selection in great detail, postulating a world governed not by the providential design of an almighty creator, but by the irrevocable laws of species' adaptation to their environment.

Darwin's emphasis on the mechanism of natural selection undermined conventional theological and philosophical assumptions about the special place of human beings in the divine order of creation. According to this view, human beings are simply a species of animal that has adapted successfully to changing conditions, thus ensuring its capacity for survival.

How will the struggle for existence, discussed too briefly in the last chapter, act in regard to variation? Can the principle of selection, which we have seen is so potent in the hands of man, apply in nature? I think we shall see that it can act most effectually. Let it be borne in mind in what an endless number of strange peculiarities our domestic productions, and, in a lesser degree, those under nature, vary; and how strong the hereditary tendency is. Under domestication, it may be truly said that the whole organisation becomes in some degree plastic. Let it be borne in mind how infinitely complex and close-fitting are the mutual relations of all organic beings to each other and to their physical conditions of life. Can it, then, be thought improbable, seeing that variations useful to man have undoubtedly occurred, that other variations useful in some way to each being in the great and complex battle of life, should sometimes occur in the course of thousands of generations? If such do occur, can we doubt (remembering that many more individuals are born than can possibly survive) that individuals having any advantage, however slight, over others, would have the best chance of surviving and of procreating their kind? On the other hand, we may feel sure that any variation in the least degree injurious would be rigidly destroyed. This preservation of favourable variations and the rejection of injurious variations, I call Natural Selection. Variations neither useful nor injurious would not be affected by natural selection, and would be left a fluctuating element, as perhaps we see in the species called polymorphic.

We shall best understand the probable course of natural selection by taking the case of a country undergoing some physical change, for instance, of climate. The proportional numbers of its inhabitants would almost immediately undergo a change, and some species might become extinct. We may conclude, from what we have seen of the intimate and complex manner in which the inhabitants of each country are bound together, that any change in the numerical proportions of some of the inhabitants, independently of the change of climate itself, would most seriously affect many of the others. If the country were open on its borders, new forms would certainly immigrate, and this also would seriously disturb the relations of some of the former inhabitants. Let it be remembered how powerful the influence of a single introduced tree or mammal has been shown to be. But in the case of an island, or of a country partly surrounded by barriers, into which new and better adapted forms could not freely enter, we should then have places in the economy of nature which would assuredly be better filled up, if some of the original inhabitants were in some manner modified; for, had the area been open to immigration, these same places would have been seized on by intruders. In such case, every slight modification, which in the course of ages chanced to arise, and which in any way favoured the individuals of any of the species, by better adapting them to their altered conditions, would tend to be preserved; and natural selection would thus have free scope for the work of improvement.

We have reason to believe, as stated in the first chapter, that a change in the conditions of life, by specially acting on the reproductive system, causes or increases variability; and in the foregoing case the conditions of life are supposed to have undergone a change, and this would manifestly be favourable to natural selection, by giving a better

chance of profitable variations occurring; and unless profitable variations do occur, natural selection can do nothing. Not that, as I believe,
any extreme amount of variability is necessary; as man can certainly
produce great results by adding up in any given direction mere individual differences, so could Nature, but far more easily, from having
incomparably longer time at her disposal. Nor do I believe that any
great physical change, as of climate, or any unusual degree of isolation
to check immigration, is actually necessary to produce new and unoccu-
pied places for natural selection to fill up by modifying and improving
some of the varying inhabitants. For as all the inhabitants of each country are struggling together with nicely balanced forces, extremely slight
modifications in the structure or habits of one inhabitant would often
give it an advantage over others; and still further modifications of the
same kind would often still further increase the advantage. No country
can be named in which all the native inhabitants are now so perfectly
adapted to each other and to the physical conditions under which they
live, that none of them could anyhow be improved; for in all countries,
the natives have been so far conquered by naturalised productions, that
they have allowed foreigners to take firm possession of the land. And as
foreigners have thus everywhere beaten some of the natives, we may
safely conclude that the natives might have been modified with advantage, so as to have better resisted such intruders.

As man can produce and certainly has produced a great result by his
methodical and unconscious means of selection, what may not nature
effect? Man can act only on external and visible characters: nature
cares nothing for appearances, except in so far as they may be useful to
any being. She can act on every internal organ, on every shade of constitutional difference, on the whole machinery of life. Man selects only
for his own good; Nature only for that of the being which she tends.
Every selected character is fully exercised by her; and the being is
placed under well-suited conditions of life. Man keeps the natives of
many climates in the same country; he seldom exercises each selected
character in some peculiar and fitting manner; he feeds a long and a
short beaked pigeon on the same food; he does not exercise a long-
backed or long-legged quadruped in any peculiar manner; he exposes
sheep with long and short wool to the same climate. He does not allow
the most vigorous males to struggle for the females. He does not rigidly
destroy all inferior animals, but protects during each varying season, as

far as lies in his power, all his productions. He often begins his selection by some half-monstrous form; or at least by some modification prominent enough to catch his eye, or to be plainly useful to him. Under nature, the slightest difference of structure or constitution may well turn the nicely-balanced scale in the struggle for life, and to be preserved. How fleeting are the wishes and efforts of man! How short his time! and consequently how poor will his products be, compared with those accumulated by nature during whole geological periods. Can we wonder, then, that nature's productions should be far 'truer' in character than man's productions; that they should be infinitely better adapted to the most complex conditions of life, and should plainly bear the stamp of far higher workmanship?

It may be said that natural selection is daily and hourly scrutinising, throughout the world, every variation, even the slightest; rejecting that which is bad, preserving and adding up all that is good; silently and insensibly working, whenever and wherever opportunity offers, at the improvement of each organic being in relation to its organic and inorganic conditions of life. We see nothing of these slow changes in progress, until the hand of time has marked the long lapses of ages, and then so imperfect is our view into long past geological ages, that we only see that the forms of life are now different from what they formerly were.

Although natural selection can act only through and for the good of each being, yet characters and structures, which we are apt to consider as of very trifling importance, may thus be acted on. When we see leaf-eating insects green, and bark-feeders mottled-grey; the alpine ptarmigan white in winter, the red-grouse the colour of heather, and the black-grouse that of peaty earth, we must believe that these tints are of service to these birds and insects in preserving them from danger. Grouse, if not destroyed at some period of their lives, would increase in countless numbers; they are known to suffer largely from birds of prey; and hawks are guided by eyesight to their prey,—so much so, that on parts of the Continent persons are warned not to keep white pigeons, as being the most liable to destruction. Hence I can see no reason to doubt that natural selection might be most effective in giving the proper colour to each kind of grouse, and in keeping that colour, when once acquired, true and constant. Nor ought we to think that the occasional destruction of an animal of any particular colour would produce little effect: we should remember how essential it is in a flock of white sheep to destroy every lamb with the faintest trace of black. In plants the down on the fruit and the colour of the flesh are considered by botanists as characters of the most trifling importance: yet we hear from an excellent horticulturist, Downing, that in the United States smooth-skinned fruits suffer far more from a beetle, a curculio, than those with down; that purple plums suffer far more from a certain disease than yellow plums; whereas another disease attacks yellow-fleshed peaches far more than those with other coloured flesh. If, with all the aids of art, these slight differences make a great difference in cultivating the several varieties, assuredly, in a state of nature, where the trees would have to struggle with other trees and with a host of enemies, such differences would effectually settle which variety, whether a smooth or downy, a yellow or purple fleshed fruit, should succeed.

In looking at many small points of difference between species, which, as far as our ignorance permits us to judge, seem to be quite unimportant, we must not forget that climate, food, &c., probably produce some slight and direct effect. It is, however far more necessary to bear in mind that there are many unknown laws of correlation of growth, which, when one part of the organisation is modified through variation, and the modifications are accumulated by natural selection for the good of the being, will cause other modifications, often of the most unexpected nature.

As we see that those variations which under domestication appear at any particular period of life, tend to reappear in the offspring at the same period; —for instance, in the seeds of the many varieties of our culinary and agricultural plants; in the caterpillar and cocoon stages of the varieties of the silkworm; in the eggs of poultry, and in the colour of the down of their chickens; in the horns of our sheep and cattle when nearly adult; —so in a state of nature, natural selection will be enabled to act on and modify organic beings at any age, by the accumulation of profitable variations at that age, and by their inheritance at a corresponding age. If it profit a plant to have its seeds more and more widely disseminated by the wind, I can see no greater difficulty in this being effected through natural selection, than in the cotton-planter increasing and improving by selection the down in the pods on his cotton-trees. Natural selection may modify and adapt the larva of an insect to a score of contingencies, wholly different from those which concern the mature insect. These modifications will no doubt affect, through the laws of correlation, the structure of the adult; and probably in the case of those insects which live only for a few hours, and which never feed, a large part of their structure is merely the correlated result of successive changes in the structure of their larvae. So, conversely, modifications in the adult will probably often affect the structure of the larva; but in all cases natural selection will ensure that modifications consequent on other modifications at a different period of life, shall not be in the least degree injurious: for if they became so, they would cause the extinction of the species.

Natural selection will modify the structure of the young in relation to the parent, and of the parent in relation to the young. In social animals it will adapt the structure of each individual for the benefit of the community; if each in consequence profits by the selected change. What natural selection cannot do, is to modify the structure of one species, without giving it any advantage, for the good of another species; and though statements to this effect may be found in works of natural history, I cannot find one case which will bear investigation. A structure used only once in an animal's whole life, if of high importance to it, might be modified to any extent by natural selection; for instance, the great jaws possessed by certain insects, and used exclusively for opening the cocoon—or the hard tip to the beak of nestling birds, used for breaking the egg. It has been asserted, that of the best short-beaked tumbler-pigeons more perish in the egg than are able to get out of it; so that fanciers assist in the act of hatching. Now, if nature had to make the beak of a full-grown pigeon very short for the bird's own advantage, the process of modification would be very slow, and there would be simultaneously the most rigorous selection of the young birds within the egg, which had the most powerful and hardest beaks, for all with weak beaks would inevitably perish: or, more delicate and more easily broken shells might be selected, the thickness of the shell being known to vary like every other structure. . . .

Illustrations of the Action of Natural Selection

In order to make it clear how, as I believe, natural selection acts, I must beg permission to give one or two imaginary illustrations. Let us take the case of a wolf, which preys on various animals, securing some by craft, some by strength, and some by fleetness; and let us suppose that the fleetest prey, a deer for instance, had from any change in the country increased in numbers, or that other prey had decreased in numbers, during that season of the year when the wolf is hardest pressed for food. I can under such circumstances see no reason to doubt that the swiftest and slimmest wolves would have the best chance of surviving, and so be preserved or selected, —provided always that they retained strength to master their prey at this or at some other period of the year, when they might be compelled to prey on other animals. I can see no more reason to doubt this, than that man can improve the fleetness of his greyhounds by careful and methodical selection, or by that unconscious selection which results from each man trying to keep the best dogs without any thought of modifying the breed.

Even without any change in the proportional numbers of the animals on which our wolf preyed, a cub might be born with an innate tendency to pursue certain kinds of prey. Nor can this be thought very improbable; for we often observe great differences in the natural tendencies of our domestic animals; one cat, for instance, taking to catch rats, another mice; one cat according to Mr. St. John, bringing home winged game, another hares or rabbits, and another hunting on marshy ground and almost nightly catching woodcocks or snipes. The tendency to catch rats rather than mice is known to be inherited. Now, if any slight innate change of habit or of structure benefited an individual wolf, it would have the best chance of surviving and of leaving offspring. Some of its young would probably inherit the same habits or structure, and by the repetition of this process, a new variety might be formed which would either supplant or coexist with the parent-form of wolf. Or, again, the wolves inhabiting a mountainous district, and those frequenting the lowlands, would naturally be forced to hunt different prey; and from the continued preservation of the individuals best fitted for the two sites, two varieties might slowly be formed. These varieties would cross and blend where they met; but to this subject of intercrossing we shall soon have to return. I may add, that, according to Mr. Pierce, there are two varieties of the wolf inhabiting the Catskill Mountains in the United States, one with a light greyhound-like form, which pursues deer, and the other more bulky, with shorter legs, which more frequently attacks the shepherd's flocks.

Let us now take a more complex case. Certain plants excrete a sweet juice, apparently for the sake of eliminating something injurious from their sap: this is effected by glands at the base of the stipules in some Leguminosae, and at the back of the leaf of the common laurel. This juice, though small in quantity, is greedily sought by insects. Let us now suppose a little sweet juice or nectar to be excreted by the inner bases of the petals of a flower. In this case insects in seeking the nectar would get dusted with pollen, and would certainly often transport the pollen from one flower to the stigma of another flower. The flowers of two distinct individuals of the same species would thus get crossed; and the act of crossing, we have good reason to believe (as will hereafter be more fully alluded to), would produce very vigorous seedlings, which consequently would have the best chance of flourishing and surviving. Some of these seedlings would probably inherit the nectar-excreting power. Those individual flowers which had the largest glands or nectaries, and which excreted most nectar, would be oftenest visited by insects and would be oftenest crossed; and so in the long-run would gain the upper hand. Those flowers, also, which had their stamens and pistils placed, in rela-tion to the size and habits of the particular insects which visited them, so as to favour in any degree the transportal of their pollen from flower to flower, would likewise be favoured or selected. We might have taken the case of insects visiting flowers for the sake of collecting pollen instead of nectar; and as pollen is formed for the sole object of fertilisa-tion, its destruction appears a simple loss to the plant; yet if a little pollen were carried, at first occasionally and then habitually, by the pollen-devouring insects from flower to flower, and a cross thus effected, although nine-tenths of the pollen were destroyed, it might still be a great gain to the plant; and those individuals which produced more and more pollen, and had larger and larger anthers, would be selected.

When our plant, by this process of the continued preservation or natural selection of more and more attractive flowers, had been ren-dered highly attractive to insects, they would, unintentionally on their part, regularly carry pollen from flower to flower; and that they can most effectually do this, I could easily show by many striking instances. I will give only one—not as a very striking case, but as likewise illustrat-ing one step in the separation of the sexes of plants, presently to be alluded to. Some holly-trees bear only male flowers, which have four stamens producing rather a small quantity of pollen, and a rudimentary pistil; other holly-trees bear only female flowers; these have a full-sized pistil, and four stamens with shrivelled anthers, in which not a grain of pollen can be detected. Having found a female tree exactly sixty yards from a male tree, I put the stigmas of twenty flowers, taken from different branches, under the microscope, and on all, without exception, there were pollen-grains, and on some a profusion of pollen. As the wind had set for several days from the female to the male tree, the pollen could not thus have been carried. The weather had been cold and boisterous, and therefore not favourable to bees, nevertheless every female flower which I examined had been effectually fertilised by the bees, accidentally dusted with pollen, having flown from tree to tree in search of nectar. But to return to our imaginary case: as soon as the plant had been rendered so highly attractive to insects that pollen was regularly carried from flower to flower, another process might commence. No naturalist doubts the advantage of what has been called the physiological division of labour; hence we may believe that it would be advantageous to a plant to produce stamens alone in one flower or on one whole plant, and pistils alone in another flower or on another plant. In plants under culture and placed under new conditions of life, sometimes the male organs and sometimes the female organs become more or less impotent; now if we suppose this to occur in ever so slight a degree under nature, then as pollen is already carried regularly from flower to flower, and as a more complete separation of the sexes of our plant would be advantageous on the principle of the division of labour, individuals with this tendency more and more increased, would be continually favoured or selected, until at last a complete separation of the sexes would be effected.

Let us now turn to the nectar-feeding insects in our imaginary case: we may suppose the plant of which we have been slowly increasing the nectar by continued selection, to be a common plant; and that certain insects depended in main part on its nectar for food. I could give many facts, showing how anxious bees are to save time; for instance, their habit of cutting holes and sucking the nectar at the bases of certain flowers, which they can, with a very little more trouble, enter by the mouth. Bearing such facts in mind, I can see no reason to doubt that an accidental deviation in the size and form of the body, or in the curvature and length of the proboscis, &c., far too slight to be appreciated by us, might profit a bee or other insect, so that an individual so characterised would be able to obtain its food more quickly, and so have a better chance of living and leaving descendants. Its descendants would probably inherit a tendency to a similar slight deviation of structure.

The tubes of the corollas of the common red and incarnate clovers (Trifolium pratense and incarnatum) do not on a hasty glance appear to differ in length; yet the hive-bee can easily suck the nectar out of the incarnate clover, but not out of the common red clover, which is visited by humble-bees alone; so that whole fields of the red clover offer in vain an abundant supply of precious nectar to the hive-bee. Thus it might be a great advantage to the hive-bee to have a slightly longer or differently constructed proboscis. On the other hand, I have found by experiment that the fertility of clover greatly depends on bees visiting and moving parts of the corolla, so as to push the pollen on to the stigmatic surface. Hence, again, if humble-bees were to become rare in any country, it might be a great advantage to the red clover to have a shorter or more deeply divided tube to its corolla, so that the hive-bee could visit its flowers. Thus I can understand how a flower and a bee might slowly become, either simultaneously or one after the other, modified and adapted in the most perfect manner to each other, by the continued preservation of individuals presenting mutual and slightly favourable deviations of structure.

I am well aware that this doctrine of natural selection, exemplified in the above imaginary instances, is open to the same objections which were at first urged against Sir Charles Lyell's noble views on 'the modern changes of the earth, as illustrative of geology;' but we now very seldom hear the action, for instance, of the coast-waves, called a trifling and insignificant cause, when applied to the excavation of gigantic valleys or to the formation of the longest lines of inland cliffs. Natural selection can act only by the preservation and accumulation of infinitesimally small inherited modifications, each profitable to the preserved being; and as modern geology has almost banished such views as the excavation of a great valley by a single diluvial wave, so will natural selection, if it be a true principle, banish the belief of the continued creation of new organic beings, or of any great and sudden modification in their structure.

Summary of Chapter

If during the long course of ages and under varying conditions of life, organic beings vary at all in the several parts of their organisation, and I think this cannot be disputed; if there be, owing to the high geometrical powers of increase of each species, at some age, season, or year, a severe struggle for life, and this certainly cannot be disputed; then, considering the infinite complexity of the relations of all organic beings to each other and to their conditions of existence, causing an infinite diversity in structure, constitution, and habits, to be advantageous to them, I think it would be a most extraordinary fact if no variation ever had occurred useful to each being's own welfare, in the same way as so many variations have occurred useful to man. But if variations useful to any organic being do occur, assuredly individuals thus characterised will have the best chance of being preserved in the struggle for life; and from the strong principle of inheritance they will tend to produce offspring similarly characterised. This principle of preservation, I have called, for the sake of brevity, Natural Selection. Natural selection, on the principle of qualities being inherited at corresponding ages, can modify the egg, seed, or young, as easily as the adult. Amongst many animals, sexual selection will give its aid to ordinary selection, by assuring to the most vigorous and best adapted males the greatest number of offspring. Sexual selection will also give characters useful to the males alone, in their struggles with other males.

Whether natural selection has really thus acted in nature, in modifying and adapting the various forms of life to their several conditions and stations, must be judged of by the general tenour and balance of evidence given in the following chapters. But we already see how it entails extinction; and how largely extinction has acted in the world's history, geology plainly declares. Natural selection, also, leads to divergence of character; for more living beings can be supported on the same area the more they diverge in structure, habits, and constitution, of which we see proof by looking at the inhabitants of any small spot or at naturalised productions. Therefore during the modification of the descendants of any one species, and during the incessant struggle of all species to increase in numbers, the more diversified these descendants become, the better will be their chance of succeeding in the battle of life. Thus the small differences distinguishing varieties of the same species, will steadily tend to increase till they come to equal the greater differences between species of the same genus, or even of distinct genera.

We have seen that it is the common, the widely-diffused, and widely-ranging species, belonging to the larger genera, which vary most; and these will tend to transmit to their modified offspring that superiority which now makes them dominant in their own countries. Natural selection, as has just been remarked, leads to divergence of character and to much extinction of the less improved and intermediate forms of life. On these principles, I believe, the nature of the affinities of all organic beings may be explained. It is a truly wonderful fact—the wonder of which we are apt to overlook from familiarity—that all animals and all plants throughout all time and space should be related to each other in group subordinate to group, in the manner which we everywhere behold—namely, varieties of the same species most closely related together, species of the same genus less closely and unequally related together, forming sections and sub-genera, species of distinct genera much less closely related, and genera related in different degrees, forming subfamilies, families, orders, sub-classes, and classes. The several subordinate groups in any class cannot be ranked in a single file, but seem rather to be clustered round points, and these round other points, and so on in almost endless cycles. On the view that each species has been independently created, I can see no explanation of this great fact in the classification of all organic beings; but, to the best of my judgment, it is explained through inheritance and the complex action of natural selection, entailing extinction and divergence of character, as we have seen illustrated in the diagram.

The affinities of all the beings of the same class have sometimes been represented by a great tree. I believe this simile largely speaks the truth. The green and budding twigs may represent existing species; and those produced during each former year may represent the long succession of extinct species. At each period of growth all the growing twigs have tried to branch out on all sides, and to overtop and kill the surrounding twigs and branches, in the same manner as species and groups of species have tried to overmaster other species in the great battle for life. The limbs divided into great branches, and these into lesser and lesser branches, were themselves once, when the tree was small, budding twigs; and this connexion of the former and present buds by ramifying branches may well represent the classification of all extinct and living species in groups subordinate to groups. Of the many twigs which flourished when the tree was a mere bush, only two or three, now grown into great branches, yet survive and bear all the other branches; so with the species which lived during long-past geological periods, very few now have living and modified descendants. From the first growth of the tree, many a limb and branch has decayed and dropped off; and these lost branches of various sizes may represent those whole orders, families, and genera which have now no living representatives, and which are known to us only from having been found in a fossil state. As we here and there see a thin straggling branch springing from a fork low down in a tree, and which by some chance has been favoured and is still alive on its summit, so we occasionally see an animal like the Ornithorhynchus or Lepidosiren, which in some small degree connects by its affinities two large branches of life, and which has apparently been saved from fatal competition by having inhabited a protected station. As buds give rise by growth to fresh buds, and these, if vigorous, branch out and overtop on all sides many a feebler branch, so by generation I believe it has been with the great Tree of Life, which fills with its dead and broken branches the crust of the earth, and covers the surface with its ever branching and beautiful ramifications.

Possibilities for Writing

1. Based on Darwin's explanations here, define "natural selection." You may quote from the text, but cast your definition primarily in your own words.
2. Focusing on the "Summary of Chapter" at the conclusion of the essay, analyze Darwin's logic. How does Darwin lay out his case and distill his primary ideas?
3. Do some research to write an essay focusing on current controversies surrounding teaching evolution in public schools. Why do Darwin's discoveries continue to trouble some, and where does the scientific community stand on the question of evolution?

*Joan Didion (b. 1934) grew up in central California, where her family had
lived for many generations. After graduating from the University of California
at Berkeley in 1956, she joined the staff of* Vogue *magazine, where she worked
until the publication of her first novel,* Run River, *in 1963. Other novels
followed—including* Play It As It Lays *(1970),* A Book of Common Prayer
(1977), and The Last Thing He Wanted *(1996)—but it is her essays,
particularly those collected in* Slouching Towards Bethlehem *(1968) and* The
White Album *(1979), that established Didion as one of the most admired voices
of her generation. A meticulous stylist who combines sharply observed detail
with wry—even bracing—irony, she has examined subjects that range from life
in Southern California to the Washington political scene to the war in
El Salvador to marriage Las Vegas–style.*

Joan Didion

Marrying Absurd

In "Marrying Absurd," Joan Didion takes a critical look at the Las Vegas
wedding industry. In keeping with the portraits of people and places throughout
her work, Didion uses carefully selected details to convey her impression of Las
Vegas and to render her judgment of its values. She uses a number of ironic
techniques to establish and sustain her satiric tone, most significantly, perhaps,
including details that mean one thing to the Las Vegas wedding people and
something quite different to the reader. Examples include the signs advertising
weddings posted throughout the city, as well as comments made by participants,
in which they condemn themselves, unwittingly. Some of the most damning
examples of this ironic use of dialogue occur in the essay's concluding paragraph.

   "Marrying Absurd," however, conveys more than Joan Didion's acerbic
criticism of Las Vegas marriages. It also suggests something of Didion's attitude
toward the larger national problem of what she describes as "venality" and a
"devotion to immediate gratification."

To be married in Las Vegas, Clark County, Nevada, a bride must swear
that she is eighteen or has parental permission and a bridegroom
that he is twenty-one or has parental permission. Someone must put up
five dollars for the license. (On Sundays and holidays, fifteen dollars.
The Clark County Courthouse issues marriage licenses at any time of
the day or night except between noon and one in the afternoon,
between eight and nine in the evening, and between four and five in the
morning.) Nothing else is required. The State of Nevada, alone among
these United States, demands neither a premarital blood test nor a

waiting period before or after the issuance of a marriage license. Driving in across the Mojave from Los Angeles, one sees the signs way out on the desert, looming up from that moonscape of rattlesnakes and mesquite, even before the Las Vegas lights appear like a mirage on the horizon: "GETTING MARRIED? Free License Information First Strip Exit." Perhaps the Las Vegas wedding industry achieved its peak operational efficiency between 9:00 p.m. and midnight of August 26, 1965, an otherwise unremarkable Thursday which happened to be, by Presidential order, the last day on which anyone could improve his draft status merely by getting married. One hundred and seventy-one couples were pronounced man and wife in the name of Clark County and the State of Nevada that night, sixty-seven of them by a single justice of the peace, Mr. James A. Brennan. Mr. Brennan did one wedding at the Dunes and the other sixty-six in his office, and charged each couple eight dollars. One bride lent her veil to six others. "I got it down from five to three minutes," Mr. Brennan said later of his feat. "I could've married them *en masse*, but they're people, not cattle. People expect more when they get married."

What people who get married in Las Vegas actually do expect— what, in the largest sense, their "expectations" are—strikes one as a curious and self-contradictory business. Las Vegas is the most extreme and allegorical of American settlements, bizarre and beautiful in its venality and in its devotion to immediate gratification, a place the tone of which is set by mobsters and call girls and ladies' room attendants with amyl nitrite poppers in their uniform pockets. Almost everyone notes that there is no "time" in Las Vegas, no night and no day and no past and no future (no Las Vegas casino, however, has taken the obliteration of the ordinary time sense quite so far as Harold's Club in Reno, which for a while issued, at odd intervals in the day and night, mimeographed "bulletins" carrying news from the world outside); neither is there any logical sense of where one is. One is standing on a highway in the middle of a vast hostile desert looking at an eighty-foot sign which blinks "Stardust" or "Caesar's Palace." Yes, but what does that explain? This geographical implausibility reinforces the sense that what happens there has no connection with "real" life; Nevada cities like Reno and Carson are ranch towns, Western towns, places behind which there is some historical imperative. But Las Vegas seems to exist only in the eye of the beholder. All of which makes it an extraordinarily stimulating and interesting place, but an odd one in which to want to wear a candlelight satin Priscilla of Boston wedding dress with Chantilly lace insets, tapered sleeves and a detachable modified train.

And yet the Las Vegas wedding business seems to appeal to precisely that impulse. "Sincere and Dignified Since 1954," one wedding chapel advertises. There are nineteen such wedding chapels in Las Vegas, intensely competitive, each offering better, faster, and, by implication, more sincere services than the next: Our Photos Best Anywhere, Your Wedding on A Phonograph Record, Candlelight with Your Ceremony, Honeymoon Accommodations, Free Transportation from Your Motel to Courthouse to Chapel and Return to Motel, Religious or Civil Ceremonies, Dressing Rooms, Flowers, Rings, Announcements, Witnesses Available, and Ample Parking. All of these services, like most others in Las Vegas (sauna baths, payroll-check cashing, chinchilla coats for sale or rent), are offered twenty-four hours a day, seven days a week, presumably on the premise that marriage, like craps, is a game to be played when the table seems hot.

But what strikes one most about the Strip chapels, with their wishing wells and stained-glass paper windows and their artificial bouvardia, is that so much of their business is by no means a matter of simple convenience, of late-night liaisons between show girls and baby Crosbys. Of course there is some of that. (One night about eleven o'clock in Las Vegas I watched a bride in an orange minidress and masses of flame-colored hair stumble from a Strip chapel on the arm of her bridegroom, who looked the part of the expendable nephew in movies like *Miami Syndicate*. "I gotta get the kids," the bride whimpered. "I gotta pick up the sitter, I gotta get to the midnight show." "What you gotta get," the bridegroom said, opening the door of a Cadillac Coupe de Ville and watching her crumple on the seat, "is sober.") But Las Vegas seems to offer something other than "convenience"; it is merchandising "niceness," the facsimile of proper ritual, to children who do not know how else to find it, how to make the arrangements, how to do it "right." All day and evening long on the Strip, one sees actual wedding parties, waiting under the harsh lights at a crosswalk, standing uneasily in the parking lot of the Frontier while the photographer hired by The Little Church of the West ("Wedding Place of the Stars") certifies the occasion, takes the picture: the bride in a veil and white satin pumps, the bridegroom usually in a white dinner jacket, and even an attendant or two, a sister or a best friend in hot-pink *peau de soie*, a flirtation veil, a carnation nosegay. "When I Fall in Love It Will Be Forever," the organist plays, and then a few bars of Lohengrin. The mother cries; the stepfather, awkward in his role, invites the chapel hostess to join them for a drink at the Sands. The hostess declines with a professional smile; she has already transferred her interest to the group waiting outside. One bride out, another in, and again the sign goes up on the chapel door: "One Moment please—Wedding."

I sat next to one such wedding party in a Strip restaurant the last time I was in Las Vegas. The marriage had just taken place; the bride still wore her dress, the mother her corsage. A bored waiter poured out a few swallows of pink champagne ("on the house") for everyone but the bride, who was too young to be served. "You'll need something with more kick than that," the bride's father said with heavy jocularity to his new son-in-law; the ritual jokes about the wedding night had a certain Pangiossian character, since the bride was clearly several months pregnant. Another round of pink champagne, this time not on the house, and the bride began to cry. "It was just as nice," she sobbed, "as I hoped and dreamed it would be."

Possibilities for Writing

1. Didion inevitably conveys an air of superiority in this essay—her purpose, after all, is to point out what she sees as the absurdity of the marriage business in Las Vegas. In an essay, analyze how you respond to this tone and this attitude towards her subjects. Use specific quotations to elaborate on the reasons for your response.

2. One of Didion's main points is that many of those who marry in Las Vegas chapels do so in order to have "the facsimile of proper ritual"; they are "children who do not know how else to find it, how to make the arrangements, how to do it 'right.' " Didion was writing in 1967. What is most people's notion of "proper ritual" today? In considering this question, think not only of weddings but of anything that is traditionally considered a "solemn occasion": graduations, church services, funerals, and the like. What do you think is the proper level of formality for such occasions?

3. Pick a setting where you think people engage in "absurd" behavior. Either spend some time observing what happens there, or re-create these activities in detail from memory. Then write an essay, as Didion does, in which you describe this setting and these activities in an ironic light. Be as specific as possible.

Annie Dillard (b. 1945) developed an interest in nature at the age of ten, after discovering The Field Book of Ponds and Streams *in a branch of the Pittsburgh library system. While studying creative writing and theology at Hollins College in rural Virginia, she began a journal of observations of natural phenomena that would eventually become the Pulitzer Prize–winning* Pilgrim at Tinker Creek *(1974), her first published work of nonfiction. This was followed by* Holy the Firm *(1977), a mystical meditation on the natural world, and* Teaching a Stone to Talk *(1982), a collection of philosophical essays. A professor at Wesleyan College, Dillard has also published several volumes of poetry, a novel, and a memoir of her youth,* An America Childhood *(1987). Her most recent book is* For the Time Being *(1999), which questions the concept of a merciful God.*

Annie Dillard
Living Like Weasels

In "Living Like Weasels," Annie Dillard describes an encounter with a weasel she had one day while resting on a log in a patch of woods near a housing development in Virginia. Dillard begins in the expository mode, detailing facts about weasels, especially their tenacity and wildness. But she shifts, before long, into a meditation on the value and necessity of instinct and tenacity in human life. Dillard's tone changes from the factual declaration of the opening into speculative wonder at the weasel's virtues and, finally, into urgent admonition. By the end of the essay Dillard has made the weasel a symbol of how human beings might live.

As a "nature writer," Dillard is compelling. She digs deep beneath the surface of her subjects, always looking for connections between the natural and human worlds. In "Living Like Weasels," these connections take the form of speculating about the connections and disjunctions between the wildness and ferocity of a little brown-bodied, furry creature, and the human need to find our necessity, lock onto it, and never let go. Dillard privileges wildness over civilization, mystical communion over separateness, instinct over intellect. She clearly values the weasel's tenacity.

I

A weasel is wild. Who knows what he thinks? He sleeps in his underground den, his tail draped over his nose. Sometimes he lives in his den for two days without leaving. Outside, he stalks rabbits, mice, muskrats, and birds, killing more bodies than he can eat warm, and often dragging the carcasses home. Obedient to instinct, he bites his prey at the neck, either splitting the jugular vein at the throat or crunching the brain at the base of the skull, and he does not let go. One naturalist refused to kill a weasel who was socketed into his hand deeply as a rattlesnake. The man could in no way pry the tiny weasel off, and he had to walk half a mile to water, the weasel dangling from his palm, and soak him off like a stubborn label.

And once, says Ernest Thompson Seton—once, a man shot an eagle out of the sky. He examined the eagle and found the dry skull of a weasel fixed by the jaws to his throat. The supposition is that the eagle had pounced on the weasel and the weasel swiveled and bit as instinct taught him, tooth to neck, and nearly won. I would like to have seen that eagle from the air a few weeks or months before he was shot: was the whole weasel still attached to his feathered throat, a fur pendant? Or did the eagle eat what he could reach, gutting the living weasel with his talons before his breast, bending his beak, cleaning the beautiful airborne bones?

II

I have been reading about weasels because I saw one last week. I startled a weasel who startled me, and we exchanged a long glance.

Twenty minutes from my house, through the woods by the quarry and across the highway, is Hollins Pond, a remarkable piece of shallowness, where I like to go at sunset and sit on a tree trunk. Hollins Pond is also called Murray's Pond; it covers two acres of bottomland near Tinker Creek with six inches of water and six thousand lily pads. In winter, brown-and-white steers stand in the middle of it, merely dampening their hooves; from the distant shore they look like miracle itself, complete with miracle's nonchalance. Now, in summer, the steers are gone. The water lilies have blossomed and spread to a green horizontal plane that is terra firma to plodding blackbirds, and tremulous ceiling to black leeches, cray fish, and carp.

This is, mind you, suburbia. It is a five-minute walk in three directions to rows of houses, though none is visible here. There's a 55 mph highway at one end of the pond, and a nesting pair of wood ducks at the other. Under every bush is a muskrat hole or a beer can. The far end is an alternating series of fields and woods, fields and woods, threaded everywhere with motorcycle tracks—in whose bare clay wild turtles lay eggs.

So, I had crossed the highway, stepped over two low barbed-wire fences, and traced the motorcycle path in all gratitude through the wild rose and poison ivy of the pond's shoreline up into high grassy fields. Then I cut down through the woods to the mossy fallen tree where I sit. This tree is excellent. It makes a dry, upholstered bench at the upper, marshy end of the pond, a plush jetty raised from the thorn shore between a shallow blue body of water and a deep blue body of sky.

The sun had just set. I was relaxed on the tree trunk, ensconced in the lap of lichen, watching the lily pads at my feet tremble and part dreamily over the thrusting path of a carp. A yellow bird appeared to my right and flew behind me. It caught my eye; I swiveled around—and the next instant, inexplicably, I was looking down at a weasel, who was looking up at me.

III

Weasel! I'd never seen one wild before. He was ten inches long, thin as a curve, a muscled ribbon, brown as fruitwood, soft-furred, alert. His face was fierce, small and pointed as a lizard's; he would have made a good arrowhead. There was just a dot of chin, maybe two brown hairs' worth, and then the pure white fur began that spread down his underside. He had two black eyes I didn't see, any more than you see a window.

The weasel was stunned into stillness as he was emerging from beneath an enormous shaggy wild rose bush four feet away. I was stunned into stillness twisted backward on the tree trunk. Our eyes locked, and someone threw away the key.

Our look was as if two lovers, or deadly enemies, met unexpectedly on an overgrown path when each had been thinking of something else: a clearing blow to the gut. It was also a bright blow to the brain, or a sudden beating of brains with all the charge and intimate grate of rubbed balloons. It emptied our lungs. It felled the forest, moved the fields, and drained the pond; the world dismantled and tumbled into that black hole of eyes. If you and I looked at each other that way, our skulls would split and drop to our shoulders. But we don't. We keep our skulls. So.

He disappeared. This was only last week, and already I don't remember what shattered the enchantment. I think I blinked, I think I retrieved my brain from the weasel's brain, and tried to memorize what

I was seeing, and the weasel felt the yank of separation, the careening splashdown into real life and the urgent current of instinct. He vanished under the wild rose. I waited motionless, my mind suddenly full of data and my spirit with pleadings, but he didn't return.

Please do not tell me about "approach-avoidance conflicts." I tell you I've been in that weasel's brain for sixty seconds, and he was in mine. Brains are private places, muttering through unique and secret tapes—but the weasel and I both plugged into another tape simultaneously, for a sweet and shocking time. Can I help it if it was a blank?

What goes on in his brain the rest of the time? What does a weasel think about? He won't say. His journal is tracks in clay, a spray of feathers, mouse blood and bone: uncollected, unconnected, loose-leaf, and blown.

IV

I would like to learn, or remember, how to live. I come to Hollins Pond not so much to learn how to live as, frankly, to forget about it. That is, I don't think I can learn from a wild animal how to live in particular—shall I suck warm blood, hold my tail high, walk with my footprints precisely over the prints of my hands?—but I might learn something of mindlessness, something of the purity of living in the physical senses and the dignity of living without bias or motive. The weasel lives in necessity and we live in choice, hating necessity and dying at the last ignobly in its talons. I would like to live as I should, as the weasel lives as he should. And I suspect that for me the way is like the weasel's: open to time and death painlessly, noticing everything, remembering nothing, choosing the given with a fierce and pointed will.

V

I missed my chance. I should have gone for the throat. I should have lunged for that streak of white under the weasel's chin and held on, held on through mud and into the wild rose, held on for a dearer life. We could live under the wild rose wild as weasels, mute and uncomprehending. I could very calmly go wild. I could live two days in the den, curled, leaning on mouse fur, sniffing bird bones, blinking, licking, breathing musk, my hair tangled in the roots of grasses. Down is a good place to go, where the mind is single. Down is out, out of your ever-loving mind and back to your careless senses. I remember muteness as a prolonged and giddy fast, where every moment is a feast of utterance received. Time and events are merely poured, unremarked, and ingested directly, like blood pulsed into my gut through a jugular vein. Could two live that way? Could two live under the wild rose, and explore by the pond, so that the smooth mind of each is as everywhere present to the other, and as received and as unchallenged, as falling snow?

We could, you know. We can live any way we want. People take vows of poverty, chastity, and obedience—even of silence—by choice. The thing is to stalk your calling in a certain skilled and supple way, to locate the most tender and live spot and plug into that pulse. This is yielding, not fighting. A weasel doesn't "attack' anything; a weasel lives as he's meant to, yielding at every moment to the perfect freedom of single necessity.

VI

I think it would be well, and proper, and obedient, and pure, to grasp your one necessity and not let it go, to dangle from it limp wherever it takes you. Then even death, where you're going no matter how you live, cannot you part. Seize it and let it seize you up aloft even, till your eyes burn out and drop; let your musky flesh fall off in shreds, and let your very bones unhinge and scatter, loosened over fields, over fields and woods, lightly, thoughtless, from any height at all, from as high as eagles.

Possibilities for Writing

1. Central to Dillard's point here are the concepts of "mindlessness" and "necessity" as opposed to consciousness and choice. In an essay, explore what Dillard means by these terms and what value she apparently finds in giving oneself over to mindlessness and necessity.

2. Dillard's essay is divided into six parts, all linked by repeated images and words. Analyze the essay to note as many of these

linkages as you can. Then explore how several of these threads function meaningfully in the essay.

3. Dillard's encounter with the weasel provides her with a profound insight about humans and the natural world. Recall a time when an encounter or experience led you to see some aspect of life in a new light. In an essay explore the circumstances of this sudden insight.

Frederick Douglass (1817–1895) was born a slave in rural Maryland and as a boy worked as a house servant in Baltimore, where his mistress taught him the rudiments of reading until her husband objected. Continuing his education surreptitiously on his own, Douglass escaped to New York when he was twenty. Within three years, he had become an ardent campaigner against slavery and for the rights of free blacks. In 1846 his freedom was officially purchased by British supporters, and in 1847 he began publishing a weekly newspaper, North Star. *During the Civil War, he promoted the use of black troops to fight the Confederacy, and following the war he held several government posts, including U. S. Minister to Haiti. Today he is best known for his autobiographical works, most notably his first publication,* Narrative of the Life of Frederick Douglass *(1845).*

Frederick Douglass
Learning to Read and Write

In this excerpt from his autobiography, Frederick Douglass, an American slave, describes how he learned to read and write, and the consequences that his literacy brought him. Douglass entwines the story of his entry into literacy with that of his enslavement. He makes clear how, by keeping black slaves ignorant through denying them literacy, white slaveowners kept them under control. In telling this part of his life story, Douglass conveys a sense of the power of literacy. Learning to read and write transformed Douglass from a passive person to an active one, from an obedient slave who accepted his lot to a thoughtful critic of the institution of slavery and a spirited rebel against it.

Douglass links the stories of how he learned to read and to write with a bridge anecdote about his resolve to run away from his master. In this section, Douglass reveals his mistrust of white people, some of whom were actually eager to help him, and he reveals as well his gradual understanding of the abolitionist movement, in which he himself would later become a prominent figure. Douglass exercised the same ingenuity and determination in learning to write as he did in learning to read. Ingenuity and determination, in fact, are central themes of Douglass's story.

I lived in Master Hugh's family about seven years. During this time, I succeeded in learning to read and write. In accomplishing this, I was compelled to resort to various stratagems. I had no regular teacher.

My mistress, who had kindly commenced to instruct me, had, in compliance with the advice and direction of her husband, not only ceased to instruct, but had set her face against my being instructed by any one else. It is due, however, to my mistress to say of her, that she did not adopt this course of treatment immediately. She at first lacked the depravity indispensable to shutting me up in mental darkness. It was at least necessary for her to have some training in the exercise of irresponsible power, to make her equal to the task of treating me as though I were a brute.

My mistress was, as I have said, a kind and tender-hearted woman; and in the simplicity of her soul she commenced, when I first went to live with her, to treat me as she supposed one human being ought to treat another. In entering upon the duties of a slaveholder, she did not seem to perceive that I sustained to her the relation of a mere chattel, and that for her to treat me as a human being was not only wrong, but dangerously so. Slavery proved as injurious to her as it did to me. When I went there, she was a pious, warm, and tender-hearted woman. There was no sorrow or suffering for which she had not a tear. She had bread for the hungry, clothes for the naked, and comfort for every mourner that came within her reach. Slavery soon proved its ability to divest her of these heavenly qualities. Under its influence, the tender heart became stone, and the lamb-like disposition gave way to one of tiger-like fierceness. The first step in her downward course was in her ceasing to instruct me. She now commenced to practise her husband's precepts. She finally became even more violent in her opposition than her husband himself. She was not satisfied with simply doing as well as he had commanded; she seemed anxious to do better. Nothing seemed to make her more angry than to see me with a newspaper. She seemed to think that here lay the danger. I have had her rush at me with a face made all up of fury, and snatch from me a newspaper, in a manner that fully revealed her apprehension. She was an apt woman; and a little experience soon demonstrated, to her satisfaction, that education and slavery were incompatible with each other.

From this time I was most narrowly watched. If I was in a separate room any considerable length of time, I was sure to be suspected of having a book, and was at once called to give an account of myself. All this, however, was too late. The first step had been taken. Mistress, in teaching me the alphabet, had given me the *inch*, and no precaution could prevent me from taking the *ell*.

The plan which I adopted, and the one by which I was most successful, was that of making friends of all the little white boys whom I met in
the street. As many of these as I could, I converted into teachers. With
their kindly aid, obtained at different times and in different places,
I finally succeeded in learning to read. When I was sent of errands, I
always took my book with me, and by going one part of my errand
quickly, I found time to get a lesson before my return. I used also to carry
bread with me, enough of which was always in the house, and to which I
was always welcome; for I was much better off in this regard than many
of the poor white children in our neighborhood. This bread I used to
bestow upon the hungry little urchins, who, in return, would give me
that more valuable bread of knowledge. I am strongly tempted to give
the names of two or three of those little boys, as a testimonial of the gratitude and affection I bear them; but prudence forbids:—not that it would
injure me, but it might embarrass them; for it is almost an unpardonable
offence to teach slaves to read in this Christian country. It is enough to
say of the dear little fellows, that they lived on Philpot Street, very near
Durgin and Bailey's ship-yard. I used to talk this matter of slavery over
with them. I would sometimes say to them, I wished I could be as free as
they would be when they got to be men. "You will be free as soon as you
are twenty-one, *but I am a slave for life!* Have not I as good a right to be
free as you have?" These words used to trouble them; they would express
for me the liveliest sympathy, and console me with the hope that something would occur by which I might be free.

I was now about twelve years old, and the thought of being *a slave
for life* began to bear heavily upon my heart. Just about this time, I
got hold of a book entitled "The Columbian Orator." Every opportunity I got, I used to read this book. Among much of other interesting
matter, I found in it a dialogue between a master and his slave. The
slave was represented as having run away from his master three
times. The dialogue represented the conversation which took place
between them, when the slave was retaken the third time. In this dialogue, the whole argument in behalf of slavery was brought forward
by the master, all of which was disposed of by the slave. The slave
was made to say some very smart as well as impressive things in reply
to his master—things which had the desired though unexpected
effect; for the conversation resulted in the voluntary emancipation of
the slave on the part of the master.

In the same book, I met with one of Sheridan's mighty speeches on and in behalf of Catholic emancipation. These were choice documents to me. I read them over and over again with unabated interest. They gave tongue to interesting thoughts of my own soul, which had frequently flashed through my mind, and died away for want of utterance. The moral which I gained from the dialogue was the power of truth over the conscience of even a slaveholder. What I got from Sheridan was a bold denunciation of slavery, and a powerful vindication of human rights. The reading of these documents enabled me to utter my thoughts, and to meet the arguments brought forward to sustain slavery; but while they relieved me of one difficulty, they brought on another even more painful than the one of which I was relieved. The more I read, the more I was led to abhor and detest my enslavers. I could regard them in no other light than a band of successful robbers, who had left their homes, and gone to Africa, and stolen us from our homes, and in a strange land reduced us to slavery. I loathed them as being the meanest as well as the most wicked of men. As I read and contemplated the subject, behold! that very discontentment which Master Hugh had predicted would follow my learning to read had already come, to torment and sting my soul to unutterable anguish. As I writhed under it, I would at times feel that learning to read had been a curse rather than a blessing. It had given me a view of my wretched condition, without the remedy. It opened my eyes to the horrible pit, but to no ladder upon which to get out. In moments of agony, I envied my fellow-slaves for their stupidity. I have often wished myself a beast. I preferred the condition of the meanest reptile to my own. Any thing, no matter what, to get rid of thinking! It was this everlasting thinking of my condition that tormented me. There was no getting rid of it. It was pressed upon me by every object within sight or hearing, animate or inanimate. The silver trump of freedom had roused my soul to eternal wakefulness. Freedom now appeared, to disappear no more forever. It was heard in every sound, and seen in every thing. It was ever present to torment me with a sense of my wretched condition. I saw nothing without seeing it, I heard nothing without hearing it, and felt nothing without feeling it. It looked from every star, it smiled in every calm, breathed in every wind, and moved in every storm.

I often found myself regretting my own existence, and wishing myself dead; and but for the hope of being free, I have no doubt but that

I should have killed myself, or done something for which I should have been killed. While in this state of mind, I was eager to hear any one speak of slavery. I was a ready listener. Every little while, I could hear something about the abolitionists. It was some time before I found what the word meant. It was always used in such connections as to make it an interesting word to me. If a slave ran away and succeeded in getting clear, or if a slave killed his master, set fire to a barn, or did any thing very wrong in the mind of a slaveholder, it was spoken of as the fruit of *abolition.* Hearing the word in this connection very often, I set about learning what it meant. The dictionary afforded me little or no help. I found it was "the act of abolishing;" but then I did not know what was to be abolished. Here I was perplexed. I did not dare to ask any one about its meaning, for I was satisfied that it was something they wanted me to know very little about. After a patient waiting, I got one of our city papers, containing an account of the number of petitions from the north, praying for the abolition of slavery in the District of Columbia, and of the slave trade between the States. From this time I understood the words *abolition* and *abolitionist,* and always drew near when that word was spoken, expecting to hear something of importance to myself and fellow-slaves. The light broke in upon me by degrees. I went one day down on the wharf of Mr. Waters; and seeing two Irishmen unloading a scow of stone, I went, unasked, and helped them. When we had finished, one of them came to me and asked me if I were a slave. I told him I was. He asked, "Are ye a slave for life?" I told him that I was. The good Irishman seemed to be deeply affected by the statement. He said to the other that it was a pity so fine a little fellow as myself should be a slave for life. He said it was a shame to hold me. They both advised me to run away to the north; that I should find friends there, and that I should be free. I pretended not to be interested in what they said, and treated them as if I did not understand them; for I feared they might be treacherous. White men have been known to encourage slaves to escape, and then, to get the reward, catch them and return them to their masters. I was afraid that these seemingly good men might use me so; but I nevertheless remembered their advice, and from that time I resolved to run away. I looked forward to a time at which it would be safe for me to escape. I was too young to think of doing so immediately; besides, I wished to learn how to write, as I might have occasion to write my own pass. I consoled myself with the hope that I should one day find a good chance. Meanwhile, I would learn to write.

The idea as to how I might learn to write was suggested to me by being in Durgin and Bailey's ship-yard, and frequently seeing the ship carpenters, after hewing, and getting a piece of timber ready for use, write on the timber the name of that part of the ship for which it was intended. When a piece of timber was intended for the larboard side, it would be marked thus—"L." When a piece was for the starboard side, it would be marked thus—"S." A piece for the larboard side forward, would be marked thus—"L. F." When a piece was for starboard side forward, it would be marked thus—"S. F." For larboard aft, it would be marked thus—"L. A." For starboard aft, it would be marked thus—"S. A." I soon learned the names of these letters, and for what they were intended when placed upon a piece of timber in the shipyard. I immediately commenced copying them, and in a short time was able to make the four letters named. After that, when I met with any boy who I knew could write, I would tell him I could write as well as he. The next word would be, "I don't believe you. Let me see you try it." I would then make the letters which I had been so fortunate as to learn, and ask him to beat that. In this way I got a good many lessons in writing, which it is quite possible I should never have gotten in any other way. During this time, my copy-book was the board fence, brick wall, and pavement; my pen and ink was a lump of chalk. With these, I learned mainly how to write. I then commenced and continued copying the Italics in Webster's Spelling Book, until I could make them all without looking on the book. By this time, my little Master Thomas had gone to school, and learned how to write, and had written over a number of copy-books. These had been brought home, and shown to some of our near neighbors, and then laid aside. My mistress used to go to class meeting at the Wilk Street meetinghouse every Monday afternoon, and leave me to take care of the house. When left thus, I used to spend the time in writing in the spaces left in Master Thomas's copy-book, copying what he had written. I continued to do this until I could write a hand very similar to that of Master Thomas. Thus, after a long, tedious effort for years, I finally succeeded in learning how to write.

Possibilities for Writing

1. In various ways throughout this essay, Douglass makes the point that education—learning to read and write—and slavery are "incompatible with each other," for both slaves and those who

own them. Using evidence from the text, as well as your own conclusions, explore why this would be so.

2. Douglass's autobiography was written before slavery was fully abolished in the United States. In what ways can his narrative be read as an argument against slavery? Consider this issue from the perspective of readers who might be slaveholders, those who were already abolitionists, and those who did not own slaves but were undecided on the question.

3. How do you respond to Douglass's situation and to the portrait he presents of himself as you read it today, more than a hundred and fifty years after it was written? Do you find that you can apply any of what he says to the world you live in today? Explain why you feel as you do.

Brian Doyle *(b. 1956) is the editor of* Portland *magazine at the University of Portland, Oregon. His essays have appeared in* The American Scholar, The Atlantic Monthly, Harper's, Orion, Commonweal, *and the* Georgia Review. *A number of his essays have been selected to appear in the annual Best American Essays series. Among his books are an edited collection of spiritual writing,* God Is Love, *and two of his own five collections of essays,* Leaping: Revelations & Epiphanies *(2004), and* The Wet Engine *(2005), in which "Joyas Voladoras" appears.*

Brian Doyle
Joyas Voladoras

In "Joyas Voladoras," Brian Doyle's characteristic wit, grace, and writerly elegance are in evidence as he explores one of life's mysteries—the beautiful jewel-like hummingbird. The essay blends scientific information with spiritual appreciation of this miniature marvel of creation. Doyle celebrates the wonders of the hummingbird, cataloging its myriad species and highlighting the intensity of its life force.

Beyond describing and celebrating the life of the hummingbird, Doyle branches out to mention other marvels of creation, especially the largest of all creatures, the blue whale. It is the heart of this great beast that interests Doyle, as well as the heart of the hummingbird, and then beyond these hearts great and small, the heart of that other marvel of creation—the human species.

Consider the hummingbird for a long moment. A hummingbird's heart beats ten times a second. A hummingbird's heart is the size of a pencil eraser. A hummingbird's heart is a lot of the hummingbird. *Joyas voladoras*, flying jewels, the first white explorers in the Americas called them, and the white men had never seen such creatures, for hummingbirds came into the world only in the Americas, nowhere else in the universe, more than three hundred species of them whirring and zooming and nectaring in hummer time zones nine times removed from ours, their hearts hammering faster than we could clearly hear if we pressed our elephantine ears to their infinitesimal chests.

Each one visits a thousand flowers a day. They can dive at sixty miles an hour. They can fly backward. They can fly more than five hundred miles without pausing to rest. But when they rest they come close to death: on frigid nights, or when they are starving, they retreat into torpor, their metabolic rate slowing to a fifteenth of their normal sleep rate, their hearts sludging nearly to a halt, barely beating, and if they are not soon warmed, if they do not soon find that which is sweet, their hearts grow cold, and they cease to be. Consider for a moment those hummingbirds who did not open their eyes again today, this very day, in the Americas: bearded helmetcrests and booted racket-tails, violet-tailed sylphs and violet-capped woodnymphs, crimson topazes and purple-crowned fairies, red-tailed comets and amethyst woodstars, rainbow-bearded thornbills and glittering-bellied emeralds, velvet-purple coronets and golden-bellied star-frontlets, fiery-tailed awlbills and Andean hillstars, spatuletails and pufflegs, each the most amazing thing you have never seen, each thunderous wild heart the size of an infant's fingernail, each mad heart silent, a brilliant music stilled.

Hummingbirds, like all flying birds but more so, have incredible enormous immense ferocious metabolisms. To drive those metabolisms they have racecar hearts that eat oxygen at an eye-popping rate. Their hearts are built of thinner, leaner fibers than ours. Their arteries are stiffer and more taut. They have more mitochondria in their heart muscles—anything to gulp more oxygen. Their hearts are stripped to the skin for the war against gravity and inertia, the mad search for food, the insane idea of flight. The price of their ambition is a life closer to death; they suffer more heart attacks and aneurysms and ruptures than any other living creature. It's expensive to fly. You burn out. You fry the machine. You melt the engine. Every creature on earth has approximately two billion heartbeats to spend in a lifetime. You can spend them slowly, like a tortoise, and live to be two hundred years old, or you can spend them fast, like a hummingbird, and live to be two years old.

The biggest heart in the world is inside the blue whale. It weighs more than seven tons. It's as big as a room. It *is* a room, with four chambers. A child could walk around in it, head high, bending only to step through the valves. The valves are as big as the swinging doors in a saloon. This house of a heart drives a creature a hundred feet long. When this creature is born it is twenty feet long and weighs four tons. It is waaaaay bigger than your car. It drinks a hundred gallons of milk from its mama every day and gains two hundred pounds a day, and when it is seven or eight years old it endures an unimaginable puberty and then it essentially disappears from human ken, for next to nothing is known of the mating habits, travel patterns, diet, social life, language, social structure, diseases, spirituality, wars, stories, despairs, and arts of the blue whale. There are perhaps ten thousand blue whales in the world, living in every ocean on earth, and of the largest mammal who ever lived we know nearly nothing. But we know this: the animals with the largest hearts in the world generally travel in pairs, and their penetrating moaning cries, their piercing yearning tongue, can be heard underwater for miles and miles.

Mammals and birds have hearts with four chambers. Reptiles and turtles have hearts with three chambers. Fish have hearts with two chambers. Insects and mollusks have hearts with one chamber. Worms have hearts with one chamber, although they may have as many as eleven single-chambered hearts. Unicellular bacteria have no hearts at all; but even they have fluid eternally in motion, washing from one side of the cell to the other, swirling and whirling. No living being is without interior liquid motion. We all churn inside.

So much held in a heart in a lifetime. So much held in a heart in a day, an hour, a moment. We are utterly open with no one, in the end—not mother and father, not wife or husband, not lover, not child, not friend. We open windows to each but we live alone in the house of the heart. Perhaps we must. Perhaps we could not bear to be so naked, for fear of a constantly harrowed heart. When young we think there will come one person who will savor and sustain us always; when we are older we know this is the dream of a child, that all hearts finally are bruised and scarred, scored and torn, repaired by time and will, patched by force of character, yet fragile and rickety forevermore, no matter how ferocious the defense and how many bricks you bring to the wall. You can brick up your heart as stout and tight and hard and cold and impregnable as you possibly can and down it comes in an instant, felled by a woman's second glance, a child's apple breath, the shatter of glass in the road, the words "I have something to tell you," a cat with a broken spine dragging itself into the forest to die, the brush of your mother's papery ancient hand in the thicket of your hair, the memory of your father's voice early in the morning echoing from the kitchen where he is making pancakes for his children.

Possibilities for Writing

1. Why do you think Doyle wrote this little essay? What is his main idea? How does his discussion of the hummingbird contribute to the development of this idea? What is the purpose of his including the description of the heart of the blue whale?

2. Take an inventory of Doyle's essay, identifying the places where his writing anchors itself in scientific detail and description, where it verges on spiritual celebration rather than the factual, and where it seems to blend or shift rapidly between the two modes of writing.

3. Write an essay in which you celebrate one of the marvels of creation. You may wish to choose something very large or very small to write about—and you may wish, like Doyle, to work in a contrast to whatever you choose to describe. You should do some research so you can present a number of factual details; and you should do some reflecting so you can provide a perspective that transcends the factual information you include.

W(illiam) E(dward) B(urghardt) DuBois (1868–1963) was born in Great Barrington, Massachusetts, and received his B.A., M.A., and Ph.D from Harvard University, an unusual achievement for a black man of his day. A tireless advocate of full civil rights for African Americans, he was a founder of the organization that would later become the National Association for the Advancement of Colored People (NAACP) and for several years edited its official magazine, Crisis. *He organized a number of international conferences on the condition of black people worldwide, and he also advised U.S. government representatives on policy issues with regard to civil rights. His writings include* The Souls of Black Folk *(1903),* The Negro *(1915), and* Color and Democracy *(1945).*

W. E. B. DuBois

Of Our Spiritual Striving

In this excerpt from *The Souls of Black Folk*, W. E. B. DuBois describes the American Negro's desire to be able "to husband and use his best powers and his latent genius," after having been freed from slavery in the 1860s and given the right to vote in 1870, by the fifteenth amendment to the Constitution. DuBois makes clear his belief in the dignity of Black people, who possess two cultures— their adopted American culture and their African ancestral culture. DuBois sees the value of not so much mingling these two cultures as of preserving each of them intact.

DuBois describes the problem of the "veil" that separates American Blacks from their African past and from their American present. He sees that to a large extent American Blacks in 1900 had yet to be integrated and accepted on their own terms into American society and culture. DuBois's ideas were revolutionary when advocated a century ago, as he urged African Americans not to deny their African heritage and roots and become culturally indistinguishable from white society. Instead, he encouraged them to preserve their distinctiveness while claiming political and social equality.

> O water, voice of my heart, crying in the sand,
>   All night long crying with a mournful cry,
> As I lie and listen, and cannot understand
>   The voice of my heart in my side or the voice of the sea,
>   O water, crying for rest, is it I, is it I?
>   All night long the water is crying to me.
>
> Unresting water, there shall never be rest
>   Till the last moon droop and the last tide fail,

And the fire of the end begin to burn in the west;
　　And the heart shall be weary and wonder and cry like the sea,
　All life long crying without avail,
　　As the water all night long is crying to me.

—*ARTHUR SYMONS*

Between me and the other world there is ever an unasked question: unasked by some through feelings of delicacy; by others through the difficulty of rightly framing it. All, nevertheless, flutter round it. They approach me in a half-hesitant sort of way, eye me curiously or compassionately, and then, instead of saying directly, How does it feel to be a problem? they say, I know an excellent colored man in my town; or, I fought at Mechanicsville; or, Do not these Southern outrages make your blood boil? At these I smile, or am interested, or reduce the boiling to a simmer, as the occasion may require. To the real question, How does it feel to be a problem? I answer seldom a word.

And yet, being a problem is a strange experience,—peculiar even for one who has never been anything else, save perhaps in babyhood and in Europe. It is the early days of rollicking boyhood that the revelation first bursts upon one, all in a day, as it were. I remember well when the shadow swept across me. I was a little thing, away up in the hills of New England, where the dark Housatonic winds between Hoosac and Taghkanic to the sea. In a wee wooden schoolhouse, something put it into the boys' and girls' heads to buy gorgeous visiting-cards—ten cents a package—and exchange. The exchange was merry, till one girl, a tall newcomer, refused my card,—refused it peremptorily, with a glance. Then it dawned upon me with a certain suddenness that I was different from the others; or like, mayhap, in heart and life and longing, but shut out from their world by a vast veil. I had thereafter no desire to tear down that veil, to creep through; I held all beyond it in common contempt, and lived above it in a region of blue sky and great wandering shadows. That sky was bluest when I could beat my mates at examination-time, or beat them at a foot-race, or even beat their stringy heads. Alas, with the years all this fine contempt began to fade; for the worlds I longed for, and all their dazzling opportunities, were theirs, not mine. But they should not keep these prizes, I said; some, all, I would wrest from them. Just how I would do it I could never decide: by reading law, by healing the sick, by telling the wonderful tales that swam in my head,—some way. With other black boys the strife was not so fiercely sunny: their youth shrunk into tasteless sycophancy, or into silent hatred of the pale world about them and mocking distrust of everything white; or wasted itself in a bitter cry, Why did God make me an outcast and a stranger in mine own house? The shades of the prison-house closed round about us all: walls strait and stubborn to the whitest, but relentlessly narrow, tall, and unscalable to sons of night who must plod darkly on in resignation, or beat unavailing palms against the stone, or steadily, half hopelessly, watch the streak of blue above.

After the Egyptian and Indian, the Greek and Roman, the Teuton and Mongolian, the Negro is a sort of seventh son, born with a veil, and gifted with second-sight in this American world,—a world which yields him no true self-consciousness, but only lets him see himself through the revelation of the other world. It is a peculiar sensation, this double-consciousness, this sense of always looking at one's self through the eyes of others, of measuring one's soul by the tape of a world that looks on in amused contempt and pity. One ever feels his two-ness,—an American, a Negro; two souls, two thoughts, two unreconciled strivings; two warring ideals in one dark body, whose dogged strength alone keeps it from being torn asunder.

The history of the American Negro is the history of this strife,—this longing to attain self-conscious manhood, to merge his double self into a better and truer self. In this merging he wishes neither of the older selves to be lost. He would not Africanize America, for America has too much to teach the world and Africa. He would not bleach his Negro soul in a flood of white Americanism, for he knows that Negro blood has a message for the world. He simply wishes to make it possible for a man to be both a Negro and an American, without being cursed and spit upon by his fellows, without having the doors of Opportunity closed roughly in his face.

This, then, is the end of his striving: to be a co-worker in the kingdom of culture, to escape both death and isolation, to husband and use his best powers and his latent genius. These powers of body and mind have in the past been strangely wasted, dispersed, or forgotten. The shadow of a mighty Negro past flits through the tale of Ethiopia the Shadowy and of Egypt the Sphinx. Throughout history, the powers of single black men flash here and there like falling stars, and die sometimes before the world has rightly gauged their brightness. Here in America, in the few days since Emancipation, the black man's turning

hither and thither in hesitant and doubtful striving has often made his
very strength to lose effectiveness, to seem like absence of power, like
weakness. And yet it is not weakness,—it is the contradiction of double
aims. The double-aimed struggle of the black artisan—on the one hand
to escape white contempt for a nation of mere hewers of wood and
drawers of water, and on the other hand to plough and nail and dig for
a poverty-stricken horde—could only result in making him a poor
craftsman, for he had but half a heart in either cause. By the poverty
and ignorance of his people, the Negro minister or doctor was tempted
toward quackery and demagogy; and by the criticism of the other
world, toward ideals that made him ashamed of his lowly tasks. The
would-be black *savant* was confronted by the paradox that the knowledge his people needed was a twice-told tale to his white neighbors,
while the knowledge which would teach the white world was Greek to
his own flesh and blood. The innate love of harmony and beauty that set
the rude souls of his people a-dancing and a-singing raised but confusion and doubt in the soul of the black artist; for the beauty revealed to
him was the soul-beauty of a race which his larger audience despised,
and he could not articulate the message of another people. This waste
of double aims, this seeking to satisfy two unreconciled ideals, has
wrought sad havoc with the courage and faith and deeds of ten thousand thousand people,—has sent them often wooing false gods and
invoking false means of salvation, and at times has even seemed about
to make them ashamed of themselves.

Away back in the days of bondage they thought to see in one divine
event the end of all doubt and disappointment; few men ever worshipped
Freedom with half such unquestioning faith as did the American Negro
for two centuries. To him, so far as he thought and dreamed, slavery was
indeed the sum of all villainies, the cause of all sorrow, the root of all
prejudice; Emancipation was the key to a promised land of sweeter
beauty than ever stretched before the eyes of wearied Israelites. In song
and exhortation swelled one refrain—Liberty; in his tears and curses the
God he implored had Freedom in his right hand. At last it came,—
suddenly, fearfully, like a dream. With one wild carnival of blood and
passion came the message in his own plaintive cadences:—

> "Shout, O children!
> Shout, you're free!
> For God has bought your liberty!"

Years have passed away since then,—ten, twenty, forty; forty years of national life, forty years of renewal and development, and yet the swarthy spectre sits in its accustomed seat at the Nation's feast. In vain do we cry to this our vastest social problem:—

> "Take any shape but that, and my firm nerves
> Shall never tremble!"

The Nation has not yet found peace from its sins; the freedman has not yet found in freedom his promised land. Whatever of good may have come in these years of change, the shadow of a deep disappointment rests upon the Negro people,—a disappointment all the more bitter because the unattained ideal was unbounded save by the simple ignorance of a lowly people.

The first decade was merely a prolongation of the vain search for freedom, the boon that seemed ever barely to elude their grasp,—like a tantalizing will-o'-the-wisp, maddening and misleading the headless host. The holocaust of war, the terrors of the Ku-Klux Klan, the lies of carpet-baggers, the disorganization of industry, and the contradictory advice of friends and foes, left the bewildered serf with no new watch-word beyond the old cry for freedom. As the time flew, however, he began to grasp a new idea. The ideal of liberty demanded for its attainment powerful means, and these the Fifteenth Amendment gave him. The ballot, which before he had looked upon as a visible sign of freedom, he now regarded as the chief means of gaining and perfecting the liberty with which war had partially endowed him. And why not? Had not votes made war and emancipated millions? Had not votes enfranchised the freedmen? Was anything impossible to a power that had done all this? A million black men started with renewed zeal to vote themselves into the kingdom. So the decade flew away, the revolution of 1876 came, and left the half-free serf weary, wondering, but still inspired. Slowly but steadily, in the following years, a new vision began gradually to replace the dream of political power,—a powerful movement, the rise of another ideal to guide the unguided, another pillar of fire by night after a clouded day. It was the ideal of "book-learning"; the curiosity, born of compulsory ignorance, to know and test the power of the cabalistic letters of the white man, the longing to know. Here at last seemed to have been discov ered the mountain path to Canaan; longer than the highway of

Emancipation and law, steep and rugged, but straight, leading to heights high enough to overlook life.

Up the new path the advance guard toiled, slowly, heavily, doggedly; only those who have watched and guided the faltering feet, the misty minds, the dull understandings, of the dark pupils of these schools know how faithfully, how piteously, this people strove to learn. It was weary work. The cold statistician wrote down the inches of progress here and there, noted also where here and there a foot had slipped or some one had fallen. To the tired climbers, the horizon was ever dark, the mists were often cold, the Canaan was always dim and far away. If, however, the vistas disclosed as yet no goal, no resting-place, little but flattery and criticism, the journey at least gave leisure for reflection and self-examination; it changed the child of Emancipation to the youth with dawning self-consciousness, self-realization, self-respect. In those sombre forests of his striving his own soul rose before him, and he saw himself,—darkly as through a veil; and yet he saw in himself some faint revelation of his power, of his mission. He began to have a dim feeling that, to attain his place in the world, he must be himself, and not another. For the first time he sought to analyze the burden he bore upon his back, that dead-weight of social degradation partially masked behind a half-named Negro problem. He felt his poverty; without a cent, without a home, without land, tools, or savings, he had entered into competition with rich, landed, skilled neighbors. To be a poor man is hard, but to be a poor race in a land of dollars is the very bottom of hardships. He felt the weight of his ignorance,—not simply of letters, but of life, of business, of the humanities; the accumulated sloth and shirking and awkwardness of decades and centuries shackled his hands and feet. Nor was his burden all poverty and ignorance. The red stain of bastardy, which two centuries of systematic legal defilement of Negro women had stamped upon his race, meant not only the loss of ancient African chastity, but also the hereditary weight of a mass of corruption from white adulterers, threatening almost the obliteration of the Negro home.

A people thus handicapped ought not to be asked to race with the world, but rather allowed to give all its time and thought to its own social problems. But alas! while sociologists gleefully count his bastards and his prostitutes, the very soul of the toiling, sweating black man is darkened by the shadow of a vast despair. Men call the shadow prejudice, and learnedly explain it as the natural defence of culture against barbarism, learning against ignorance, purity against crime, the "higher" against the "lower" races. To which the Negro cries Amen! and swears that to so much of this strange prejudice as is founded on just homage to civilization, culture, righteousness, and progress, he humbly bows and meekly does obeisance. But before that nameless prejudice that leaps beyond all this he stands helpless, dismayed, and well-nigh speechless; before that personal disrespect and mockery, the ridicule and systematic humiliation, the distortion of fact and wanton license of fancy, the cynical ignoring of the better and the boisterous welcoming of the worse, the all-pervading desire to inculcate disdain for everything black, from Toussaint to the devil,—before this there rises a sickening despair that would disarm and discourage any nation save that black host to whom "discouragement" is an unwritten word.

But the facing of so vast a prejudice could not but bring the inevitable self-questioning, self-disparagement, and lowering of ideals which ever accompany repression and breed in an atmosphere of contempt and hate. Whisperings and portents came borne upon the four winds: Lo! we are diseased and dying, cried the dark hosts; we cannot write, our voting is vain; what need of education, since we must always cook and serve? And the Nation echoed and enforced this self-criticism, saying: Be content to be servants, and nothing more; what need of higher culture for half-men? Away with the black man's ballot, by force or fraud,—and behold the suicide of a race! Nevertheless, out of the evil came something of good,—the more careful adjustment of education to real life, the clearer perception of the Negroes' social responsibilities, and the sobering realization of the meaning of progress.

So dawned the time of *Sturm und Drang:* storm and stress to-day rocks our little boat on the mad waters of the world-sea; there is within and without the sound of conflict, the burning of body and rending of soul; inspiration strives with doubt, and faith with vain questionings. The bright ideals of the past,—physical freedom, political power, the training of brains and the training of hands,—all these in turn have waxed and waned, until even the last grows dim and overcast. Are they all wrong,—all false? No, not that, but each alone was over-simple and incomplete,—the dreams of a credulous race-childhood, or the fond imaginings of the other world which does not know and does not want to know our power. To be really true, all these ideals must be melted and welded into one. The training of the schools we need to-day more than ever,—the training of deft hands, quick eyes and ears, and above all the broader, deeper, higher culture of gifted minds and pure hearts. The power of the ballot we need in sheer self-defence,—else what shall save us from a second slavery? Freedom, too, the long-sought, we still seek,—the freedom of life and limb, the freedom to work and think, the freedom to love and aspire. Work, culture, liberty,—all these we need, not singly but together, not successively but together, each growing and aiding each, and all striving toward that vaster ideal that swims before the Negro people, the ideal of human brotherhood, gained through the unifying ideal of Race; the ideal of fostering and developing the traits and talents of the Negro, not in opposition to or contempt for other races, but rather in large conformity to the greater ideals of the American Republic, in order that some day on American soil two world-races may give each to each those characteristics both so sadly lack. We the darker ones come even now not altogether empty-handed: there are to-day no truer exponents of the pure human spirit of the Declaration of Independence than the American Negroes; there is no true American music but the wild sweet melodies of the Negro slave; the American fairy tales and folklore are Indian and African; and, all in all, we black men seem the sole oasis of simple faith and reverence in a dusty desert of dollars and smartness. Will America be poorer if she replace her brutal dyspeptic blundering with light-hearted but determined Negro humility? or her coarse and cruel wit with loving jovial good-humor? or her vulgar music with the soul of the Sorrow Songs?

Merely a concrete test of the underlying principles of the great republic is the Negro Problem, and the spiritual striving of the freedmen's sons is the travail of souls whose burden is almost beyond the measure of their strength, but who bear it in the name of an historic race, in the name of this the land of their fathers' fathers, and in the name of human opportunity.

And now what I have briefly sketched in large outline let me on coming pages tell again in many ways, with loving emphasis and deeper detail, that men may listen to the striving in the souls of black folk.

Possibilities for Writing

1. What are DuBois's main themes here, and how does he relate them to the past, to his present day, and to a possible future?

2. DuBois's later paragraphs focus on "the shadow prejudice." What does he see as the causes and results of prejudice? How, in his view, can prejudice be overcome?

3. DuBois was one of the first defenders of full social and civil equality for African Americans. How are the ideas he puts forth here reflected in contemporary cultural reality and societal attitudes?

Gretel Ehrlich (b. 1946), a native Californian, attended Bennington College and later the film school at New York University. Her work as a documentary filmmaker took her to Wyoming in 1979, and she found herself drawn to the state's sweeping open countryside and to the people who inhabit it. During her seventeen years working as a rancher there, she produced several books of reflections on her experiences, including The Solace of Open Spaces *(1985) and* A Match to the Heart *(1994), as well a novel and other works. Currently dividing her time between California and Wyoming, she has most recently published* Questions from Heaven *(1997), an account of her pilgrimage as a Buddhist to shrines in China, and* John Muir: Nature's Visionary *(2000), a biography of the great American naturalist and conservationist.*

Gretel Ehrlich
About Men

Ehrlich's brief essay, "About Men," originally appeared in *Time* magazine, and was included in her first essay collection, *The Solace of Open Spaces.* Ehrlich's primary purpose in the essay is to reconsider some basic stereotypes about men—particularly western men, including, of course, "cowboys." Through a series of carefully chosen examples graced by vivid description, revealing dialogue, and sharply etched details, Ehrlich reveals the complex nature of the American cowboy. She suggests that cowboys, usually thought of as rugged and tough, are kind and tender hearted. In debunking stereotypes about cowboys, Ehrlich encourages readers to consider how manliness is a quality which, for cowboys, also requires a balancing of more conventionally typical feminine qualities, such as caring and compassion. The cowboys Ehrlich knows and describes are, as she writes, "androgynous at the core."

    While describing what cowboys are really like, Ehrlich also conveys a powerful impression of the natural world, which so dramatically and inescapably affects their lives. She describes the sheer beauty of nature, while not ignoring the darker dangers it poses for beasts and men alike. But it's clear from her tone of respectful admiration, she wouldn't trade her western world and the western men she describes for anything, regardless of the challenges both nature and cowboys present.

When I'm in New York but feeling lonely for Wyoming I look for the Marlboro ads in the subway. What I'm aching to see is horseflesh, the glint of a spur, a line of distant mountains, brimming creeks, and a reminder of the ranchers and cowboys I've ridden with for the last eight years. But the men I see in those posters with their stern, humorless looks remind me of no one I know here. In our hellbent earnestness to romanticize the cowboy we've ironically disesteemed his true character.

If he's "strong and silent" it's because there's probably no one to talk to. If he "rides away into the sunset" it's because he's been on horseback since four in the morning moving cattle and he's trying, fifteen hours later, to get home to his family. If he's "a rugged individualist" he's also part of a team: ranch work is teamwork and even the glorified open-range cowboys of the 1880s rode up and down the Chisholm Trail in the company of twenty or thirty other riders. Instead of the macho, trigger-happy man our culture has perversely wanted him to be, the cowboy is more apt to be convivial, quirky, and softhearted. To be "tough" on a ranch has nothing to do with conquests and displays of power. More often than not, circumstances—like the colt he's riding or an unexpected blizzard—are overpowering him. It's not toughness but "toughing it out" that counts. In other words, this macho, cultural artifact the cowboy has become is simply a man who possesses resilience, patience, and an instinct for survival. "Cowboys are just like a pile of rocks—everything happens to them. They get climbed on, kicked, rained and snowed on, scuffed up by wind. Their job is 'just to take it,' " one old-timer told me.

A cowboy is someone who loves his work. Since the hours are long—ten to fifteen hours a day—and the pay is $30 he has to. What's required of him is an odd mixture of physical vigor and maternalism. His part of the beef-raising industry is to birth and nurture calves and take care of their mothers. For the most part his work is done on horseback and in a lifetime he sees and comes to know more animals than people. The iconic myth surrounding him is built on American notions of heroism: the index of a man's value as measured in physical courage. Such ideas have perverted manliness into a self-absorbed race for cheap thrills. In a rancher's world, courage has less to do with facing danger than with acting spontaneously—usually on behalf of an animal or another rider. If a cow is stuck in a boghole he throws a loop around her neck, takes his dally (a half hitch around the saddle horn), and pulls her out with horsepower. If a calf is born sick, he may take her home, warm her in front of the kitchen fire, and massage her legs until dawn. One friend, whose favorite horse was trying to swim a lake with hobbles on, dove under water and cut her legs loose with a knife, then swam her to shore, his arm around her neck lifeguard-style, and saved her from drowning. Because these incidents are usually linked to someone or something outside himself, the westerner's courage is selfless, a form of compassion.

The physical punishment that goes with cowboying is greatly under-played. Once fear is dispensed with, the threshold of pain rises to meet the demands of the job. When Jane Fonda asked Robert Redford (in the film *Electric Horseman*) if he was sick as he struggled to his feet one morning, he replied, "No, just bent." For once the movies had it right. The cowboys I was sitting with laughed in agreement. Cowboys are rarely complainers; they show their stoicism by laughing at themselves.

If a rancher or cowboy has been thought of as a "man's man"—laconic, hard-drinking, inscrutable—there's almost no place in which the balancing act between male and female, manliness and femininity, can be more natural. If he's gruff, handsome, and physically fit on the outside, he's androgynous at the core. Ranchers are midwives, hunters, nurturers, providers, and conservationists all at once. What we've interpreted as toughness—weathered skin, calloused hands, a squint in the eye and a growl in the voice—only masks the tenderness inside. "Now don't go telling me these lambs are cute," one rancher warned me the first day I walked into the football-field-sized lambing sheds. The next thing I knew he was holding a black lamb. "Ain't this little rat good-lookin'?"

So many of the men who came to the West were southerners—men looking for work and a new life after the Civil War—that chivalrousness and strict codes of honor were soon thought of as western traits. There were very few women in Wyoming during territorial days, so when they did arrive (some as mail-order brides from places like Philadelphia) there was a stand-offishness between the sexes and a formality that per-sists now. Ranchers still tip their hats and say, "Howdy, ma'am" instead of shaking hands with me.

Even young cowboys are often evasive with women. It's not that they're Jekyll and Hyde creatures—gentle with animals and rough on women—but rather, that they don't know how to bring their tenderness into the house and lack the vocabulary to express the complexity of what they feel. Dancing wildly all night becomes a metaphor for the explosive emotions pent up inside, and when these are, on occasion, released, they're so battery-charged and potent that one caress of the face or one "I love you" will peal for a long while.

The geographical vastness and the social isolation here make emo-tional evolution seem impossible. Those contradictions of the heart between respectability, logic, and convention on the one hand, and impulse, passion, and intuition on the other, played out wordlessly against the paradisical beauty of the West, give cowboys a wide-eyed but drawn look. Their lips pucker up, not with kisses but with immutability. They may want to break out, staying up all night with a lover just to talk, but they don't know how and can't imagine what the consequences will be. Those rare occasions when they do bare themselves result in confusion. "I feel as if I'd sprained my heart," one friend told me a month after such a meeting.

My friend Ted Hoagland wrote, "No one is as fragile as a woman but no one is as fragile as a man." For all the women here who use "fragileness" to avoid work or as a sexual ploy, there are men who try to hide theirs, all the while clinging to an adolescent dependency on women to cook their meals, wash their clothes, and keep the ranch house warm in winter. But there is true vulnerability in evidence here. Because these men work with animals, not machines or numbers, because they live outside in landscapes of torrential beauty, because they are confined to a place and a routine embellished with awesome variables, because calves die in the arms that pulled others into life, because they go to the mountains as if on a pilgrimage to find out what makes a herd of elk tick, their strength is also a softness, their toughness, a rare delicacy.

Possibilities for Writing

1. What does Ehrlich find so admirable and so sympathetic about the cowboys and ranchers she encounters in Wyoming? What does this suggest about her view of male roles more generally in our culture? Using specific examples from her essay, explore her central themes.

2. Cowboys, as Ehrlich describes them, seem to have trouble communicating with and relating to women, yet cling to an "adolescent dependency" on women to take care of them. How does Ehrlich square this with her positive image of cowboys? Do you think she does so effectively, or does this point diminish her image of cowboys in your eyes?

3. The media depict many different stereotypes in terms of gender, ethnicity, and so on. Choose a particular stereotype you have encountered, describe it and how it is exemplified in the media, then, as Ehrlich does, question the stereotype based on your own experiences.

Ralph Ellison (1914–1994) was born in Oklahoma City, the grandson of slaves. Named for Ralph Waldo Emerson, Ellison was a voracious reader from an early age, a strong student, and well trained in music. He attended the Tuskegee Institute on a music scholarship but moved to Harlem in 1936, a year shy of graduating. There he began to write reviews and short stories under the tutelage of Richard Wright. His major work is Invisible Man *(1952), a novel that has continued to receive wide critical acclaim. A professor at New York University for many years, Ellison also published several highly regarded collections of essays, including* Shadow and Act *(1964) and* Going to the Territory *(1986). His second, unfinished novel,* Juneteenth, *was published posthumously in 1999 in a controversial edited version.*

Ralph Ellison
Living with Music

In "Living with Music," Ellison describes himself as a young man living between two musical worlds—the world of classical music and the world of jazz. As a young writer struggling to find his voice and hone his art, Ellison lived amidst the sounds of musicians practicing and performing music in these diverse styles and forms. As a lover of music, Ellison was, by turns, distracted and inspired by what he heard from these musicians, who themselves were perfecting their own art through intense practice and inspired performance.

Ellison's essay mixes humor with reverence as he tells stories about musicians and about his own experiences as a budding trumpeter. Ellison explains the power of music to soothe and ennoble humanity, and he highlights the inspiration we can take from musicians who struggle daily with their art, much as Ellison himself does with his writing. Nor does Ellison ignore the cultural context of the music he describes or its historical significance, claiming no less than that music helps us understand ourselves, gives order and meaning to our lives, and contributes, as well, to our social and cultural identity.

In those days it was either live with music or die with noise, and we chose rather desperately to live. In the process our apartment—what with its booby-trappings of audio equipment, wires, discs and tapes—came to resemble the Collier mansion, but that was later. First there was the neighborhood, assorted drunks and a singer.

We were living at the time in a tiny ground-floor-rear apartment in which I was also trying to write. I say "trying" advisedly. To our right, separated by a thin wall, was a small restaurant with a juke box the size of the Roxy. To our left, a night-employed swing enthusiast who took his lullaby music so loud that every morning promptly at nine Basie's brasses started blasting my typewriter off its stand. Our living room looked out across a small back yard to a rough stone wall to an apartment building which, towering above, caught every passing thoroughfare sound and rifled it straight down to me. There were also howling cats and barking dogs, none capable of music worth living with, so we'll pass them by.

But the court behind the wall, which on the far side came knee-high to a short Iroquois, was a forum for various singing and/or preaching drunks who wandered back from the corner bar. From these you sometimes heard a fair barbershop style "Bill Bailey," free-wheeling versions of "The Bastard King of England," the saga of Uncle Bud, or a deeply felt rendition of Leroy Carr's "How Long Blues." The preaching drunks took on any topic that came to mind: current events, the fate of the long-sunk *Titanic* or the relative merits of the Giants and the Dodgers. Naturally there was great argument and occasional fighting—none of it fatal but all of it loud.

I shouldn't complain, however, for these were rather entertaining drunks, who like the birds appeared in the spring and left with the first fall cold. A more dedicated fellow was there all the time, day and night, come rain, come shine. Up on the corner lived a drunk of legend, a true phenomenon, who could surely have qualified as the king of all the world's winos—not excluding the French. He was neither poetic like the others nor ambitious like the singer (to whom we'll presently come) but his drinking bouts were truly awe-inspiring and he was not without his sensitivity. In the throes of his passion he would shout to the whole wide world one concise command, "Shut up!" Which was disconcerting enough to all who heard (except, perhaps, the singer), but such were the labyrinthine acoustics of courtyards and areaways that he seemed to direct his command at me. The writer's block which this produced is indescribable. On one heroic occasion he yelled his obsessive command without one interruption longer than necessary to take another drink (and with no appreciable loss of volume, penetration or authority) for three long summer days and nights, and shortly afterwards he died. Just how many lines of agitated prose he cost me I'll never know, but in all that chaos of sound I sympathized with his obsession, for I, too, hungered and thirsted for quiet. Nor did he inspire me to a painful identification, and for that I was thankful.

Identification, after all, involves feelings of guilt and responsibility, and since I could hardly hear my own typewriter keys I felt in no way accountable for his condition. We were simply fellow victims of the madding crowd. May he rest in peace.

No, these more involved feelings were aroused by a more intimate source of noise, one that got beneath the skin and worked into the very structure of one's consciousness—like the "fate" motif in Beethoven's Fifth or the knocking-at-the-gates scene in *Macbeth*. For at the top of our pyramid of noise there was a singer who lived directly above us, you might say we had a singer on our ceiling.

Now, I had learned from the jazz musicians I had known as a boy in Oklahoma City something of the discipline and devotion to his art required of the artist. Hence I knew something of what the singer faced. These jazzmen, many of them now world-famous, lived for and with music intensely. Their driving motivation was neither money nor fame, but the will to achieve the most eloquent expression of idea-emotions through the technical mastery of their instruments (which, incidentally, some of them wore as a priest wears the cross) and the give and take, the subtle rhythmical shaping and blending of idea, tone and imagination demanded of group improvisation. The delicate balance struck between strong individual personality and the group during those early jam sessions was a marvel of social organization. I had learned too that the end of all this discipline and technical mastery was the desire to express an affirmative way of life through its musical tradition and that this tradition insisted that each artist achieve his creativity within its frame. He must learn the best of the past, and add to it his personal vision. Life could be harsh, loud and wrong if it wished, but they lived it fully, and when they expressed their attitude toward the world it was with a fluid style that reduced the chaos of living to form.

The objectives of these jazzmen were not at all those of the singer on our ceiling, but though a purist committed to the mastery of the *bel canto* style, German *lieder*, modern French art songs and a few American slave songs sung as if *bel canto*, she was intensely devoted to her art. From morning to night she vocalized, regardless of the condition of her voice, the weather or my screaming nerves. There were times when her notes, sifting through her floor and my ceiling, bouncing down the walls and ricocheting off the building in the rear, whistled like tenpenny nails, buzzed like a saw, wheezed like the asthma of a Hercules, trumpeted like an enraged African elephant—and the squeaky pedal of her piano rested plumb center above my typing chair. After a year of non-co-operation from the neighbor on my left I became desperate enough to cool down the hot blast of his phongraph by calling the cops, but the singer presented a serious ethical problem: Could I, an aspiring artist, complain against the hard work and devotion to craft of another aspiring artist?

Then there was my sense of guilt. Each time I prepared to shatter the ceiling in protest I was restrained by the knowledge that I, too, during my boyhood, had tried to master a musical instrument and to the great distress of my neighbors—perhaps even greater than that which I now suffered. For while our singer was concerned basically with a single tradition and style, I had been caught actively between two: that of the Negro folk music, both sacred and profane, slave song and jazz, and that of Western classical music. It was most confusing; the folk tradition demanded that I play what I heard and felt around me, while those who were seeking to teach the classical tradition in the schools insisted that I play strictly according to the book and express that which I was *supposed* to feel. This sometimes led to heated clashes of wills. Once during a third-grade music appreciation class a friend of mine insisted that it was a large green snake he saw swimming down a quiet brook instead of the snowy bird the teacher felt that Saint-Saëns' *Carnival of the Animals* should evoke. The rest of us sat there and lied like little black, brown and yellow Trojans about that swan, but our stalwart classmate held firm to his snake. In the end he got himself spanked and reduced the teacher to tears, but truth, reality and our environment were redeemed. For we were all familiar with snakes, while a swan was simply something the Ugly Duckling of the story grew up to be. Fortunately some of us grew up with a genuine appreciation of classical music *despite* such teaching methods. But as an inspiring trumpeter I was to wallow in sin for years before being awakened to guilt by our singer.

Caught mid-range between my two traditions, where one attitude often clashed with the other and one technique of playing was by the other opposed, I caused whole blocks of people to suffer.

Indeed, I terrorized a good part of an entire city section. During summer vacation I blew sustained tones out of the window for hours, usually starting—especially on Sunday mornings—before breakfast. I sputtered whole days through M. Arban's (he's the great authority on the instrument) double- and triple-tonguing exercises—with an effect like that of a jackass hiccupping off a big meal of briars. During school-term mornings I practiced a truly exhibitionist "Reveille" before leaving for school, and in the evening I generously gave the ever-listening world a long, slow version of "Taps," ineptly played but throbbing with what I in my adolescent vagueness felt was a romantic sadness. For it was farewell to day and a love song to life and a peace-be-with-you to all the dead and dying.

On hot summer afternoons I tormented the ears of all not blessedly deaf with imitations of the latest hot solos of Hot Lips Paige (then a local hero), the leaping right hand of Earl "Fatha" Hines, or the rowdy poetic flights of Louis Armstrong. Naturally I rehearsed also such school-band standbys as the *Light Cavalry* Overture, Sousa's "Stars and Stripes Forever," the *William Tell* Overture, and "Tiger Rag." (Not even an after-school job as office boy to a dentist could stop my efforts. Frequently, by way of encouraging my development in the proper cultural direction, the dentist asked me proudly to render Schubert's *Serenade* for some poor devil with his jaw propped open in the dental chair. When the drill got going, or the forceps bit deep, I blew real strong.)

Sometimes, inspired by the even then considerable virtuosity of the late Charlie Christian (who during our school days played marvelous riffs on a cigar box banjo), I'd give whole summer afternoons and the evening hours after heavy suppers of black-eyed peas and turnip greens, cracklin' bread and buttermilk, lemonade and sweet potato cobbler, to practicing hard-driving blues. Such food oversupplied me with bursting energy, and from listening to Ma Rainey, Ida Cox and Clara Smith, who made regular appearances in our town, I knew exactly how I wanted my horn to sound. But in the effort to make it do so (I was no embryo Joe Smith or Tricky Sam Nanton) I sustained the curses of both Christian and infidel— along with the encouragement of those more sympathetic citizens who understood the profound satisfaction to be found in expressing oneself in the blues.

Despite those who complained and cried to heaven for Gabriel to blow a chorus so heavenly sweet and so hellishly hot that I'd forever put down my horn, there were more tolerant ones who were willing to pay in present pain for future pride.

For who knew what skinny kid with his chops wrapped around a trumpet mouthpiece and a faraway look in his eyes might become the next Armstrong? Yes, and send you, at some big dance a few years hence, into an ecstasy of rhythm and memory and brassy affirmation of the goodness of being alive and part of the community? Someone had to; for it was part of the group tradition—though that was not how they said it.

"Let that boy blow," they'd say to the protesting ones. "He's got to talk baby talk on that thing before he can preach on it. Next thing you know he's liable to be up there with Duke Ellington. Sure, plenty Oklahoma boys are up there with the big bands. Son, let's hear you try those "Trouble in Mind Blues." Now try and make it sound like ole Ida Cox sings it."

And I'd draw in my breath and do Miss Cox great violence.

Thus the crimes and aspirations of my youth. It had been years since I had played the trumpet or irritated a single ear with other than the spoken or written word, but as far as my singing neighbor was concerned I had to hold my peace. I was forced to listen, and in listening I soon became involved to the point of identification. If she sang badly I'd hear my own futility in the windy sound; if well, I'd stare at my typewriter and despair that I should ever make my prose so sing. She left me neither night nor day, this singer on our ceiling, and as my writing languished I became more and more upset. Thus one desperate morning I decided that since I seemed doomed to live within a shrieking chaos I might as well contribute my share; perhaps if I fought noise with noise I'd attain some small peace. Then a miracle: I turned on my radio (an old Philco AM set connected to a small Pilot FM tuner) and I heard the words

> Art thou troubled?
> Music will calm thee . . .

I stopped as though struck by the voice of an angel. It was Kathleen Ferrier, that loveliest of singers, giving voice to the aria from Handel's *Rodelinda*. The voice was so completely expressive of words and music that I accepted it without question—what lover of the vocal art could resist her?

Yet it was ironic, for after giving up my trumpet for the typewriter I had avoided too close a contact with the very art which she recommended as balm. For I had started music early and lived with it daily, and when I broke I tried to break clean. Now in this magical moment all the old love, the old fascination with music superbly rendered, flooded back. When she finished I realized that with such music in my own apartment, the chaotic sounds from without and above had sunk, if not into silence, then well below the level where they mattered. Here was a way out. If I was to live and write in that apartment, it would be only through the grace of music. I had tuned in a Ferrier recital, and when it ended I rushed out for several of her records, certain that now deliverance was mine.

But not yet. Between the hi-fi record and the ear, I learned, there was a new electronic world. In that realization our apartment was well on its way toward becoming an audio booby trap. It was 1949 and I rushed to the Audio Fair. I have, I confess, as much gadget-resistance as the next American of my age, weight and slight income; but little did I dream of the test to which it would be put. I had hardly entered the fair before I heard David Sarser's and Mel Sprinkle's Musician's Amplifier, took a look at its schematic and, recalling a boyhood acquaintance with such matters, decided that I could build one. I did, several times before it measured within specifications. And still our system was lacking. Fortunately my wife shared my passion for music, so we went on to buy, piece by piece, a fine speaker system, a first-rate AM-FM tuner, a transcription turntable and a speaker cabinet. I built half a dozen or more preamplifiers and record compensators before finding a commercial one that satisfied my ear, and, finally, we acquired an arm, a magnetic cartridge and—glory of the house—a tape recorder. All this plunge into electronics, mind you, had as its simple end the enjoyment of recorded music as it was intended to be heard. I was obsessed with the idea of reproducing sound with such fidelity that even when using music as a defense behind which I could write, it would reach the unconscious levels of the mind with the least distortion. And it didn't come easily. There were wires and pieces of equipment all over the tiny apartment (I became a compulsive experimenter) and it was worth your life to move about without first taking careful bearings. Once we were almost crushed in our sleep by the tape machine, for which there was space only on a shelf at the head of our bed. But it was worth it.

For now when we played a recording on our system even the drunks on the wall could recognize its quality. I'm ashamed to admit, however, that I did not always restrict its use to the demands of pleasure or defense. Indeed, with such marvels of science at my control I lost my humility. My ethical consideration for the singer up above shriveled like a plant in too much sunlight. For instead of soothing, music seemed to release the beast in me. Now when jarred from my writer's reveries by some especially enthusiastic flourish of our singer, I'd rush to my music system with blood in my eyes and burst a few decibels in her direction. If she defied me with a few more pounds of pressure against her diaphragm, then a war of decibels was declared.

If, let us say, she were singing *"Depuis le Jour"* from *Louise*, I'd put on a tape of Bidu Sayão performing the same aria, and let the rafters ring. If it was some song by Mahler, I'd match her spitefully with Marian Anderson or Kathleen Ferrier; if she offended with something from *Der Rosenkavalier*, I'd attack her flank with Lotte Lehmann. If she brought me up from my desk with art songs by Ravel or Rachmaninoff, I'd defend myself with Maggie Teyte or Jennie Tourel. If she polished a spiritual to a meaningless artiness I'd play Bessie Smith to remind her of the earth out of which we came. Once in a while I'd forget completely that I was supposed to be a gentleman and blast her with Strauss' *Zarathustra*, Bartók's *Concerto for Orchestra*, Ellington's "Flaming Sword," the famous crescendo from *The Pines of Rome*, or Satchmo scatting, "I'll be Glad When You're Dead" (you rascal you!). Oh, I was living with music with a sweet vengeance.

One might think that all this would have made me her most hated enemy, but not at all. When I met her on the stoop a few weeks after my rebellion, expecting her fully to slap my face, she astonished me by complimenting our music system. She even questioned me concerning the artists I had used against her. After that, on days when the acoustics were right, she'd stop singing until the piece was finished and then applaud—not always, I guessed, without a justifiable touch of sarcasm. And although I was now getting on with my writing, the unfairness of this business bore in upon me. Aware that I could not have withstood a similar comparison with literary artists of like caliber, I grew remorseful. I also came to admire the singer's courage and control, for she was neither intimidated into silence nor goaded into undisciplined screaming; she persevered, she marked the phrasing of the great singers I sent her way, she improved her style.

Better still, she vocalized more softly, and I, in turn, used music less and less as a weapon and more for its magic with mood and memory. After a while a simple twirl of the volume control up a few decibels and down again would bring a live-and-let-live reduction of her volume. We have long since moved from that apartment and that most interesting neighborhood and now the floors and walls of our present apartment are adequately thick and there is even a closet large enough to house the audio system; the only wire visible is that leading from the closet to the corner speaker system. Still we are indebted to the singer and the old environment for forcing us to discover one of the most deeply satisfying aspects of our living. Perhaps the enjoyment of music is always suffused with past experience; for me, at least, this is true.

It seems a long way and a long time from the glorious days of Oklahoma jazz dances, the jam sessions at Halley Richardson's place on Deep Second, from the phonographs shouting the blues in the back alleys I knew as a delivery boy and from the days when watermelon men with voices like mellow bugles shouted their wares in time with the rhythm of their horses' hoofs and farther still from the washerwomen singing slave songs as they stirred sooty tubs in sunny yards, and a long time, too, from those intense, conflicting days when the school music program of Oklahoma City was tuning our earthy young ears to classical accents—with music appreciation classes and free musical instruments and basic instruction for any child who cared to learn and uniforms for all who made the band. There was a mistaken notion on the part of some of the teachers that classical music had nothing to do with the rhythms, relaxed or hectic, of daily living, and that one should crook the little finger when listening to such refined strains. And the blues and the spirituals—jazz—? they would have destroyed them and scattered the pieces. Nevertheless, we learned some of it all, for in the United States when traditions are juxtaposed they tend, regardless of what we do to prevent it, irresistibly to merge. Thus musically at least each child in our town was an heir of all the ages. One learns by moving from the familiar to the unfamiliar, and while it might sound incongruous at first, the step from the spirituality of the spirituals to that of the Beethoven of the symphonies or the Bach of the chorales is not as vast as it seems. Nor is the romanticism of a Brahms or Chopin completely unrelated to that of Louis Armstrong. Those who know their native culture and love it unchauvinistically are never lost when encountering the unfamiliar.

Living with music today we find Mozart and Ellington, Kirsten Flagstad and Chippie Hill, William L. Dawson and Carl Orff all forming part of our regular fare. For all exalt life in rhythm and melody; all add to its significance. Perhaps in the swift change of American society in which the meanings of one's origin are so quickly lost, one of the chief values of living with music lies in its power to give us an orientation in time. In doing so, it gives significance to all those indefinable aspects of experience which nevertheless help to make us what we are. In the swift whirl of time music is a constant, reminding us of what we were and of that toward which we aspired. Art thou troubled? Music will not only calm, it will ennoble thee.

Possibilities for Writing

1. Ellison suggests that music has meant many things to him over the course of his life, from the days of his childhood to the years in the apartment he describes here to the time when he was writing this essay. Focusing on each of these stages in his life, analyze his various feelings about music.

2. Ellison's tone in this essay ranges from serious to light, from outraged to self-deprecating, from "classical" to "jazzy." Analyze these various elements of his voice and how they work together to help make his larger point.

3. Write an essay of your own about "living with music," focusing the music you grew up with, were taught in school, learned to play yourself, listen to now, and so forth. Try to draw some larger conclusions, as Ellison does, about your relationship with music.

Richard Feynman (1918–1988) grew up in Far Rockaway, New York, where he attended school and became interested in science at an early age. He received a Doctor of Philosophy in Physics from Princeton University in 1942. During the Second World War Feynman played an important role in the development of the atomic bomb, an experience he discusses a number of times in his works. After the war, Feynman taught at Cornell University and the California Institute of Technology. In 1965, he was awarded the Nobel Prize in Physics for his research in quantum electrodynamics. And after the explosion of the Challenger in 1986, Feynman was consulted to identify the cause of the disaster. In addition to his work as a physicist, Feynman was an artist, bongo player, raconteur, and safecracker. He was an engaging and entertaining lecturer on physics, with many of his lecturers having been published. Among his best known books are Six Easy Pieces; Six Not So Easy Pieces; Surely, You Are Joking, Mr. Feynman; *and* The Pleasure of Finding Things Out, *from which "The Value of Science" has been taken.*

Richard Feynman
The Value of Science

In "The Value of Science," a lecture for fellow scientists, Richard Feynman considers why science is important and why scientists should focus the great bulk of their energy and attention on scientific questions, rather than on social problems. He argues that scientific knowledge is morally neutral, that although people can use scientific knowledge either for good or for ill, science is not something that can be ignored or stopped.

Among the values Feynman assigns to scientific investigations are its practical results, including technological advances and applications that flow from scientific discoveries. Besides the many practical benefits of science, such as medical applications, for example, Feynman argues for the value of science in stimulating the imagination, in providing intellectual enjoyment, which he calls simply, "the pleasure of finding things out." But the most important value of science, in Feynman's view, is in its capacity to doubt, to use doubt and uncertainty to investigate all manner of unanswered and partly answered questions.

From time to time, people suggest to me that scientists ought to give more consideration to social problems—especially that they should be more responsible in considering the impact of science upon society. This same suggestion must be made to many other scientists, and it seems to be generally believed that if the scientists would only look at these very difficult social problems and not spend so much time fooling with the less vital scientific ones, great success would come of it.

It seems to me that we do think about these problems from time to time, but we don't put full-time effort into them—the reason being that we know we don't have any magic formula for solving problems, that social problems are very much harder than scientific ones, and that we usually don't get anywhere when we do think about them.

I believe that a scientist looking at nonscientific problems is just as dumb as the next guy—and when he talks about a nonscientific matter, he will sound as naive as anyone untrained in the matter. Since the question of the value of science is not a scientific subject, this discussion is dedicated to proving my point—by example.

The first way in which science is of value is familiar to everyone. It is that scientific knowledge enables us to do all kinds of things and to make all kinds of things. Of course if we make good things, it is not only to the credit of science; it is also to the credit of the moral choice which led us to good work. Scientific knowledge is an enabling power to do either good or bad—but it does not carry instructions on how to use it. Such power has evident value—even though the power may be negated by what one does.

I learned a way of expressing this common human problem on a trip to Honolulu. In a Buddhist temple there, the man in charge explained a little bit about the Buddhist religion for tourists, and then ended his talk by telling them he had something to say to them that they would *never* forget—and I have never forgotten it. It was a proverb of the Buddhist religion:

"To every man is given the key to the gates of heaven; the same key opens the gates of hell."

What, then, is the value of the key to heaven? It is true that if we lack clear instructions that determine which is the gate to heaven and which the gate to hell, the key may be a dangerous object to use, but it obviously has value. How can we enter heaven without it?

The instructions, also, would be of no value without the key. So it is evident that, in spite of the fact that science could produce enormous horror in the world, it is of value because it *can* produce *something*.

Another value of science is the fun called intellectual enjoyment which some people get from reading and learning and thinking about it, and which others get from working in it. This is a very real and important point and one which is not considered enough by those who tell us it is our social responsibility to reflect on the impact of science on society.

Is this mere personal enjoyment of value to society as a whole? No! But it is also a responsibility to consider the value of society itself. Is it, in the last analysis, to arrange things so that people can enjoy things? If so, the enjoyment of science is as important as anything else.

But I would like *not* to underestimate the value of the worldview which is the result of scientific effort. We have been led to imagine all sorts of things infinitely more marvelous than the imaginings of poets and dreamers of the past. It shows that the imagination of nature is far, far greater than the imagination of man. For instance, how much more remarkable it is for us all to be stuck—half of us upside down—by a mysterious attraction, to a spinning ball that has been swinging in space for billions of years, than to be carried on the back of an elephant supported on a tortoise swimming in a bottomless sea.

I have thought about these things so many times alone that I hope you will excuse me if I remind you of some thoughts that I am sure you have all had—or this type of thought—which no one could ever have had in the past, because people then didn't have the information we have about the world today.

For instance, I stand at the seashore, alone, and start to think. There are the rushing waves . . . mountains of molecules, each stupidly minding its own business . . . trillions apart . . . yet forming white surf in unison.

Ages on ages . . . before any eyes could see . . . year after year . . . thunderously pounding the shore as now. For whom, for what? . . . on a dead planet, with no life to entertain.

Never at rest . . . tortured by energy . . . wasted prodigiously by the sun . . . poured into space. A mite makes the sea roar.

Deep in the sea, all molecules repeat the patterns of one another till complex new ones are formed. They make others like themselves . . . and a new dance starts.

Growing in size and complexity . . . living things, masses of atoms, DNA, protein . . . dancing a pattern ever more intricate.

Out of the cradle onto the dry land . . . here it is standing . . . atoms with consciousness . . . matter with curiosity.

Stands at the sea . . . wonders at wondering . . . I . . . a universe of atoms . . . an atom in the universe.

The Grand Adventure

The same thrill, the same awe and mystery, come again and again when we look at any problem deeply enough. With more knowledge comes deeper, more wonderful mystery, luring one on to penetrate deeper still. Never concerned that the answer may prove disappointing, but with pleasure and confidence we turn over each new stone to find unimagined strangeness leading on to more wonderful questions and mysteries—certainly a grand adventure!

It is true that few unscientific people have this particular type of religious experience. Our poets do not write about it; our artists do not try to portray this remarkable thing. I don't know why. Is nobody inspired by our present picture of the universe? The value of science remains unsung by singers, so you are reduced to hearing—not a song or a poem, but an evening lecture about it. This is not yet a scientific age.

Perhaps one of the reasons is that you have to know how to read the music. For instance, the scientific article says, perhaps, something like this: "The radioactive phosphorus content of the cerebrum of the rat decreases to one-half in a period of two weeks." Now, what does that mean?

It means that phosphorus that is in the brain of a rat (and also in mine, and yours) is not the same phosphorus as it was two weeks ago, but that all of the atoms that are in the brain are being replaced, and the ones that were there before have gone away.

So what is this mind, what are these atoms with consciousness? Last week's potatoes! That is what now can *remember* what was going on in my mind a year ago—a mind which has long ago been replaced.

That is what it means when one discovers how long it takes for the atoms of the brain to be replaced by other atoms, to note that the thing which I call my individuality is only a pattern or dance. The atoms come into my brain, dance a dance, then go out; always new atoms but always doing the same dance, remembering what the dance was yesterday.

The Remarkable Idea

When we read about this in the newspaper, it says, "The scientist says that this discovery may have importance in the cure of cancer." The paper is only interested in the use of the idea, not the idea itself. Hardly anyone can understand the importance of an idea, it is so remarkable. Except that, possibly, some children catch on. And when a child catches on to an idea like that, we have a scientist. These ideas do filter down (in spite of all the conversation about TV replacing thinking), and lots of kids get the spirit—and when they have the spirit you have a scientist. It's too late for them to get the spirit when they are in our universities, so we must attempt to explain these ideas to children.

I would now like to turn to a third value that science has. It is a little more indirect, but not much. The scientist has a lot of experience with ignorance and doubt and uncertainty, and this experience is of very great importance, I think. When a scientist doesn't know the answer to a problem, he is ignorant. When he has a hunch as to what the result is, he is uncertain. And when he is pretty darn sure of what the result is going to be, he is in some doubt. We have found it of paramount importance that in order to progress we must recognize the ignorance and leave room for doubt. Scientific knowledge is a body of statements of varying degrees of certainty—some most unsure, some nearly sure, none *absolutely* certain.

Now, we scientists are used to this, and we take it for granted that it is perfectly consistent to be unsure—that it is possible to live and *not* know. But I don't know whether everyone realizes that this is true. Our freedom to doubt was born of a struggle against authority in the early days of science. It was a very deep and strong struggle. Permit us to question—to doubt, that's all—not to be sure. And I think it is important that we do not forget the importance of this struggle and thus perhaps lose what we have gained. Here lies a responsibility to society.

We are all sad when we think of the wondrous potentialities human beings seem to have, as contrasted with their small accomplishments. Again and again people have thought that we could do much better. They of the past saw in the nightmare of their times a dream for the future. We, of their future, see that their dreams, in certain ways surpassed, have in many ways remained dreams. The hopes for the future today are, in good share, those of yesterday.

Education, for Good and Evil

Once some thought that the possibilities people had were not developed because most of those people were ignorant. With education universal, could all men be Voltaires? Bad can be taught at least as efficiently as good. Education is a strong force, but for either good or evil.

Communications between nations must promote understanding: So went another dream. But the machines of communication can be channeled or choked. What is communicated can be truth or lie. Communication is a strong force also, but for either good or bad.

The applied sciences should free men of material problems at least. Medicine controls diseases. And the record here seems all to the good. Yet there are men patiently working to create great plagues and poisons. They are to be used in warfare tomorrow.

Nearly everybody dislikes war. Our dream today is peace. In peace, man can develop best the enormous possibilities he seems to have. But maybe future men will find that peace, too, can be good and bad. Perhaps peaceful men will drink out of boredom. Then perhaps drink will become the great problem which seems to keep man from getting all he thinks he should out of his abilities.

Clearly, peace is a great force, as is sobriety, as are material power, communication, education, honesty, and the ideals of many dreamers.

We have more of these forces to control than did the ancients. And maybe we are doing a little better than most of them could do. But what we ought to be able to do seems gigantic compared with our confused accomplishments.

Why is this? Why can't we conquer ourselves?

Because we find that even great forces and abilities do not seem to carry with them clear instructions on how to use them. As an example, the great accumulation of understanding as to how the physical world behaves only convinces one that this behavior seems to have a kind of meaninglessness. The sciences do not directly teach good and bad.

Through all ages men have tried to fathom the meaning of life. They have realized that if some direction or meaning could be given to our actions, great human forces would be unleashed. So, very many answers must have been given to the question of the meaning of it all. But they have been of all different sorts, and the proponents of one answer have looked with horror at the actions of the believers in another. Horror, because from a disagreeing point of view all the great potentialities of the race were being channeled into a false and confining blind alley. In fact, it is from the history of the enormous monstrosities created by false belief that philosophers have realized the apparently infinite and wondrous capacities of human beings. The dream is to find the open channel.

What, then, is the meaning of it all? What can we say to dispel the mystery of existence?

If we take everything into account, not only what the ancients knew, but all of what we know today that they didn't know, then I think that we must frankly admit that *we do not know*.

But, in admitting this, we have probably found the open channel.

This is not a new idea; this is the idea of the age of reason. This is the philosophy that guided the men who made the democracy that we live under. The idea that no one really knew how to run a government led to the idea that we should arrange a system by which new ideas could be developed, tried out, tossed out, more new ideas brought in; a trial and error system. This method was a result of the fact that science was already showing itself to be a successful venture at the end of the 18th century. Even then it was clear to socially minded people that the openness of the possibilities was an opportunity, and that doubt and discussion were essential to progress into the unknown. If we want to solve a problem that we have never solved before, we must leave the door to the unknown ajar.

Our Responsibility as Scientists

We are at the very beginning of time for the human race. It is not unreasonable that we grapple with problems. There are tens of thousands of years in the future. Our responsibility is to do what we can, learn what we can, improve the solutions and pass them on. It is our responsibility to leave the men of the future a free hand. In the impetuous youth of humanity, we can make grave errors that can stunt our growth for a long time. This we will do if we say we have the answers now, so young and ignorant; if we suppress all discussion, all criticism, saying, "This is it, boys, man is saved!" and thus doom man for a long time to the chains of authority, confined to the limits of our present imagination. It has been done so many times before.

It is our responsibility as scientists, knowing the great progress and great value of a satisfactory philosophy of ignorance, the great progress that is the fruit of freedom of thought, to proclaim the value of this freedom, to teach how doubt is not to be feared but welcomed and discussed, and to demand this freedom as our duty to all coming generations.

Possibilities for Writing

1. Summarize the key points Feynman makes about the value of science. Identify the values of science and provide a brief explanation of each.
2. To what extent to you agree with the values Feynman sees in science? Are there any you would dispute or modify? Are there any you would add? Explain.
3. Write an essay in which you consider the benefits and the dangers of scientific knowledge. You might wish to focus on a particular area of scientific investigation, such as stem cell research and its relation to cloning.

Benjamin Franklin (1706–1790), one of the most versatile and widely admired figures in American history, was born in Boston and apprenticed at an early age to a printer and newpaper publisher. As a young man, he moved to Philadelphia to make his fortune, eventually acquiring his own printing and newspaper house where he produced the popular Poor Richard's Almanack from 1732 to 1757. Essentially self-taught, Franklin helped to establish what became the American Philosophical Society and the University of Pennsylvania, and his experiments with electricity were noted worldwide. A leading figure in the American Revolution and the establishment of the United States as a democracy, Franklin has been referred to as the "wisest American." His autobiography of his early years is considered a classic of American literature.

Benjamin Franklin
Arriving at Perfection

In "Arriving at Perfection," an excerpt from his *Autobiography*, Benjamin Franklin lays out a plan for his own self-improvement. Franklin was a conscious and a conscientious perfectionist. His little essay on self-improvement reflects the enlightenment ideals of his time with their emphasis on reason and progress. But it also reflects an older tendency in American culture: the tendency toward self-examination and self-correction, a meditative cast of mind Franklin inherited from his Puritan ancestors. Franklin weds these two tendencies toward self-examination and toward self-improvement, toward the moral and the practical.

Franklin's goal for what he calls this "bold and arduous Project" is to live each day without committing any faults. As a rationalist, he sees no reason why he shouldn't be able to live according to a standard of moral propriety. He comes to realize, however, that there are many ways he can lapse from his high standard—through habit, carelessness, inclination, and bad example.

It was about this time that I conceiv'd the bold and arduous Project of arriving at moral Perfection. I wish'd to live without committing any Fault at any time; I would conquer all that either Natural Inclination, Custom, or Company might lead me into. As I knew, or thought I knew, what was right and wrong, I did not see why I might not *always* do the one and avoid the other. But I soon found I had undertaken a Task of more Difficulty than I had imagined: While my Care was employ'd in guarding against one Fault, I was often surpriz'd by another. Habit took the Advantage of Inattention. Inclination was sometimes too strong for

Reason. I concluded at length, that the mere speculative Conviction that it was our Interest to be compleatly virtuous, was not sufficient to prevent our Slipping, and that the contrary Habits must be broken and good Ones acquired and established, before we can have any Dependance on a steady uniform Rectitude of Conduct. For this purpose I therefore contriv'd the following Method.

In the various Enumerations of the moral Virtues I had met with in my Reading, I found the Catalogue more or less numerous, as different Writers included more or fewer Ideas under the same Name. Temperance, for Example, was by some confin'd to Eating and Drinking, while by others it was extended to mean the moderating every other Pleasure, Appetite, Inclination or Passion, bodily or mental, even to our Avarice and Ambition. I propos'd to myself, for the sake of Clearness, to use rather more Names with fewer Ideas annex'd to each, than a few Names with more Ideas; and I included after Thirteen Names of Virtues all that at that time occurr'd to me as necessary or desirable, and annex'd to each a short Precept, which fully express'd the Extent I gave to its Meaning.

These Names of Virtues with their Precepts were

1. *Temperance.* Eat not to Dulness. Drink not to Elevation.
2. *Silence.* Speak not but what may benefit others or your self. Avoid trifling conversation.
3. *Order.* Let all your Things have their Places. Let each Part of your Business have its Time.
4. *Resolution.* Resolve to perform what you ought. Perform without fail what you resolve.
5. *Frugality.* Make no Expence but to do good to others or yourself: i.e. Waste nothing.
6. *Industry.* Lose no Time. Be always employ'd in something useful. Cut off all unnecessary Actions.
7. *Sincerity.* Use no hurtful Deceit. Think innocently and justly; and, if you speak; speak accordingly.
8. *Justice.* Wrong none, by doing Injuries or omitting the Benefits that are your Duty.
9. *Moderation.* Avoid Extreams. Forbear resenting Injuries so much as you think they deserve.
10. *Cleanliness.* Tolerate no Uncleanness in Body, Cloaths or Habitation.
11. *Tranquility.* Be not disturbed at Trifles, or at Accidents common or unavoidable.

12. *Chastity*: Rarely use Venery but for Health or Offspring; Never to Dulness, Weakness, or the Injury of your own or another's Peace or Reputation.

13. *Humility*. Imitate Jesus and Socrates.

My intention being to acquire the *Habitude* of all these Virtues, I judg'd it would be well not to distract my Attention by attempting the whole at once, but to fix it on one of them at a time, and when I should be Master of that, then to proceed to another, and so on till I should have gone thro' the thirteen. And as the previous Acquisition of some might facilitate the Acquisition of certain others, I arrang'd them with that View as they stand above. *Temperance* first, as it tends to procure that Coolness and Clearness of Head, which is so necessary where constant Vigilance was to be kept up, and Guard maintained, against the unremitting Attraction of ancient Habits, and the Force of perpetual Temptations. This being acquir'd and establish'd, *Silence* would be more easy, and my Desire being to gain Knowledge at the same time that I improv'd in Virtue, and considering that in Conversation it was obtain'd rather by the Use of the Ears than of the Tongue, and therefore wishing to break a Habit I was getting into of Prattling, Punning and Joking, which only made me acceptable to trifling Company, I gave *Silence* the second Place. This, and the next, *Order*, I expected would allow me more Time for attending to my Project and my Studies; RESOLUTION once become habitual, would keep me firm in my Endeavors to obtain all the subsequent Virtues; *Frugality* and *Industry*, by freeing me from my remaining Debt, and producing Affluence and Independance would make more easy the Practice of *Sincerity* and *Justice*, etc. etc. Conceiving then that agreable to the Advice of Pythagoras in his Golden Verses, daily examination would be necessary, I contriv'd the following Method for conducting that Examination.

I made a little Book in which I allotted a Page for each of the Virtues. I rul'd each Page with red Ink so as to have seven Columns, one for each Day of the Week, marking each Column with a Letter for the Day. I cross'd these Columns with thirteen red Lines, marking the Beginning of each Line with the first Letter of one of the Virtues, on which Line and in its proper Column I might mark by a little black Spot every Fault I found upon Examination, to have been committed respecting that Virtue upon that Day.

TEMPERANCE						
Eat not to Dulness. Drink not to Elevation.						
	S	M	T	W	T	F	S
T							
S	••	•		•		•	
O	•	•	•		•	•	•
R			•			•	
F		•			•		
I			•				
S							
J							
M							
Cl.							
T							
Ch.							
H							

I determined to give a Week's strict Attention to each of the Virtues successively. Thus in the first Week my great Guard was to avoid every the least Offence against Temperance, leaving the other Virtues to their ordinary Chance, only marking every Evening the faults of the Day. Thus if in the first Week I could keep my first Line marked T clear of Spots, I suppos'd the Habit of that Virtue so much strengthen'd and its opposite weaken'd, that I might venture extending my Attention to include the next, and for the following Week keep both Lines clear of Spots. Proceeding thus to the last, I could go thro' a Course compleat in Thirteen Weeks, and four Courses in a Year. And like him who having a Garden to weed, does not attempt to eradicate all the bad Herbs at once, which would exceed his Reach and his Strength, but works on one of the Beds at a time, and having accomplish'd the first proceeds to a second; so I should have, (I hoped) the encouraging Pleasure of seeing on my Pages the Progress I made in Virtue, by clearing successively my Lines of their Spots, till in the End by a Number of Courses.

I should be happy in viewing a clean Book after a thirteen Weeks daily Examination. . . .

Possibilities for Writing

1. Revise, reorder, and supplement Franklin's list of practical virtues as a guide for contemporary college students. Why do you make any changes that you do?
2. Compare Franklin's program for self-improvement with contemporary self-improvement books found in the advice section of a bookstore. To what extent are the values expressed similiar and different?
3. Franklin's goal here is not just moral behavior but moral "perfection." Why do you think so few people today believe in such perfection?

*John Lewis Gaddis (b. 1942) is the Robert A. Lovett Professor of Military
and Naval History at Yale University. He is a noted historian of the Cold
War and grand strategy. He is also the official biographer of the twentieth-
century statesman George F. Kennan. Gaddis received his doctorate from
the University of Texas at Austin. Before moving to Yale, he taught at the
Naval War College, Ohio University, where he founded and directed
the Contemporary History Institute. In 2005 he received the National
Humanities Medal. His books include* We Now Know, The Long Peace,
Strategies of Containment, *and* The Landscape of History: How
Historians Map the Past, *from which "The Landscape of History" has
been taken.*

John Lewis Gaddis
The Landscape of History

In "The Landscape of History," John Lewis Gaddis provides an overview of the
historian's craft, along with an explanation for why historical investigation and
knowledge matter. Gaddis investigates the method historians use to "map" the
past, using a metaphor from cartography to explain how historians work to
represent rather than re-create or replicate the past.

Like Richard Feynman's lecture/essay, "The Value of Science," which
highlights the reasons for doing science, Gaddis's "The Landscape of History"
argues for and explains a series of reasons for reading and writing history.
Among these are an enlargement of experience and a deeper understanding of
the world and its peoples by means of the historian's creation of a wider
perspective on the past.

A young man stands hatless in a black coat on a high rocky point.
His back is turned toward us, and he is bracing himself with a walking stick against the wind that blows his hair in tangles. Before him
lies a fog-shrouded landscape in which the fantastic shapes of more
distant promontories are only partly visible. The far horizon reveals
mountains off to the left, plains to the right, and perhaps very far
away—one can't be sure—an ocean. But maybe it's just more fog,
merging imperceptibly into clouds. The painting, which dates from
1818, is a familiar one: Caspar David Friedrich's *The Wanderer
above a Sea of Fog.* The impression it leaves is contradictory, suggesting at once mastery over a landscape and the insignificance of
an individual within it. We see no face, so it's impossible to know

whether the prospect confronting the young man is exhilarating, or terrifying, or both.

Paul Johnson used Friedrich's painting some years ago as the cover for his book *The Birth of the Modern*, to evoke the rise of romanticism and the advent of the industrial revolution. I should like to use it here to summon up something, more personal, which is my own sense—admittedly idiosyncratic—of what historical consciousness is all about. The logic of beginning with a landscape may not be immediately obvious. But consider the power of metaphor, on the one hand, and the particular combination of economy and intensity with which visual images can express metaphors, on the other.

The best introduction I know to the scientific method, John *Ziman's Reliable Knowledge: An Exploration of the Grounds for Belief in Science*, points out that scientific insights often arise from such realizations as "that the behavior of an electron in an atom is 'like' the vibration of air in a spherical container, or that the random configuration of the long chain of atoms in a polymer molecule is 'like' the motion of a drunkard across a village green." "Reality is still to be embraced and reported without flinching," the sociobiologist Edward O. Wilson has added. "But it is also best delivered the same way it was discovered, retaining a comparable vividness and play of the emotions." It's here, I think, that science, history, and art have something in common: they all depend on metaphor, on the recognition of patterns, on the realization that something is "like" something else.

For me, the posture of Friedrich's wanderer—this striking image of a back turned toward the artist and all who have since seen his work—is "like" that of historians. Most of us consider it our business, after all, to turn our back on wherever it is we may be going, and to focus our attention, from whatever vantage point we can find, on where we've been. We pride ourselves on *not* trying to predict the future, as our colleagues in economics, sociology, and political science attempt to do. We resist letting contemporary concerns influence us—the term "presentism," among historians, is no compliment. We advance bravely into the future with our eyes fixed firmly on the past: the image we present to the world is, to put it bluntly, that of a rear end.

I.

Historians do, to be sure, assume *some* things about what's to come. It's a good bet, for example, that time will continue to pass, that gravity will continue to extend itself through space, and that Michaelmas term at Oxford will continue to be, as it has been for well over seven hundred years, dreary, dark, and damp. But we know these things about the future only from having learned about the past: without it we'd have no sense of even these fundamental truths, to say nothing of the words with which to express them, or even of who or where or what we are. We know the future only by the past we project into it. History, in this sense, is all we have.

But the past, in another sense, is something we can never have. For by the time we've become aware of what has happened it's already inaccessible to us; we cannot relive, retrieve, or rerun it as we might some laboratory experiment or computer simulation. We can only *represent* it. We can portray the past as a near or distant landscape, much as Friedrich has depicted what his wanderer sees from his lofty perch. We can perceive shapes through the fog and mist, we can speculate as to their significance, and sometimes we can even agree among ourselves as to what these are. Barring the invention of a time machine, though, we can never go back there to see for sure.

Science fiction, of course, has invented time machines. Indeed two recent novels, Connie Willis's *Doomsday Book* and Michael Crichton's *Timelines*, feature graduate students in history at, respectively, Oxford and Yale, who use these devices to project themselves back to England and France in the fourteenth century for the purpose of researching their dissertations. Both authors suggest some things time travel might do for us. It could, for example, give us a "feel" for a particular time and place: the novels evoke the denser forests, clearer air, and much louder singing birds of medieval Europe, as well as the muddy roads, rotting food, and smelly people. What they don't show is that we could easily detect the larger patterns of a period by visiting it, because the characters keep getting caught up in complications of everyday life that tend to limit perspective. Like catching the plague, or being burned at the stake, or getting their heads chopped off.

Maybe this is just what it takes to keep the novel exciting, or to make the movie rights marketable. I'm inclined to think, though, that there's a larger point lurking here: it is that the direct experience of events isn't necessarily the best path toward understanding them, because your field of vision extends no further than your own immediate senses. You lack the capacity, when trying to figure out how to survive a famine, or flee a band of brigands, or fight from within a suit of armor, to function as a historian might do. You're not likely to take the time to contrast conditions in fourteenth-century France with those under Charlemagne or the Romans, or to compare what might have been parallels in Ming China or pre-Columbian Peru. Because the individual is "narrowly restricted by his senses and power of concentration," Marc Bloch writes in *The Historian's Craft*, he "never perceives more than a tiny patch of the vast tapestry of events. . . . In this respect, the student of the present is scarcely any better off than the historian of the past.

I'd argue, indeed, that the historian of the past is *much better off* than the participant in the present, from the simple fact of having an expanded horizon. Gertrude Stein got close to the reason in her brief 1938 biography of Picasso: "When I was in America I for the first time travelled pretty much all the time in an airplane and when I looked at the earth I saw all the lines of cubism made at a time when not any painter had ever gone up in an airplane. I saw there on earth the mingling lines of Picasso, coming and going, developing and destroying themselves. What was happening here, quite literally, was detachment from, and consequent elevation above, a landscape: a departure from the normal that provided a new perception of what was real. It was what the Montgolfier brothers saw from their balloon over Paris in 1783, or the Wright brothers from their first "Flyer" in 1903, or the Apollo astronauts when they flew around the moon at Christmas 1968, thus becoming the first humans to view the earth set against the darkness of space. It's also, of course, what Friedrich's wanderer sees from his mountaintop, as have countless others for whom elevation, by shifting perspective, has enlarged experience.

This brings us around, then, to one of the things historians do. For if you think of the past as a landscape, then history is the way we represent it, and it's that act of representation that lifts us above the familiar to let us experience vicariously what we can't experience directly: a wider view.

II.

What, though, do we gain from such a view? Several things, I think, the first of which is a sense of identity that parallels the process of growing up. Taking off in an airplane makes you feel both large and small at the same time. You can't help but have a sense of mastery as your airline of choice detaches you from the ground, lifts you above the traffic jams surrounding the airport, and reveals vast horizons stretching out beyond it—assuming, of course, that you have a window seat, it isn't a cloudy day, and you aren't one of those people whose fear of flying causes them to keep their eyes clamped shut from takeoff to landing. But as you gain altitude, you also can't help noticing how small you are in relation to the landscape that lies before you. The experience is at once exhilarating and terrifying.

So is life. We are born, each of us, with such self-centeredness that only the fact of being babies, and therefore cute, saves us. Growing up is largely a matter of growing out of that condition: we soak in impressions, and as we do so we dethrone ourselves—or at least most of us do—from our original position at the center of the universe. It's like taking off in an airplane: the establishment of identity requires recognizing our relative insignificance in the larger scheme of things. Remember how it felt to have your parents unexpectedly produce a younger sibling, or abandon you to the tender mercies of kindergarten? Or what it was like to enter your first public or private school, or to arrive at places like Oxford, or Yale, or the Hogwarts School of Witchcraft and Wizardry? Or as a teacher to confront your first classroom filled with sullen, squirmy, slumbering, solipsistic students? Just as you've cleared one hurdle another is set before you. Each event diminishes your authority at just the moment at which you think you've become an authority.

If that's what maturity means in human relationships—the arrival at identity by way of insignificance—then I would define historical consciousness as the projection of that maturity through time. We understand how much has preceded us, and how unimportant we are in relation to it. We learn our place, and we come to realize that it isn't a large one. "Even a superficial acquaintance with the existence, through millennia of time, of numberless human beings," the historian Geoffrey Elton has pointed out, "helps to correct the normal adolescent inclination to relate the world to oneself instead of relating oneself to the world." History teaches "those adjustments and insights which help the adolescent to become adult, surely a worthy service in the education of youth." Mark Twain put it even better:

That it took a hundred million years to prepare the world for [man] is proof that that is what it was done for. I suppose it is. I dunno. If the Eiffel Tower were now representing the world's age, the skin of paint on the pinnacle knob at its summit would represent man's share of that age; and anybody would perceive that the skin was what the tower was built for. I reckon they would, I dunno.

Here too, though, there's a paradox, for although the discovery of geologic or "deep" time diminished the significance of human beings in the overall history of the universe, it also, in the eyes of Charles Darwin, T. H. Huxley, Mark Twain, and many others, dethroned God from *his* position at its center—which left no one else around but man. The recognition of human insignificance did not, as one might have expected, enhance the role of divine agency in explaining human affairs: it had just the opposite effect. It gave rise to a secular consciousness that, for better or for worse, placed the responsibility for what happens in history squarely on the people who live through history.

What I'm suggesting, therefore, is that just as historical consciousness demands detachment from—or if you prefer, elevation above—the landscape that is the past, so it also requires a certain displacement: an ability to shift back and forth between humility and mastery. Niccolò Machiavelli made the point precisely in his famous preface to *The Prince*: how was it, he asked his patron Lorenzo de' Medici, that "a man from a low and mean state dares to discuss and give rules for the governments of princes?" Being Machiavelli, he then answered his own question:

> For just as those who sketch landscapes place themselves down in the plain to consider the nature of mountains and high places and to consider the nature of low places place themselves high atop mountains, similarly to know well the nature of peoples one needs to be [a] prince, and to know well the nature of princes one needs to be of the people.

You feel small, whether as a courtier or an artist or a historian, because you recognize your insignificance in an infinite universe. You know you can never yourself rule a kingdom, or capture on canvas everything you see on a distant horizon, or recapture in your books and lectures everything that's happened in even the most particular part of the past. The best you can do, whether with a prince or a landscape or the past, is to *represent* reality: to smooth over the details, to look for larger patterns, to consider how you can use what you see for your own purposes.

That very act of representation, though, makes you feel large, because you yourself are in charge of the representation: it's you who must make complexity comprehensible, first to yourself, then to others. And the power that resides in representation can be great indeed, as Machiavelli certainly understood. For how much influence today does Lorenzo de' Medici have, compared to the man who applied to be his tutor?

Historical consciousness therefore leaves you, as does maturity itself, with a simultaneous sense of your own significance and insignificance. Like Friedrich's wanderer, you dominate a landscape even as you're diminished by it. You're suspended between sensibilities that are at odds with one another; but it's precisely within that suspension that your own identity—whether as a person or a historian—tends to reside. Self-doubt must always precede self-confidence. It should never, however, cease to accompany, challenge, and by these means discipline self-confidence.

III.

Machiavelli, who so strikingly combined both qualities, wrote *The Prince*, as he immodestly informed Lorenzo de' Medici, "considering that no greater gift could be made by me than to give you the capacity to be able to understand in a very short time all that I have learned and understood in so many years and with so many hardships and dangers for myself." The purpose of his representation was *distillation*: he sought to "package" a large body of information into a compact usable form so that his patron could quickly master it. It's no accident that the book is a short one. What Machiavelli offered was a compression of historical experience that would vicariously enlarge personal experience. "For since men almost always walk on paths beaten by others . . . , a prudent man should always . . . imitate those who have been most excellent, so that if his own virtue does not reach that far, it is at least in the odor of it."

This is as good a summary of the uses of historical consciousness as I have found. I like it because it makes two points: first, that we're bound to learn from the past whether or not we make the effort, since it's the only data base we have; and second, that we might as well try to do so systematically. E. H. Carr elaborated on the first of these arguments when he observed, in *What Is History?*, that the size and reasoning capacity of the human brain are probably no greater now than they were five thousand years ago, but that very few human beings live now as they did then. The effectiveness of human thinking, he continued, "has been multiplied many times by learning and incorporating . . . the experience of the intervening generations." The inheritance of acquired characteristics may not work in biology, but it does in human affairs: "History is progress through the transmission of acquired skills from one generation to another."

As his biographer Jonathan Haslam has pointed out, Carr's idea of "progress" in twentieth-century history tended disconcertingly to associate that quality with the accumulation of power in the hands of the state. But in *What Is History?* Carr was making a larger and less controversial argument: that if we can widen the range of experience beyond what we as individuals have encountered, if we can draw upon the experiences of others who've had to confront comparable situations in the past, then— although there are no guarantees—our *chances* of acting wisely should increase proportionately.

This brings us to Machiavelli's second point, which is that we should learn from the past systematically. Historians ought not to delude themselves into thinking that they provide the *only* means by which acquired skills—and ideas—are transmitted from one generation to the next. Culture, religion, technology, environment, and tradition can all do this. But history is arguably the best method of enlarging experience in such a way as to command the widest possible consensus on what the significance of that experience might be.

I know that statement will raise eyebrows, because historians so often and so visibly disagree with one another. We relish revisionism and distrust orthodoxy, not least because were we to do otherwise, we might put ourselves out of business. We have, in recent years, embraced postmodernist insights about the relative character of all historical judgments—the inseparability of the observer from that which is being observed—although some of us feel that we've known this all along. Historians appear, in short, to have only squishy ground upon which to stand, and hence little basis for claiming any consensus at all on what the past might tell us with respect to the present and future.

Except when you ask the question: compared to what? No other mode of inquiry comes any closer to producing such a consensus, and most fall far short of it. The very fact that orthodoxies so dominate the realms of religion and culture suggests the absence of agreement from below, and hence the need to impose it from above. People adapt to technology and environment in so many different ways as to defy generalization. Traditions manifest themselves so variously across such diverse institutions and cultures that they provide hardly any consistency on what the past should signify. The historical method, in this sense, beats all the others.

Nor does it demand agreement, among its practitioners, as to precisely what the "lessons" of history are: a consensus can incorporate contradictions. It's part of growing up to learn that there are competing versions of truth, and that you yourself must choose which to embrace. It's part of historical consciousness to learn the same thing: that there is no "correct" interpretation of the past, but that the act of interpreting is itself a vicarious enlargement of experience from which you can benefit. It would ill serve any prince to be told that the past offers simple lessons—or even, for some situations, any lessons at all. "The prince can gain the people to himself in many modes," Machiavelli wrote at one point, "for which one cannot give certain rules because the modes vary according to circumstances." The general proposition still holds, though, that "for a prince it is necessary to have the people friendly; otherwise he has no remedy in adversity.

This gets us close to what historians do—or at least, to echo Machiavelli, should have the odor of doing: it is to interpret the past for the purposes of the present with a view to managing the future, but to do so without suspending the capacity to assess the particular circumstances in which one might have to act, or the relevance of past actions to them. To accumulate experience is not to endorse its automatic application, for part of historical consciousness is the ability to see differences as well as similarities, to understand that generalizations do not always hold in particular circumstances.

That sounds pretty daunting—until you consider another arena of human activity in which this distinction between the general and the particular is so ubiquitous that we hardly even think about it: it's the wide world of sports. To achieve proficiency in basketball, baseball, or even bridge, you have to know the rules of the game, and you have to practice. But these rules, together with what your coach can teach you about applying them, are nothing more than a distillation of accumulated experience: they serve the same function that Machiavelli intended

The Prince to serve for Lorenzo de' Medici. They're generalizations: compressions and distillations of the past in order to make it usable in the future.

Each game you play, however, will have its own characteristics: the skill of your opponent, the adequacy of your own preparation, the circumstances in which the competition takes place. No competent coach would lay out a plan to be mechanically followed throughout the game: you have to leave a lot to the discretion—and the good judgment—of the individual players. The fascination of sports resides in the intersection of the general with the particular. The practice of life is much the same.

Studying the past is no sure guide to predicting the future. What it does do, though, is to *prepare* you for the future by expanding experience, so that you can increase your skills, your stamina—and, if all goes well, your wisdom. For while it may be true, as Machiavelli estimated, "that fortune is the arbiter of half our actions," it's also the case that "she leaves the other half, or close to it, for us to govern." Or, as he also put it, "God does not want to do everything."

IV.

Just how, though, do you present historical experience for the purpose of enlarging personal experience? To include too little information can render the whole exercise irrelevant. To include too much can overload the circuits and crash the system. The historian has got to strike a balance, and that means recognizing a trade-off between literal and abstract representation. Let me illustrate this with two well-known artistic portrayals of the same subject.

The first is Jan van Eyck's great double portrait *The Marriage of Giovanni Arnolfini*, from 1434, which documents a relationship between a man and a woman in such precise detail that we can see every fold in their clothes, every frill in the lace, the apples on the windowsill, the shoes on the floor, the individual hairs on the little dog, and even the artist himself reflected in the mirror. The picture is striking because it's as close as anything we have to photographic realism four hundred years before photography was invented. This can only have been 1434, these can only have been the Arnolfinis, and they can only have been painted in Bruges. We get the vicarious experience of a distant but very particular time and place.

Two representations of the same subject,
one from a particular time and the other for all time.
Jan van Eyck, The Marriage of Giovanni Arnolfini, 1434,
London, National Gallery (Alinari/Art Resource, New York), and Pablo
Picasso, The Lovers, 1904, Musée Picasso, Paris (Réunion des Musées
Nationaux/Art Resource, New York; © 2002 Estate of Pablo Picasso/
Artists Rights Society (ARS), New York).

Now, contrast this with Picasso's *The Lovers*, an ink, watercolor, and charcoal drawing dashed off quickly in 1904. The image, like van Eyck's, leaves little doubt as to the subject. But here everything has been stripped away: background, furnishings, shoes, dog, even clothes, and we're down to the essence of the matter. What we have is a transmission of vicarious experience so generic that anyone from Adam and Eve onward would immediately understand it. The very point of this drawing is the abstraction that flows from its absence of context, and it's this that projects it so effectively across time and space.

Switch now, if you can manage this leap, to Thucydides, in whom I find both the particularity of a van Eyck and the generality of a Picasso. He is, at times, so photographic in his narrative that he could be writing a modern screenplay. He tells us, for example, of a Plataean attempt against a Peloponnesian wall in which the soldiers advanced with only their left feet shod to keep from slipping in the mud, and in which the inadvertent dislodgment of a single roof tile raised the alarm. He places us in the middle of the Athenian attack on Pylos in 425 B.C. just as precisely as those remarkable first moments of Steven Spielberg's film *Saving Private Ryan* place us on the Normandy beaches in 1944 A.D. He makes us hear the sick and wounded Athenians on Sicily "loudly calling to each individual comrade or relative whom they could see, hanging upon the necks of their tent-fellows in the act of departure, and following as far as they could, and when their bodily strength failed them, calling again and again upon heaven and shrieking aloud as they were left behind." There is, in short, an authenticity in this particularity that puts us there at least as effectively as one of Michael Crichton's time machines.

But Thucydides, unlike Crichton, is also a great generalizer. He meant his work, he tells us, for those inquirers "who desire an exact knowledge of the past as an aid to the interpretation of the future, which in the course of human things must resemble if it does not reflect it." He knew that abstraction—we might even call it a Picasso-like separation from context—is what makes generalizations hold up over time. Hence he has the Athenians telling the rebellious Melians, as a timeless principle, that "the strong do what they can and the weak suffer what they must": it follows that the Athenians "put to death all the grown men whom they took, and sold the women and children for slaves, and subsequently sent out five hundred colonists and inhabited the place themselves." Thucydides also shows us, though, that there are exceptions to any rule: when the Mityleneans rebel and the Athenians conquer them, the strong suddenly have second thoughts and send out a second ship to overtake the first, countermanding the order to slaughter or enslave the weak.

This tension between particularization and generalization—between literal and abstract representation—comes with the territory, I think, when you're transmitting vicarious experience. A simple chronicle of details, however graphic, locks you into a particular time and place. You move beyond it by abstracting, but abstracting is an artificial exercise, involving an oversimplification of complex realities. It's analogous to what happened in the world of art once it began, in the late nineteenth century, to depart from the literal representation of reality. One objective of impressionism, cubism, and futurism was to find a way to represent motion from within the necessarily static media of paint, canvas, and frame. Abstraction arose as a form of liberation, a new view of reality that suggested something of the flow of time. It worked, though, only by distorting space.

Historians, in contrast, employ abstraction to overcome a different constraint, which is their separation in time from their subjects. Artists coexist with the objects they're representing, which means that it's always possible for them to shift the view, adjust the light, or move the model. Historians can't do this: because what they represent is in the past, they can never alter it. But they can, by that means of the particular form of abstraction we know as *narrative*, portray movement through time, something an artist can only hint at.

There's always a balance to be struck, though, for the more time the narrative covers, the less detail it can provide. It's like the Heisenberg uncertainty principle, in which the precise measurement of one variable renders another one imprecise. This then, is yet another of the polarities involved in historical consciousness: the tension between the literal and the abstract, between the detailed depiction of what lies at some point in the past, on the one hand, and the sweeping sketch of what extends over long stretches of it, on the other.

V.

Which brings me back to Friedrich's *Wanderer*, a representation in art that comes close to suggesting visually what historical consciousness is all about. The back turned toward us. Elevation from, not immersion in, a distant landscape. The tension between significance and insignificance, the way you feel both large and small at the same time. The polarities of generalization and particularization, the gap between abstract and literal representation. But there's something else here as well: a sense of curiosity mixed with awe mixed with a determination to find things out—to penetrate the fog, to distill experience, to *depict* reality—that is as much an artistic vision as a scientific sensibility.

Harold Bloom has written of Shakespeare that he created our concept of ourselves by discovering ways—never before achieved—of portraying human nature on the stage. John Madden's film *Shakespeare in Love*, I think, shows that actually happening: it's the moment when *Romeo and Juliet* has been staged for the first time, when the last lines have been delivered, and when the audience, utterly amazed, sits silently with eyes bulging and mouths agape, unsure of what to do. Confronting uncharted territory, whether in theater, history, or human affairs, produces something like that sense of wonder. Which is probably why *Shakespeare in*

Love ends at the beginning of *Twelfth Night*, with Viola shipwrecked on an uncharted continent, filled with dangers but also with infinite possibilities. And as in Friedrich's *Wanderer*, it's a backside we see in that last long shot as she wades ashore.

Now, I don't mean to suggest that historians can, with any credibility, play the role of Gwyneth Paltrow. We're supposed to be solid, dispassionate chroniclers of events, not given to allowing our emotions and our intuitions to affect what we do, or so we've traditionally been taught. I worry, though, that if we don't allow for these things, and for the sense of excitement and wonder they bring to the doing of history, then we're missing much of what the field is all about. The first lines Shakespeare has Viola speak, filled as they are with intelligence, curiosity, and some dread, could well be the starting point for any historian contemplating the landscape of history: "What country, friends, is this?"

Possibilities for Writing

1. Write a summary of the central ideas Gaddis advances in "The Landscape of History." Identify the qualities or characteristics Gaddis highlights as aspects of what he calls "historical consciousness."

2. Consider one of the dualities Gaddis suggests that historians have to balance when they write history: subjectivity and objectivity; the particular and the general; simplicity and complexity; narrative and explanation; elevation above and immersion in the past.

3. Write an essay in which you explain the values of and the limits of the kind of historical consciousness Gaddis describes. You may wish to use Gaddis's ideas as a starting point to develop some additional ideas of your own, perhaps agreeing or disagreeing with Gaddis on particular points, perhaps modifying what he says.

Ellen Goodman (b. 1941) is a native of Newton, Massachusetts, and a graduate of Radcliffe College. After working as a reporter for several news organizations, she joined the Boston Globe *in 1967 and has been on the staff there ever since. She writes an editorial column titled "At Large" that mixes the personal with the political in a way that has achieved broad appeal among readers; it is currently syndicated in more than 250 newspapers nationwide. These columns have been collected in several volumes, and most recently she was coauthor of* I Know Just What You Mean: The Power of Friendship in Women's Lives *(2000). Goodman won the Pulitzer Prize for commentary in 1980.*

Ellen Goodman
The Company Man

In "The Company Man," Ellen Goodman presents a sketch of a character who sacrifices everything for his work. He gives up all pretension to a social life and becomes disconnected from his wife and family, while keeping his focus entirely on his job as a corporate vice president.

Goodman tells the story of "Phil," the company man, the phrase itself conveying the extent of his commitment to his career. She keeps her language general, making Phil a symbol of company men (and now women too) everywhere. Describing him as a "type A" workaholic who lives for his work on the job, Goodman simplifies the man and the choices he makes. What she loses in presenting Phil as a complete and complex human being, she gains in making a point about what matters, or should matter, most in our lives.

He worked himself to death, finally and precisely, at 3:00 A.M. Sunday morning.

The obituary didn't say that, of course. It said that he died of a coronary thrombosis—I think that was it—but everyone among his friends and acquaintances knew it instantly. He was a perfect Type A, a workaholic, a classic, they said to each other and shook their heads—and thought for five or ten minutes about the way they lived.

This man who worked himself to death finally and precisely at 3:00 A.M. Sunday morning—on his day off—was fifty-one years old and a vice-president. He was, however, one of six vice-presidents, and one of three who might conceivably—if the president died or retired soon enough—have moved to the top spot. Phil knew that.

He worked six days a week, five of them until eight or nine at night, during a time when his own company had begun the four-day week for everyone but the executives. He worked like the Important People. He had no outside "extracurricular interests," unless, of course, you think about a monthly golf game that way. To Phil, it was work. He always ate egg salad sandwiches at his desk. He was, of course, overweight, by 20 or 25 pounds. He thought it was okay, though, because he didn't smoke.

On Saturdays, Phil wore a sports jacket to the office instead of a suit, because it was the weekend.

He had a lot of people working for him, maybe sixty, and most of them liked him most of the time. Three of them will be seriously considered for his job. The obituary didn't mention that.

But it did list his "survivors" quite accurately. He is survived by his wife, Helen, forty-eight years old, a good woman of no particular marketable skills, who worked in an office before marrying and mothering. She had, according to her daughter, given up trying to compete with his work years ago, when the children were small. A company friend said, "I know how much you will miss him." And she answered, "I already have."

"Missing him all these years," she must have given up part of herself which had cared too much for the man. She would be "well taken care of."

His "dearly beloved" eldest of the "dearly beloved" children is a hard-working executive in a manufacturing firm down South. In the day and a half before the funeral, he went around the neighborhood researching his father, asking the neighbors what he was like. They were embarrassed.

His second child is a girl, who is twenty-four and newly married. She lives near her mother and they are close, but whenever she was alone with her father, in a car driving somewhere, they had nothing to say to each other.

The youngest is twenty, a boy, a high-school graduate who has spent the last couple of years, like a lot of his friends, doing enough odd jobs to stay in grass and food. He was the one who tried to grab at his father, and tried to mean enough to him to keep the man at home. He was his father's favorite. Over the last two years, Phil stayed up nights worrying about the boy.

The boy once said, "My father and I only board here."

At the funeral, the sixty-year-old company president told the forty-eight-year-old widow that the fifty-one-year-old deceased had meant much to the company and would be missed and would be hard to replace. The widow didn't look him in the eye. She was afraid he would read her bitterness and, after all, she would need him to straighten out the finances—the stock options and all that.

Phil was overweight and nervous and worked too hard. If he wasn't at the office, he was worried about it. Phil was a Type A, a heart-attack natural. You could have picked him out in a minute from a lineup.

So when he finally worked himself to death, at precisely 3:00 A.M. Sunday morning, no one was really surprised.

By 5:00 P.M. the afternoon of the funeral, the company president had begun, discreetly of course, with care and taste, to make inquiries about his replacement. One of three men. He asked around: "Who's been working the hardest?"

Possibilities for Writing

1. Goodman's essay is marked by irony throughout. Analyze the use of irony here—in language, in juxtapositions of images, and within scenes. Do you find the level of irony appropriate, or does it ever strike you as heavy-handed?

2. Goodman wrote this essay in the early 1970s. What values and social constructs does it suggest were common at the time? Using evidence from your own experience, would you say that things today are different or pretty much the same?

3. Using Goodman as a model, write an ironic portrait of a personality type you know well. You may base your portrait on a real person or on a composite of different people. If appropriate to your subject, you may wish to focus more on humorous aspects of this personality type.

Mary Gordon (b. 1949) grew up in a working-class Catholic neighborhood in Far Rockaway, New York. She shocked her family by insisting on attending Barnard College rather than a school closer to home, and she later received a master's degree from Syracuse University. Her first novel, Final Payments *(1978), was an immediate critical and popular success, and she followed this with the equally well received* The Company of Women *(1981) and* The Other Side *(1989), as well as several collections of short stories. Much of her fiction focuses on tightly-knit ethnic families like her own. Gordon has also published several essay collections, including* Good Boys and Dead Girls *(1992) and* Seeing through Places: Reflections on Geography and Identity *(2000), as well as a memoir. She currently teaches at Barnard.*

Mary Gordon

More than Just a Shrine— Ellis Island

In "More than Just a Shrine—Ellis Island," Mary Gordon describes a visit she made to Ellis Island, the gateway to America for immigrants throughout the last century. Ellis Island, the place, however, does not interest Gordon as much as the people who passed through it. Gordon imagines their dreams and their hopes as they pursued their destinies in a new and foreign land.

For Gordon, Ellis Island is an emblem, a shrine to the people who arrived in America with little more than their hopes of finding and making better lives than the ones they left behind in their native countries. Gordon does not sentimentalize either the people or the place. Rather, she tries to understand both as she celebrates their courage and their humanity.

I once sat in a hotel in Bloomsbury trying to have breakfast alone. A Russian with a habit of compulsively licking his lips asked if he could join me. I was afraid to say no; I thought it might be bad for détente. He explained to me that he was a linguist and that he always liked to talk to Americans to see if he could make any connection between their speech and their ethnic background. When I told him about my mixed ancestry—my mother is Irish and Italian, my father was a Lithuanian Jew—he began jumping up and down in his seat, rubbing his hands together and licking his lips even more frantically.

"Ah," he said, "so you are really somebody who comes from what is called the boiling pot of America." Yes, I told him; yes, I was; but I quickly rose to leave. I thought it would be too hard to explain to him the relation of the boiling potters to the main course, and I wanted to get to the British Museum. I told him that the only thing I could think of that united people whose backgrounds, histories, and points of view were utterly diverse was that their people had landed at a place called Ellis Island.

I didn't tell him that Ellis Island was the only American landmark I'd ever visited. How could I describe to him the estrangement I'd always felt from the kind of traveler who visits shrines to America's past greatness, those rebuilt forts with muskets behind glass and sabers mounted on the walls and gift shops selling maple sugar candy in the shape of Indian headdresses, those reconstructed villages with tables set for fifty and the Paul Revere silver gleaming? All that Americana— Plymouth Rock, Gettysburg, Mount Vernon, Valley Forge—it all inhabits for me a zone of blurred abstraction with far less hold on my imagination than the Bastille or Hampton Court. I suppose I've always known that my uninterest in it contains a large component of the willed: I am American, and those places purport to be my history. But they are not mine.

Ellis Island is, though; it's the one place I can be sure my people are connected to. And so I made a journey there to find my history, like any Rotarian traveling in his Winnebago to Antietam to find his. I had become part of that humbling democracy of people looking in some site for a past that has grown unreal. The monument I traveled to was not, however, a tribute to some old glory. The minute I set foot upon the island I could feel all that it stood for: insecurity, obedience, anxiety, dehumanization, the terrified and careful deference of the displaced. I hadn't traveled to the Battery and boarded a ferry across from the Statue of Liberty to raise flags or breathe a richer, more triumphant air. I wanted to do homage to the ghosts.

I felt them everywhere, from the moment I disembarked and saw the building with its high-minded brick, its hopeful little lawn, its ornamental cornices. The place was derelict when I arrived; it had not functioned for more than thirty years—almost as long as the time it had operated at full capacity as a major immigration center. I was surprised to learn what a small part of history Ellis Island had occupied. The main building was constructed in 1892, then rebuilt between 1898 and 1900 after a fire. Most of the immigrants who arrived during the latter half of the nineteenth century, mainly northern and western Europeans, landed not at Ellis Island but on the western tip of the Battery, at Castle Garden, which had opened as a receiving center for immigrants in 1855.

By the 1880s, the facilities at Castle Garden had grown scandalously inadequate. Officials looked for an island on which to build a new immigration center, because they thought that on an island immigrants could be more easily protected from swindlers and quickly transported to railroad terminals in New Jersey. Bedloe's Island was considered, but New Yorkers were aghast at the idea of a "Babel" ruining their beautiful new treasure, "Liberty Enlightening the World." The statue's sculptor, Frédéric-Auguste Bartholdi, reacted to the prospect of immigrants landing near his masterpiece in horror; he called it a "monstrous plan." So much for Emma Lazarus.

Ellis Island was finally chosen because the citizens of New Jersey petitioned the federal government to remove from the island an old naval powder magazine that they thought dangerously close to the Jersey shore. The explosives were removed; no one wanted the island for anything. It was the perfect place to build an immigration center.

I thought about the island's history as I walked into the building and made my way to the room that was the center in my imagination of the Ellis Island experience: the Great Hall. It had been made real for me in the stark, accusing photographs of Louis Hine and others, who took those pictures to make a point. It was in the Great Hall that everyone had waited—waiting, always, the great vocation of the dispossessed. The room was empty, except for me and a handful of other visitors and the park ranger who showed us around. I felt myself grow insignificant in that room, with its huge semicircular windows, its air, even in dereliction, of solid and official probity.

I walked in the deathlike expansiveness of the room's disuse and tried to think of what it might have been like, filled and swarming. More than sixteen million immigrants came through that room; approximately 250,000 were rejected. Not really a large proportion, but the implications for the rejected were dreadful. For some, there was nothing to go back to, or there was certain death; for others, who left as adventurers, to return would be to adopt in local memory the fool's role, and the failure's. No wonder that the island's history includes reports of three thousand suicides.

Sometimes immigrants could pass through Ellis Island in mere hours, though for some the process took days. The particulars of the experience in the Great Hall were often influenced by the political events and attitudes on the mainland. In the 1890s and the first years of the new century, when cheap labor was needed, the newly built receiving center took in its immigrants with comparatively little question. But as the century progressed, the economy worsened, eugenics became both scientifically respectable and popular, and World War I made American xenophobia seem rooted in fact.

Immigration acts were passed; newcomers had to prove, besides moral correctness and financial solvency, their ability to read. Quota laws came into effect, limiting the number of immigrants from southern and eastern Europe to less than 14 percent of the total quota. Intelligence tests were biased against all non-English-speaking persons, and medical examinations became increasingly strict, until the machinery of immigration nearly collapsed under its own weight. The Second Quota Law of 1924 provided that all immigrants be inspected and issued visas at American consular offices in Europe, rendering the center almost obsolete.

On the day of my visit, my mind fastened upon the medical inspections, which had always seemed to me most emblematic of the ignominy and terror the immigrants endured. The medical inspectors, sometimes dressed in uniforms like soldiers, were particularly obsessed with a disease of the eyes called trachoma, which they checked for by flipping back the immigrants' top eyelids with a hook used for buttoning gloves—a method that sometimes resulted in the transmission of the disease to healthy people. Mothers feared that if their children cried too much, their red eyes would be mistaken for a symptom of the disease and the whole family would be sent home. Those immigrants suspected of some physical disability had initials chalked on their coats. I remembered the photographs I'd seen of people standing, dumbstruck and innocent as cattle, with their manifest numbers hung around their necks and initials marked in chalk upon their coats: "E" for eye trouble, "K" for hernia, "L" for lameness, "X" for mental defects, "H" for heart disease.

I thought of my grandparents as I stood in the room: my seventeen-year-old grandmother, coming alone from Ireland in 1896, vouched for by a stranger who had found her a place as a domestic servant to some Irish who had done well. I tried to imagine the assault it all must have been for her; I've been to her hometown, a collection of farms with a main street—smaller than the athletic field of my local public school.

She must have watched the New York skyline as the first- and second-class passengers were whisked off the gangplank with the most cursory of inspections while she was made to board a ferry to the new immigration center.

What could she have made of it—this buff-painted wooden structure with its towers and its blue slate roof, a place *Harper's Weekly* described as "a latter-day watering place hotel"? It would have been the first time she had heard people speaking something other than English. She would have mingled with people carrying baskets on their heads and eating foods unlike any she had ever seen—dark-eyed people, like the Sicilian she would marry ten years later, who came over with his family at thirteen, the man of the family, responsible even then for his mother and sister. I don't know what they thought, my grandparents, for they were not expansive people, nor romantic; they didn't like to think of what they called "the hard times," and their trip across the ocean was the single adventurous act of lives devoted after landing to security, respectability, and fitting in.

What is the potency of Ellis Island for someone like me—an American, obviously, but one who has always felt that the country really belonged to the early settlers, that, as J. F. Powers wrote in *Morte D'Urban*, it had been "handed down to them by the Pilgrims, George Washington and others, and that they were taking a risk in letting you live in it." I have never been the victim of overt discrimination; nothing I have wanted has been denied me because of the accidents of blood. But I suppose it is part of being an American to be engaged in a somewhat tiresome but always self-absorbing process of national definition. And in this process, I have found in traveling to Ellis Island an important piece of evidence that could remind me I was right to feel my differentness. Something had happened to my people on that island, a result of the eternal wrongheadedness of American protectionism and the predictabilities of simple greed. I came to the island, too, so I could tell the ghosts that I was one of them, and that I honored them—their stoicism, and their innocence, the fear that turned them inward, and their pride. I wanted to tell them that I liked them better than I did the Americans who made them pass through the Great Hall and stole their names and chalked their weaknesses in public on their clothing. And to tell the ghosts what I have always thought: that American history was a very classy party that was not much fun until they arrived, brought the good food, turned up the music, and taught everyone to dance.

Possibilities for Writing

1. Gordon's visit to Ellis Island evokes in her a variety of negative impressions, yet the overall experience does not seem to be a negative one for her. Analyze the essay to explore this apparent contradiction. What does she gain from the experience?

2. In this essay Gordon mixes personal narration, description, reporting of historical detail and images from her imagination, along with personal analysis and reflection. Look carefully at how she develops these strands of the essay, provides transitions, and moves from point to point. In an essay analyze and evaluate her technique.

3. Reflect on own sense of your heritage as an American. Are there any "shrines"—whether public or private—that have special meaning to you? Do you feel more an insider or an outsider? (If you are not a citizen, you may wish to reflect on what your experience has led you to believe it means to be an American.)

William Hazlitt (1778–1830), one of the most popular writers of his day, worked during his early years as a journalist and theatrical critic for a variety of London publications. Later in life, he was particularly noted for his writings on the history of English literature in such collections as Characters of Shakespeare's Plays *(1817),* Lectures on the English Comic Writers *(1819), and* Dramatic Literature of the Age of Elizabeth *(1820). But Hazlitt is best remembered today for his many and varied personal essays: witty, sophisticated, and highly graceful meditations on a variety of subjects ranging from the grand to the homely.*

William Hazlitt

On the Pleasure of Hating

In "On the Pleasure of Hating," William Hazlitt catalogues the many ways human beings express and act out their anger and antipathy toward other creatures and toward one another. Hazlitt explores the reasons why hatred and its associated feelings fascinate and excite us. In the process Hazlitt shows people to be nasty, mean-spirited, and vengeful, enjoying the suffering of others as idle amusement.

Hazlitt's long paragraphs are replete with instances of humanity's splenetic nature and habits. He piles on example upon example, from our fear of and disgust with insects and spiders to our fascination with disasters such as fires, our cruelty toward those different from ourselves, and our eagerness to maintain old animosities and hostilities whose original causes are long buried in history. According to Hazlitt, we even enjoy hating our old friends, amusing ourselves with their weaknesses and eccentricities. He writes, "We grow tired of every thing but turning others into ridicule, and congratulating ourselves on their defects."

There is a spider crawling along the matted floor of the room where I sit (not the one which has been so well allegorised in the admirable *Lines to a Spider*, but another of the same edifying breed); he runs with heedless, hurried haste, he hobbles awkwardly towards me, he stops—he sees the giant shadow before him, and, at a loss whether to retreat or proceed, meditates his huge foe—but as I do not start up and seize upon the straggling caitiff, as he would upon a hapless fly within his toils, he takes heart, and ventures on with mingled cunning, impudence, and fear. As he passes me, I lift up the matting to assist his escape, am glad to get rid of the unwelcome intruder, and shudder at the recollection after he is gone. A child, a woman, a clown, or a moralist a century ago, would have crushed the little reptile to death—my philosophy has got beyond that—I bear the creature no ill-will, but still I hate the very sight of it. The spirit of malevolence survives the practical exertion of it. We learn to curb our will and keep our overt actions within the bounds of humanity, long before we can subdue our sentiments and imaginations to the same mild tone. We give up the external demonstration, the *brute* violence, but cannot part with the essence or principle of hostility. We do not tread upon the poor little animal in question (that seems barbarous and pitiful!) but we regard it with a sort of mystic horror and superstitious loathing. It will ask another hundred years of fine writing and hard thinking to cure us of the prejudice, and make us feel towards this ill-omened tribe with something of "the milk of human kindness," instead of their own shyness and venom.

Nature seems (the more we look into it) made up of antipathies: without something to hate, we should lose the very spring of thought and action. Life would turn to a stagnant pool, were it not ruffled by the jarring interests, the unruly passions, of men. The white streak in our own fortunes is brightened (or just rendered visible) by making all around it as dark as possible; so the rainbow paints its form upon the cloud. Is it pride? Is it envy? Is it the force of contrast? Is it weakness or malice? But so it is, that there is a secret affinity [with], a *hankering* after, evil in the human mind, and that it takes a perverse, but a fortunate delight in mischief, since it is a never-failing source of satisfaction. Pure good soon grows insipid, wants variety and spirit. Pain is a bitter-sweet, which never surfeits. Love turns, with a little indulgence, to indifference or disgust: hatred alone is immortal. Do we not see this principle at work everywhere? Animals torment and worry one another without mercy: children kill flies for sport: every one reads the accidents and offences in a newspaper as the cream of the jest: a whole town runs to be present at a fire, and the spectator by no means exults to see it extinguished. It is better to have it so, but it diminishes the interest; and our feelings take part with our passions rather than with our understandings. Men assemble in crowds, with eager enthusiasm, to witness a tragedy: but if there were an execution going forward in the next street, as Mr. Burke observes, the theatre would be left empty. A strange cur in a village, an idiot, a crazy woman, are set upon and baited by the whole community. Public nuisances are in the nature of public benefits. How long did the Pope, the Bourbons, and the Inquisition keep the people of

England in breath, and supply them with nicknames to vent their spleen upon! Had they done us any harm of late? No: but we have always a quantity of superfluous bile upon the stomach, and we wanted an object to let it out upon. How loth were we to give up our pious belief in ghosts and witches, because we liked to persecute the one, and frighten ourselves to death with the other! It is not the quality so much as the quantity of excitement that we are anxious about: we cannot bear a state of indifference and *ennui:* the mind seems to abhor a *vacuum* as much as ever nature was supposed to do. Even when the spirit of the age (that is, the progress of intellectual refinement, warring with our natural infirmities) no longer allows us to carry our vindictive and headstrong humours into effect, we try to revive them in description, and keep up the old bugbears, the phantoms of our terror and our hate, in imagination. We burn Guy Fawx in effigy, and the hooting and buf-feting and maltreating that poor tattered figure of rags and straw makes a festival in every village in England once a year. Protestants and Papists do not now burn one another at the stake: but we subscribe to new editions of Fox's *Book of Martyrs;* and the secret of the success of the *Scotch Novels* is much the same—they carry us back to the feuds, the heart-burnings, the havoc, the dismay, the wrongs, and the revenge of a barbarous age and people—to the rooted prejudices and deadly animosities of sects and parties in politics and religion, and of contend-ing chiefs and clans in war and intrigue. We feel the full force of the spirit of hatred with all of them in turn. As we read, we throw aside the trammels of civilization, the flimsy veil of humanity. "Off, you lend-ings!" The wild beast resumes its sway within us, we feel like hunting-animals, and as the hound starts in his sleep and rushes on the chase in fancy, the heart rouses itself in its native lair, and utters a wild cry of joy, at being restored once more to freedom and lawless, unrestrained impulses. Every one has his full swing, or goes to the Devil his own way. Here are no Jeremy Bentham Panopticons, none of Mr. Owen's impassable Parallelograms (Rob Roy would have spurned and poured a thousand curses on them), no long calculations of self-interest—the will takes its instant way to its object, as the mountain-torrent flings itself over the precipice: the greatest possible good of each individual consists in doing all the mischief he can to his neighbour: that is charming, and finds a sure and sympathetic chord in every breast! So Mr. Irving, the celebrated preacher, has rekindled the old, original, almost exploded hell-fire in the aisles of the Caledonian Chapel, as they introduce the real water of the New River at Sadler's Wells, to the delight and astonishment of his fair audience. *'Tis pretty, though a plague*, to sit and peep into the pit of Tophet, to play at *snap-dragon* with flames and brimstone (it gives a smart electrical shock, a lively filip to delicate constitutions), and to see Mr. Irving, like a huge Titan, looking as grim and swarthy as if he had to forge tortures for all the damned! What a strange being man is! Not content with doing all he can to vex and hurt his fellows here, "upon this bank and shoal of time," where one would think there were heartaches, pain, disappointment, anguish, tears, sighs, and groans enough, the bigoted maniac takes him to the top of the high peak of school divinity to hurl him down the yawning gulf of penal fire; his speculative malice asks eternity to wreak its infinite spite in, and calls on the Almighty to execute its relentless doom! The cannibals burn their enemies and eat them in good-fellowship with one another: meek Christian divines cast those who differ from them but a hair's-breadth, body and soul into hell-fire for the glory of God and the good of His creatures! It is well that the power of such persons is not co-ordinate with their wills: indeed, it is from the sense of their weakness and inability to control the opinions of others, that they thus "outdo termagant," and endeavour to frighten them into conformity by big words and monstrous denunciations.

The pleasure of hating, like a poisonous mineral, eats into the heart of religion, and turns it to rankling spleen and bigotry; it makes patriotism an excuse for carrying fire, pestilence, and famine into other lands: it leaves to virtue nothing but the spirit of censoriousness, and a narrow, jealous, inquisitorial watchfulness over the actions and motives of others. What have the different sects, creeds, doctrines in religion been but so many pretexts set up for men to wrangle, to quarrel, to tear one another in pieces about, like a target as a mark to shoot at? Does any one suppose that the love of country in an Englishman implies any friendly feeling or disposition to serve another bearing the same name? No, it means only hatred to the French or the inhabitants of any other country that we happen to be at war with for the time. Does the love of virtue denote any wish to discover or amend our own faults? No, but it atones for an obstinate adherence to our own vices by the most virulent intolerance to human frailties. This principle is of a most universal application. It extends to good as well as evil: if it makes us hate folly, it makes us no less dissatisfied with distinguished merit. If it inclines us to resent the wrongs of others, it impels us to be as impatient of their prosperity. We revenge injuries: we repay benefits with ingratitude. Even our strongest partialities and likings soon take this turn. "That which was luscious as locusts, anon becomes bitter as coloquintida;" and love and friendship melt in their own fires. We hate old friends: we hate old books: we hate old opinions; and at last we come to hate ourselves.

I have observed that few of those whom I have formerly known most intimate, continue on the same friendly footing, or combine the steadiness with the warmth of attachment. I have been acquainted with two or three knots of inseparable companions, who saw each other "six days in the week," that have broken up and dispersed. I have quarrelled with almost all my old friends, (they might say this is owing to my bad temper, but) they have also quarrelled with one another. What is become of "that set of whist-players," celebrated by ELIA in his notable *Epistle to Robert Southey, Esq.* (and now I think of it—that I myself have celebrated in this very volume) "that for so many years called Admiral Burney friend? They are scattered, like last year's snow. Some of them are dead, or gone to live at a distance, or pass one another in the street like strangers, or if they stop to speak, do it as coolly and try to *cut* one another as soon as possible." Some of us have grown rich, others poor. Some have got places under Government, others a *niche* in the *Quarterly Review*. Some of us have dearly earned a name in the world; whilst others remain in their original privacy. We despise the one, and envy and are glad to mortify the other. Times are changed; we cannot revive our old feelings; and we avoid the sight, and are uneasy in the presence of, those who remind us of our infirmity, and put us upon an effort at seeming cordiality which embarrasses ourselves, and does not impose upon our *quondam* associates. Old friendships are like meats served up repeatedly, cold, comfortless, and distasteful, The stomach turns against them. Either constant intercourse and familiarity breed weariness and contempt; or, if we meet again after an interval of absence, we appear no longer the same. One is too wise, another too foolish, for us; and we wonder we did not find this out before. We are disconcerted and kept in a state of continual alarm by the wit of one, or tired to death of the dullness of another. The *good things* of the first (besides leaving stings behind them) by repetition grow stale, and lose their startling effect; and the insipidity of the last becomes intolerable. The most amusing or instructive companion is at best like a favourite volume, that we wish after a time to *lay upon the shelf*; but as our friends are not willing to be laid there, this produces a misunderstanding and ill-blood between us. Or if the zeal and integrity of friendship is not abated, [n]or its career interrupted by any obstacle arising out of its own nature, we look out for other subjects of complaint and sources of dissatisfaction. We begin to criticize each other's dress, looks, and general character. "Such a one is a pleasant fellow, but it is a pity he sits so late!" Another fails to keep his appointments, and that is a sore that never heals. We get acquainted with some fashionable young men or with a mistress, and wish to introduce our friend; but he is awkward and a sloven, the interview does not answer, and this throws cold water on our intercourse. Or he makes himself obnoxious to opinion; and we shrink from our own convictions on the subject as an excuse for not defending him. All or any of these causes mount up in time to a ground of coolness or irritation; and at last they break out into open violence as the only amends we can make ourselves for suppressing them so long, or the readiest means of banishing recollections of former kindness so little compatible with our present feelings. We may try to tamper with the wounds or patch up the carcase of departed friendship; but the one will hardly bear the handling, and the other is not worth the trouble of embalming! The only way to be reconciled to old friends is to part with them for good: at a distance we may chance to be thrown back (in a waking dream) upon old times and old feelings: or at any rate we should not think of renewing our intimacy, till we have fairly *spit our spite*, or said, thought, and felt all the ill we can of each other. Or if we can pick a quarrel with some one else, and make him the scape-goat, this is an excellent contrivance to heal a broken bone. I think I must be friends with Lamb again, since he has written that magnanimous Letter to Southey, and told him a piece of his mind! I don't know what it is that attaches me to H——— so much, except that he and I, whenever we meet, sit in judgment on another set of old friends, and "carve them as a dish fit for the Gods." There was L[eigh] [Hunt], John Scott, Mrs. [Montagu], whose dark raven locks make a picturesque background to our discourse, B———, who is grown fat, and is, they say, married, R[ickman]; these had all separated long ago, and their foibles are the common link that holds us together. We do not affect to condole or whine over their follies; we enjoy, we laugh at them, till we are ready to burst our sides, "*sans* intermission, for hours by the dial." We serve up a course of anecdotes, *traits*, master-strokes of character, and cut and hack at them till we are weary. Perhaps some of them are even with us. For my own part, as I once said, I like a friend the better for having faults that one can talk about. "Then," said Mrs. [Montagu], "you will never cease to be a philanthropist!" Those in question were some of the choice-spirits of the age, not "fellows of no mark or likelihood"; and we so far did them justice: but it is well they did not hear what we sometimes said of them. I care little what any one says of me, particularly behind my back, and in the way of critical and analytical discussion: it is looks of dislike and scorn that I answer with the worst venom of my pen. The expression of the face wounds me more than the expressions of the tongue. If I have in one instance mistaken this expression, or resorted to this remedy where I ought not, I am sorry for it. But the face was too fine over which it mantled, and I am too old to have misunderstood it! . . . I sometimes go up to ———'s; and as often as I do, resolve never to go again. I do not find the old homely welcome. The ghost of friendship meets me at the door, and sits with me all dinner-time. They have got a set of fine notions and new acquaintance. Allusions to past occurrences are thought trivial, nor is it always safe to touch upon more general subjects. M. does not begin as he formerly did every five minutes, "Fawcett used to say," &c. That topic is something worn. The girls are grown up, and have a thousand accomplishments. I perceive there is a jealousy on both sides. They think I give myself airs, and I fancy the same of them. Every time I am asked, "If I do not think Mr. Washington Irving a very fine writer?" I shall not go again till I receive an invitation for Christmas Day in company with Mr. Liston. The only intimacy I never found to flinch or fade was a purely intellectual one. There was none of the cant of candour in it, none of the whine of mawkish sensibility. Our mutual acquaintance were considered merely as subjects of conversation and knowledge, not at all of affection. We regarded them no more in our experiments than "mice in an air-pump:" or like malefactors, they were regularly cut down and given over to the dissecting-knife. We spared neither friend nor foe. We sacrificed human infirmities at the shrine of truth. The skeletons of character might be seen, after the juice was extracted, dangling in the air like flies in cobwebs: or they were kept for future inspection in some refined acid. The demonstration was as beautiful as it was new. There is no surfeiting on gall: nothing keeps so well as a decoction of spleen. We grow tired of every thing but turning others into ridicule, and congratulating ourselves on their defects.

We take a dislike to our favourite books, after a time, for the same reason. We cannot read the same works for ever. Our honey-moon, even though we wed the Muse, must come to an end; and is followed by indifference, if not by disgust. There are some works, those indeed that produce the most striking effect at first by novelty and boldness of outline, that will not bear reading twice: others of a less extravagant character, and that excite and repay attention by a greater nicety of details, have hardly interest enough to keep alive our continued enthusiasm. The popularity of the most successful writers operates to wean us from them, by the cant and fuss that is made about them, by hearing their names everlastingly repeated, and by the number of ignorant and indiscriminate admirers they draw after them:—we as little like to have to drag others from their unmerited obscurity, lest we should be exposed to the charge of affectation and singularity of taste. There is nothing to be said respecting an author that all the world have made up their minds about: it is a thankless as well as hopeless task to recommend one that nobody has ever heard of. To cry up Shakespear as the god of our idolatry, seems like a vulgar national prejudice: to take down a volume of Chaucer, or Spenser, or Beaumont and Fletcher, or Ford, or Marlowe, has very much the look of pedantry and egotism. I confess it makes me hate the very name of Fame and Genius, when works like these are "gone into the wastes of time," while each successive generation of fools is busily employed in reading the trash of the day, and women of fashion gravely join with their waiting-maids in discussing the preference between the *Paradise Lost* and Mr. Moore's *Loves of the Angels*. I was pleased the other day on going into a shop to ask, "If they had any of the *Scotch Novels?*" to be told—"That they had just sent out the last, *Sir Andrew Wylie!*"—Mr. Galt will also be pleased with this answer! The reputation of some books is raw and *unaired:* that of others is worm-eaten and mouldy. Why fix our affections on that which we cannot bring ourselves to have faith in, or which others have long ceased to trouble themselves about? I am half afraid to look into *Tom Jones*, lest it should not answer my expectations at this time of day; and if it did not, I should certainly be disposed to fling it into the fire, and never look into another novel while I lived. But surely, it may be said, there are some works that, like nature, can never grow old; and that must always touch the imagination and passions alike! Or there are passages that seem as if we might brood over them all our lives, and not exhaust the sentiments of love and admiration they excite: they become favourites, and we are fond of them to a sort of dotage. Here is one:

> —"Sitting in my window
> Printing my thoughts in lawn, I saw a god,
> I thought (but it was you), enter our gates;
> My blood flew out and back again, as fast
> As I had puffed it forth and sucked it in
> Like breath; then was I called away in haste
> To entertain you: never was a man
> Thrust from a sheepcote to a sceptre, raised
> So high in thoughts as I; you left a kiss
> Upon these lips then, which I mean to keep
> From you for ever. I did hear you talk
> Far above singing!"

A passage like this, indeed, leaves a taste on the palate like nectar, and we seem in reading it to sit with the Gods at their golden tables: but if we repeat it often in ordinary moods, it loses its flavour, becomes vapid, "the wine of *poetry* is drank, and but the lees remain." Or, on the other hand, if we call in the aid of extraordinary circumstances to set it off to advantage, as the reciting it to a friend, or after having our feelings excited by a long walk in some romantic situation, or while we

> —"play with Amaryllis in the shade,
> Or with the tangles of Neaera's hair"—

we afterwards miss the accompanying circumstances, and instead of transferring the recollection of them to the favourable side, regret what we have lost, and strive in vain to bring back "the irrevocable hour"— wondering in some instances how we survive it, and at the melancholy blank that is left behind! The pleasure rises to its height in some moment of calm solitude or intoxicating sympathy, declines ever after, and from the comparison and a conscious falling-off, leaves rather a sense of satiety and irksomeness behind it. . . . "Is it the same in pictures?" I confess it is, with all but those from Titian's hand. I don't know why, but an air breathes from his landscapes, pure, refreshing, as if it came from other years; there is a look in his faces that never passes away. I saw one the other day. Amidst the heartless desolation and glittering finery of Fonthill, there is a portfolio of the Dresden Gallery. It opens, and a young female head looks from it; a child, yet woman grown; with an air of rustic innocence and the graces of a princess, her eyes like those of doves, the lips about to open, a smile of pleasure dimpling the whole face, the jewels sparkling in her crisped hair, her youthful shape compressed in a rich antique dress, as the bursting leaves contain the April buds! Why do I not call up this image of gentle sweetness, and place it as a perpetual barrier between mischance and me?—It is because pleasure asks a greater effort of the mind to support it than pain; and we turn after a little idle dalliance from what we love to what we hate!

As to my old opinions, I am heartily sick of them. I have reason, for they have deceived me sadly. I was taught to think, and I was willing to believe, that genius was not a bawd, that virtue was not a mask, that liberty was not a name, that love had its seat in the human heart. Now I would care little if these words were struck out of the dictionary, or if I had never heard them. They are become to my ears a mockery and a dream. Instead of patriots and friends of freedom, I see nothing but the tyrant and the slave, the people linked with kings to rivet on the chains of despotism and superstition. I see folly join with knavery, and together make up public spirit and public opinions. I see the insolent Tory, the blind Reformer, the coward Whig! If mankind had wished for what is right, they might have had it long ago. The theory is plain enough; but they are prone to mischief, "to every good work reprobate." I have seen all that had been done by the mighty yearnings of the spirit and intellect of men, "of whom the world was not worthy," and that promised a proud opening to truth and good through the vista of future years, undone by one man, with just glimmering of understanding enough to feel that he was a king, but not to comprehend how he could be king of a free people! I have seen this triumph celebrated by poets, the friends of my youth and the friends of man, but who were carried away by the infuriate tide that, setting in from a throne, bore down every distinction of right reason before it; and I have seen all those who did not join in applauding this insult and outrage on humanity proscribed, hunted down (they and their friends made a byword of), so that it has become an understood thing that no one can live by his talents or knowledge who is not ready to prostitute those talents and that knowledge to betray his species, and prey upon his fellowman. "This was some time a mystery: but the time gives evidence of it." The echoes of liberty had awakened once more in Spain, and the morning of human hope dawned again: but that dawn has been overcast by the foul breath of bigotry, and those reviving sounds stifled by fresh cries from the time-rent towers of the Inquisition—man yielding (as it is fit he should) first to brute force, but more to the innate perversity and dastard spirit of his own nature which leaves no room for farther hope or disappointment. And England, that arch-reformer, that heroic deliverer, that mouther about liberty, and tool of power, stands gaping by, not feeling the blight and mildew coming over it, nor its very bones crack and turn to a paste under the grasp and circling folds of this new monster, Legitimacy! In private life do we not see hypocrisy, servility, selfishness, folly, and impudence succeed, while modesty shrinks from the encounter, and merit is trodden under foot? How often is "the rose plucked from the forehead of a virtuous love to plant a blister there!" What chance is there of the success of real passion? What certainty of its continuance? Seeing all this as I do, and unravelling the web of human life into its various threads of meanness, spite, cowardice, want of feeling, and want of understanding, of indifference towards others, and ignorance of ourselves—seeing custom prevail over all excellence, itself giving way to infamy—mistaken as I have been in my public and private hopes, calculating others from myself, and calculating wrong; always disappointed where I placed most reliance; the dupe of friendship, and the fool of love;—have I not reason to hate and to despise myself? Indeed I do; and chiefly for not having hated and despised the world enough.

Possibilities for Writing

1. As expressed here, are Hazlitt's views those of a pessimist, a realist, or something in between? How do you respond to the writer's views of hating?

2. "Hating" takes on a variety of meanings here, some more intense than others. Explore these various meanings, using examples from the text to explain your reasoning.

3. Pick a passage or two from Hazlitt's essay that you find relevant to contemporary life and write an essay exploring its implications for the world today.

Michael Hogan (b. 1943) was born in Newport, Rhode Island. He is the author of fourteen books of fiction, poetry, and nonficion, including Teaching from the Heart, *a collection of his essays and speeches, and the seminal work on the Irish Soldiers in the Mexican War of 1846–1848. His poetry and prose have been published in such literary magazines as* The Paris Review, *the* Harvard Review, *the* Iowa Review, *and the* American Poetry Review. *He is the recipient of numerous awards, including the NEA Creative Writing Fellowship and two Puschcart Prizes. He lives in Guadalajara, Mexico, with the well-known textile artist Lucinda Mayo.*

Michael Hogan
The Colonel

In "The Colonel," Michael Hogan describes his experiences in watching, learning, and playing tennis from his boyhood years into late middle age. Hogan's essay focuses on an army colonel, whose war stories induced the twelve-year-old Hogan to give up the pleasures of baseball, football, and basketball for the rigors of tennis. Colonel Flack taught the young Hogan not only the rudiments of the game, but also important lessons about sportsmanship, competitiveness, courage, and grace.

Hogan conveys these and other lessons about the discipline of the game in a clear, direct, and graceful style, which echoes the way he plays the game. And he suggests that played over a lifetime with diligence, passion, and attentive devotion, tennis can make a difference in a person's quality of life, a difference for which Hogan expresses "a sure sense of gratitude."

Tennis is so popular these days and so much a part of the average teenager's sports experience, that it is difficult for most of them to imagine a time when it was not. Yet, in the post–war period and the Fifties of my childhood, tennis was considered more a rich man's sport played at country clubs and exclusive resorts. Competitive singles was largely a sport of the male sex and, although women had been competing for years at Wimbledon and other international venues, most were amateurs and the few professionals who did compete got paid so little it was laughable. It wasn't until Billie Jean King's assertiveness in 1967 and the Virginia Slim tournaments of the 1970s that the sport opened up for generations of Chris Everts and Steffi Grafs, and finally grew to include million-dollar players like Venus Williams who changed the sport forever making it the dream of every athletic boy and girl.

The courts in my hometown of Newport, RI, were mostly off-limits to working class kids like me. The excellent grass center courts and the red clay courts of the private Newport Casino where the National Doubles Championships were held, were open only to wealthy members who paid a hefty annual fee. The courts at the Newport Country Club were restricted to those few rich families who were members, as were those at the even more exclusive Bailey's Beach. At the Brenton Village navy facility inside Fort Adams there were courts for officers and their dependents but these were not accessible to locals. Both composition and clay courts were available at Salve Regina College but only for registered students and faculty. So that left two casually-maintained asphalt courts at the city park on Carroll Avenue where during the summer, students home from college would bang away in lusty volleys and dominate the courts in rugged comradery.

A twelve-year-old working at a summer job, I had little interest in tennis. To me, pickup games of basketball and football were more fun and interesting. I played both at the Carroll Street Park and at the YMCA, and in the prolonged light of New England summer evenings practicing shots alone in the backyard with a hoop hung from the front of the garage. As fall approached and football season began, I'd play touch games with my friends and rougher tackle games with boys from uptown in the same park that abutted the tennis area. On occasion we might glance over at the courts if a particular cute coed was playing doubles. Sometimes we would head over to the water fountains close by to get a drink and watch a game or two. "Love-fifteen. Love-thirty. Deuce." We had no idea what this absurd scoring method could signify. It was remote from our experience, as were the crisp white shorts, the spotless tennis shoes, and the white sports shirts which were *de rigueur* in those days. We were ragamuffins, I suppose; heady youth, and tennis seemed effete, subtle, complex and sophisticated—more like an elaborate dance than a sport, a dance to which we would never be invited.

So, it came as a surprise to me when an Army colonel who lived up the street from us began talking about tennis one day with my Dad. "Does the boy play?" I heard him ask. "No," my Dad said, "but he loves sports and plays basketball, baseball, football." "Well," replied the Colonel, "if he ever wants a lesson tell him to stop by. I was an Army champion in my day."

Later my Dad would mention it, and when I replied that I thought it was a sissy game, he would begin to tell me of some of the great players of the day: Poncho Gonzalez, Jack Kramer, Ken Rosewell, but the names meant little to me. But I did like the old Colonel who had great stories to tell about the War which was not too distant in memory. My father's brother Harry had died in the forests of Belgium in 1944 during the last German push. A Little League baseball field in our neighborhood carried his name. War games in the local hills were still very much a part of our youthful pastimes. So, on a Saturday afternoon, home from a half day's labor at my summer job with a landscape company, I stopped by to talk to the Colonel. When the subject turned to tennis, his eyes lit up as he described the competition he faced in college and in the service. He regaled me with stories of tournaments, matches with famous players, games played at officer clubs in remote parts of the world. He said, "Tennis is the one game that, once you learn it, you will be able to play for the rest of your life. When your knees go out and you can't play football, when there is no gang of boys around for the pickup game of basketball or baseball, you can always find someone to play tennis with." So he convinced me. Or, perhaps it was his enthusiasm, my love for his stories and respect for his retired rank, his war experiences, or his genial personality and his enthusiasm, that I just felt I didn't want to disappoint. However it was, we agreed.

He loaned me one of his wooden rackets in its complicated screw-down press and the following day, right after early mass on a Sunday morning, he began teaching me the basics. In between suggestions about how to hold the racket and how to volley, he lectured me on the history of the sport, taught me how to score, how to adjust the net, how to anticipate the ball, how to refrain from cussing or displaying untoward emotional behavior. I think he probably bought me my first set of tennis whites that summer as well, although the first few games I'm sure I played in T-shirt and Levi cutoffs much to his distaste. That July was my thirteenth birthday and my father bought me my own racket, a Bancroft wood—expensive, highly polished and tightly strung with catgut and protected in a standard wooden press with butterfly screw-downs. The racket would be re-strung many times over the four years that I owned it. I would play with it in local matches, city tournaments, and even one memorable morning at the Newport Casino, where I got to volley with Poncho Gonzalez on the grass center court, courtesy of my father who owned a business next door and had persuaded the famous champion to trade a few strokes with his son.

The Colonel was, I suppose, in his mid-sixties which seemed ancient to me then. I could not imagine, as I improved in my tennis skills, and learned to volley deep, hit cross-court passing shots and top-spin lobs, that he would be able to keep up with me. Surely, the student would outplay the master any day now. But it never happened. Colonel Flack had a whole repertoire of moves; drop shots, slices, topspin backhands, corkscrew serves, and high-bouncing serves which just cut the end of the line. He knew the angles and limits of the court and, comfortable with these absorbed geometries, kept his young opponent racing from the net to the baseline, ragged and breathless.

As the summer passed, I improved, the muscles on my right forearm grew oversized, my lung capacity deepened, and my strokes improved from the gradual anticipation of the slides and twists that the ball would take as it came off the Colonel's racket. My service improved as well, so that I sometimes caught him wrong-footed and could come to the net quickly and put the ball away. I still didn't win a set but the games were closer and I noticed the Colonel was flushed and winded more and more often.

We played less the following year as I found new and younger competition among military dependants, boys from De La Salle Academy, and returning college players. I was often on the courts for hours each evening and on the weekends. With only two courts to play on, you had to win to keep the court and I was often a winner. Sometimes I would generously concede to play mixed doubles with couples who were waiting patiently on the sidelines.

Then one afternoon, shortly after my fourteenth birthday, all of that changed. A new boy appeared on the block; redheaded, cocky, with an easy confidence and grace and a powerful serve that could knock a poorly-gripped racket clear out of your hand. Tommy Gallagher was a compact, good-looking Irish boy who appeared from nowhere and had all the natural moves of a champion. I was blown off the court again and again in swift, blurred games of intense ferocity. I began to learn the difference between a "club player" as opposed to a "show player" or competitive athlete. Tommy played like he was born to it. There was nothing you could hit to him that he could not return. When I tried to play his game he beat me ruthlessly, contemptuously, as if I were wasting his time.

On one of those occasions, the semifinals of a citywide tournament, Colonel Flack was in the audience. Shamed by the 6–1, 6–0 defeat, I did not look him in the eye as I retreated back to the bench. "I'm not going to try and console you, Mike," he said. "You got sent to hell and back by that lad. And if you play him again, he'll beat you again. He's one of these kids who's a natural. But don't let him take away your pleasure in the game; don't let him do that to you. You're a club player and a decent one. Play your own game, take the shots you can, don't get caught up in his game. And don't be intimidated."

I was to play Tommy Gallagher several times over the next two years. He beat me, as he beat most of his competitors, but he won less easily as time went by, and never with the contemptuous indifference I had felt in that one semifinal. More importantly, losing to him did not take away from me the love of the game or my sense of myself as a player. Partly this was true because Colonel Flack and I returned to our early morning volleys interspersed with lessons. But now the lessons had more to do with eliminating distractions, watching the ball, and feeling the sun, the sweat on my skin, the slight breeze from the ocean, hearing the thwock of the perfectly hit ball coming off the strings. He taught me to be totally present in the moment, totally aware, totally focused.

He also trained me to go after every ball regardless of whether it seemed returnable or not. He taught me to play according to my skill level, placing shots carefully, not overhitting because of a desire to put it away like a pro, but stroking with the steady grace and pressure of a good club player who often tires out his more ambitious, more aggressive opponent.

Finally, he taught me that graciousness is what saves the game from savagery and ugliness. He instructed me not to give in to the temptation to call a ball out when it was in, to always give the opponent the benefit of the doubt, and that it was better to lose than to win unfairly. He reminded me to hold my temper in check, to always be polite, to return the balls in a single bounce to the server when there was no one to fetch balls.

But what he couldn't teach me and what I learned for myself over the years was that all of this was a gift. Tennis would change with the Australian 100 mph serves of Rod Laver, the aluminum and then titanium rackets, the oversized head rackets, with Wilson and Adidas logos covering every piece of equipment and raiment. Bad boys like John McEnroe would cuss out line judges and umpires, as aggressiveness had its day and then subsided ... though never completely. Competitive tennis would be enshrined in every high school and university; tennis camps would groom a new generation of players like Pete Sampras and Andre Agassi intent on making millions as they made their mark in the sport. Still, I would go right on playing my 3.5 club-level game. I would play tennis in the dry heat of the Sonoran deserts of Tucson and on the mile-high courts of Denver. I would play in Argentina and Panama. I would play after clearing the debris off a hurricane-littered court in Florida; I would hit the low-bounce ball while bundled in a jacket in up-state New York after sweeping off the snow-covered court, and—year after year—I would sweat through grueling sets in the tropical heat of May in Guadalajara. I would play through days of political unrest and assassination in my twenties, through the bitter, rancorous divorce in my thirties, through the crushing death of a beloved child in my forties, then through uncertain days of financial disasters and overseas currency devaluations in my fifties.

Now here I am in my sixties, approaching inexorably the age of my mentor, Colonel Flack, who on a summer morning took a skinny twelve-year old out to the concrete courts of a seaside town to give him the gift of lifelong victory. It is a way of maintaining both physical and psychological fitness, but also a way of moving through life with a focus, with grace and a sure sense of gratitude. One of those ineffable spiritual gifts which continue to give again and again when I walk on to a sun-speckled court, go over to measure the net with my "stick" (a Wilson H-26 titanium racket), and all the world narrows down to the clear geometries of the white lines, to the sound of the thwock as the ball hits the strings, as my muscles respond again in their dependable way to the known rhythms of the game, and everything is suddenly whole and perfect, and the world completely intelligible.

Possibilities for Writing

1. Write a brief character sketch of Colonel Flack. Try to convey a sense of the colonel as a man and as a teacher.

2. Summarize the lessons Hogan learned from the colonel. To what extent do you think that these lessons are valuable for life as well as for tennis? Explain.

3. Write an essay about a sport, game, hobby, or other leisure pursuit for which you have a passion. Explain how you became involved in it and what values it holds for you.

Langston Hughes (1902–1967) was born in Joplin, Missouri, to a prominent African-American family. Interested in poetry from childhood, he attended Columbia University as an engineering major but dropped out after his first year to pursue his literary aspirations (he later graduated from Lincoln University). Spurred by the flourishing of black artists known as the Harlem Renaissance, he quickly found a distinctive voice that reflected the culture of everyday life, and he had published his first works before he was out of his teens. Hughes is best known for his poetry, which often employs vernacular language and jazz-like rhythms, but he also wrote popular works of fiction, essays, plays, books for children, and several volumes of autobiography, including The Big Sea *(1940), focusing on his childhood and teenage years.*

Langston Hughes
Salvation

In "Salvation," Hughes describes a memorable incident from his youth, one that had a decisive impact on his view of the world. In the span of just a few pages, Hughes tells a story of faith and doubt, of belief and disbelief, of how he was "saved from sin" when he was going on thirteen. "But not really saved." This paradoxical opening to "Salvation" establishes a tension that characterizes the essay, which culminates in an ironic reversal of expectations for the reader, and a life-altering realization for Hughes.

The power of Hughes's "Salvation" derives not only from its language, but also from the irony of its action, as well as its blend of humor and sadness, the humor of the child's literal understanding of what his aunt tells him to expect, and the sadness of his disappointed belief, which ironically, turns against itself. In restricting the point-of-view to that of a twelve-year-old child, Hughes enhances the credibility of his narrative and increases its dramatic power. His concluding paragraph is a quietly resounding tour-de-force of irony and epiphany.

I was saved from sin when I was going on thirteen. But not really saved. It happened like this. There was a big revival at my Auntie Reed's church. Every night for weeks there had been much preaching, singing, praying, and shouting, and some very hardened sinners had been brought to Christ, and the membership of the church had grown by leaps and bounds. Then just before the revival ended, they held a special meeting for children, "to bring the young lambs to the fold." My aunt spoke of it for days ahead. That night I was escorted to the front row and placed on the mourners' bench with all the other young sinners, who had not yet been brought to Jesus.

My aunt told me that when you were saved you saw a light, and something happened to you inside! And Jesus came into your life! And God was with you from then on! She said you could see and hear and feel Jesus in your soul. I believed her. I had heard a great many old people say the same thing and it seemed to me they ought to know. So I sat there calmly in the hot, crowded church, waiting for Jesus to come to me.

The preacher preached a wonderful rhythmical sermon, all moans and shouts and lonely cries and dire pictures of hell, and then he sang a song about the ninety and nine safe in the fold, but one little lamb was left out in the cold. Then he said: "Won't you come? Won't you come to Jesus? Young lambs, won't you come?" And he held out his arms to all us young sinners there on the mourners' bench. And the little girls cried. And some of them jumped up and went to Jesus right away. But most of us just sat there.

A great many old people came and knelt around us and prayed, old women with jet-black faces and braided hair, old men with work-gnarled hands. And the church sang a song about the lower lights are burning, some poor sinners to be saved. And the whole building rocked with prayer and song.

Still I kept waiting to *see* Jesus.

Finally all the young people had gone to the altar and were saved, but one boy and me. He was a rounder's son named Westley. Westley and I were surrounded by sisters and deacons praying. It was very hot in the church, and getting late now. Finally Westley said to me in a whisper: "God damn! I'm tired o' sitting here. Let's get up and be saved." So he got up and was saved.

Then I was left all alone on the mourners' bench. My aunt came and knelt at my knees and cried, while prayers and songs swirled all around me in the little church. The whole congregation prayed for me alone, in a mightly wail of moans and voices. And I kept waiting serenely for Jesus, waiting, waiting—but he didn't come. I wanted to see him, but nothing happened to me. Nothing! I wanted something to happen to me, but nothing happened.

I heard the songs and the minister saying: "Why don't you come? My dear child, why don't you come to Jesus? Jesus is waiting for you. He wants you. Why don't you come? Sister Reed, what is this child's name?"

"Langston," my aunt sobbed.

"Langston, why don't you come? Why don't you come and be saved? Oh, Lamb of God! Why don't you come?"

Now it was really getting late. I began to be ashamed of myself, holding everything up so long. I began to wonder what God thought about Westley, who certainly hadn't seen Jesus either, but who was now sitting proudly on the platform, swinging his knickerbockered legs and grinning down at me, surrounded by deacons and old women on their knees praying. God had not struck Westley dead for taking his name in vain or for lying in the temple. So I decided that maybe to save further trouble, I'd better lie, too, and say that Jesus had come, and get up and be saved.

So I got up.

Suddenly the whole room broke into a sea of shouting, as they saw me rise. Waves of rejoicing swept the place. Women leaped in the air. My aunt threw her arms around me. The minister took me by the hand and led me to the platform.

When things quieted down, in a hushed silence, punctuated by a few ecstatic "Amens," all the new young lambs were blessed in the name of God. Then joyous singing filled the room.

That night, for the last time in my life but one—for I was a big boy twelve years old—I cried. I cried, in bed alone, and couldn't stop. I buried my head under the quilts, but my aunt heard me. She woke up and told my uncle I was crying because the Holy Ghost had come into my life, and because I had seen Jesus. But I was really crying because I couldn't bear to tell her that I had lied, that I had deceived everybody in the church, and I hadn't seen Jesus, and that now I didn't believe there was a Jesus any more, since he didn't come to help me.

Possibilities for Writing

1. Recall a time when, like Hughes, you did something you didn't really believe in because you found it easier to go along with the crowd. In an essay, narrate the experience, focusing on the situation, the other people involved, your feelings at the time, and the aftermath of the incident.

2. In this brief narration, Hughes does a great deal to re-create his experience vividly and concretely. Analyze Hughes's use of language—specific nouns, verbs, and adjectives—as well as his use of dialogue and repetition to add punch to his story.

3. Hughes ends his narration on a note of disillusionment: "now I didn't believe there was a Jesus any more, since he didn't come to help me." Have you ever been disillusioned about a deeply held and cherished belief? In an essay, explore that experience and its consequences in detail. How did you eventually cope with your disappointment?

Pico Iyer (b. 1957) was born in England to Indian parents, grew up in California, attended Eton and Oxford, and has lived in suburban Japan. Iyer is the author of half a dozen books along with essays and journalism that have appeared in Time, Harper's, The New Yorker, The New York Review of Books, *and many other publications around the world. He has described himself as a "multinational soul on a multicultural globe," and his writing frequently probes the meaning of personal identity in a global context. His most recent books are* The Global Soul: Jet Lag, Shopping Malls, and the Search for Home *(2000) and* Abandon: A Romance *(2003).*

Pico Iyer
Nowhere Man

In "Nowhere Man," Iyer describes an "entirely new breed of people" who do not live in a single place, but instead have multiple places of residences, often in different countries and continents. These individuals, many of them relatively young, find themselves learning about and living in quite different cultures, and thus become both multilingual and multicultural. Iyer describes both the up and down sides of such multiple cultural identities.

One of the more interesting features of "Nowhere Man" is Iyer's exploration of the consequences of being without a distinct national identity. Using himself as an example, Iyer highlights the advantages and drawbacks, the benefits and limitations of being a man without a country. Iyer's essay is distinctively modern in its references to technology, and how the new breed of rootless, international travelers he describes are connected to each other and to their far-flung quasi-residences via cell phones, faxes, and the Internet, while keeping abreast of world events via CNN, and eating in internationally franchised restaurants.

By the time I was nine, I was already used to going to school by plane, to sleeping in airports, to shuttling back and forth, three times a year, between my home in California and my boarding school in England. While I was growing up, I was never within six thousand miles of the nearest relative—and came, therefore, to learn how to define relations in nonfamilial ways. From the time I was a teenager, I took it for granted that I could take my budget vacation (as I did) in Bolivia and Tibet, China and Morocco. It never seemed strange to me that a girlfriend might be half a world (or ten hours flying time) away, that my closest friends might be on the other side of a continent or sea. It was only recently that I realized that all these habits of mind and life would scarcely have been imaginable in my parents' youth, that the very facts and facilities that shape my world are all distinctly new developments, and mark me as a modern type.

It was only recently, in fact, that I realized that I am an example, perhaps, of an entirely new breed of people, a transcontinental tribe of wanderers that is multiplying as fast as international telephone lines and frequent flier programs. We are the transit loungers, forever heading to the departure gate. We buy our interests duty-free, we eat our food on plastic plates, we watch the world through borrowed headphones. We pass through countries as through revolving doors, resident aliens of the world, impermanent residents of nowhere. Nothing is strange to us, and nowhere is foreign. We are visitors even in our own homes.

The modern world seems increasingly made for people like me. I can plop myself down anywhere and find myself in the same relation of familiarity and strangeness: Lusaka is scarcely more strange to me than the England in which I was born, the America where I am registered as an "alien," and the almost unvisited India that people tell me is my home. All have Holiday Inns, direct-dial phones, CNN, and DHL. All have sushi, Thai restaurants, and Kentucky Fried Chicken.

This kind of life offers an unprecedented sense of freedom and mobility: Tied down nowhere, we can pick and choose among locations. Ours is the first generation that can go off to visit Tibet for a week, or meet Tibetans down the street; ours is the first generation to be able to go to Nigeria for a holiday—to find our roots or to find that they are not there. At a superficial level, this new internationalism means that I can meet, in the Hilton coffee shop, an Indonesian businessman who is as conversant as I am with Magic Johnson and Madonna. At a deeper level, it means that I need never feel estranged. If all the world is alien to us, all the world is home.

And yet I sometimes think that this mobile way of life is as disquietingly novel as high-rises, or as the video monitors that are rewiring our consciousness. Even as we fret about the changes our progress wreaks in the air and on the airwaves, in forests and on streets, we hardly worry about the change it is working in ourselves, the new kind of soul that is being born out of a new kind of life. Yet this could be the most dangerous development of all, and the least examined.

For us in the transit lounge, disorientation is as alien as affiliation. We become professional observers, able to see the merits and deficiencies of anywhere, to balance our parents' viewpoints with their enemies' position. Yes, we say, of course it's terrible, but look at the situation from Saddam's point of view. I understand how you feel, but the Chinese had their own cultural reasons for Tiananmen Square. Fervor comes to seem to us the most foreign place of all.

Seasoned experts at dispassion, we are less good at involvement, or suspension of disbelief; at, in fact, the abolition of distance. We are masters of the aerial perspective, but touching down becomes more difficult. Unable to get stirred by the raising of a flag, we are sometimes unable to see how anyone could be stirred. I sometimes think that this is how Salman Rushdie, the great analyst of this condition, somehow became its victim. He had juggled homes for so long, so adroitly, that he forgot how the world looks to someone who is rooted—in country or in belief. He had chosen to live so far from affiliation that he could no longer see why people choose affiliation in the first place. Besides, being part of no society means one is accountable to no one, and need respect no laws outside one's own. If single-nation people can be fanatical as terrorists, we can end up ineffectual as peacekeepers.

We become, in fact, strangers to belief itself, unable to comprehend many of the rages and dogmas that animate (and unite) people. I could not begin to fathom why some Muslims would think of murder after hearing about *The Satanic Verses*; yet sometimes I force myself to recall that it is we, in our floating skepticism, who are the exceptions, that in China or Iran, in Korea or Peru, it is not so strange to give up one's life for a cause.

We end up, then, a little like nonaligned nations, confirming our reservations at every step. We tell ourselves, self-servingly, that nationalism breeds monsters, and choose to ignore the fact that internationalism breeds them too. Ours is the culpability not of the assassin, but of the bystander who takes a snapshot of the murder. Or, when the revolution catches fire, hops on the next plane out.

I wonder, sometimes, if this new kind of nonaffiliation may not be alien to something fundamental in the human state. Refugees at least harbor passionate feeling about the world they have left—and generally seek to return there. The exile at least is propelled by some kind of strong emotion away from the old country and toward the new; indifference is not an exile emotion. But what does the transit lounger feel? What are the issues that we would die for? What are the passions that we would live for?

Airports are among the only sites in public life where emotions are hugely sanctioned. We see people weep, shout, kiss in airports; we see them at the furthest edges of excitement and exhaustion. Airports are privileged spaces where we can see the primal states writ large—fear, recognition, hope. But there are some of us, perhaps, sitting at the departure gate, boarding passes in hand, who feel neither the pain of separation nor the exultation of wonder; who alight with the same emotions with which we embarked; who go down to the baggage carousel and watch our lives circling, circling, circling, waiting to be claimed.

Possibilities for Writing

1. Discuss your perception of what Iyer describes as an "entirely new breed of people," the "nowhere man" of his title. What characterizes this new type of person? To what extent are you familiar with it? What consequences of "the transit lounge" syndrome does Iyer identify? Can you think of others?

2. Explain Iyer's remark that "being part of no society means one is accountable to no one." According to Iyer, what are the consequences of being rootless, of lacking a sense of being rooted in a particular place that one can call home? Do you agree with him? Why or why not?

3. The flip side of the rootlessness that Iyer describes is a strong sense of pride that people feel for their countries and for their nationalities. What dangers and what benefits does Iyer see as resulting from an intense pride in one's place of origin and/or residence? To what extent do you agree with his assessment? Explain.

Martin Luther King, Jr. (1929–1968), the most revered leader of the civil rights movement, was born in Atlanta, the son of a Baptist clergyman. A graduate of Morehouse College and Boston University, King was himself ordained in 1947 and became the minister at a church in Montgomery, Alabama, in 1954. There he spearheaded a year-long boycott of segregated city buses, which eventually resulted in the system's integration, and as head of the Southern Christian Leadership Conference, he took his crusade against segregation to other Southern cities. Noted for his commitment to peaceful demonstration and nonviolent resistance, King and those who protested with him often ended up in jail. An international figure by the 1960s, he was awarded a Nobel Peace Prize in 1964. King was assassinated in 1968 in Memphis, Tennessee.

Martin Luther King, Jr.

Letter from Birmingham Jail

King's "Letter" is a response to criticism made against his effort to use peaceful, nonviolent demonstrations as forms of public disruption to advance the cause of racial integration. King addresses his letter to an audience of clergymen, whom he assures from the start that he respects their sincerity and good will in presenting their criticism. But he quickly seizes the moral ground by explaining why he came to Birmingham, linking himself with the biblical prophets, who preached against social injustice. Developing his argument carefully, King answers their actual questions and anticipates their additional potential questions.

King takes up complex issues, including whether it is right to break a law to achieve a desired end, citing a roster of Christian and Jewish theologians and quoting the Roman Catholic theologian St. Augustine who wrote that "an unjust law is no law at all." He also cites examples of revolutionary thinkers whose ideas and example changed history—from Socrates and Martin Luther to Thoreau and Mahatma Gandhi, whose civil disobedience in the form of nonviolent protest was politically effective.

My Dear Fellow Clergymen:

While confined here in the Birmingham city jail, I came across your recent statement calling my present activities "unwise and untimely." Seldom do I pause to answer criticism of my work and ideas. If I sought to answer all the criticisms that cross my desk, my secretaries would have little time for anything other than such correspondence in the course of the day, and I would have no time for constructive work. But since I feel that you are men of genuine good will and that your criticisms are sincerely set forth, I want to try to answer your statement in what I hope will be patient and reasonable terms.

I think I should indicate why I am here in Birmingham, since you have been influenced by the view which argues against "outsiders coming in." I have the honor of serving as president of the Southern Christian Leadership Conference, an organization operating in every southern state, with headquarters in Atlanta, Georgia. We have some eighty-five affiliated organizations across the South, and one of them is the Alabama Christian Movement for Human Rights. Frequently we share staff, educational, and financial resources with our affiliates. Several months ago the affiliate here in Birmingham asked us to be on call to engage in a nonviolent direct-action program if such were deemed necessary. We readily consented, and when the hour came we lived up to our promise. So I, along with several members of my staff, am here because I was invited here. I am here because I have organizational ties here.

But more basically, I am in Birmingham because injustice is here. Just as the prophets of the eighth century B.C. left their villages and carried their "thus saith the Lord" far beyond the boundaries of their home towns, and just as the Apostle Paul left his village of Tarsus and carried the gospel of Jesus Christ to the far corners of the Greco-Roman world, so am I compelled to carry the gospel of freedom beyond my own home town. Like Paul, I must constantly respond to the Macedonian call for aid.

Moreover, I am cognizant of the interrelatedness of all communities and states. I cannot sit idly by in Atlanta and not be concerned about what happens in Birmingham. Injustice anywhere is a threat to justice everywhere. We are caught in an inescapable network of mutuality, tied in a single garment of destiny. Whatever affects one directly, affects all indirectly. Never again can we afford to live with the narrow, provincial "outside agitator" idea. Anyone who lives inside the United States can never be considered an outsider anywhere within its bounds.

You deplore the demonstrations taking place in Birmingham. But your statement, I am sorry to say, fails to express a similar concern for the conditions that brought about the demonstrations. I am sure that none of you would want to rest content with the superficial kind of social analysis that deals merely with effects and does not grapple with underlying causes. It is unfortunate that demonstrations are taking place in Birmingham, but it is even more unfortunate that the city's white power structure left the Negro community with no alternative.

In any nonviolent campaign there are four basic steps: collection of the facts to determine whether injustices exist; negotiation; self-purification; and direct action. We have gone through all these steps in Birmingham. There can be no gainsaying the fact that racial injustice engulfs this community. Birmingham is probably the most thoroughly segregated city in the United States. Its ugly record of brutality is widely known. Negroes have experienced grossly unjust treatment in the courts. There have been more unsolved bombings of Negro homes and churches in Birmingham than in any other city in the nation. These are the hard, brutal facts of the case. On the basis of these conditions, Negro leaders sought to negotiate with the city fathers. But the latter consistently refused to engage in good-faith negotiation.

Then, last September, came the opportunity to talk with leaders of Birmingham's economic community. In the course of the negotiations, certain promises were made by the merchants—for example, to remove the stores' humiliating racial signs. On the basis of these promises, the Reverend Fred Shuttlesworth and the leaders of the Alabama Christian Movement for Human Rights agreed to a moratorium on all demonstrations. As the weeks and months went by, we realized that we were the victims of a broken promise. A few signs, briefly removed, returned; the others remained.

As in so many past experiences, our hopes had been blasted, and the shadow of deep disappointment settled upon us. We had no alternative except to prepare for direct action, whereby we would present our very bodies as a means of laying our case before the conscience of the local and the national community. Mindful of the difficulties involved, we decided to undertake a process of self-purification. We began a series of workshops on nonviolence, and we repeatedly asked ourselves: "Are you able to accept blows without retaliating?" "Are you able to endure the ordeal of jail?" We decided to schedule our direct-action program for the Easter season, realizing that except for Christmas, this is the main shopping period of the year. Knowing that a strong economic-withdrawal program would be the by-product of direct action, we felt that this would be the best time to bring pressure to bear on the merchants for the needed change.

Then it occurred to us that Birmingham's mayoral election was coming up in March, and we speedily decided to postpone action until after election day. When we discovered that the Commissioner of Public Safety, Eugene "Bull" Connor, had piled up enough votes to be in the run-off, we decided again to postpone action until the day after the run-off so that the demonstrations could not be used to cloud the issues. Like many others, we wanted to see Mr. Connor defeated, and to this end we endured postponement after postponement. Having aided in this community need, we felt that our direct-action program could be delayed no longer.

You may well ask, "Why direct action? Why sit-ins, marches, and so forth? Isn't negotiation a better path?" You are quite right in calling for negotiation. Indeed, this is the very purpose of direct action. Nonviolent direct action seeks to create such a crisis and foster such a tension that a community which has constantly refused to negotiate is forced to confront the issue. It seeks so to dramatize the issue that it can no longer be ignored. My citing the creation of tension as part of the work of the nonviolent-resister may sound rather shocking. But I must confess that I am not afraid of the word "tension." I have earnestly opposed violent tension, but there is a type of constructive, nonviolent tension which is necessary for growth. Just as Socrates felt that it was necessary to create a tension in the mind so that individuals could rise from the bondage of myths and half-truths to the unfettered realm of creative analysis and objective appraisal, so must we see the need for nonviolent gadflies to create the kind of tension in society that will help men rise from the dark depths of prejudice and racism to the majestic heights of understanding and brotherhood.

The purpose of our direct-action program is to create a situation so crisis-packed that it will inevitably open the door to negotiation. I therefore concur with you in your call for negotiation. Too long has our beloved Southland been bogged down in a tragic effort to live in monologue rather than dialogue.

One of the basic points in your statement is that the action that I and my associates have taken in Birmingham is untimely. Some have asked: "Why didn't you give the new city administration time to act?" The only answer that I can give to this query is that the new Birmingham administration must be prodded about as much as the outgoing one, before it will act. We are sadly mistaken if we feel that the election of Albert Boutwell as mayor will bring the millennium to Birmingham. While

Mr. Boutwell is a much more gentle person than Mr. Connor, they are both segregationists, dedicated to maintenance of the status quo. I have hoped that Mr. Boutwell will be reasonable enough to see the futility of massive resistance to desegregation. But he will not see this without pressure from devotees of civil rights. My friends, I must say to you that we have not made a single gain in civil rights without determined legal and nonviolent pressure. Lamentably, it is an historical fact that privileged groups seldom give up their privileges voluntarily. Individuals may see the moral light and voluntarily give up their unjust posture, but, as Reinhold Niebuhr has reminded us, groups tend to be more immoral than individuals.

We know through painful experience that freedom is never voluntarily given by the oppressor; it must be demanded by the oppressed. Frankly, I have yet to engage in a direct-action campaign that was "well timed" in the view of those who have not suffered unduly from the disease of segregation. For years now I have heard the word "Wait!" It rings in the ear of every Negro with piercing familiarity. This "Wait" has almost always meant "Never." We must come to see, with one of our distinguished jurists, that "justice too long delayed is justice denied."

We have waited for more than 340 years for our constitutional and God-given rights. The nations of Asia and Africa are moving with jet-like speed toward gaining political independence, but we still creep at horse-and-buggy pace toward gaining a cup of coffee at a lunch counter. Perhaps it is easy for those who have never felt the stinging darts of segregation to say, "Wait." But when you have seen vicious mobs lynch your mothers and fathers at will and drown your sisters and brothers at whim; when you have seen hate-filled policemen curse, kick, and even kill your black brothers and sisters; when you see the vast majority of your twenty million Negro brothers smothering in an airtight cage of poverty in the midst of an affluent society; when you suddenly find your tongue twisted and your speech stammering as you seek to explain to your six-year-old daughter why she can't go to the public amusement park that has just been advertised on television, and see tears welling up in her eyes when she is told that Funtown is closed to colored children, and see ominous clouds of inferiority beginning to form in her little mental sky, and see her beginning to distort her personality by developing an unconscious bitterness toward white people; when you have to concoct an answer for a five-year-old son who is asking, "Daddy, why do white people treat colored people so mean?"; when you take a cross-country drive and find it necessary to sleep night after night in the uncomfortable corners of your automobile because no motel will accept you; when you are humiliated day in and day out by nagging signs reading "white" and "colored"; when your first name becomes "nigger," your middle name becomes "boy" (however old you are) and your last name becomes "John," and your wife and mother are never given the respected title "Mrs."; when you are harried by day and haunted by night by the fact that you are a Negro, living constantly at tiptoe stance, never quite knowing what to expect next, and are plagued with inner fears and outer resentments; when you are forever fighting a degenerating sense of "nobodiness"—then you will understand why we find it difficult to wait. There comes a time when the cup of endurance runs over, and men are no longer willing to be plunged into the abyss of despair. I hope, sirs, you can understand our legitimate and unavoidable impatience.

You express a great deal of anxiety over our willingness to break laws. This is certainly a legitimate concern. Since we so diligently urge people to obey the Supreme Court's decision of 1954 outlawing segregation in the public schools, at first glance it may seem rather paradoxical for us consciously to break laws. One may well ask: "How can you advocate breaking some laws and obeying others?" The answer lies in the fact that there are two types of laws: just and unjust. I would be the first to advocate obeying just laws. One has not only a legal but a moral responsibility to obey just laws. Conversely, one has a moral responsibility to disobey unjust laws. I would agree with St. Augustine that "an unjust law is no law at all."

Now, what is the difference between the two? How does one determine whether a law is just or unjust? A just law is a man-made code that squares with the moral law or the law of God. An unjust law is a code that is out of harmony with the moral law. To put it in the terms of St. Thomas Aquinas: An unjust law is a human law that is not rooted in eternal law and natural law. Any law that uplifts human personality is just. Any law that degrades human personality is unjust. All segregation statutes are unjust because segregation distorts the soul and damages the personality. It gives the segregator a false sense of superiority and the segregated a false sense of inferiority. Segregation, to use the terminology of the Jewish philosopher Martin Buber, substitutes an "I-it" relationship for an "I-thou" relationship and ends up relegating persons to the status of things. Hence segregation is not only politically, economically, and sociologically unsound, it is morally wrong and sinful. Paul Tillich has said that sin is separation. Is not segregation an existential expression of man's tragic separation, his awful estrangement, his terrible sinfulness? Thus it is that I can urge men to obey the 1954 decision of the Supreme Court, for it is morally right; and I can urge them to disobey segregation ordinances, for they are morally wrong.

Let us consider a more concrete example of just and unjust laws. An unjust law is a code that a numerical or power majority group compels a minority group to obey but does not make binding on itself. This is *difference* made legal. By the same token, a just law is a code that a majority compels a minority to follow and that it is willing to follow itself. This is *sameness* made legal.

Let me give another explanation. A law is unjust if it is inflicted on a minority that, as a result of being denied the right to vote, had no part in enacting or devising the law. Who can say that the legislature of Alabama which set up that state's segregation laws was democratically elected? Throughout Alabama all sorts of devious methods are used to prevent Negroes from becoming registered voters, and there are some counties in which, even though Negroes constitute a majority of the population, not a single Negro is registered. Can any law enacted under such circumstances be considered democratically structured?

Sometimes a law is just on its face and unjust in its application. For instance, I have been arrested on a charge of parading without a permit. Now, there is nothing wrong in having an ordinance which requires a permit for a parade. But such an ordinance becomes unjust when it is used to maintain segregation and to deny citizens the First-Amendment privilege of peaceful assembly and protest.

I hope you are able to see the distinction I am trying to point out. In no sense do I advocate evading or defying the law, as would the rabid segregationist. That would lead to anarchy. One who breaks an unjust law must do so openly, lovingly, and with a willingness to accept the penalty. I submit that an individual who breaks a law that conscience tells him is unjust, and who willingly accepts the penalty of imprisonment in order to arouse the conscience of the community over its injustice, is in reality expressing the highest respect for law.

Of course, there is nothing new about this kind of civil disobedience. It was evidenced sublimely in the refusal of Shadrach, Meshach, and Abednego to obey the laws of Nebuchadnezzar, on the ground that a higher moral law was at stake. It was practiced superbly by the early Christians, who were willing to face hungry lions and the excruciating pain of chopping blocks rather than submit to certain unjust laws of the Roman Empire. To a degree, academic freedom is a reality today because Socrates practiced civil disobedience. In our own nation, the Boston Tea Party represented a massive act of civil disobedience.

We should never forget that everything Adolf Hitler did in Germany was "legal" and everything the Hungarian freedom fighters did in Hungary was "illegal." It was "illegal" to aid and comfort a Jew in Hitler's Germany. Even so, I am sure that, had I lived in Germany at the time, I would have aided and comforted my Jewish brothers. If today I lived in a Communist country where certain principles dear to the Christian faith are suppressed, I would openly advocate disobeying that country's anti-religious laws.

I must make two honest confessions to you, my Christian and Jewish brothers. First, I must confess that over the past few years I have been gravely disappointed with the white moderate. I have almost reached the regrettable conclusion that the Negro's great stumbling block in his stride toward freedom is not the White Citizen's Counciler or the Ku Klux Klanner, but the white moderate, who is more devoted to "order" than to justice; who prefers a negative peace which is the absence of tension to a positive peace which is the presence of justice; who constantly says, "I agree with you in the goal you seek, but I cannot agree with your methods of direct action"; who paternalistically believes he can set the timetable for another man's freedom; who lives by a mythical concept of time and who constantly advises the Negro to wait for a "more convenient season." Shallow understanding from people of good will is more frustrating than absolute misunderstanding from people of ill will. Lukewarm acceptance is much more bewildering than outright rejection.

I had hoped that the white moderate would understand that law and order exist for the purpose of establishing justice and that when they fail in this purpose they become the dangerously structured dams that block the flow of social progress. I had hoped that the white moderate would understand that the present tension in the South is a necessary phase of the transition from an obnoxious negative peace, in which the Negro passively accepted his unjust plight, to a substantive and positive peace, in which all men will respect the dignity and worth of human personality. Actually, we who engage in nonviolent direct action are not the creators of tension. We merely bring to the surface the hidden tension that is already alive. We bring it out in the open, where it can be seen and dealt with. Like a boil that can never be cured so long as it is covered up but must be opened with all its ugliness to the natural medicines of air and light, injustice must be exposed, with all the tension its exposure creates, to the light of human conscience and the air of national opinion, before it can be cured.

In your statement you assert that our actions, even though peaceful, must be condemned because they precipitate violence. But is this a logical assertion? Isn't this like condemning a robbed man because his possession of money precipitated the evil act of robbery? Isn't this like condemning Socrates because his unswerving commitment to truth and his philosophical inquiries precipitated the act by the misguided populace in which they made him drink hemlock? Isn't this like condemning Jesus because his unique God-consciousness and never-ceasing devotion to God's will precipitated the evil act of crucifixion? We must come to see that, as the federal courts have consistently affirmed, it is wrong to urge an individual to cease his efforts to gain his basic constitutional rights because the quest may precipitate violence. Society must protect the robbed and punish the robber.

I had also hoped that the white moderate would reject the myth concerning time in relation to the struggle for freedom. I have just received a letter from a white brother in Texas. He writes: "All Christians know that the colored people will receive equal rights eventually, but it is possible that you are in too great a religious hurry. It has taken Christianity almost two thousand years to accomplish what it has. The teachings of Christ take time to come to earth." Such an attitude stems from a tragic misconception of time, from the strangely irrational notion that there is something in the very flow of time that will inevitably cure all ills. Actually, time itself is neutral; it can be used either destructively or constructively. More and more I feel that the people of ill will have used time much more effectively than have the people of good will. We will have to repent in this generation not merely for the hateful words and actions of the bad people, but for the appalling silence of the good people. Human progress never rolls in on wheels of inevitability; it comes through the tireless efforts of men willing to be co-workers with God, and without this hard work, time itself becomes an ally of the forces of social stagnation. We must use time creatively, in the knowledge that the time is always ripe to do right. Now is the time to make real the promise of democracy and transform our pending national elegy into a creative psalm of brotherhood. Now is the time to lift our national policy from the quicksand of racial injustice to the solid rock of human dignity.

You speak of our activity in Birmingham as extreme. At first I was rather disappointed that fellow clergymen would see my nonviolent efforts as those of an extremist. I began thinking about the fact that I stand in the middle of two opposing forces in the Negro community. One is a force of complacency, made up in part of Negroes who, as a result of long years of oppression, are so drained of self-respect and a sense of "somebodiness" that they have adjusted to segregation; and in part of a few middle-class Negroes who, because of a degree of academic and economic security and because in some ways they profit by segregation, have become insensitive to the problems of the masses. The other force is one of bitterness and hatred, and it comes perilously close to advocating violence. It is expressed in the various black nationalist groups that are springing up across the nation, the largest and best-known being Elijah Muhammad's Muslim movement. Nourished by the Negro's frustration over the continued existence of racial discrimination, this movement is made up of people who have lost faith in America, who have absolutely repudiated Christianity, and who have concluded that the white man is an incorrigible "devil."

I have tried to stand between these two forces, saying that we need emulate neither the "do-nothingism" of the complacent nor the hatred and despair of the black nationalist. For there is the more excellent way of love and nonviolent protest. I am grateful to God that, through the influence of the Negro church, the way of nonviolence became an integral part of our struggle.

If this philosophy had not emerged, by now many streets of the South would, I am convinced, be flowing with blood. And I am further convinced that if our white brothers dismiss as "rabblerousers" and "outside agitators" those of us who employ nonviolent direct action, and if they refuse to support our nonviolent efforts, millions of Negroes will, out of frustration and despair, seek solace and security in black-nationalist ideologies—a development that would inevitably lead to a frightening racial nightmare.

Oppressed people cannot remain oppressed forever. The yearning for freedom eventually manifests itself, and that is what has happened to the American Negro. Something within has reminded him of his birthright of freedom, and something without has reminded him that it can be gained. Consciously or unconsciously, he has been caught up by the *Zeitgeist*, and with his black brothers of Africa and his brown and yellow brothers of Asia, South America, and the Caribbean, the United States Negro is moving with a sense of great urgency toward the promised land of racial justice. If one recognizes this vital urge that has engulfed the Negro community, one should readily understand why public demonstrations are taking place. The Negro has many pent-up resentments and latent frustrations, and he must release them. So let him march; let him make prayer pilgrimages to the city hall; let him go on freedom rides—and try to understand why he must do so. If his repressed emotions are not released in nonviolent ways, they will seek expression through violence; this is not a threat but a fact of history. So I have not said to my people, "Get rid of your discontent." Rather, I have tried to say that this normal and healthy discontent can be channeled into the creative outlet of nonviolent direct action. And now this approach is being termed extremist.

But though I was initially disappointed at being categorized as an extremist, as I continued to think about the matter I gradually gained a measure of satisfaction from the label. Was not Jesus an extremist for love: "Love your enemies, bless them that curse you, do good to them that hate you, and pray for them which despitefully use you, and persecute you." Was not Amos an extremist for justice: "Let justice roll down like waters and righteousness like an ever-flowing stream." Was not Paul an extremist for the Christian gospel: "I bear in my body the marks of the Lord Jesus." Was not Martin Luther an extremist: "Here I stand; I cannot do otherwise, so help me God." And John Bunyan: "I will stay in jail to the end of my days before I make a butchery of my conscience." And Abraham Lincoln: "This nation cannot survive half slave and half free." And Thomas Jefferson: "We hold these truths to be self-evident, that all men are created equal. . . ." So the question is not whether we will be extremists, but what kind of extremists we will be. Will we be extremists for hate or for love? Will we be extremists for the preservation of injustice or for the extension of justice? In that dramatic scene on Calvary's hill three men were crucified. We must never forget that all three were crucified for the same crime—the crime of extremism. Two were extremists for immorality, and thus fell below their environment. The other, Jesus Christ, was an extremist for love, truth, and goodness, and thereby rose above his environment. Perhaps the South, the nation, and the world are in dire need of creative extremists.

I had hoped that the white moderate would see this need. Perhaps I was too optimistic; perhaps I expected too much. I suppose I should have realized that few members of the oppressor race can understand the deep groans and passionate yearnings of the oppressed race, and still fewer have the vision to see that injustice must be rooted out by strong, persistent, and determined action. I am thankful, however, that some of our white brothers in the South have grasped the meaning of this social revolution and committed themselves to it. They are still all too few in quantity, but they are big in quality. Some—such as Ralph McGill, Lillian Smith, Harry Golden, James McBridge Dabbs, Ann Braden, and Sarah Patton Boyle—have written about our struggle in eloquent and prophetic terms. Others have marched with us down nameless streets of the South. They have languished in filthy, roach-infested jails, suffering the abuse and brutality of policemen who view them as "dirty nigger-lovers." Unlike so many of their moderate brothers and sisters, they have recognized the urgency of the moment and sensed the need for powerful "action" antidotes to combat the disease of segregation.

Let me take note of my other major disappointment. I have been so greatly disappointed with the white church and its leadership. Of course, there are some notable exceptions. I am not unmindful of the fact that each of you has taken some significant stands on this issue. I commend you, Reverend Stallings, for your Christian stand on this past Sunday, in welcoming Negroes to your worship service on a nonsegregated basis. I commend the Catholic leaders of this state for integrating Spring Hill College several years ago.

But despite these notable exceptions, I must honestly reiterate that I have been disappointed with the church. I do not say this as one of those negative critics who can always find something wrong with the church. I say this as a minister of the gospel, who loves the church; who was nurtured in its bosom; who has been sustained by its spiritual blessings and who will remain true to it as long as the cord of life shall lengthen.

When I was suddenly catapulted into the leadership of the bus protest in Montgomery, Alabama, a few years ago, I felt we would be supported by the white church. I felt that the white ministers, priests, and rabbis of the South would be among our strongest allies. Instead, some have been outright opponents, refusing to understand the freedom movement and misrepresenting its leaders; all too many others have been more cautious than courageous and have remained silent behind the anesthetizing security of stainedglass windows.

In spite of my shattered dreams, I came to Birmingham with the hope that the white religious leadership of this community would see the justice of our cause and, with deep moral concern, would serve as the channel through which our just grievances could reach the power structure. I had hoped that each of you would understand. But again I have been disappointed.

I have heard numerous southern religious leaders admonish their worshipers to comply with a desegregation decision because it is the law, but I have longed to hear white ministers declare: "Follow this decree because integration is morally right and because the Negro is your brother." In the midst of blatant injustices inflicted upon the Negro, I have watched white churchmen stand on the sideline and mouth pious irrelevancies and sanctimonious trivialities. In the midst of a mighty struggle to rid our nation of racial and economic injustice, I have heard many ministers say: "Those are social issues, with which the gospel has no real concern." And I have watched many churches commit themselves to a completely otherworldly religion which makes a strange, un-Biblical distinction between body and soul, between the sacred and the secular.

I have traveled the length and breadth of Alabama, Mississippi, and all the other southern states. On sweltering summer days and crisp autumn mornings I have looked at the South's beautiful churches with their lofty spires pointing heavenward. I have beheld the impressive outlines of her massive religious-education buildings. Over and over I have found myself asking: "What kind of people worship here? Who is their God? Where were their voices when the lips of Governor Barnett dripped with words of interposition and nullification? Where were they when Governor Wallace gave a clarion call for defiance and hatred? Where were their voices of support when bruised and weary Negro men and women decided to rise from the dark dungeons of complacency to the bright hills of creative protest?"

Yes, these questions are still in my mind. In deep disappointment I have wept over the laxity of the church. But be assured that my tears have been tears of love. There can be no deep disappointment where there is not deep love. Yes, I love the church. How could I do otherwise? I am in the rather unique position of being the son, the grandson, and the great-grandson of preachers. Yes, I see the church as the body of Christ. But, oh! How we have blemished and scarred that body through social neglect and through fear of being nonconformists.

There was a time when the church was very powerful—in the time when the early Christians rejoiced at being deemed worthy to suffer for what they believed. In those days the church was not merely a thermometer that recorded the ideas and principles of popular opinion; it was a thermostat that transformed the mores of society. Whenever the early Christians entered a town, the people in power became disturbed and immediately sought to convict the Christians for being "disturbers of the peace" and "outside agitators." But the Christians pressed on, in the conviction that they were "a colony of heaven," called to obey God rather than man. Small in number, they were big in commitment. They were too God-intoxicated to be "astronomically intimidated." By their effort and example they brought an end to such ancient evils as infanticide and gladiatorial contests.

Things are different now. So often the contemporary church is a weak, ineffectual voice with an uncertain sound. So often it is an archdefender of the status quo. Far from being disturbed by the presence of the church, the power structure of the average community is consoled by the church's silent—and often even vocal—sanction of things as they are.

But the judgment of God is upon the church as never before. If today's church does not recapture the sacrificial spirit of the early church, it will lose its authenticity, forfeit the loyalty of millions, and be dismissed as an irrelevant social club with no meaning for the twentieth century. Every day I meet young people whose disappointment with the church has turned into outright disgust.

Perhaps I have once again been too optimistic. Is organized religion too inextricably bound to the status quo to save our nation and the world? Perhaps I must turn my faith to the inner spiritual church, the church within the church, as the true *ekklesia* and the hope of the world. But again I am thankful to God that some noble souls from the ranks of organized religion have broken loose from the paralyzing chains of conformity and joined us as active partners in the struggle for freedom. They have left their secure congregations and walked the streets of Albany, Georgia, with us. They have gone down the highways of the South on tortuous rides for freedom. Yes, they have gone to jail with us. Some have been dismissed from their churches, have lost the support of their bishops and fellow ministers. But they have acted in the faith that right defeated is stronger than evil triumphant. Their witness has been the spiritual salt that has preserved the true meaning of the gospel in these troubled times. They have carved a tunnel of hope through the dark mountain of disappointment.

I hope the church as a whole will meet the challenge of this decisive hour. But even if the church does not come to the aid of justice, I have no despair about the future. I have no fear about the outcome of our struggle in Birmingham, even if our motives are at present misunderstood. We will reach the goal of freedom in Birmingham and all over the nation, because the goal of America is freedom. Abused and scorned though we may be, our destiny is tied up with America's destiny. Before the pilgrims landed at Plymouth, we were here. Before the pen of Jefferson etched the majestic words of the Declaration of Independence across the pages of history, we were here. For more than two centuries our forebears labored in this country without wages: they made cotton king; they built the homes of their masters while suffering gross injustice and shameful humiliation—and yet out of a bottomless vitality they continued to thrive and develop. If the inexpressible cruelties of slavery could not stop us, the opposition we now face will surely fail. We will win our freedom because the sacred heritage of our nation and the eternal will of God are embodied in our echoing demands.

Before closing I feel impelled to mention one other point in your statement that has troubled me profoundly. You warmly commended the Birmingham police force for keeping "order" and "preventing violence." I doubt that you would have so warmly commended the police force if you had seen its dogs sinking their teeth into unarmed, nonviolent Negroes. I doubt that you would so quickly commend the policemen if you were to observe their ugly and inhumane treatment of Negroes here in the city jail; if you were to watch them push and curse old Negro women and young Negro girls; if you were to see them slap and kick old Negro men and young boys; if you were to observe them, as they did on two occasions, refuse to give us food because we wanted to sing our grace together. I cannot join you in your praise of the Birmingham police department.

It is true that the police have exercised a degree of discipline in handling the demonstrators. In this sense they have conducted themselves rather "nonviolently" in public. But for what purpose? To preserve the evil system of segregation. Over the past few years I have consistently preached that nonviolence demands that the means we use must be as pure as the ends we seek. I have tried to make clear that it is wrong to use immoral means to attain moral ends. But now I must affirm that it is just as wrong, or perhaps even more so, to use moral means to preserve immoral ends. Perhaps Mr. Connor and his policemen have been rather nonviolent in public, as was Chief Pritchett in Albany, Georgia, but they have used the moral means of nonviolence to maintain the immoral end of racial injustice. As T. S. Eliot has said. "The last temptation is the greatest treason: To do the right deed for the wrong reason."

I wish you had commended the Negro sit-inners and demonstrators of Birmingham for their sublime courage, their willingness to suffer, and their amazing discipline in the midst of great provocation. One day the South will recognize its real heroes. They will be the James Merediths, with the noble sense of purpose that enables them to face jeering and hostile mobs, and with the agonizing loneliness that characterizes the life of the pioneer. They will be old, oppressed, battered Negro women, symbolized in a seventy-two-year-old woman in Montgomery, Alabama, who rose up with a sense of dignity and with her people decided not to ride segregated buses, and who responded with ungrammatical profundity to one who inquired about her weariness: "My feets is tired, but my soul is at rest." They will be the young high school and college students, the young ministers of the gospel and a host of their elders, courageously and nonviolently sitting in at lunch counters and willingly going to jail for conscience' sake. One day the South will know that when these disinherited children of God sat down at lunch counters, they were in reality standing up for what is best in the American dream and for the most sacred values in our Judaeo-Christian heritage, thereby bringing our nation back to those great wells of democracy which were dug deep by the founding fathers in their formulation of the Constitution and the Declaration of Independence.

Never before have I written so long a letter. I'm afraid it is much too long to take your precious time. I can assure you that it would have been much shorter if I had been writing from a comfortable desk, but what else can one do when he is alone in a narrow jail cell, other than write long letters, think long thoughts, and pray long prayers?

If I have said anything in this letter that overstates the truth and indicates an unreasonable impatience, I beg you to forgive me. If I have said anything that understates the truth and indicates my having a patience that allows me to settle for anything less than brotherhood, I beg God to forgive me.

I hope this letter finds you strong in the faith. I also hope that circumstances will soon make it possible for me to meet each of you, not as an integrationist or a civil-rights leader but as a fellow clergyman and a Christian brother. Let us all hope that the dark clouds of racial prejudice will soon pass away and the deep fog of misunderstanding will be lifted from our fear-drenched communities, and in some not too distant tomorrow the radiant stars of love and brotherhood will shine over our great nation with all their scintillating beauty.

> Yours for the cause of Peace and Brotherhood,
> MARTIN LUTHER KING, JR.

Possibilities for Writing

1. King's letter is a classic example of refutation, taking arguments made against one's opinions or actions and showing why they are wrong or incomplete. In an essay, note each point made in the statement condemning King's actions that King sets out to refute. How does he go about doing so? How do you respond to his arguments?

2. King is writing here to white moderates who say, in his words, "I agree with you in the goal you seek, but I cannot agree with your methods of direct action." In what ways has he tailored his arguments to such an audience? How does his tone reveal his understanding of this audience?

3. King makes a distinction between "just" and "unjust" laws. How does he define an "unjust" law? Do you agree with his definition? Point to any current examples of laws that you think are unjust, and explain why you feel as you do.

Maxine Hong Kingston (b. 1940) grew up in Stockton, California, the daughter of Chinese immigrants in a close-knit Asian community; her first language was a dialect of Chinese. She graduated from the University of California at Berkeley and went on to teach high school English in California and Hawaii. Her award-winning The Woman Warrior: Memoirs of a Childhood Among Ghosts *(1976) is an impressionistic remembrance of the stories she grew up with concerning women in her culture, both real and legendary. Its companion volume focusing on images of manhood,* China Men, *followed in 1980. Kingston has also published a novel,* Tripmaster Monkey: His Fake Book *(1989). She is currently a senior lecturer at her alma mater and was awarded a National Humanities Medal by President Clinton in 1997.*

Maxine Hong Kingston
On Discovery

"On Discovery" is an unusual piece of writing. An excerpt from Kingston's book *China Men*, "On Discovery" tells the story of a man who became a woman. Encased within Kingston's hybrid factual/fictional prose of the book, as a whole, is this parable about gender and identity. It's a prose piece that invites consideration of how gender identity is formed and why it is such a powerful cultural construct.

Tang Ao's odyssey takes him/her on a journey that could only be imagined, and one that ends with a shift in how Tang Ao imagines him/her self. In Tang Ao's transformation from man to woman, Tang Ao undergoes as much an inner, psychological change as an external one.

In Tang Ao's case, the transformation was neither desired not sought. But neither was it resisted when it was forced upon Tang Ao. It is a metamorphosis that Kingston's readers can hardly believe and certainly never forget.

Once upon a time, a man, named Tang Ao, looking for the Gold Mountain, crossed an ocean, and came upon the Land of Women. The women immediately captured him, not on guard against ladies. When they asked Tang Ao to come along, he followed; if he had had male companions, he would've winked over his shoulder.

"We have to prepare you to meet the queen," the women said. They locked him in a canopied apartment equipped with pots of makeup, mirrors, and a woman's clothes. "Let us help you off with your armor and boots," said the women. They slipped his coat off his shoulders, pulled it down his arms, and shackled his wrists behind him. The women who kneeled to take off his shoes chained his ankles together.

A door opened, and he expected to meet his match, but it was only two old women with sewing boxes in their hands. "The less you struggle, the less it'll hurt," one said, squinting a bright eye as she threaded her needle. Two captors sat on him while another held his head. He felt an old woman's dry fingers trace his ear; the long nail on her little finger scraped his neck. "What are you doing?" he asked. "Sewing your lips together," she joked, blackening needles in a candle flame. The ones who sat on him bounced with laughter. But the old woman did not sew his lips together. They pulled his earlobes taut and jabbed a needle through each of them. They had to poke and probe before puncturing the layers of skin correctly, the hole in the front of the lobe in line with one in back, the layers of skin sliding about so. They worked the needle through—a last jerk for the needle's wide eye ("needle's nose" in Chinese). They strung his raw flesh with silk threads; he could feel the fibers.

The women who sat on him turned to direct their attention to his feet. They bent his toes so far backward that his arched foot cracked. The old ladies squeezed each foot and broke many tiny bones along the sides. They gathered his toes, toes over and under one another like a knot of ginger root. Tang Ao wept with pain. As they wound the bandages tight and tighter around his feet, the women sang foot-binding songs to distract him: "Use aloe for binding feet and not for scholars."

During the months of a season, they fed him on women's food: the tea was thick with white chrysanthemums and stirred the cool female winds inside his body; chicken wings made his hair shine; vinegar soup improved his womb. They drew the loops of thread through the scabs that grew daily over the holes in his earlobes. One day they inserted gold hoops. Every night they unbound his feet, but his veins had shrunk, and the blood pumping through them hurt so much, he begged to have his feet rewrapped tight. They forced him to wash his used bandages, which were embroidered with flowers and smelled of rot and cheese. He hung the bandages up to dry, streamers that drooped and draped wall to wall. He felt embarrassed; the wrapping were like underwear, and they were his.

One day his attendants changed his gold hoops to jade studs and strapped his feet to shoes that curved like bridges. They plucked out each hair on his face, powdered him white, painted his eyebrows like a moth's wings, painted his cheeks and lips red. He served a meal at the queen's court. His hips swayed and his shoulders swiveled because of his shaped feet. "She's pretty, don't you agree?" the diners said, smacking their lips at his dainty feet as he bent to put dishes before them.

In the Women's Land there are no taxes and no wars. Some scholars say that that country was discovered during the reign of Empress Wu (A.D. 694–705), and some say earlier than that, A.D. 441, and it was in North America.

Possibilities for Writing

1. What is Kingston's central idea in "On Discovery"? To what extent is this piece about gender switching? About gender roles? About power?
2. What ironies does Kingston play up in "On Discovery"? Consider both verbal irony and irony of situation—that is, ironic comments and ironic developments in the action.
3. Discuss the following comment by Simone de Beauvoir in relation to "On Discovery": "One is not born a woman; one becomes a woman."

Charles Lamb (1775–1834) was born in London, where he focused his literary career. As a critic, he was noted for his Specimens of English Dramatic Poets *(1808), and he and his sister collaborated on the highly successful* Tales from Shakespeare *(1807). A playwright and contributor to many periodicals, Lamb is best remembered today for his* Essays of Elia, *written for* London Magazine *between 1820 and 1825 and published in collections in 1823 and 1833. His individual style, ranging from deeply felt personal observations to whimsical flights of fancy, made his work widely popular in his day, and he has long been considered one of the greatest of English essayists.*

Charles Lamb

A Bachelor's Complaint

In "A Bachelor's Complaint," Charles Lamb protests against the married state as superior to and happier than the state of bachelorhood. Lamb amuses himself and his readers by laying out the many reasons why he believes marriage to be both less interesting and less attractive than bachelorhood as a way of life. Lamb takes affront on every side, from a married woman's difference of opinion with him to the complacency and self-sufficiency of the married, a complacency and self-sufficiency that he, by implied contrast, is not fit to share.

Lamb reserves his most serious criticism and his loudest complaints for married couples with children, not because he has anything against children in and of themselves, but because, as a bachelor, he is presumed either to be uninterested in them, or is expected to find joy in their presence simply because they are the children of his friends. What troubles Lamb most, however, as a bachelor friend of a married couple, is that the nature of his friendship with the husband is irreparably altered by the injection of the wife into the equation. Yet however much Lamb catalogues his complaints against marriage, children, and family life, he does so in a comic spirit.

As a single man, I have spent a good deal of my time in noting down the infirmities of Married People, to console myself for those superior pleasures, which they tell me I have lost by remaining as I am.

I cannot say that the quarrels of men and their wives ever made any great impression upon me, or had much tendency to strengthen me in those antisocial resolutions, which I took up long ago upon more substantial considerations. What oftenest offends me at the houses of married persons where I visit, is an error of quite a different description; it is that they are too loving.

Not too loving neither: that does not explain my meaning. Besides, why should that offend me? The very act of separating themselves from the rest of the world, to have the fuller enjoyment of each other's society, implies that they prefer one another to all the world.

But what I complain of is, that they carry this preference so undisguisedly, they perk it up in the faces of us single people so shamelessly, you cannot be in their company a moment without being made to feel, by some indirect hint or open avowal, that you are not the object of this preference. Now there are some things which give no offence, while implied or taken for granted merely; but expressed, there is much offence in them.

If a man were to accost the first homely-featured or plain-dressed young woman of his acquaintance, and tell her bluntly, that she was not handsome or rich enough for him, and he could not marry her, he would deserve to be kicked for his ill manners; yet no less is implied in the fact, that having access and opportunity of putting the question to her, he has never yet thought fit to do it. The young woman understands this as clearly as if it were put into words; but no reasonable young woman would think of making this the ground of a quarrel. Just as little right have a married couple to tell me by speeches, and looks that are scarce less plain than speeches, that I am not the happy man—the lady's choice. It is enough that I know I am not: I do not want this perpetual reminding.

The display of superior knowledge or riches may be made sufficiently mortifying; but these admit of a palliative. The knowledge which is brought out to insult me, may accidentally improve me: and in the rich man's houses and pictures, his parks and gardens, I have a temporary usufruct at least. But the display of married happiness has none of these palliatives: it is throughout pure, unrecompensed, unqualified insult.

Marriage by its best title is a monopoly, and not of the least invidious sort. It is the cunning of most possessors of any exclusive privilege to keep their advantage as much out of sight as possible, that their less favoured neighbours, seeing little of the benefit, may the less be disposed to question the right. But these married monopolists thrust the most obnoxious part of their patent into our faces.

Nothing is to me more distasteful than that entire complacency and satisfaction which beam in the countenances of a new-married couple—in that of the lady particularly: it tells you, that her lot is disposed of in this world: that you can have no hopes of her. It is true, I have none: nor wishes either, perhaps; but this is one of those truths which ought, as I said before, to be taken for granted, not expressed.

The excessive airs which those people give themselves, founded on the ignorance of us unmarried people, would be more offensive if they were less irrational. We will allow them to understand the mysteries belonging to their own craft better than we, who have not had the happiness to be made free of the company: but their arrogance is not content within these limits. If a single person presume to offer his opinion in their presence, though upon the most indifferent subject, he is immediately silenced as an incompetent person. Nay, a young married lady of my acquaintance, who, the best of the jest was, had not changed her condition above a fortnight before, in a question on which I had the misfortune to differ from her, respecting the properest mode of breeding oysters for the London market, had the assurance to ask with a sneer, how such an old Bachelor as I could pretend to know anything about such matters!

But what I have spoken of hitherto is nothing to the airs these creatures give themselves when they come, as they generally do, to have children. When I consider how little of a rarity children are—that every street and blind alley swarms with them—that the poorest people commonly have them in most abundance—that there are few marriages that are not blest with at least one of these bargains—how often they turn out ill, and defeat the fond hopes of their parents, taking to vicious courses, which end in poverty, disgrace, the gallows, etc.—I cannot for my life tell what cause for pride there can possibly be in having them. If they were young phoenixes, indeed, that were born but one in a year, there might be a pretext. But when they are so common . . . .

I do not advert to the insolent merit which they assume with their husbands on these occasions. Let *them* look to that. But why we who are not their natural-born subjects, should be expected to bring our spices, myrrh, and incense—our tribute and homage of admiration—I do not see.

"Like as the arrows in the hand of the giant, even so are the young children": so says the excellent office in our Prayer-book appointed for the churching of women. "Happy is the man that hath his quiver full of them." So say I; but then don't let him discharge his quiver upon us that are weaponless; let them be arrows, but not to gall and stick us. I have generally observed that these arrows are double-headed: they have two forks, to be sure to hit with one or the other. As for instance, where you come into a house which is full of children, if you happen to take no notice of them (you are thinking of something else, perhaps, and turn a deaf ear to their innocent caresses), you are set down as untractable, morose, a hater of children. On the other hand, if you find them more than usually engaging—if you are taken with their pretty manners, and set about in earnest to romp and play with them, some pretext or other is sure to be found for sending them out of the room; they are too noisy or boisterous, or Mr. ——— does not like children. With one or other of these folks the arrow is sure to hit you.

I could forgive their jealousy, and dispense with toying with their brats, if it gives them any pain; but I think it unreasonable to be called upon to *love* them, where I see no occasion—to love a whole family, perhaps eight, nine, or ten, indiscriminately—to love all the pretty dears, because children are so engaging!

I know there is a proverb. "Love me, love my dog": that is not always so very practicable, particularly if the dog be set upon you to tease you or snap at you in sport. But a dog, or a lesser thing—any inanimate substance, as a keepsake, a watch or a ring, a tree, or the place where we last parted when my friend went away upon a long absence, I can make shift to love, because I love him, and anything that reminds me of him; provided it be in its nature indifferent, and apt to receive whatever hue fancy can give it. But children have a real character, and an essential being of themselves: they are amiable or unamiable *per se;* I must love or hate them as I see cause for either in their qualities.

A child's nature is too serious a thing to admit of its being regarded as a mere appendage to another being, and to be loved or hated accordingly: they stand with me upon their own stock, as much as men and women do. Oh! but you will say, sure it is an attractive age—there is something in the tender years of infancy that of itself charms us? This is the very reason why I am more nice about them. I know that a sweet child is the sweetest thing in nature, not even excepting the delicate creatures which bear them; but the prettier the kind of a thing is, the more desirable it is that it should be pretty of its kind. One daisy differs not much from another in glory; but a violet should look and smell the daintiest. I was always rather squeamish in my women and children.

But this is not the worst: (one must be admitted into their familiarity at least, before they can complain of inattention.) It implies visits, and some kind of intercourse. But if the husband be a man with whom you have lived on a friendly footing before marriage—if you did not come in on the wife's side—if you did not sneak into the house in her train, but were an old friend in fast habits of intimacy before their courtship was so much as thought on—look about you—your tenure is precarious—before a twelvemonth shall roll over your head, you shall find your old friend gradually grow cool and altered towards you, and at last seek opportunities of breaking with you.

I have scarce a married friend of my acquaintance, upon whose firm faith I can rely, whose friendship did not commence *after the period of his marriage.* With some limitations, they can endure that; but that the good man should have dared to enter into a solemn league of friendship in which they were not consulted, though it happened before they knew him—before they that are now man and wife ever met—this is intolerable to them. Every long friendship, every old authentic intimacy, must be brought into their office to be new stamped with their currency, as a sovereign prince calls in the good old money that was coined in some reign before he was born or thought of, to be new marked and minted with the stamp of his authority, before he will let it pass current in the world. You may guess what luck generally befalls such a rusty piece of metal as I am in these *new mintings.*

Innumerable are the ways which they take to insult and worm you out of their husband's confidence. Laughing at all you say with a kind of wonder, as if you were a queer kind of fellow that said good things, *but an oddity,* is one of the ways—they have a particular kind of stare for the purpose—till at last the husband, who used to defer to your judgment, and would pass over some excrescences of understanding and manner for the sake of a general vein of observation (not quite vulgar) which he perceived in you, begins to suspect whether you are not altogether a humourist—a fellow well enough to have consorted with in his bachelor days, but not quite so proper to be introduced to ladies. This may be called the staring way; and is that which has oftenest been put in practice against me.

Then there is the exaggerating way, or the way of irony: that is, where they find you an object of especial regard with their husband, who is not so easily to be shaken from the lasting attachment founded on esteem which he has conceived towards you, by never qualified exaggerations to cry up all that you say or do, till the good man, who understands well enough that it is all done in compliment to him, grows weary of the debt of gratitude which is due to so much candour, and by relaxing a little on his part, and taking down a peg or two in his enthusiasm, sinks at length to the kindly level of moderate esteem—that "decent affection and complacent kindness" towards you, where she herself can join in sympathy with him without much stretch and violence to her sincerity.

Another way (for the ways they have to accomplish so desirable a purpose are infinite) is, with a kind of innocent simplicity, continually to mistake what it was which first made their husband fond of you. If an esteem for something excellent in your moral character was that which riveted the chain which she is to break, upon any imaginary discovery of a want of poignancy in your conversation, she will cry, "I thought, my dear, you described your friend, Mr. ———, as a great wit?" If, on the other hand, it was for some supposed charm in your conversation that he first grew to like you, and was content for this to overlook some trifling irregularities in your moral deportment, upon the first notice of any of these she as readily exclaims, "This, my dear, is your good Mr. ———!"

One good lady whom I took the liberty of expostulating with for not showing me quite so much respect as I thought due to her husband's old friend, had the candour to confess to me that she had often heard Mr. ——— speak of me before marriage, and that she had conceived a great desire to be acquainted with me, but that the sight of me had very much disappointed her expectations; for from her husband's representations of me, she had formed a notion that she was to see a fine, tall, officer-like-looking man (I use her very words), the very reverse of which proved to be the truth.

This was candid; and I had the civility not to ask her in return, how she came to pitch upon a standard of personal accomplishments for her husband's friends which differed so much from his own; for my friend's dimensions as near as possible approximate to mine: he standing five feet five in his shoes, in which I have the advantage of him by about half an inch; and he no more than myself exhibiting any indications of a martial character in his air or countenance.

These are some of the mortifications which I have encountered in the absurd attempt to visit at their houses. To enumerate them all would be a vain endeavour; I shall therefore just glance at the very common impropriety of which married ladies are guilty—of treating us as if we were their husbands, and vice versa. I mean, when they use us with familiarity, and their husbands with ceremony. *Testacea*, for instance, kept me the other night two or three hours beyond my usual time of supping, while she was fretting because Mr. —— did not come home, till the oysters were all spoiled, rather than she would be guilty of the impoliteness of touching one in his absence.

This was reversing the point of good manners: for ceremony is an invention to take off the uneasy feeling which we derive from knowing ourselves to be less the object of love and esteem with a fellow-creature than some other person is. It endeavours to make up, by superior attentions in little points, for that invidious preference which it is forced to deny in the greater. Had *Testacea* kept the oysters back for me, and withstood her husband's importunities to go to supper, she would have acted according to the strict rules of propriety.

I know no ceremony that ladies are bound to observe to their husbands, beyond the point of a modest behaviour and decorum: therefore I must protest against the vicarious gluttony of *Cerasia*, who at her own table sent away a dish of Morellas, which I was applying to with great goodwill, to her husband at the other end of the table, and recommended a plate of less extraordinary gooseberries to my unwedded palate in their stead. Neither can I excuse the wanton affront of ——.

But I am weary of stringing up all my married acquaintances by Roman denominations. Let them amend and change their manners, or I promise to record the full-length English of their names, to the terror of all such desperate offenders in future.

Possibilities for Writing

1. Explore Lamb's specific complaints about married couples here. How can you tell the extent to which he is serious or is exaggerating for comic effect?

2. Would unmarried friends today offer similar complaints about their married friends and their children? Are there any additional complaints that are pertinent to contemporary life?

3. Write an essay in which you describe some chronic complaints of your own relating to the behavior of a certain group of people that you number among your friends.

Chang-Rae Lee *(b. 1965) was born in Seoul, South Korea, and his family immigrated to the United States when he was three. He grew up in New York's Westchester County, where his father was a successful psychiatrist. After graduating from Yale University, he worked for a year as an analyst on Wall Street before completing his M.F.A. at the University of Oregon. He currently teaches in the creative writing program at Hunter College of the City University of New York. His works, which focus on the lives of contemporary Asian Americans, include the prize-winning* Native Speaker *(1995),* A Gesture Life *(1999), and* Aloft *(2004).*

Chang-Rae Lee
Coming Home Again

In "Coming Home Again," Chang-Rae Lee describes living at home with his family after attending boarding school and college. Lee's sister is living at home too, having recently resigned from her job in the city, and his father, a psychiatrist who typically worked until late in the evening seeing his patients, is returning from work in the late afternoon. The reason is simply that Lee's mother is dying of cancer, and he, with the others, is pitching in to try to lend an air of normalcy to their family lives.

The heart of Lee's essay is his description of his mother cooking. Lee flashes back to the time when, as a six- or seven-year-old child, he would "enter the kitchen quietly and stand beside her, [his] chin lodging upon the point of her hip." Lee presents in meticulous and vivid detail his mother's virtuoso movements with knives—dicing, slicing, mincing, scoring, and otherwise readying meat and poultry for seasoning and soaking in her specially prepared marinades. He learns to cook by watching her, and he inherits her knack for knowing just how much of each ingredient to include, just how much seasoning to add, and just how long to cook each of his mother's Korean specialties.

When my mother began using the electronic pump that fed her liquids and medication, we moved her to the family room. The bedroom she shared with my father was upstairs, and it was impossible to carry the machine up and down all day and night. The pump itself was attached to a metal stand on casters, and she pulled it along wherever she went. From anywhere in the house, you could hear the sound of the wheels clicking out a steady time over the grout lines of the slate-tiled foyer, her main thoroughfare to the bathroom and the kitchen. Sometimes you would hear her halt after only a few steps, to catch her breath or steady her balance, and whatever you were doing was instantly suspended by a pall of silence.

I was usually in the kitchen, preparing lunch or dinner, poised over the butcher block with her favorite chef's knife in my hand and her old yellow apron slung around my neck. I'd be breathless in the sudden quiet, and, having ceased my mincing and chopping, would stare blankly at the brushed sheen of the blade. Eventually, she would clear her throat or call out to say she was fine, then begin to move again, starting her rhythmic *ka-jug*; and only then could I go on with my cooking, the world of our house turning once more, wheeling through the black.

I wasn't cooking for my mother but for the rest of us. When she first moved downstairs she was still eating, though scantily, more just to taste what we were having than from any genuine desire for food. The point was simply to sit together at the kitchen table and array ourselves like a family again. My mother would gently set herself down in her customary chair near the stove. I sat across from her, my father and sister to my left and right, and crammed in the center was all the food I had made—a spicy codfish stew, say, or a casserole of gingery beef, dishes that in my youth she had prepared for us a hundred times.

It had been ten years since we'd all lived together in the house, which at fifteen I had left to attend boarding school in New Hampshire. My mother would sometimes point this out, by speaking of our present time as being "just like before Exeter," which surprised me, given how proud she always was that I was a graduate of the school.

My going to such a place was part of my mother's not so secret plan to change my character, which she worried was becoming too much like hers. I was clever and able enough, but without outside pressure I was readily given to sloth and vanity. The famous school —which none of us knew the first thing about—would prove my mettle. She was right, of course, and while I was there I would falter more than a few times, academically and otherwise. But I never thought that my leaving home then would ever be a problem for her, a private quarrel she would have even as her life waned.

Now her house was full again. My sister had just resigned from her job in New York City, and my father, who typically saw his psychiatric patients until eight or nine in the evening, was appearing in the driveway at four-thirty. I had been living at home for nearly a year and was in the final push of work on what would prove a dismal failure of a novel. When I wasn't struggling over my prose, I kept occupied with the things she usually did—the daily errands, the grocery shopping, the vacuuming and the cleaning, and, of course, all the cooking.

When I was six or seven years old, I used to watch my mother as she prepared our favorite meals. It was one of my daily pleasures. She shooed me away in the beginning, telling me that the kitchen wasn't my place, and adding, in her half-proud, half-deprecating way, that her kind of work would only serve to weaken me. "Go out and play with your friends," she'd snap in Korean, "or better yet, do your reading and homework." She knew that I had already done both, and that as the evening approached there was no place to go save her small and tidy kitchen, from which the clatter of her mixing bowls and pans would ring through the house.

I would enter the kitchen quietly and stand beside her, my chin lodging upon the point of her hip. Peering through the crook of her arm, I beheld the movements of her hands. For *kalbi*, she would take up a butchered short rib in her narrow hand, the flinty bone shaped like a section of an airplane wing and deeply embedded in gristle and flesh, and with the point of her knife cut so that the bone fell away, though not completely, leaving it connected to the meat by the barest opaque layer of tendon. Then she methodically butterflied the flesh, cutting and unfolding, repeating the action until the meat lay out on her board, glistening and ready for seasoning. She scored it diagonally, then sifted sugar into the crevices with her pinched fingers, gently rubbing in the crystals. The sugar would tenderize as well as sweeten the meat. She did this with each rib, and then set them all aside in a large shallow bowl. She minced a half-dozen cloves of garlic, a stub of ginger-root, sliced up a few scallions, and spread it all over the meat. She wiped her hands and took out a bottle of sesame oil, and, after pausing for a moment, streamed the dark oil in two swift circles around the bowl. After adding a few splashes of soy sauce, she thrust her hands in and kneaded the flesh, careful not to dislodge the bones. I asked her why it mattered that they remain connected. "The meat needs the bone nearby," she said, "to borrow its richness." She wiped her hands clean of the marinade, except for her little finger, which she would flick with her tongue from time to time, because she knew that the flavor of a good dish developed not at once but in stages.

Whenever I cook, I find myself working just as she would, readying the ingredients—a mash of garlic, a julienne of red peppers, fantails of shrimp—and piling them in little mounds about the cutting surface. My mother never left me any recipes, but this is how I learned to make her food, each dish coming not from a list or a card but from the aromatic spread of a board.

I've always thought it was particularly cruel that the cancer was in her stomach, and that for a long time at the end she couldn't eat. The last meal I made for her was on New Year's Eve, 1990. My sister suggested that instead of a rib roast or a bird, or the usual overflow of Korean food, we make all sorts of finger dishes that our mother might fancy and pick at.

We set the meal out on the glass coffee table in the family room. I prepared a tray of smoked-salmon canapés, fried some Korean bean cakes, and made a few other dishes I thought she might enjoy. My sister supervised me, arranging the platters, and then with some pomp carried each dish in to our parents. Finally, I brought out a bottle of champagne in a bucket of ice. My mother had moved to the sofa and was sitting up, surveying the low table. "It looks pretty nice," she said. "I think I'm feeling hungry."

This made us all feel good, especially me, for I couldn't remember the last time she had felt any hunger or had eaten something I cooked. We began to eat. My mother picked up a piece of salmon toast and took a tiny corner in her mouth. She rolled it around for a moment and then pushed it out with the tip of her tongue, letting it fall back onto her plate. She swallowed hard, as if to quell a gag, then glanced up to see if we had noticed. Of course we all had. She attempted a bean cake, some cheese, and then a slice of fruit, but nothing was any use.

She nodded at me anyway, and said, "Oh, it's very good." But I was already feeling lost and I put down my plate abruptly, nearly shattering it on the thick glass. There was an ugly pause before my father asked me in a weary, gentle voice if anything was wrong, and I answered that it was nothing, it was the last night of a long year, and we were together, and I was simply relieved. At midnight, I poured out glasses of champagne, even one for my mother, who took a deep sip. Her manner grew playful and light, and I helped her shuffle to her mattress, and she lay down in the place where in a brief week she was dead.

My mother could whip up most anything, but during our first years of living in this country we ate only Korean foods. At my harangue-like behest, my mother set herself to learning how to cook exotic American dishes. Luckily, a kind neighbor, Mrs. Churchill, a tall, florid young woman with flaxen hair, taught my mother her most trusted recipes. Mrs. Churchill's two young sons, palish, weepy boys with identical crew cuts, always accompanied her, and though I liked them well enough, I would slip away from them after a few minutes, for I knew that the real action would be in the kitchen, where their mother was playing guide. Mrs. Churchill hailed from the state of Maine, where the finest Swedish meatballs and tuna casserole and angel food cake in America are made. She readily demonstrated certain techniques—how to layer wet sheets of pasta for a lasagna or whisk up a simple roux, for example. She often brought gift shoeboxes containing curious ingredients like dried oregano, instant yeast, and cream of mushroom soup. The two women, though at ease and jolly with each other, had difficulty communicating, and this was made worse by the often confusing terminology of Western cuisine ("corned beef," "deviled eggs"). Although I was just learning the language myself, I'd gladly play the interlocutor, jumping back and forth between their places at the counter, dipping my fingers into whatever sauce lay about.

I was an insistent child, and, being my mother's firstborn, much too prized. My mother could say no to me, and did often enough, but anyone who knew us—particularly my father and sister—could tell how much the denying pained her. And if I was overconscious of her indulgence even then, and suffered the rushing pangs of guilt that she could inflict upon me with the slightest wounded turn of her lip, I was too happily obtuse and venal to let her cease. She reminded me daily that I was her sole son, her reason for living, and that if she were to lose me, in either body or spirit, she wished that God would mercifully smite her, strike her down like a weak branch.

In the traditional fashion, she was the house accountant, the maid, the launderer, the disciplinarian, the driver, the secretary, and, of course, the cook. She was also my first basketball coach. In South Korea, where girls' high school basketball is a popular spectator sport, she had been a star, the point guard for the national high school team that once won the all-Asia championships. I learned this one Saturday during the summer, when I asked my father if he would go down to the schoolyard and shoot some baskets with me. I had just finished the fifth grade, and wanted desperately to make the middle school team the coming fall. He called for my mother and sister to come along. When we arrived, my sister immediately ran off to the swings, and I recall being annoyed that my mother wasn't following her. I dribbled clumsily around the key, on the verge of losing control of the ball, and flung a flat shot that caromed wildly off the rim. The ball bounced to my father, who took a few not so graceful dribbles and made an easy layup. He dribbled out and then drove to the hoop for a layup on the other side. He rebounded his shot and passed the ball to my mother, who had been watching us from the foul line. She turned from the basket and began heading the other way.

"Um-mah," I cried at her, my exasperation already bubbling over, "the basket's over *here!"*

After a few steps she turned around, and from where the professional three-point line must be now, she effortlessly flipped the ball up in a two-handed set shot, its flight truer and higher than I'd witnessed from any boy or man. The ball arced cleanly into the hoop, stiffly popping the chain-link net. All afternoon, she rained in shot after shot, as my father and I scrambled after her.

When we got home from the playground, my mother showed me the photograph album of her team's championship run. For years I kept it in my room, on the same shelf that housed the scrapbooks I made of basketball stars, with magazine clippings of slick players like Bubbles Hawkins and Pistol Pete and George (the Iceman) Gervin.

It puzzled me how much she considered her own history to be immaterial, and if she never patently diminished herself, she was able to finesse a kind of self-removal by speaking of my father whenever she could. She zealously recounted his excellence as a student in medical school and reminded me, each night before I started my homework, of how hard he drove himself in his work to make a life for us. She said that because of his Asian face and imperfect English, he was "working two times the American doctors." I knew that she was building him up, buttressing him with both genuine admiration and her own brand of anxious braggadocio, and that her overarching concern was that I might fail to see him as she wished me to—in the most dawning light, his pose steadfast and solitary.

In the year before I left for Exeter, I became weary of her oft-repeated accounts of my father's success. I was a teenager, and so ever inclined to be dismissive and bitter toward anything that had to do with family and home. Often enough, my mother was the object of my derision. Suddenly, her life seemed so small to me. She was there, and sometimes, I thought, *always* there, as if she were confined to the four walls of our house. I would even complain about her cooking. Mostly, though, I was getting more and more impatient with the difficulty she encountered in doing everyday things. I was afraid for her. One day, we got into a terrible argument when she asked me to call the bank, to question a discrepancy she had discovered in the monthly statement. I asked her why she couldn't call herself. I was stupid and brutal, and I knew exactly how to wound her.

"Whom do I talk to?" she said. She would mostly speak to me in Korean, and I would answer in English.

"The bank manager, who else?"

"What do I say?"

"Whatever you want to say."

"Don't speak to me like that!" she cried.

"It's just that you should be able to do it yourself," I said.

"You know how I feel about this!"

"Well, maybe then you should consider it *practice*," I answered lightly, using the Korean word to make sure she understood.

Her face blanched, and her neck suddenly became rigid, as if I were throttling her. She nearly struck me right then, but instead she bit her lip and ran upstairs. I followed her, pleading for forgiveness at her door. But it was the one time in our life that I couldn't convince her, melt her resolve with the blandishments of a spoiled son.

When my mother was feeling strong enough, or was in particularly good spirits, she would roll her machine into the kitchen and sit at the table and watch me work. She wore pajamas day and night, mostly old pairs of mine.

She said, "I can't tell, what are you making?"

"*Mahn-doo* filling."

"You didn't salt the cabbage and squash."

"Was I supposed to?"

"Of course. Look, it's too wet. Now the skins will get soggy before you can fry them."

"What should I do?"

"It's too late. Maybe it'll be OK if you work quickly. Why didn't you ask me?"

"You were finally sleeping."

"You should have woken me."

"No way."

She sighed, as deeply as her weary lungs would allow.

"I don't know how you were going to make it without me."

"I don't know, either. I'll remember the salt next time."

"You better. And not too much."

We often talked like this, our tone decidedly matter-of-fact, chin up, just this side of being able to bear it. Once, while inspecting a potato fritter batter I was making, she asked me if she had ever done anything that I wished she hadn't done. I thought for a moment, and told her no. In the next breath, she wondered aloud if it was right of her to have let me go to Exeter, to live away from the house while I was so young. She tested the batter's thickness with her finger and called for more flour. Then she asked if, given a choice, I would go to Exeter again.

I wasn't sure what she was getting at, and I told her that I couldn't be certain, but probably yes, I would. She snorted at this and said it was my leaving home that had once so troubled our relationship. "Remember how I had so much difficulty talking to you? Remember?"

She believed back then that I had found her more and more ignorant each time I came home. She said she never blamed me, for this was the way she knew it would be with my wonderful new education. Nothing I could say seemed to quell the notion. But I knew that the problem wasn't simply the *education*; the first time I saw her again after starting school, barely six weeks later, when she and my father visited me on Parents Day, she had already grown nervous and distant. After the usual campus events, we had gone to the motel where they were staying in a nearby town and sat on the beds in our room. She seemed to sneak looks at me, as though I might discover a horrible new truth if our eyes should meet.

My own secret feeling was that I had missed my parents greatly, my mother especially, and much more than I had anticipated. I couldn't tell them that these first weeks were a mere blur to me, that I felt completely overwhelmed by all the studies and my much brighter friends and the thousand irritating details of living alone, and that I had really learned nothing, save perhaps how to put on a necktie while sprinting to class. I felt as if I had plunged too deep into the world, which, to my great horror, was much larger than I had ever imagined.

I welcomed the lull of the motel room. My father and I had nearly dozed off when my mother jumped up excitedly, murmured how stupid she was, and hurried to the closet by the door. She pulled out our old metal cooler and dragged it between the beds. She lifted the top and began unpacking plastic containers, and I thought she would never stop. One after the other they came out, each with a dish that traveled well—a salted stewed meat, rolls of Korean-style sushi. I opened a container of radish kimchi and suddenly the room bloomed with its odor, and I reveled in the very peculiar sensation (which perhaps only true kimchi lovers know) of simultaneously drooling and gagging as I breathed it all in. For the next few minutes, they watched me eat. I'm not certain that I was even hungry. But after weeks of pork parmigiana and chicken patties and wax beans, I suddenly realized that I had lost all the savor in my life. And it seemed I couldn't get enough of it back. I ate and I ate, so much and so fast that I actually went to the bathroom and vomited. I came out dizzy and sated with the phantom warmth of my binge.

And beneath the face of her worry, I thought, my mother was smiling.

From that day, my mother prepared a certain meal to welcome me home. It was always the same. Even as I rode the school's shuttle bus from Exeter to Logan airport, I could already see the exact arrangement of my mother's table.

I knew that we would eat in the kitchen, the table brimming with plates. There was the *kalbi* of course, broiled or grilled depending on the season. Leaf lettuce, to wrap the meat with. Bowls of garlicky clam broth with miso and tofu and fresh spinach. Shavings of cod dusted in flour and then dipped in egg wash and fried. Glass noodles with onions and shiitake. Scallion-and-hot-pepper pancakes. Chilled steamed shrimp. Seasoned salads of bean sprouts, spinach, and white radish. Crispy squares of seaweed. Steamed rice with barley and red beans. Homemade kimchi. It was all there—the old flavors I knew, the beautiful salt, the sweet, the excellent taste.

After the meal, my father and I talked about school, but I could never say enough for it to make any sense. My father would often recall his high school principal, who had gone to England to study the methods and traditions of the public schools, and regaled students with stories of the great Eton man. My mother sat with us, paring fruit, not saying a word but taking everything in. When it was time to go to bed, my father said good night first. I usually watched television until the early morning. My mother would sit with me for an hour or two, perhaps until she was accustomed to me again, and only then would she kiss me and head upstairs to sleep.

During the following days, it was always the cooking that started our conversations. She'd hold an inquest over the cold leftovers we ate at lunch, discussing each dish in terms of its balance of flavors or what might have been prepared differently. But mostly I begged her to leave the dishes alone. I wish I had paid more attention. After her death, when my father and I were the only ones left in the house, drifting through the rooms like ghosts, I sometimes tried to make that meal for him. Though it was too much for two, I made each dish anyway, taking as much care as I could. But nothing turned out quite right—not the color, not the smell. At the table, neither of us said much of anything. And we had to eat the food for days.

I remember washing rice in the kitchen one day and my mother's saying in English, from her usual seat, "I made a big mistake."

"About Exeter?"

"Yes. I made a big mistake. You should be with us for that time. I should never let you go there."

"So why did you?" I said.

"Because I didn't know I was going to die."

I let her words pass. For the first time in her life, she was letting herself speak her full mind, so what else could I do?

"But you know what?" she spoke up. "It was better for you. If you stayed home, you would not like me so much now."

I suggested that maybe I would like her even more.

She shook her head. "Impossible."

Sometimes I still think about what she said, about having made a mistake. I would have left home for college, that was never in doubt, but those years I was away at boarding school grew more precious to her as her illness progressed. After many months of exhaustion and pain and the haze of the drugs, I thought that her mind was beginning to fade, for more and more it seemed that she was seeing me again as her fifteen-year-old boy, the one she had dropped off in New Hampshire on a cloudy September afternoon.

I remember the first person I met, another new student, named Zack, who walked to the welcome picnic with me. I had planned to eat with my parents—my mother had brought a coolerful of food even that first day—but I learned of the cookout and told her that I should probably go. I wanted to go, of course. I was excited, and no doubt fearful and nervous, and I must have thought I was only thinking ahead. She agreed wholeheartedly, saying I certainly should. I walked them to the car, and perhaps I hugged them, before saying goodbye. One day, after she died, my father told me what happened on the long drive home to Syracuse.

He was driving the car, looking straight ahead. Traffic was light on the Massachusetts Turnpike, and the sky was nearly dark. They had driven for more than two hours and had not yet spoken a word. He then heard a strange sound from her, a kind of muffled chewing noise, as if something inside her were grinding its way out.

"So, what's the matter?" he said, trying to keep an edge to his voice.

She looked at him with her ashen face and she burst into tears. He began to cry himself, and pulled the car over onto the narrow shoulder of the turnpike, where they stayed for the next half hour or so, the blank-faced cars droning by them in the cold, onrushing night.

Every once in a while, when I think of her, I'm driving alone somewhere on the highway. In the twilight, I see their car off to the side, a blue Olds coupe with a landau top, and as I pass them by I look back in the mirror and I see them again, the two figures huddling together in the front seat. Are they sleeping? Or kissing? Are they all right?

Possibilities for Writing

1. Analyze Lee's essay in terms of its references to food and eating. How does the writer use food as a means of suggesting character and relationships?

2. What is your response to Lee's mother as he presents her here? To Lee's behavior toward his mother? Explain how Lee's biographical techniques contribute to your impressions.

3. Write an essay in which you explore family memories of your own that revolve around food, cooking, and eating.

Abraham Lincoln (1809–1865) was born in virtual poverty in rural Kentucky and spent most of his childhood in what is now Spencer County, Indiana. In 1827 he settled in New Salem, Illinois, where he worked in a general store and managed a mill. Almost completely self-educated, he spent much of his spare time during these years studying law and was elected to the state legislature in 1834, serving four terms. While in private practice as a lawyer, he ran unsuccessfully for national office several times, most notably a campaign for the Senate in which he emerged as a forceful opponent of the extension of slavery. Based on this, he was nominated for the Presidency by the Republican Party in 1860, winning with less than a majority of the popular vote. Commander and chief of the Northern forces during the Civil War, Lincoln was assassinated in its final year. His speeches are among the classics of American literature.

Abraham Lincoln
The Gettysburg Address

Abraham Lincoln's "Gettysburg Address," a little over two minutes long, was occasioned by the battle of Gettysburg, which took place the first three days of July, 1863, during the American Civil War. At the battle of Gettysburg, Union soldiers were victorious over their Confederate opponents. But both sides suffered heavy losses of life. Lincoln memorializes the soldiers who died at Gettysburg with language that is elevated, formal, and ceremonial. Each of Lincoln's sentences is carefully structured, with word balancing word, phrase balancing phrase, and clause balancing clause. Using contrast and repetition as well as balanced phrasing, Lincoln created a speech that is as memorable as it is beautiful.

Lincoln's speech begins with a formal phrase "Four score and seven years ago" that refers to an exalted moment in American history, 1776, the creation of the United States of America. His second sentence shifts to the present, to the country's immersion in the Civil War. It is followed by a few simple sentences that identify the occasion of Lincoln's presence and his remarks. These opening sentences set the stage for the glorious elaboration that follows, in which Lincoln celebrates the sacrifice made by those who gave their lives for the cause of freedom.

Four score and seven years ago our fathers brought forth on this continent, a new nation, conceived in Liberty, and dedicated to the proposition that all men are created equal.

Now we are engaged in a great civil war, testing whether that nation, or any nation so conceived and so dedicated, can long endure. We are met on a great battle-field of that war. We have come to dedicate a portion of that field, as a final resting place for those who here gave their lives that that nation might live. It is altogether fitting and proper that we should do this.

But, in a larger sense, we can not dedicate—we can not consecrate—we can not hallow—this ground. The brave men, living and dead, who struggled here, have consecrated it, far above our poor power to add or detract. The world will little note, nor long remember what we say here, but it can never forget what they did here. It is for us the living, rather, to be dedicated here to the unfinished work which they who fought here have thus far so nobly advanced. It is rather for us to be here dedicated to the great task remaining before us—that from these honored dead we take increased devotion to that cause for which they gave the last full measure of devotion—that we here highly resolve that these dead shall not have died in vain—that this nation, under God, shall have a new birth of freedom—and that government of the people, by the people, for the people, shall not perish from the earth.

Possibilities for Writing

1. The Gettysburg Address was composed for a very specific occasion, yet it has come to be considered one of the most profound statements in American political history. What in the speech gives it weight beyond simply honoring those who were killed during the battle of Gettysburg? In what ways does it capture elements essential to the American ideal?

2. Analyze Lincoln's use of repetition, contrast, and balanced phrasing in the Gettysburg Address. Using examples of each from the text, explore their contributions to the overall effect of the speech.

3. Do some research about the composition of the Gettysburg address, initial public response to it, and how it was popularized. In an essay, report on the history of this document. You might wish to consult Gary Wills's book *Lincoln at Gettysburg*.

Niccolò Machiavelli (1469–1527), one of the major thinkers of the Italian Renaissance, was born in Florence, the son of a noble family fallen on hard times. After the despotic Medicis fled the city in 1498, he joined the newly established republican government and became a highly trusted diplomat and secretary of defense. In 1513, after the return of Medici rule, he was accused of treason, suffering imprisonment and torture before being allowed to retire to his country estate. There he produced works of history, literature, and, most notably, political discourse. The most famous of these is The Prince *(written in 1513, but not published until 1531), a treatise in which Machiavelli explains that, in order to maintain power, princes must do anything necessary, however immoral. Read as a lesson in realpolitick, the book is seen as the first example of modern political theory.*

Niccolò Machiavelli
The Morals of the Prince

Niccolò Machiavelli wrote *The Prince* in 1513 as a guidebook for Guiliano de Medici, one of a family of Renaissance rulers of Florence. During the sixteenth century, Italy was a fragmented country, composed of various warring city-states all vying for power. Machiavelli believed that if the country were ever to be unified and brought to peace, it would take a strong ruler, an ideal prince, to do that. His book was the prescription for creating such a successful monarch.

Machiavelli's advice to the ideal prince is designed to be effective in gaining and maintaining political power. For Machiavelli, power is the end or goal, and whatever means are necessary to acquire and preserve that power are entirely justified. The morals of the prince are not a consideration, any more than is his desire for popularity. The only concern is securing and staying in power. And if this requires pretense, so be it. Let the prince pretend to be whatever he needs to be—as long as he effectively maintains his position of power.

On the Reasons Why Men Are Praised or Blamed—Especially Princes

It remains now to be seen what style and principles a prince ought to adopt in dealing with his subjects and friends. I know the subject has been treated frequently before, and I'm afraid people will think me rash for trying to do so again, especially since I intend to differ in this discussion from what others have said. But since I intend to write something useful to an understanding reader, it seemed better to go after the real truth of the matter than to repeat what people have imagined. A great many men have imagined states and princedoms such as nobody ever saw or knew in the real world, for there's such a difference between the way we really live and the way we ought to live that the man who neglects the real to study the ideal will learn how to accomplish his ruin, not his salvation. Any man who tries to be good all the time is bound to come to ruin among the great number who are not good. Hence a prince who wants to keep his post must learn how not to be good, and use that knowledge, or refrain from using it, as necessity requires.

Putting aside, then, all the imaginary things that are said about princes, and getting down to the truth, let me say that whenever men are discussed (and especially princes because they are prominent), there are certain qualities that bring them either praise or blame. Thus some are considered generous, others stingy (I use a Tuscan term, since "greedy" in our speech means a man who wants to take other people's goods. We call a man "stingy" who clings to his own); some are givers, others grabbers: some cruel, others merciful; one man is treacherous, another faithful; one is feeble and effeminate, another fierce and spirited; one humane, another proud; one lustful, another chaste; one straightforward, another sly; one harsh, another gentle; one serious, another playful; one religious, another skeptical, and so on. I know everyone will agree that among these many qualities a prince certainly ought to have all those that are considered good. But since it is impossible to have and exercise them all, because the conditions of human life simply do not allow it, a prince must be shrewd enough to avoid the public disgrace of those vices that would lose him his state. If he possibly can, he should also guard against vices that will not lose him his state; but if he cannot prevent them, he should not be too worried about indulging them. And furthermore, he should not be too worried about incurring blame for any vice without which he would find it hard to save his state. For if you look at matters carefully, you will see that something resembling virtue, if you follow it, may be your ruin, while something else resembling vice will lead, if you follow it, to your security and well-being.

On Liberality and Stinginess

Let me begin, then, with the first of the qualities mentioned above, by saying that a reputation for liberality is doubtless very fine; but the generosity that earns you that reputation can do you great harm. For if you exercise your generosity in a really virtuous way, as you should, nobody will know of it, and you cannot escape the odium of the opposite vice. Hence if you wish to be widely known as a generous man, you must seize every opportunity to make a big display of your giving. A prince of this character is bound to use up his entire revenue in works of ostentation. Thus, in the end, if he wants to keep a name for generosity, he will have to load his people with exorbitant taxes and squeeze money out of them in every way he can. This is the first step in making him odious to his subjects; for when he is poor, nobody will respect him. Then, when his generosity has angered many and brought rewards to a few, the slightest difficulty will trouble him, and at the first approach of danger, down he goes. If by chance he foresees this, and tries to change his ways, he will immediately be labeled a miser.

Since a prince cannot use this virtue of liberality in such a way as to become known for it unless he harms his own security, he won't mind, if he judges prudently of things, being known as a miser. In due course he will be thought the more liberal man, when people see that his parsimony enables him to live on his income, to defend himself against his enemies, and to undertake major projects without burdening his people with taxes. Thus he will be acting liberally toward all those people from whom he takes nothing (and there are an immense number of them), and in a stingy way toward those people on whom he bestows nothing (and they are very few). In our times, we have seen great things being accomplished only by men who have had the name of misers; all the others have gone under. Pope Julius II, though he used his reputation as a generous man to gain the papacy, sacrificed it in order to be able to make war; the present king of France has waged many wars without levying a single extra tax on his people, simply because he could take care of the extra expenses out of the savings from his long parsimony. If the present king of Spain had a reputation for generosity, he would never have been able to undertake so many campaigns, or win so many of them.

Hence a prince who prefers not to rob his subjects, who wants to be able to defend himself, who wants to avoid poverty and contempt, and who doesn't want to become a plunderer, should not mind in the least if people consider him a miser; this is simply one of the vices that enable him to reign. Someone may object that Caesar used a reputation for generosity to become emperor, and many other people have also risen in the world, because they were generous or were supposed to be so. Well, I answer, either you are a prince already, or you are in the process of becoming one; in the first case, this reputation for generosity is harmful to you, in the second case it is very necessary. Caesar was one of those who wanted to become ruler in Rome; but after he had reached his goal, if he had lived, and had not cut down on his expenses, he would have ruined the empire itself. Someone may say: there have been plenty of princes, very successful in warfare, who have had a reputation for generosity. But I answer; either the prince is spending his own money and that of his subjects, or he is spending someone else's. In the first case, he ought to be sparing; in the second case, he ought to spend money like water. Any prince at the head of his army, which lives on loot, extortion, and plunder, disposes of other people's property, and is bound to be very generous; otherwise, his soldiers would desert him. You can always be a more generous giver when what you give is not yours or your subjects'; Cyrus, Caesar, and Alexander were generous in this way. Spending what belongs to other people does no harm to your reputation, rather it enhances it; only spending your own substance harms you. And there is nothing that wears out faster than generosity; even as you practice it, you lose the means of practicing it, and you become either poor and contemptible or (in the course of escaping poverty) rapacious and hateful. The thing above all against which a prince must protect himself is being contemptible and hateful; generosity leads to both. Thus, it's much wiser to put up with the reputation of being a miser, which brings you shame without hate, than to be forced—just because you want to appear generous—into a reputation for rapacity, which brings shame on you and hate along with it.

On Cruelty and Clemency: Whether It Is Better to Be Loved or Feared

Continuing now with our list of qualities, let me say that every prince should prefer to be considered merciful rather than cruel, yet he should be careful not to mismanage this clemency of his. People thought Cesare Borgia was cruel, but that cruelty of his reorganized the Romagna, united it, and established it in peace and loyalty. Anyone who views the matter realistically will see that this prince was much more merciful than the people of Florence who, to avoid the reputation of cruelty, allowed Pistoia to be destroyed. Thus, no prince should mind being called cruel for what he does to keep his subjects united and loyal; he may make examples of a very few, but he will be more merciful in reality than those who, in their tenderheartedness, allow disorders to occur, with their attendant murders and lootings. Such turbulence brings harm to an entire community, while the executions ordered by a prince affect only one individual at a time. A new prince, above all others, cannot possibly avoid a name for cruelty, since new states are always in danger. And Virgil, speaking through the mouth of Dido says:

> My cruel fate
> And doubts attending an unsettled state
> Force me to guard my coast from foreign foes.

Yet a prince should be slow to believe rumors and to commit himself to action on the basis of them. He should not be afraid of his own thoughts; he ought to proceed cautiously, moderating his conduct with prudence and humanity, allowing neither overconfidence to make him careless, nor overtimidity to make him intolerable.

Here the question arises: is it better to be loved than feared, or vice versa? I don't doubt that every prince would like to be both; but since it is hard to accommodate these qualities, if you have to make a choice, to be feared is much safer than to be loved. For it is a good general rule about men, that they are ungrateful, fickle, liars and deceivers, fearful of danger and greedy for gain. While you serve their welfare, they are all yours, offering their blood, their belongings, their lives, and their children's lives, as we noted above—so long as the danger is remote. But when the danger is close at hand, they turn against you. Then, any prince who has relied on their words and has made no other preparations will come to grief; because friendships that are bought at a price, and not with greatness and nobility of soul, may be paid for but they are not acquired, and they cannot be used in time of need. People are less concerned with offending a man who makes himself loved than one who makes himself feared: the reason is that love is a link of obligation which men, because they are rotten, will break any time they think doing so serves their advantage; but fear involves dread of punishment, from which they can never escape.

Still, a prince should make himself feared in such a way that, even if he gets no love, he gets no hate either; because it is perfectly possible to be feared and not hated, and this will be the result if only the prince will keep his hands off the property of his subjects or citizens, and off their women. When he does have to shed blood, he should be sure to have a strong justification and manifest cause; but above all, he should not confiscate people's property, because men are quicker to forget the death of a father than the loss of a patrimony. Besides, pretexts for confiscation are always plentiful, it never fails that a prince who starts living by plunder can find reasons to rob someone else. Excuses for proceeding against someone's life are much rarer and more quickly exhausted.

But a prince at the head of his armies and commanding a multitude of soldiers should not care a bit if he is considered cruel; without such a reputation, he could never hold his army together and ready for action. Among the marvelous deeds of Hannibal, this was prime: that, having an immense army, which included men of many different races and nations, and which he led to battle in distant countries, he never allowed them to fight among themselves or to rise against him, whether his fortune was good or bad. The reason for this could only be his inhuman cruelty, which, along with his countless other talents, made him an object of awe and terror to his soldiers; and without the cruelty, his other qualities would never have sufficed. The historians who pass snap judgments on these matters admire his accomplishments and at the same time condemn the cruelty which was their main cause.

When I say, "His other qualities would never have sufficed," we can see that this is true from the example of Scipio, an outstanding man not only among those of his own time, but in all recorded history; yet his armies revolted in Spain, for no other reason than his excessive leniency in allowing his soldiers more freedom than military discipline permits. Fabius Maximus rebuked him in the senate for this failing, calling him the corrupter of the Roman armies. When a lieutenant of Scipio's plundered the Locrians, he took no action in behalf of the people, and did nothing to discipline that insolent lieutenant; again, this was the result of his easygoing nature. Indeed, when someone in the senate wanted to excuse him on this occasion, he said there are many men who knew better how to avoid error themselves than how to correct error in others. Such a soft temper would in time have tarnished the fame and glory of Scipio, had he brought it to the office of emperor; but as he lived under the control of the senate, this harmful quality of his not only remained hidden but was considered creditable.

Returning to the question of being feared or loved, I conclude that since men love at their own inclination but can be made to fear at the inclination of the prince, a shrewd prince will lay his foundations on what is under his own control, not on what is controlled by others. He should simply take pains not to be hated, as I said.

The Way Princes Should Keep Their Word

How praiseworthy it is for a prince to keep his word and live with integrity rather than by craftiness, everyone understands; yet we see from recent experience that those princes have accomplished most who paid little heed to keeping their promises, but who knew how craftily to manipulate the minds of men. In the end, they won out over those who tried to act honestly.

You should consider then, that there are two ways of fighting, one with laws and the other with force. The first is properly a human method, the second belongs to beasts. But as the first method does not always suffice, you sometimes have to turn to the second. Thus a prince must know how to make good use of both the beast and the man. Ancient writers made subtle note of this fact when they wrote that Achilles and many other princes of antiquity were sent to be reared by Chiron the centaur, who trained them in his discipline. Having a teacher who is half man and half beast can only mean that a prince must know how to use both these two natures, and that one without the other has no lasting effect.

Since a prince must know how to use the character of beasts, he should pick for imitation the fox and the lion. As the lion cannot protect himself from traps, and the fox cannot defend himself from wolves, you have to be a fox in order to be wary of traps, and a lion to overawe the wolves. Those who try to live by the lion alone are badly mistaken. Thus a prudent prince cannot and should not keep his word when to do so would go against his interest, or when the reasons that made him pledge it no longer apply. Doubtless if all men were good, this rule would be bad; but since they are a sad lot, and keep no faith with you, you in your turn are under no obligation to keep it with them.

Besides, a prince will never lack for legitimate excuses to explain away his breaches of faith. Modern history will furnish innumerable examples of this behavior, showing how many treaties and promises have been made null and void by the faithlessness of princes, and how the man succeeded best who knew best how to play the fox. But it is a necessary part of this nature that you must conceal it carefully; you must be a great liar and hypocrite. Men are so simple of mind and so much dominated by their immediate needs, that a deceitful man will always find plenty who are ready to be deceived. One of many recent examples calls for mention. Alexander VI never did anything else, never had another thought, except to deceive men, and he always found fresh material to work on. Never was there a man more convincing in his assertions, who sealed his promises with more solemn oaths, and who observed them less. Yet his deceptions were always successful, because he knew exactly how to manage this sort of business.

In actual fact, a prince may not have all the admirable qualities we listed, but it is very necessary that he should seem to have them. Indeed, I will venture to say that when you have them and exercise them all the time, they are harmful to you; when you just seem to have them, they are useful. It is good to appear merciful, truthful, humane, sincere, and religious; it is good to be so in reality. But you must keep your mind so disposed that, in case of need, you can turn to the exact contrary. This has to be understood: a prince, and especially a new prince, cannot possibly exercise all those virtues for which men are called "good." To preserve the state, he often has to do things against his word, against charity, against humanity, against religion. Thus he has to have a mind ready to shift as the winds of fortune and the varying circumstances of life may dictate. And as I said above, he should not depart from the good if he can hold to it, but he should be ready to enter on evil if he has to.

Hence a prince should take great care never to drop a word that does not seem imbued with the five good qualities noted above; to anyone who sees or hears him, he should appear all compassion, all honor, all humanity, all integrity, all religion. Nothing is more necessary than to seem to have this last virtue. Men in general judge more by the sense of sight than by the sense of touch, because everyone can see but only a few can test by feeling. Everyone sees what you seem to be, few know what you really are; and those few do not dare take a stand against the general opinion, supported by the majesty of the government. In the actions of all men, and especially of princes who are not subject to a court of appeal, we must always look to the end. Let a prince, therefore, win victories and uphold his state; his methods will always be considered worthy, and everyone will praise them, because the masses are always impressed by the superficial appearance of things, and by the outcome of an enterprise. And the world consists of nothing but the masses; the few who have no influence when the many feel secure. A certain prince of our own time, whom it's just as well not to name, preaches nothing but peace and mutual trust, yet he is the determined enemy of both; and if on several different occasions he had observed either, he would have lost both his reputation and his throne.

Possibilities for Writing

1. What seems to be Machiavelli's attitude toward those whom princes rule, and how does this factor into his advice? In developing your answer, cite specific passages from the text.

2. How do you respond to Machiavelli's characterization of morality here? In general, do you think that "moral" behavior is situational, that the morals one practices should depend on the situation one finds oneself in? Why or why not?

3. Consider what constitutes political power today—whether in a democracy such as the United States or under another political system with which you are familiar. To what extent does Machiavelli's advice apply under such a system, and to what extent does it not? Be as specific as possible in your use of examples.

James McBride (b. 1957) is a professional jazz musician and a writer. A former staff writer for a number of magazines, including Essence, People, *and* Rolling Stone, *as well as a writer for major national newspapers, such as* The Boston Globe *and* The Washington Post, *McBride was the 1993 recipient of the American Music Theater Festival Stephen Sondheim Award. A graduate of Oberlin College, he holds a master's degree in journalism from Columbia University. He has published two books:* Miracle at St. Anne, *a novel, and* The Color of Water, *a dual biography/autobiography of his mother and himself, from which "Shul/School" has been taken.*

James McBride
Shul

In "Shul/School," James McBride describes, first, his mother's Jewish school, "shul" in Yiddish, and then the school he attended in lower Manhattan. McBride describes his mother's experience attending a white school as distinguished from the synagogue-related shul for Jewish children. Issues of race play out significantly during his mother's grade school years.

Racial issues play a significant role in McBride's early education as well. As the child of a black father and a Jewish mother, McBride moved between the two racial and cultural worlds. He describes how he negotiated his dual identity and how he related to the white non-Jewish students in his school.

In Suffolk, they had a white folks' school and a black folks' school and a Jewish school. You called the Jewish school "shul" in Yiddish. It wasn't really a school. It was just the synagogue where Tatch taught Hebrew lessons and gave Bible study to children and taught cantoring to boys and that sort of thing. He'd practice his singing around the house sometimes, singing "do re mi fa sol," and all that. You know, they'd let him circumcise children too. That was part of his job as a rabbi, to go to people's houses and circumcise their kids. He had special knives for it. He'd also kill cows in the kosher faith for the Jews in town to eat, and we often kept a cow in the yard behind the store. We'd lead the cow to the Jaffe slaughterhouse down the road and the butchers would tie it from the ceiling by its hind legs. Tatch would open his knife case—he had a special velvet case with knives just for this purpose—and carefully select one of those big, shiny knives. Then he'd utter a quick prayer and plunge the knife blade into the cow's neck. The cow would shudder violently and blood would spurt down his neck and through his nose into a drain in the cement floor and he'd die. The butchers would then set upon him and slit his stomach and yank out his intestines, heart, liver, and innards.

I was almost grown before I could eat meat. The sight of my father plunging his knife into that cow was enough to make me avoid it for years. I was terrified of my father. He put the fear of God in me.

The Jewish school didn't really count with the white folks, so I went to the white school, Thomas Jefferson Elementary. If it was up to Tateh he would have kept me out of school altogether. "That gentile school won't teach you anything you can use," he scoffed. He paid for us to take private lessons in sewing and knitting and record keeping from other people. He was tight with his money, but when it came to that kind of thing, he wasn't cheap, I'll say that for him. He would rather pay for us to study privately than to go to school with gentiles, but the law was the law, so I had to go to school with the white folks. It was a problem from the moment I started, because the white kids hated Jews in my school. "Hey, Ruth, when did you start being a dirty Jew?" they'd ask. I couldn't stand being ridiculed. I even changed my name to try to fit in more. My real name was Rachel, which in Yiddish is Ruckla, which is what my parents called me—but I used the name Ruth around white folk, because it didn't sound so Jewish, though it never stopped the other kids from teasing me.

Nobody liked me. That's how I felt as a child. I know what it feels like when people laugh at you walking down the street, or snicker when they hear you speaking Yiddish, or just look at you with hate in their eyes. You know a Jew living in Suffolk when I was coming up could be lonely even if there were fifteen of them standing in the room, I don't know why; it's that feeling that nobody likes you; that's how I felt, living in the South. You were different from everyone and liked by very few. There were white sections of Suffolk, like the Riverview section, where Jews weren't allowed to own property. It said that on the deeds and you can look them up. They'd say "for White Anglo-Saxon Protestants only." That was the law there and they meant it. The Jews in Suffolk did stick together, but even among Jews my family was low because we dealt with *shvartses*. So I didn't have a lot of Jewish friends either.

When I was in the fourth grade, a girl came up to me in the school-yard during recess and said, "You have the prettiest hair. Let's be friends." I said, "Okay." Heck, I was glad someone wanted to be my friend. Her name was Frances. I'll never forget Frances for as long as I live. She was thin, with light brown hair and blue eyes. She was a quiet gentle person. I was actually forbidden to play with her because she was a gentile, but I'd sneak over to her house anyway and sneak her over to mine. Actually I didn't have to sneak into Frances's house because I was always welcome there. She lived past the cemetery on the other side of town in a frame house that we entered from the back door. It seemed that dinner was always being served at Frances's house. Her mother would serve it on plates she took out of a wooden china closet; ham, chicken, potatoes, corn, string beans, sliced tomatoes, lima beans, white bread, and hot biscuits with lots of butter—and I couldn't eat any of it. It was *treyf*, not kosher for a Jew to eat. The first time her mother served me dinner I said, "I can't eat this," and I was embarrassed until Frances piped out, "I don't like this food either. My favorite food is mayonnaise on white bread." That's how she was. She'd do little things to let you know she was on your side. It didn't bother her one bit that I was Jewish, and if she was around, no one in school would tease me.

I would take pennies from the store cash register so Frances and I could go to the Chadwick Movie Theater—it cost only ten cents. Or we would cut through the town cemetery on the way home from school so Tateh wouldn't see us; we'd spend a lot of afternoons sitting on the headstones talking. You know I'm spooked around dead folks. To this day you can't get me near a graveyard. But when I was with Frances, it didn't bother me a bit. It seemed like the easiest, most natural thing in the world, to sit on somebody's headstone under the cool shade of a tree and chat. We always lingered till the last minute and when it was time to go, we'd have to run in separate directions to get home, so I'd watch her go first to make sure no ghosts were trying to catch her. She'd back away, facing me, asking, "Any ghosts behind me, Ruth? Is it clear?" I'd say, "Yeah. It's clear."

Then she'd turn around and scamper off, dodging the headstones and yelling over her shoulder, "You still watching, Ruth? Watch out for me!"

"I'm watching! No ghosts!" I'd shout. Then after a few seconds I'd yell, "I'm counting now!" I'd count to ten like this: "One two three four five . . . ten!"—and fly home! Fly through that cemetery!

Frances's family wasn't rich. They were like a lot of white folks back then. Farming-type folks, poor. Not poor like you see today. Back then it was a different kind of poor. A better kind of poor, but poor just the same. What I mean by that is you didn't need money as much, but you didn't have any neither. Just about everyone I knew was poor. A lot of our customers were so poor it wasn't funny. Black and white were poor. They got their food from the Nansemond River down the hill from our store. The men would go fishing and crabbing at the wharf and catch huge turtles and take them home and make soup and stew out of them. There was a man who all he did was haul in turtles. He'd walk home carrying a huge turtle under his arm the way you carry a schoolbook, and me and Dee-Dee would gawk. Sometimes he'd stop at the store and buy various ingredients for his turtle soup, various spices and garnishes. That turtle would still be alive, kicking and trying to get away while the man was standing in the store, poring over the vegetables, buying garlics and peppers to cook it up with. I used to feel sorry for the turtles. I wanted him to throw them back in the water, but I wouldn't say that. You crazy? Shoot! He wouldn't throw them back in the water for nobody. They were his dinner.

Folks were poor, and starving. And I have to admit I never starved like a lot of people did. I never had to eat turtles and crabs out of the wharf like a lot of folks did. I never starved for food till I got married. But I was starving in another way. I was starving for love and affection. I didn't get none of that.

School

Back in the 1960s, when she had money, which was hardly ever, Mommy would take us down to Delancey Street on Manhattan's Lower East Side to shop for school clothes. "You have to go where the deals are," she said. "They won't come to you."

"Where are the deals?" we asked.

"The Jews have the deals."

I thought Jews were something that was in the Bible. I'd heard about them in Sunday school, through Jesus and such. I told Ma I didn't know they were still around.

"Oh, they're around," she said. She had a funny look on her face.

The Hasidic Jewish merchants in their black yarmulkes would stare in shock as Mommy walked in, trailed by five or six of us. When they recovered enough to make money, she would drive them to the wall, haggling them to death, lapsing into Yiddish when the going got tough. "I know what's happening here! I know what's happening!" she snapped when the merchants lapsed into Yiddish amongst themselves during negotiations over a pair of shoes. She angrily whipped off some gibberish and the merchants gawked even more. We were awed.

The first time it happened, we asked, "Ma, how'd you learn to talk like that?"

"Mind your own business," she said. "Never ask questions or your mind will end up like a rock. Some of these Jews can't stand you."

Looking back, I realize that I never felt any kinetic relationship to Jews. We were insulated from their world and any other world but our own. Yet there was a part of me that recognized Jews as slightly different from other white folks, partly through information gleaned from Mommy, who consciously and unconsciously sought many things Jewish, and partly through my elder siblings. My sister Rosetta's college education at the all-black Howard University was completely paid for—tuition, books, even school clothes—by the Joseph L. Fisher Foundation, which was run out of the Stephen Wise Free Synagogue of Manhattan. In addition, my oldest brother, Dennis, guru of wisdom and source of much of our worldly news in the 1960s, came home from college with respect for Jewish friends he'd met. "They support the civil rights movement," he reported. Mommy was for anything involving the improvement of our education and condition, and while she would be quick to point out that "some Jews can't stand you," she also, in her crazy contradictory way, communicated the sense to us that if we were lucky enough to come across the right Jew in our travels—a teacher, a cop, a merchant—he would be kinder than other white folks. She never spoke about Jewish people as white. She spoke about them as Jews, which made them somehow different. It was a feeling every single one of us took into adulthood, that Jews were different from white people somehow. Later as an adult when I heard folks talk of the love/hate relationship between blacks and Jews I understood it to the bone not because of any outside sociological study, but because of my own experience with Jewish teachers and classmates—some who were truly kind, genuine, and sensitive, others who could not hide their distaste for my black face—people I'd met during my own contacts with the Jewish world, which Mommy tacitly arranged by forcing every one of us to go to predominantly Jewish public schools.

It was in her sense of education, more than any other, that Mommy conveyed her Jewishness to us. She admired the way Jewish parents raised their children to be scholastic standouts, insulating them from a potentially harmful and dangerous public school system by clustering together within certain communities, to attend certain schools, to be taught by certain teachers who enforced discipline and encouraged learning, and she followed their lead. During the school year she gave us careful instructions to bring home every single paper that the teachers handed out at school, especially in January, and failure to follow these instructions resulted in severe beatings. When we dutifully arrived with the papers, she would pore over them carefully, searching—"Okay . . . okay . . . here it is!"—grabbing the little form and filling it out. Every year the mighty bureaucratic dinosaur known as the New York City Public School System would belch forth a tiny diamond: they slipped a little notice to parents giving them the opportunity to have their kids bused to different school districts if they wanted; but there was a limited time to enroll, a short window of opportunity that lasted only a few days. Mommy stood poised over that option like a hawk. She invariably chose predominantly Jewish public schools: P.S. 138 in Rosedale, J.H.S. 231 in Springfield Gardens, Benjamin Cardozo, Francis Lewis, Forest Hills, Music and Art. Every morning we hit the door at six-thirty, fanning out across the city like soldiers, armed with books, T squares, musical instruments, an "S" bus pass that allowed you to ride the bus and subway for a nickel, and a free-school-lunch coupon in our pocket. Even the tiniest of us knew the subway and local city bus sched-ules and routes by heart. *The number 3 bus lets you off at the corner, but the 3A turns, so you have to get off* . . . By age twelve, I was traveling an hour and a half one way to junior high school by myself, taking two buses each direction every day. My homeroom teacher, Miss Allison, a young white woman with glasses who generally ignored me, would shrug as I walked in ten minutes late, apologizing about a delayed bus. The white kids stared at me in the cafeteria as I gobbled down the horrible school lunch. Who cared. It was all I had to eat.

In this pre-busing era, my siblings and I were unlike most other kids in our neighborhood, traveling miles and miles to largely white, Jewish communities to attend school while our friends walked to the neighbor-hood school. We grew accustomed to being the only black, or "Negro," in school and were standout students, neat and well-mannered, despite the racist attitudes of many of our teachers, who were happy to knock our 95 test scores down to 85's and 80's over the most trivial mistakes. Being the token Negro was something I was never entirely comfortable with. I was the only black kid in my fifth-grade class at P.S. 138 in the then all-white enclave of Rosedale, Queens, and one afternoon as the teacher dutifully read aloud from our history book's one page on "Negro history," someone in the back of the class whispered, "James is a nigger!" followed by a ripple of tittering and giggling across the room. The teacher shushed him and glared, but the damage had been done. I felt the blood rush to my face and sank low in my chair, seething inside, yet I did nothing. I imagined what my siblings would have done. They would have gone wild. They would have found that punk and bum-rushed him. They never would've allowed anyone to call them a nigger. But I was not them. I was shy and passive and quiet, and only later did the anger come bursting out of me, roaring out of me with such blast-furnace force that I would wonder who that person was and where it all came from.

Music arrived in my life around that time, and books. I would dis-appear inside whole worlds comprised of *Gulliver's Travels*, *Shane*, and books by Beverly Cleary. I took piano and clarinet lessons in school, often squirreling myself away in some corner with my clarinet to practice, wandering away in Tchaikovsky or John Philip Sousa, try-ing to improvise like jazz saxophonist James Moody, only to blink back to reality an hour or two later. To further escape from painful reality, I created an imaginary world for myself. I believed my true self was a boy who lived in the mirror. I'd lock myself in the bathroom and spend long hours playing with him. He looked just like me. I'd stare at him. Kiss him. Make faces at him and order him around. Unlike my siblings, he had no opinions. He would listen to me. "If I'm here and you're me, how can *you* be there at the same time?" I'd ask. He'd shrug and smile. I'd shout at him, abuse him verbally. "Give me an answer!" I'd snarl. I would turn to leave, but when I wheeled around he was always there, waiting for me. I had an ache inside, a longing, but I didn't know where it came from or why I had it. The boy in the mirror, he didn't seem to have an ache. He was free. He was never hungry, he had his own bed probably, and his mother wasn't white. I hated him. "Go away!" I'd shout. "Hurry up! Get on out!" but he'd never leave. My siblings would hold their ears to the bathroom door and laugh as I talked to myself. "What a doofus you are," my brother Richie snickered.

Even though my siblings called me "Big Head" because I had a big head and a skinny body, to the outer world I was probably on the "most likely to succeed" list. I was a smart kid. I read a lot. I played music well. I went to church. I had what black folks called "good" hair, because it was curly as opposed to nappy. I was light-skinned or brown-skinned, and girls thought I was cute despite my shyness. Yet I myself had no idea who I was. I loved my mother yet looked nothing like her. Neither did I look like the role models in my life—my stepfather, my godparents, other relatives—all of whom were black. And *they* looked nothing like the other heroes I saw, the guys in the movies, white men like Steve McQueen and Paul Newman who beat the bad guys and in the end got the pretty girl—who, incidentally, was always white.

One afternoon I came home from school and cornered Mommy while she was cooking dinner. "Ma, what's a tragic mulatto?" I asked.

Anger flashed across her face like lightning and her nose, which tends to redden and swell in anger, blew up like a balloon. "Where'd you hear that?" she asked.

"I read it in a book."

"For God's sake, you're no tragic mul—What book is this?"

"Just a book I read."

"Don't read that book anymore." She sucked her teeth. "Tragic mulatto. What a stupid thing to call somebody! Somebody called you that?"

"No."

"Don't ever ever use that term."

"Am I black or white?"

"You're a human being," she snapped. "Educate yourself or you'll be a nobody!"

"Will I be a black nobody or just a nobody?"

"If you're a nobody," she said dryly, "it doesn't matter what color you are."

"That doesn't make sense," I said.

She sighed and sat down. "I bet you never heard the joke about the teacher and the beans," she said. I shook my head. "The teacher says to the class, 'Tell us about different kinds of beans.'

"The first little boy says, 'There's pinto beans.'

" 'Correct,' says the teacher.

"Another boy raises his hand. 'There's lima beans.'

" 'Very good,' says the teacher.

"Then a little girl in the back raises her hand and says, 'We're all *human* beans!' "

She laughed. "That's what you are, a *human* bean! And a *fartbuster* to boot!" She got up and went back to cooking, while I wandered away, bewildered.

Perplexed to the point of bursting, I took the question to my elder siblings. Although each had drawn from the same bowl of crazy logic Mommy served up, none seemed to share my own confusion. "Are we black or white?" I asked my brother David one day.

"*I'm* black," said David, sporting his freshly grown Afro the size of Milwaukee. "But *you* may be a Negro. You better check with Billy upstairs."

I approached Billy, but before I could open my mouth, he asked, "Want to see something?"

"Sure," I said.

He led me through our house, past Mommy, who was absorbed in changing diapers, past a pile of upended chairs, books, music stands, and musical instruments that constituted the living room, up the stairs into the boys' bedroom, and over to a closet which was filled, literally, from floor to ceiling, with junk. He stuck his head inside, pointed to the back, and said, "Look at this." When I stuck my head in, he shoved me in from behind and slammed the door, holding it shut. "Hey, man! It's dark in here!" I shouted, banging at the door and trying to keep the fear out of my voice. Suddenly, in the darkness, I felt hands grabbing me and heard a monster roar. My panic zoomed into high-level terror and I frantically pounded on the door with all my might, screaming in a high-pitched, fervent squawk, "BILLLLYYYYYYYY!" He released the door and I tore out of the closet, my brother David tumbling out behind me. My two brothers fell to the floor laughing, while I ran around the house crying for Ma, zooming from room to room, my circuits blown.

The question of race was like the power of the moon in my house. It's what made the river flow, the ocean swell, and the tide rise, but it was a silent power, intractable, indomitable, indisputable, and thus

completely ignorable. Mommy kept us at a frantic living pace that left
no time for the problem. We thrived on thought, books, music, and art,
which she fed to us instead of food. At every opportunity she loaded five
or six of us onto the subway, paying one fare and pushing the rest of us
through the turnstiles while the token-booth clerks frowned and subway
riders stared, parading us to every free event New York City offered: festivals, zoos, parades, block parties, libraries, concerts. We walked for
hours through the city, long meandering walks that took in whole neigh-
borhoods which we would pass through without buying a thing or
speaking to anyone. Twice a year she marched us to the Guggenheim
dental clinic in Manhattan for free care, where foreign dental students
wearing tunics and armed with drills, picks, and no novocaine, manned
a row of dental chairs and reduced each of us to a screaming mass of
tears while the others waited in line, watching, horrified. They pulled
teeth like maniacs, barking at us in whatever their native tongues were
while they yanked our heads back and forth like rag dolls'. They once
pulled my brother Billy's tooth and then sent him out to Ma in the waiting room, whereupon she looked into the mouth full of gauze and blood
and discovered they had yanked the wrong tooth. She marched back in
and went wild. In summer she was the Pied Piper, leading the whole
pack of us to public swimming pools, stripping down to her one-piece
bathing suit and plunging into the water like a walrus, the rest of us following her like seals, splashing and gurgling in terror behind her as
Mommy flailed along, seemingly barely able to swim herself until one of
us coughed and sputtered, at which time she whipped through the water
and grabbed the offending child, pulling him out and slapping him on
the back, laughing. We did not consider ourselves poor or deprived, or
depressed, for the rules of the outside world seemed meaningless to us
as children. But as we grew up and fanned out into the world as
teenagers and college students, we brought the outside world home with
us, and the world that Mommy had so painstakingly created began to
fall apart.

The sixties roared through my house like a tidal wave. My sister
Helen's decision to drop out of school and run off at age fifteen, though
she returned home five years later with a nursing degree and a baby
girl, was the first sign of impending doom. Now the others began to act
out, and the sense of justice and desire for equal rights that Mommy and
my father had imparted to us began to backfire. Kind, gentle, Sunday

school children who had been taught to say proudly, "I am a Negro," and recite the deeds of Jackie Robinson and Paul Robeson now turned to Malcolm X and H. Rap Brown and Martin Luther King for inspiration. Mommy was the wrong color for black pride and black power, which nearly rent my house in two.

One by one, my elder siblings broke with her rules, coming home bearing fruits of their own confusion, which we jokingly called their "revolution." An elder brother disappeared to Europe. Another sister had an affair at college and came home with a love child, fairly big news in 1967. My brother Richie got married at eighteen over Mommy's objections, divorced, then entered college, and was home on summer break when he got stopped by two cops while walking down the street with a friend. A group of boys who were walking about ten yards in front of Richie and his friend had ditched what appeared to be a bag of heroin as the cop car approached. The cops grouped the boys together, lined them up against a fence, and demanded to know which of them had jettisoned the bag, which later turned out to be filled with quinine, not heroin. All denied it, so the cops searched them all and found ninety dollars of Richie's college-bank-loan money in his pocket. When the policeman asked him where he got the money from, Richie told him it was his college money and he'd forgotten he'd had it. If you knew Richie, you'd nod and say, "Uh-huh," because it was perfectly in character for him to forget he was carrying around ninety precious dollars, which was a huge sum in those days. We used to call him "the Mad Scientist" when he was little. His science experiments would nearly blow up the house because whatever he created, he'd leave it bubbling and boiling while he went to search for food, forgetting it completely. He could remember the toughest calculus formulas and had nearly perfect pitch as a musician, but he literally could not remember to put his pants on. He would play John Coltrane-type solos on his sax for hours and be dressed in a winter jacket and gym shorts the whole time. He was that kind of kid, absentminded, and very smart, and later in life he became a chemist. But to the cops, he was just another black perpetrator with a story, and he was arrested and jailed.

Mommy paced the house all night when she got the news. She showed up early at Richie's arraignment the next day and took a seat right behind the defense table. When they brought him out in handcuffs and she saw him cuffed and dirty after being in the holding pen all night, she could not contain her grief and began muttering like a crazy woman, wringing her hands. Through her reverie of mumbo jumbo she heard the court-appointed lawyer lean over to Richie and offer two words of legal advice: "Plead guilty." She jumped up and screamed, "Wait!" She charged past the court officers, shouting to the judge that it was a mistake, that none of her kids had ever been in trouble with the law before, that her son was a college student, and so forth. The white judge, who had noticed Mommy sitting in the largely black courtroom, released Richie to her custody and the charges were later dropped.

But that experience made Mommy bear down on the younger ones like me even more. She was, in retrospect, quite brilliant when it came to manipulating us. She depended heavily on the "king/queen system" which she established in our house long before I was born: the eldest sibling was the king or queen and you could not defy him or her, because you were a slave. When the eldest left for college, the next ascended to the throne. The king/queen system gave us a sense of order, rank, and self. It gave the older ones the sense that they were in charge, when in actuality it was Mommy who ruled the world. It also harked back to her own traditional Orthodox upbringing where the home was run by one dominating figure with strict rules and regulations. Despite the orchestrated chaos of our home, we always ate meals at a certain time, always did homework at a certain time, and always went to bed at a certain time. Mommy also aligned her-self with any relative or friend who had any interest in any of her children and would send us off to stay with whatever relative promised to straighten us out, and many did. The extended black family was Mommy's hole card, and she played it as often as the times demanded because her family was not available to her. As I grew older, it occurred to me at some point that we had some relatives I had never seen. "How come we don't have any aunts and uncles on your side?" I asked her one day.

"I had a brother who died and my sister . . . I don't know where she is," she said.

"Why not?"

"We got separated."

"How's that?"

"I'm removed from my family."

"Removed?"

"Removed. Dead."

"Who's dead?'

"I'm dead. They're dead too by now probably. What's the difference? They didn't want me to marry on the black side."

"But if you're black already, how can they be mad at you?"

Boom. I had her. But she ignored it. "Don't ask me any more questions."

My stepfather, a potential source of information about her background, was not helpful. "Oh, your mama, you mind her," he grunted when I asked him. He loved her. He seemed to have no problem with her being white, which I found odd, since she was clearly so different from him. Whereas he was largely easygoing and open-minded about most worldly matters, she was suspicious, strict, and inaccessible. Whenever she stepped out of the house with us, she went into a sort of mental zone where her attention span went no farther than the five kids trailing her and the tightly balled fist in which she held her small bit of money, which she always counted to the last penny. She had absolutely no interest in a world that seemed incredibly agitated by our presence. The stares and remarks, the glances and cackles that we heard as we walked about the world went right over her head, but not over mine. By age ten, I was coming into my own feelings about myself and my own impending manhood, and going out with Mommy, which had been a privilege and an honor at age five, had become a dreaded event. I had reached a point where I was ashamed of her and didn't want the world to see my white mother. When I went out with my friends, I'd avoid telling her where we were playing because I didn't want her coming to the park to fetch me. I grew secretive, cautious, passive, angry, and fearful, always afraid that the baddest cat on the block would call her a "honky," in which case I'd have to respond and get my ass kicked. "Come and let's walk to the store," she said one afternoon.

"I can go by myself," I said. The intent was to hide my white mom and go it alone.

"Okay," she said. She didn't seem bothered by my new-found independence. Relieved, I set off to a neighborhood grocery store. The store owner was a gruff white man who, like many of the whites in St. Albans, was on his way out as we blacks began to move in. He did not seem to like black children and he certainly took no particular liking to or interest in me. When I got home, Mommy placed the quart of milk he sold me on the table, opened it up, and the smell of sour milk filled the room. She closed the carton and handed it to me. "Take it back and get my money back."

"Do I have to?"

"Take it back." It was an order. I was a Little Kid in my house, not a Big Kid who could voice opinions and sway the master. I had to take orders.

I dragged myself back to the store, dreading the showdown I knew was coming. The owner glared at me when I walked in. "I have to return this," I said.

"Not here," he said. "The milk is opened. I'm not taking it back."

I returned home. Ten minutes later Mommy marched into the store, doing her "madwalk," the bowlegged strut that meant thunder and lightning was coming—body pitched forward, jaw jutted out, hands balled into tight fists, nose red, stomping like Cab Calloway with the Billy Eckstein band blowing full blast behind him. I followed her sheepishly, my plan to go it alone and hide my white mother now completely awash, backfired in the worst way.

She angrily placed the milk on the counter. The merchant looked at her, then at me. Then back at her. Then at me again. The surprise written on his face changed to anger and disgust, and it took me completely by surprise. I thought the man would see Ma, think they had something in common, then give her the dough and we'd be off. "That milk is sold," he said.

"Smell it," Ma said. "It's spoiled."

"I don't smell milk. I sell milk."

Right away they were at each other, I mean really going at it. A crowd of black kids gathered, watching my white mother arguing with this white man. I wanted to sink into the floor and disappear. "It's okay, Ma . . ." I said. She ignored me. In matters of money, of which she had so little, I knew it was useless. She was going full blast— ". . . fool . . . think you are . . . idiot!"—her words flying together like gibberish, while the neighborhood kids howled, woofing like dogs and enjoying the show.

After a while it was clear the man was not going to return her money, so she grabbed my hand and was heading toward the door, when he made another remark, something that I missed, something he murmured beneath his breath so softly that I couldn't hear, but it made the crowd murmur "Ooohhhh." Ma stiffened. Still holding the milk in her right hand, she turned around and flung it at him like a football.

He ducked and the milk missed him, smashing into the cigarette cabinet behind him and sending milk and cigarettes splattering everywhere.

I could not understand such anger. I could not understand why she didn't just give up the milk. Why cause a fuss? I thought. My own embarrassment overrode all other feelings. As I walked home, holding Mommy's hand while she fumed, I thought it would be easier if we were just one color, black or white. I didn't want to be white. My siblings had already instilled the notion of black pride in me. I would have preferred that Mommy were black. Now, as a grown man, I feel privileged to have come from two worlds. My view of the world is not merely that of a black man but that of a black man with something of a Jewish soul. I don't consider myself Jewish, but when I look at Holocaust photographs of Jewish women whose children have been wrenched from them by Nazi soldiers, the women look like my own mother and I think to myself, *There but for the grace of God goes my own mother—and by extension, myself.* When I see two little Jewish old ladies giggling over coffee at a Manhattan diner, it makes me smile, because I hear my own mother's laughter beneath theirs. Conversely, when I hear black "leaders" talking about "Jewish slave owners" I feel angry and disgusted, knowing that they're inflaming people with lies and twisted history, as if all seven of the Jewish slave owners in the antebellum South, or however few there were, are responsible for the problems of African-Americans now. Those leaders are no better than their Jewish counterparts who spin statistics in marvelous ways to make African-Americans look like savages, criminals, drags on society, and "animals" (a word quite popular when used to describe blacks these days). I don't belong to any of those groups. I belong to the world of one God, one people. But as a kid, I preferred the black side, and often wished that Mommy had sent me to black schools like my friends. Instead I was stuck at that white school, P.S. 138, with white classmates who were convinced I could dance like James Brown. They constantly badgered me to do the "James Brown" for them, a squiggling of the feet made famous by the "Godfather of Soul" himself, who back in the sixties was bigger than life. I tried to explain to them that I couldn't dance. I have always been one of the worst dancers that God has ever put upon this earth. My sisters would spend hours at home trying out new dances to Archie Bell and the Drells, Martha Reeves, King Curtis, Curtis Mayfield, Aretha Franklin, and the Spinners. "Come on and dance!" they'd shout, boogying across the room. Even Ma would join in, sashaying across the floor, but when I joined in I looked so odd and stupid they fell to the floor laughing. "Give it up," they said. "You can't dance."

The white kids in school did not believe me, and after weeks of encouragement I found myself standing in front of the classroom on talent day, wearing my brother's good shoes and hitching up my pants, soul singer–style like one of the Temptations, as someone dropped the needle on a James Brown record. I slid around the way I'd seen him do, shouting "Owww—shabba-na!" They were delighted. Even the teacher was amused. They really believed I could dance! I had them fooled. They screamed for more and I obliged, squiggling my feet and slip-sliding across the wooden floor, jumping into the air and landing in a near split by the blackboard, shouting "Eeeee-yowwww!" They went wild, but even as I sat down with their applause ringing in my ears, with laughter on my face, happy to feel accepted, to be part of them, knowing I had pleased them, I saw the derision on their faces, the clever smiles, laughing at the oddity of it, and I felt the same ache I felt when I gazed at the boy in the mirror. I remembered him, and how free he was, and I hated him even more.

Possibilities for Writing

1. Describe how the two school stories—of McBride and of his mother—are related. To what extent is the Shul section of the essay about school and to what extent are other elements prominent? Explain what McBride and his mother learn from their respective grade school educations.
2. What educational values are emphasized in McBride's story? To what extent do Jewish educational values influence the young James McBride? McBride's mother often took her children to zoos, parades, libraries, festivals, and concerts; to what extent did these trips shape her son's future education and life?
3. Write an essay in which you describe an aspect of your early education—either in school or outside of it. Consider the values that your schooling or extracurricular education imparted. Consider as well any special relationships you may have developed with teachers or mentors who helped foster your educational development.

N. Scott Momaday (b. 1934) was born in Lawton, Oklahoma, of Kiowa ancestry and grew up on a reservation in New Mexico. A graduate of the University of New Mexico and of Stanford University, he won a Pulitzer Prize for his first novel, House Made of Dawn *(1968). Author of many genres in addition to fiction, Momaday has published volumes of poetry, including* The Gourd Dancer *(1976), and the memoirs* The Way to Rainy Mountain *(1969) and* The Names *(1976), as well as children's books, essay collections, and plays. He is also an artist whose work has been widely exhibited. For many years a professor at the University of Arizona, Momaday often takes as his subject the history and culture of Native Americans and, in particular, their relationship with the physical environment. His most recent collection is* The Man Made of Words *(1997).*

N. Scott Momaday
The Way to Rainy Mountain

In his autobiographical memoir, *The Way to Rainy Mountain*, N. Scott Momaday celebrates his Kiowa Native American heritage. Momaday describes both a place and a person in this essay from his memoir. He describes Rainy Mountain as a place saturated in the history of the Kiowa people. It is a place every aspect of which bears significance.

But it is not only place that is celebrated in Momaday's essay/memoir. He also memorializes his grandmother, who is, herself, a repository of Kiowa history and culture. Momaday's moving portrait captures her dignity and nobility as an individual and as a representative of her vanishing Kiowa world. In language at once reverential and wonderfully precise, Momaday describes the holy regard that his grandmother held for the sun, an awe and a reverence reflected in the sun dances of Kiowa cultural tradition.

A single knoll rises out of the plain in Oklahoma, north and west of the Wichita Range. For my people, the Kiowas, it is an old landmark, and they gave it the name Rainy Mountain. The hardest weather in the world is there. Winter brings blizzards, hot tornadic winds arise in the spring, and in summer the prairie is an anvil's edge. The grass turns brittle and brown, and it cracks beneath your feet. There are green belts along the rivers and creeks, linear groves of hickory and pecan, willow and witch hazel. At a distance in July or August the steaming foliage seems almost to writhe in fire. Great green and yellow grasshoppers are everywhere in the tall grass, popping up like corn to sting the flesh, and tortoises crawl about on the red earth, going nowhere in the plenty of time. Loneliness is an aspect of the land. All things in the plain are isolate; there is no confusion of objects in the eye, but *one* hill or *one* tree or *one* man. To look upon that landscape in the early morning, with the sun at your back, is to lose the sense of proportion. Your imagination comes to life, and this, you think, is where Creation was begun.

I returned to Rainy Mountain in July. My grandmother had died in the spring, and I wanted to be at her grave. She had lived to be very old and at last infirm. Her only living daughter was with her when she died, and I was told that in death her face was that of a child.

I like to think of her as a child. When she was born, the Kiowas were living the last great moment of their history. For more than a hundred years they had controlled the open range from the Smoky Hill River to the Red, from the headwaters of the Canadian to the fork of the Arkansas and Cimarron. In alliance with the Comanches, they had ruled the whole of the southern Plains. War was their sacred business, and they were among the finest horsemen the world has ever known. But warfare for the Kiowas was preeminently a matter of disposition rather than of survival, and they never understood the grim, unrelenting advance of the U.S. Cavalry. When at last, divided and ill-provisioned, they were driven onto the Staked Plains in the cold rains of autumn, they fell into panic. In Palo Duro Canyon they abandoned their crucial stores to pillage and had nothing then but their lives. In order to save themselves, they surrendered to the soldiers at Fort Sill and were imprisoned in the old stone corral that now stands as a military museum. My grandmother was spared the humiliation of those high gray walls by eight or ten years, but she must have known from birth the affliction of defeat, the dark brooding of old warriors.

Her name was Aho, and she belonged to the last culture to evolve in North America. Her forebears came down from the high country in western Montana nearly three centuries ago. They were a mountain people, a mysterious tribe of hunters whose language has never been positively classified in any major group. In the late seventeenth century they began a long migration to the south and east. It was a journey toward the dawn, and it led to a golden age. Along the way the Kiowas were befriended by the Crows, who gave them the culture and religion of the Plains. They acquired horses, and their ancient nomadic spirit was suddenly free of the ground. They acquired Tai-me, the sacred Sun Dance doll, from that moment the object and symbol of their worship, and so shared in the divinity of the sun. Not least, they acquired the sense of destiny, therefore courage and pride. When they entered upon the southern Plains they had been transformed. No longer were they slaves to the simple necessity of survival; they were a lordly and dangerous society of fighters and thieves, hunters and priests of the sun. According to their origin myth, they entered the world through a hollow log. From one point of view, their migration was the fruit of an old prophecy, for indeed they emerged from a sunless world.

Although my grandmother lived out her long life in the shadow of Rainy Mountain, the immense landscape of the continental interior lay like memory in her blood. She could tell of the Crows, whom she had never seen, and of the Black Hills, where she had never been. I wanted to see in reality what she had seen more perfectly in the mind's eye, and traveled fifteen hundred miles to begin my pilgrimage.

Yellowstone, it seemed to me, was the top of the world, a region of deep lakes and dark timber, canyons and waterfalls. But, beautiful as it is, one might have the sense of confinement there. The skyline in all directions is close at hand, the high wall of the woods and deep cleavages of shade. There is a perfect freedom in the mountains, but it belongs to the eagle and the elk, the badger and the bear. The Kiowas reckoned their stature by the distance they could see, and they were bent and blind in the wilderness.

Descending eastward, the highland meadows are a stairway to the plain. In July the inland slope of the Rockies is luxuriant with flax and buckwheat, stonecrop and larkspur. The earth unfolds and the limit of the land recedes. Clusters of trees, and animals grazing far in the distance, cause the vision to reach away and wonder to build upon the mind. The sun follows a longer course in the day, and the sky is immense beyond all comparison. The great billowing clouds that sail upon it are the shadows that move upon the grain like water, dividing light. Farther down, in the land of the Crows and Blackfeet, the plain is yellow. Sweet clover takes hold of the hills and bends upon itself to cover and seal the soil. There the Kiowas paused on their way; they had come to the place where they must change their lives. The sun is at home on the plains. Precisely there does it have the certain character of a god. When the Kiowas came to the land of the Crows, they could see the dark lees of the hills at dawn across the Bighorn River, the profusion of light on the grain shelves, the oldest deity ranging after the solstices. Not yet would they veer southward to the caldron of the land that lay below; they must wean their blood from the northern winter and hold the mountains a while longer in their view. They bore Tai-me in procession to the east.

A dark mist lay over the Black Hills, and the land was like iron. At the top of a ridge I caught sight of Devil's Tower upthrust against the gray sky as if in the birth of time the core of the earth had broken through its crust and the motion of the world was begun. There are things in nature that engender an awful quiet in the heart of man; Devil's Tower is one of them. Two centuries ago, because they could not do otherwise, the Kiowas made a legend at the base of the rock. My grandmother said:

> Eight children were there at play, seven sisters and their brother. Suddenly the boy was struck dumb; he trembled and began to run upon his hands and feet. His fingers became claws, and his body was covered with fur. Directly there was a bear where the boy had been. The sisters were terrified; they ran, and the bear after them. They came to the stump of a great tree, and the tree spoke to them. It bade them climb upon it, and as they did so it began to rise into the air. The bear came to kill them, but they were just beyond its reach. It reared against the tree and scored the bark all around with its claws. The seven sisters were borne into the sky, and they became the stars of the Big Dipper.

From that moment, and so long as the legend lives, the Kiowas have kinsmen in the night sky. Whatever they were in the mountains, they could be no more. However tenuous their well-being, however much they had suffered and would suffer again, they had found a way out of the wilderness.

My grandmother had a reverence for the sun, a holy regard that now is all but gone out of mankind. There was a wariness in her, and an ancient awe. She was a Christian in her later years, but she had come a long way about, and she never forgot her birthright. As a child she had been to the Sun Dances; she had taken part in those annual rites, and by them she had learned the restoration of her people in the presence of Tai-me. She was about seven when the last Kiowa Sun Dance was held in 1887 on the Washita River above Rainy Mountain Creek. The buffalo were gone. In order to consummate the ancient sacrifice—to impale the head of a buffalo bull upon the medicine tree—a delegation of old men journeyed into Texas, there to beg and barter for an animal from the Goodnight herd. She was ten when the Kiowas came together for the last time as a living Sun Dance culture. They could find no buffalo; they had to hang an old hide from the sacred tree. Before the dance could begin, a company of soldiers rode out from Fort Sill under orders to disperse the tribe. Forbidden without cause the essential act of their faith, having seen the wild herds slaughtered and left to rot upon the ground, the Kiowas backed away forever from the medicine tree. That was July 20, 1890, at the great bend of the Washita. My grandmother was there. Without bitterness, and for as long as she lived, she bore a vision of deicide.

Now that I can have her only in memory, I see my grandmother in the several postures that were peculiar to her: standing at the wood stove on a winter morning and turning meat in a great iron skillet: sitting at the south window, bent above her beadwork, and afterwards, when her vision failed, looking down for a long time into the fold of her hands; going out upon a cane, very slowly as she did when the weight of age came upon her; praying. I remember her most often at prayer. She made long, rambling prayers out of suffering and hope, having seen many things. I was never sure that I had the right to hear, so exclusive were they of all mere custom and company. The last time I saw her she prayed standing by the side of her bed at night, naked to the waist, the light of a kerosene lamp moving upon her dark skin. Her long, black hair, always drawn and braided in the day, lay upon her shoulders and against her breasts like a shawl. I do not speak Kiowa, and I never understood her prayers, but there was something inherently sad in the sound, some merest hesitation upon the syllables of sorrow. She began in a high and descending pitch, exhausting her breath to silence; then again and again—and always the same intensity of effort, of something that is, and is not, like urgency in the human voice. Transported so in the dancing light among the shadows of her room, she seemed beyond the reach of time. But that was illusion; I think I knew then that I should not see her again.

Houses are like sentinels in the plain, old keepers of the weather watch. There, in a very little while, wood takes on the appearance of great age. All colors wear soon away in the wind and rain, and then the wood is burned gray and the grain appears and the nails turn red with rust. The windowpanes are black and opaque; you imagine there is nothing within, and indeed there are many ghosts, bones given up to the land. They stand here and there against the sky, and you approach them for a longer time than you expect. They belong in the distance; it is their domain.

Once there was a lot of sound in my grandmother's house, a lot of coming and going, feasting and talk. The summers there were full of excitement and reunion. The Kiowas are a summer people; they abide the cold and keep to themselves, but when the season turns and the land becomes warm and vital they cannot hold still; an old love of going returns upon them. The aged visitors who came to my grandmother's house when I was a child were made of lean and leather, and they bore themselves upright. They wore great black hats and bright ample shirts that shook in the wind. They rubbed fat upon their hair and wound their braids with strips of colored cloth. Some of them painted their faces and carried the scars of old and cherished enmities. They were an old council of warlords, come to remind and be reminded of who they were. Their wives and daughters served them well. The women might indulge themselves; gossip was at once the mark and compensation of their servitude. They made loud and elaborate talk among themselves, full of jest and gesture, fright and false alarm. They went abroad in fringed and flowered shawls, bright beadwork and German silver. They were at home in the kitchen, and they prepared meals that were banquets.

There were frequent prayer meetings, and great nocturnal feasts. When I was a child I played with my cousins outside, where the lamplight fell upon the ground and the singing of the old people rose up around us and carried away into the darkness. There were a lot of good things to eat, a lot of laughter and surprise. And afterwards, when the quiet returned, I lay down with my grandmother and could hear the frogs away by the river and feel the motion of the air.

Now there is a funeral silence in the rooms, the endless wake of some final word. The walls have closed in upon my grandmother's house. When I returned to it in mourning, I saw for the first time in my life how small it was. It was late at night, and there was a white moon, nearly full. I sat for a long time on the stone steps by the kitchen door. From there I could see out across the land; I could see the long row of trees by the creek, the low light upon the rolling plains, and the stars of the Big Dipper. Once I looked at the moon and caught sight of a strange thing. A cricket had perched upon the handrail, only a few inches away from me. My line of vision was such that the creature filled the moon like a fossil. It had gone there, I thought, to live and die, for there, of all places, was its small definition made whole and eternal. A warm wind rose up and purled like the longing within me.

The next morning I awoke at dawn and went out on the dirt road to Rainy Mountain. It was already hot, and the grasshoppers began to fill the air. Still, it was early in the morning, and the birds sang out of the shadows. The long yellow grass on the mountain shone in the bright light, and a scissortail hied above the land. There, where it ought to be, at the end of a long and legendary way, was my grandmother's grave. Here and there on the dark stones were ancestral names. Looking back once, I saw the mountain and came away.

Possibilities for Writing

1. Momaday traces the migration of the Kiowa from Montana to the Great Plains in terms of both physical landscape and of spiritual development. For him, how are the two related in the rise and fall of Kiowa history and culture? What is the significance of his ending the story of his journey at his grandmother's grave?

2. What does his grandmother represent for Momaday? Why, for example, does he begin his pilgrimage to her grave from Yellowstone, fifteen hundred miles away? How do his memories of her, as he describes them, help develop this image?

3. Explore the ways in which a grandparent or other older relative provides you with ties to your history and culture. Like Momaday, you may wish to develop the influence of a particular place associated with that person as well.

*Michel de Montaigne (1533–1592), the father of the modern essay, was born
in Perigord, France, to a family of wealthy landowners. He studied law at the
University of Guyenne in Bordeaux and during his career served as a local
magistrate and later as mayor of Bordeaux. In 1580 he published the first of
his collected* Essais, *which were revised and added to in 1588. These
"attempts" or "trials," as he termed them, dealt with a wide range of subjects
and were intended as personal, but at the same time universal, reflections on
the human condition. Intensely intellectual, the* essais *are nonetheless written
in concrete, everyday language and marked by a great deal of humor. His
works were highly influential throughout Europe, not only in terms of their
subject matter but also as exemplars of this unique literary form.*

Michel de Montaigne
Of Smells

Michel de Montaigne originated a unique style that is at once both personal
and reflective. Montaigne's "Of Smells," though one of his shortest essays,
exemplifies his characteristic method. It begins with a few general thoughts on
the nature of odors that human beings give off. It moves quickly to a series of
quotations from Montaigne's reading in classic writers from the past. And it
includes a number of observations based on Montaigne's experience—his
autobiographical perspective on what he himself has noticed about the way
people smell, including the way he himself smells.

The unpretentiousness of this little essay is part of its charm. "Of Smells"
wears its learning lightly. And it leans lightly, too, on what Montaigne has
experienced in the realm of the olfactory. It never pretends to be anything more
than a brief set of notes on what is noteworthy about smell. Montaigne's essay is
suggestive without being insistent. It presents opportunities for readers to notice
what Montaigne himself has noticed. But it doesn't force the issue; it doesn't
argue in any systematic or methodical way. Nonetheless, "Of Smells" makes a
good case for the influence of smell in our everyday lives.

It is said of some, as of Alexander the Great, that their sweat emitted a
sweet odor, owing to some rare and extraordinary constitution of theirs,
of which Plutarch and others seek the cause. But the common make-up
of bodies is the opposite, and the best condition they may have is to be
free of smell. The sweetness even of the purest breath has nothing more
excellent about it than to be without any odor that offends us, as is that
of very healthy children. That is why, says Plautus,

A woman smells good when she does not smell.

The most perfect smell for a woman is to smell of nothing, as they say that her actions smell best when they are imperceptible and mute, And perfumes are rightly considered suspicious in those who use them, and thought to be used to cover up some natural defect in that quarter. Whence arise these nice sayings of the ancient poets: To smell good is to stink:

> You laugh at us because we do not smell.
> I'd rather smell of nothing than smell sweet.
>
> MARTIAL

And elsewhere:

> Men who smell always sweet, Posthumus, don't smell good.
>
> MARTIAL

However, I like very much to be surrounded with good smells, and I hate bad ones beyond measure, and detect them from further off than anyone else:

> My scent will sooner be aware
> Where goat-smells, Polypus, in hairy arm-pits lurk,
> Than keen hounds scent a wild boar's lair.
>
> HORACE

The simplest and most natural smells seem to me the most agreeable. And this concern chiefly affects the ladies. Amid the densest barbarism, the Scythian women, after washing, powder and plaster their whole body and face with a certain odoriferous drug that is native to their soil; and having removed this paint to approach the men, they find themselves both sleek and perfumed.

Whatever the odor is, it is a marvel how it clings to me and how apt my skin is to imbibe it. He who complains of nature that she has left man without an instrument to convey smells to his nose is wrong, for they convey themselves. But in my particular case my mustache, which is thick, performs that service. If I bring my gloves or my handkerchief near it, the smell will stay there a whole day. It betrays the place I come from. The close kisses of youth, savory, greedy, and sticky, once used to adhere to it and stay there for several hours after. And yet, for all that, I find myself little subject to epidemics, which are caught by communication and bred by the contagion of the air; and I have escaped those of my time, of which there have been many sorts in our cities and our armies. We read of Socrates that though he never left Athens during many recurrences of the plague which so many times tormented that city, he alone never found himself the worse for it.

The doctors might, I believe, derive more use from odors than they do; for I have often noticed that they make a change in me and work upon my spirits according to their properties; which makes me approve of the idea that the use of incense and perfumes in churches, so ancient and widespread in all nations and religions, was intended to delight us and arouse and purify our senses to make us more fit for contemplation.

I should like, in order to judge of it, to have shared the art of those cooks who know how to add a seasoning of foreign odors to the savor of foods, as was particularly remarked in the service of the king of Tunis, who in our time landed at Naples to confer with the Emperor Charles. They stuffed his foods with aromatic substances, so sumptuously that one peacock and two pheasants came to a hundred ducats to dress them in that manner; and when they were carved, they filled not only the dining hall but all the rooms in his palace, and even the neighboring houses, with sweet fumes which did not vanish for some time.

The principal care I take in my lodgings is to avoid heavy, stinking air. Those beautiful cities Venice and Paris weaken my fondness for them by the acrid smell of the marshes of the one and of the mud of the other.

Possibilities for Writing

1. Trace closely the arc of this brief essay, exploring the sequence of thoughts from beginning to end. Do you find a coherent pattern here? If so, explain the pattern you find. If not, how does this fact affect your reading of the essay?

2. Write an essay of your own titled "Of Smells." Focus on your personal responses to the odors you encounter at home, in public, and in man-made and natural settings, as well as on how our culture seems to define good and bad smells. Don't be afraid to be whimsical.

3. Using Montaigne as a model, write an impressionistic essay on a topic that is common to everyone's experience but that would not normally be thought of as the subject of an essay: hands or feet, say, or tears, or refrigerators, or dust. Use your imagination. Incorporate quotations as you may find them.

Nuala O'Faolain *(b. 1942) was born in Dublin, the second eldest of nine children of a journalist who became Ireland's first social columnist, writing* Dubliner's Diary. *O'Faolain received her university education in Dublin and studied both English and French, receiving a Master of Arts. She also received a scholarship to attend the University of Hull in England, where she specialized in medieval literature, and at Oxford University, where she received a Bachelor of Philosophy in literature. O'Faolain has worked as a book reviewer for the* London Times, *a producer for the British Broadcasting Corporation, a university lecturer in the United States and Ireland, and a columnist for the* Irish Times. *Her books include* Are You Somebody? *(1998), a memoir;* My Dream of You *(2000), a novel;* Almost There: The Onward Journey of a Dublin Woman *(2002), the second installment of her autobiography; and* The Story of Chicago May *(2005).*

Nuala O'Faolain
Are You Somebody?

In "Are You Somebody," the introduction to Nuala O'Faolain's memoir of the same title, the author introduces the themes and identifies the question that serves as a catalyst for her book. O'Faolain's goal was to identify the person behind the author of the columns she wrote for the *Irish Times*, to let her readers know who she was and what she was like. First identifying herself as a "nobody," a girl who became a woman in a country where men were the measure of all things important, she resisted this definition with a pressing sense of individuality and selfhood.

O'Faolain's style is honest and direct and her tone absent of sentimentality. Paradoxically, in writing about herself and her sense of her individual self, her stories transcend her personal experience to resonate with the lives of her readers.

I was born in a Dublin that was much more like something from an earlier century than like the present day. I was one of nine children, when nine was not even thought of as a big family, among the teeming, penniless, anonymous Irish of the day. I was typical: a nobody, who came of an unrecorded line of nobodies. In a conservative Catholic country, which feared sexuality and forbade me even information about my body, I could expect difficulty in getting through my life as a girl and a woman. But at least—it would have been assumed—I wouldn't have the burden of having to earn a good wage. Eventually some man would marry me and keep me.

But there are no typical people. And places don't stay the same. The world changed around Ireland, and even Ireland changed, and I was to be both an agent of change and a beneficiary of it. I didn't see that, until I wrote out my story. I was immured in the experience of my own life. Most of the time I just went blindly from day to day, and though what I was doing must have looked ordinary enough—growing up in the countryside, getting through school, falling in love, discovering lust, learning, working, travelling, moving in and out of health and happiness—to myself I was usually barely hanging on. I never stood back and looked at myself and what I was doing. I didn't value myself enough—take myself seriously enough—to reflect even privately on whether my existence had any pattern, any meaning. I took it for granted that like most of the billions of people who are born and die on this planet I was just an accident. There was no reason for me.

Yet my life burned inside me. Even such as it was, it was the only record of me, and it was my only creation, and something in me would not accept that it was insignificant. Something in me must have been waiting to stand up and demand to be counted. Because eventually, when I was presented with an opportunity to talk about myself, I grasped at it. I'm on my own anyway, I thought. What have I to lose? But I needed to speak, too. I needed to howl.

What happened was that in my forties, back in the Dublin of my birth, I began working for the most respected newspaper in the country—*The Irish Times*—as an opinion columnist. This was a wonderful job to have, and a quite unexpected one. The very idea of an Irishwoman opinion columnist would have been unthinkable for most of my life. The columns were usually about politics or social questions or moments in popular culture—they weren't personal at all. They used a confident, public voice. My readers probably thought I was as confident as that all the time, but I knew the truth. My private life was solitary. My private voice was apologetic. In terms of national influence I mattered, in Ireland. But I possessed nothing of what has traditionally mattered to women and what had mattered to me during most of my life. I had no lover, no child. It seemed to me that I had nothing to look back on but failure.

But when I'd been writing my columns for ten years or so, a publisher came to me and asked whether he could put some of them together in book form. I said that was fine. No one would track my work through the back numbers of the newspaper, but a book gets around. It might be the only thing to read in a trekker's hut in Nepal. It would be catalogued in the National Library. It would be there for my grandniece, who is only a baby now. But I wasn't interested in the old columns. I was interested in what I would say in the personal introduction I'd promised to write. What would I say about myself, the person who *wrote* the columns? Now that I had the opportunity, how would I introduce myself?

I'm fairly well known in Ireland. I've been on television a lot, and there's a photo of me in the paper, at the top of my column. But I'm no star. People have to look at me twice or three times to put a name on me. Sometimes when I'm drinking in a lounge bar, a group of women, say, across the room, may look at me and send one of their number over to me, or when I'm in the grocery store someone who has just passed me by turns back and comes right up to me and scrutinises my face. "Are you somebody?" they ask. Well—am I somebody? I'm not anybody in terms of the world, but then, who decides what a somebody is? How is a somebody made? I've never done anything remarkable; neither have most people. Yet most people, like me, feel remarkable. That self-importance welled up inside me. I had the desire to give an account of my life. I was finished with furtiveness. I sat down to write the introduction, and I summoned my pride. I turned it into a memoir.

I imagined the hostile response I'd get in my little Irish world. "Who does she think she is?" I could hear the reviewers saying. But it turned out not to be like that at all. The world my story went out to turned out to be much, much bigger than I'd ever thought. And it turned out to be full of people who knew me, who were sisters and brothers although we had never met, who were there to welcome me coming out of the shadows, and who wanted to throw off the shadows that obscured their own lives, too. My small voice was answered by a rich chorus of voices: my voice, which had once been mute! Of all the places where my story might start, even, it started itself at a point in my life when I could not speak at all . . . .

Possibilities for Writing

1. O'Faolain calls herself a "nobody" and says that she is "typical." How does she use these terms to set up her piece? To what extent are these terms effective ones for her purpose? What other words and phrases echo and support these?

2. What motivated O'Faolain to write "Are You Somebody?"? What motivated her to write her newspaper columns? From the evidence of this short piece, to what extent does O'Faolain consider herself a writer? What kind of writer?

3. Imagine that you were invited to write your autobiography—a memoir of your life so far. Write the introduction, or preliminary setup chapter, using O'Faolain's "Are You Somebody?" as a model.

George Orwell
Shooting an Elephant

George Orwell's "Shooting an Elephant," one of the most frequently
anthologized and analyzed of all modern essays, has achieved the status of a
modern classic. The essay describes Orwell's experience in Burma, when he
served as a sub-divisional police officer for Burma's colonial master, England.
Through an incident that involved his shooting of an elephant, Orwell conveys
his ambivalence about the people he supervises and the country he serves.

At the climactic moment of the essay, Orwell describes in harrowing detail
the agony of the elephant in its death throes. At this point Orwell has so slowed
the pace of the essay as to create a cinematic effect of slow motion, which
highlights the elephant's agony and intensifies the emotional effect upon the
reader. Then with the narrative drive halted and the harrowing description over,
Orwell speculates on the larger significance of this most unusual experience.

In Moulmein, in Lower Burma, I was hated by large numbers of
people—the only time in my life that I have been important enough for
this to happen to me. I was sub-divisional police officer of the town, and
in an aimless, petty kind of way anti-European feeling was very bitter.
No one had the guts to raise a riot, but if a European woman went
through the bazaars alone somebody would probably spit betel juice
over her dress. As a police officer I was an obvious target and was baited
whenever it seemed safe to do so. When a nimble Burman tripped me
up on the football field and the referee (another Burman) looked the
other way, the crowd yelled with hideous laughter. This happened more
than once. In the end the sneering yellow faces of young men that met
me everywhere, the insults hooted after me when I was at a safe distance, got badly on my nerves. The young Buddhist priests were the
worst of all. There were several thousands of them in the town and none
of them seemed to have anything to do except stand on street corners
and jeer at Europeans.

All this was perplexing and upsetting. For at that time I had already
made up my mind that imperialism was an evil thing and the sooner
I chucked up my job and got out of it the better. Theoretically—and
secretly, of course—I was all for the Burmese and all against their
oppressors, the British. As for the job I was doing, I hated it more bitterly
than I can perhaps make clear. In a job like that you see the dirty work

of Empire at close quarters. The wretched prisoners huddling in the stinking cages of the lock-ups, the grey, cowed faces of the long-term convicts, the scarred buttocks of the men who had been flogged with bamboos—all these oppressed me with an intolerable sense of guilt. But I could get nothing into perspective. I was young and ill-educated and I had had to think out my problems in the utter silence that is imposed on every Englishman in the East. I did not even know that the British Empire is dying, still less did I know that it is a great deal better than the younger empires that are going to supplant it. All I knew was that I was stuck between my hatred of the empire I served and my rage against the evil-spirited little beasts who tried to make my job impossible. With one part of my mind I thought of the British Raj as an unbreakable tyranny, as something clamped down, in *saecula saeculorum* upon the will of prostrate peoples; with another part I thought that the greatest joy in the world would be to drive a bayonet into a Buddhist priest's guts. Feelings like these are the normal by-products of imperialism; ask any Anglo-Indian official, if you can catch him off duty.

One day something happened which in a roundabout way was enlightening. It was a tiny incident in itself, but it gave me a better glimpse than I had had before of the real nature of imperialism—the real motives for which despotic governments act. Early one morning the sub-inspector at a police station the other end of the town rang me up on the 'phone and said that an elephant was ravaging the bazaar. Would I please come and do something about it? I did not know what I could do, but I wanted to see what was happening and I got on to a pony and started out. I took my rifle, an old .44 Winchester and much too small to kill an elephant, but I thought the noise might be useful *in terrorem*. Various Burmans stopped me on the way and told me about the elephant's doings. It was not, of course, a wild elephant, but a tame one which had gone "must." It had been chained up, as tame elephants always are when their attack of "must" is due, but on the previous night it had broken its chain and escaped. Its mahout, the only person who could manage it when it was in that state, had set out in pursuit, but had taken the wrong direction and was now twelve hours' journey away, and in the morning the elephant had suddenly reappeared in the town. The Burmese population had no weapons and were quite helpless against it. It had already destroyed somebody's bamboo hut, killed a cow and raided some fruit-stalls and devoured the stock; also it had met the municipal rubbish van and, when the driver jumped out and took to his heels, had turned the van over and inflicted violences upon it.

The Burmese sub-inspector and some Indian constables were waiting for me in the quarter where the elephant had been seen. It was a very poor quarter, a labyrinth of squalid bamboo huts, thatched with palm-leaf, winding all over a steep hillside. I remember that it was a cloudy, stuffy morning at the beginning of the rains. We began questioning the people as to where the elephant had gone and, as usual, failed to get any definite information. That is invariably the case in the East; a story always sounds clear enough at a distance, but the nearer you get to the scene of events the vaguer it becomes. Some of the people said that the elephant had gone in one direction, some said that he had gone in another, some professed not even to have heard of any elephant. I had almost made up my mind that the whole story was a pack of lies, when we heard yells a little distance away. There was a loud, scandalized cry of "Go away, child! Go away this instant!" and an old woman with a switch in her hand came round the corner of a hut, violently shooing away a crowd of naked children. Some more women followed, clicking their tongues and exclaiming; evidently there was something that the children ought not to have seen. I rounded the hut and saw a man's dead body sprawling in the mud. He was an Indian, a black Dravidian coolie, almost naked, and he could not have been dead many minutes. The people said that the elephant had come suddenly upon him round the corner of the hut, caught him with its trunk, put its foot on his back and ground him into the earth. This was the rainy season and the ground was soft, and his face had scored a trench a foot deep and a couple of yards long. He was lying on his belly with arms crucified and head sharply twisted to one side. His face was coated with mud, the eyes wide open, the teeth bared and grinning with an expression of unendurable agony. (Never tell me, by the way, that the dead look peaceful. Most of the corpses I have seen looked devilish.) The friction of the great beast's foot had stripped the skin from his back as neatly as one skins a rabbit. As soon as I saw the dead man I sent an orderly to a friend's house nearby to borrow an elephant rifle. I had already sent back the pony, not wanting it to go mad with fright and throw me if it smelt the elephant.

The orderly came back in a few minutes with a rifle and five car-tridges, and meanwhile some Burmans had arrived and told us that the elephant was in the paddy fields below, only a few hundred yards away. As I started forward practically the whole population of the quarter flocked out of the houses and followed me. They had seen the rifle and were all shouting excitedly that I was going to shoot the elephant. They had not shown much interest in the elephant when he was merely rav-aging their homes, but it was different now that he was going to be shot. It was a bit of fun to them, as it would be to an English crowd; besides they wanted the meat. It made me vaguely uneasy. I had no intention of shooting the elephant—I had merely sent for the rifle to defend myself if necessary—and it is always unnerving to have a crowd following you. I marched down the hill, looking and feeling a fool, with the rifle over my shoulder and an ever-growing army of people jostling at my heels. At the bottom, when you got away from the huts, there was a metalled road and beyond that a miry waste of paddy fields a thousand yards across, not yet ploughed but soggy from the first rains and dotted with coarse grass. The elephant was standing eight yards from the road, his left side towards us. He took not the slightest notice of the crowd's approach. He was tearing up bunches of grass, beating them against his knees to clean them and stuffing them into his mouth.

I had halted on the road. As soon as I saw the elephant I knew with perfect certainty that I ought not to shoot him. It is a serious matter to shoot a working elephant—it is comparable to destroying a huge and costly piece of machinery—and obviously one ought not to do it if it can possibly be avoided. And at that distance, peacefully eating, the ele-phant looked no more dangerous than a cow. I thought then and I think now that his attack of "must" was already passing off; in which case he would merely wander harmlessly about until the mahout came back and caught him. Moreover, I did not in the least want to shoot him. I decided that I would watch him for a little while to make sure that he did not turn savage again, and then go home.

But at that moment I glanced round at the crowd that had followed me. It was an immense crowd, two thousand at the least and growing every minute. It blocked the road for a long distance on either side. I looked at the sea of yellow faces above the garish clothes—faces all happy and excited over this bit of fun, all certain that the elephant was going to be shot. They were watching me as they would watch a conjurer about to perform a trick. They did not like me, but with the magical rifle in my hands I was momentarily worth watching. And suddenly I realized that I should have to shoot the elephant after all. The people expected it of me and I had got to do it; I could feel their two thousand wills pressing me forward, irresistibly. And it was at this moment, as I stood there with the rifle in my hands, that I first grasped the hollowness, the futility of the white man's dominion in the East. Here was I, the white man with his gun, standing in front of the unarmed native crowd—seemingly the leading actor of the piece; but in reality I was only an absurd puppet pushed to and fro by the will of those yellow faces behind. I perceived in this moment that when the white man turns tyrant it is his own freedom that he destroys. He becomes a sort of hollow, posing dummy, the conventionalized figure of a sahib. For it is the condition of his rule that he shall spend his life in trying to impress the "natives," and so in every crisis he has got to do what the "natives" expect of him. He wears a mask, and his face grows to fit it. I had got to shoot the elephant. I had committed myself to doing it when I sent for the rifle. A sahib has got to act like a sahib; he has got to appear resolute, to know his own mind and do definite things. To come all that way, rifle in hand, with two thousand people marching at my heels, and then to trail feebly away, having done nothing—no, that was impossible. The crowd would laugh at me. And my whole life, every white man's life in the East, was one long struggle not to be laughed at.

But I did not want to shoot the elephant. I watched him beating his bunch of grass against his knees, with that preoccupied grandmotherly air that elephants have. It seemed to me that it would be murder to shoot him. At that age I was not squeamish about killing animals, but I had never shot an elephant and never wanted to. (Somehow it always seems worse to kill a *large* animal.) Besides, there was the beast's owner to be considered. Alive, the elephant was worth at least a hundred pounds; dead, he would only be worth the value of his tusks, five pounds, possibly. But I had got to act quickly. I turned to some experienced-looking Burmans who had been there when we arrived, and asked them how the elephant had been behaving. They all said the same thing: he took no notice of you if you left him alone, but he might charge if you went too close to him.

It was perfectly clear to me what I ought to do. I ought to walk up to within, say, twenty-five yards of the elephant and test his behavior. If he charged, I could shoot; if he took no notice of me, it would be safe to leave him until the mahout came back. But also I knew that I was going to do no such thing. I was a poor shot with a rifle and the ground was soft mud into which one would sink at every step. If the elephant charged and I missed him, I should have about as much chance as a toad under a steam-roller. But even then I was not thinking particularly of my own skin, only of the watchful yellow faces behind. For at that moment, with the crowd watching me, I was not afraid in the ordinary sense, as I would have been if I had been alone. A white man mustn't be frightened in front of "natives"; and so, in general, he isn't frightened. The sole thought in my mind was that if anything went wrong those two thousand Burmans would see me pursued, caught, trampled on and reduced to a grinning corpse like that Indian up the hill. And if that happened it was quite probable that some of them would laugh. That would never do. There was only one alternative. I shoved the cartridges into the magazine and lay down on the road to get a better aim.

The crowd grew very still, and a deep, low, happy sigh, as of people who see the theatre curtain go up at last, breathed from innumerable throats. They were going to have their bit of fun after all. The rifle was a beautiful German thing with cross-hair sights. I did not then know that in shooting an elephant one would shoot to cut an imaginary bar running from ear-hole to ear-hole. I ought, therefore, as the elephant was sideways on, to have aimed straight at his ear-hole; actually I aimed several inches in front of this, thinking the brain would be further forward.

When I pulled the trigger I did not hear the bang or feel the kick—one never does when a shot goes home—but I heard the devilish roar of glee that went up from the crowd. In that instant, in too short a time, one would have thought, even for the bullet to get there, a mysterious, terrible change had come over the elephant. He neither stirred nor fell, but every line of his body had altered. He looked suddenly stricken, shrunken, immensely old, as though the frightful impact of the bullet had paralysed him without knocking him down. At last, after what seemed a long time—it might have been five seconds, I dare say—he sagged flabbily to his knees. His mouth slobbered. An enormous senility seemed to have settled upon him. One could have imagined him thousands of years old. I fired again into the same spot. At the second shot he did not collapse but climbed with desperate slowness to his feet and stood weakly upright, with legs sagging and head drooping. I fired a third time. That was the shot that did for him. You could see the agony of it jolt his whole body and knock the last remnant of strength from his legs. But in falling he seemed for a moment to rise, for as his hind legs collapsed beneath him he seemed to tower upward like a huge rock toppling, his trunk reaching skywards like a tree. He trumpeted, for the first and only time. And then down he came, his belly towards me, with a crash that seemed to shake the ground even where I lay.

I got up. The Burmans were already racing past me across the mud. It was obvious that the elephant would never rise again, but he was not dead. He was breathing very rhythmically with long rattling gasps, his great mound of a side painfully rising and falling. His mouth was wide open—I could see far down into caverns of pale pink throat. I waited a long time for him to die, but his breathing did not weaken. Finally I fired my two remaining shots into the spot where I thought his heart must be. The thick blood welled out of him like red velvet, but still he did not die. His body did not even jerk when the shots hit him, the tortured breathing continued without a pause. He was dying, very slowly and in great agony, but in some world remote from me where not even a bullet could damage him further. I felt that I had got to put an end to that dreadful noise. It seemed dreadful to see the great beast lying there, powerless to move and yet powerless to die, and not even to be able to finish him. I sent back for my small rifle and poured shot after shot into his heart and down his throat. They seemed to make no impression. The tortured gasps continued as steadily as the ticking of a clock.

In the end I could not stand it any longer and went away. I heard later that it took him half an hour to die. Burmans were bringing dahs and baskets even before I left, and I was told they had stripped his body almost to the bones by the afternoon.

Afterwards, of course, there were endless discussions about the shooting of the elephant. The owner was furious, but he was only an Indian and could do nothing. Besides, legally I had done the right thing, for a mad elephant has to be killed, like a mad dog, if its owner fails to control it. Among the Europeans opinion was divided. The older men said I was right, the younger men said it was a damn shame to shoot an elephant for killing a coolie, because an elephant was worth more than any damn Coringhee coolie. And afterwards I was very glad that the coolie had been killed; it put me legally in the right and it gave me a sufficient pretext for shooting the elephant. I often wondered whether any of the others grasped that I had done it solely to avoid looking a fool.

Possibilities for Writing

1. Orwell makes the point in his second paragraph that he had come to believe that "imperialism was an evil thing," and he goes on to explain why he believes this both explicitly, through his own thoughts, and implicitly, through the circumstances of the story he tells. In an essay, examine Orwell's views of the evils of imperialism, both for the natives and for the colonizers.

2. Analyze Orwell's essay to consider the sense of ambivalence he felt in his position as part of the imperial police force. What does this ambivalence contribute to the tone of the essay and to Orwell's central point?

3. Orwell describes acting against his better judgment "solely to avoid looking like a fool." Have you ever done anything you believed to be wrong in order to save face, to avoid looking like a fool? Describe such an experience and what it led you to understand about yourself and about the pressure to save face.

Cynthia Ozick (b. 1928) was born in New York City and earned her Bachelor of Arts at New York University. After earning a Master of Arts at The Ohio State University, she began writing fiction and essays. Her essay collection Quarrel & Quandary *won the 2001 National Book Critics Circle Award, and her collection* Fame & Folly *was a finalist for the 1996 Pulitzer Prize. Her most recent novel,* Heir to the Glimmering World, *was a New York Times Notable Book and a Book Sense pick, which was also chosen by NBC's Today Book Club. Her most recent collection of essays is* The Din in the Head, *from which the following essay of the same title has been taken.*

Cynthia Ozick
The Din in the Head

In "The Din in the Head," Cynthia Ozick contemplates the incessant inner voice that hums in our heads—at least when we are alone and quiet, and not hooked up to a cell phone, ipod, or other technological device. Ozick regards the new technologies, like the older ones of telephone and radio and television, as threats to the development of innerness, as enemies of thoughtfulness and imagination.

In place of the many electronic gadgets that beckon for our attention, Ozick suggests that we read fiction, especially novels, for in them she finds "the last trustworthy vessel of the inner life." Ozick's essay, in fact, turns into a defense of the novel, a kind of apologia, or argument for its many virtues, which include, not least, a form of lifelike art that prizes interiority and that can save us from atrophy of the imagination.

On a gray afternoon I sit in a silent room and contemplate din. In the street a single car passes—a rapid bass vowel—and then it is quiet again. So what is this uproar, this hubbub, this heaving rumble of zigzag static I keep hearing? This echo chamber spooling out spirals of chaos? An unmistakable noise as clearly mine as fingerprint or twist of DNA: the thrum of regret, of memory, of defeat, of mutability, of bitter fear, made up of shame and ambition and anger and vanity and wishing. The sound-track of a movie of the future, an anticipatory ribbon of scenes long dreaded, or daydreams without a prayer of materializing. Or else: the replay of unforgotten conversations, humiliating, awkward, indelible. Mainly it is the buzz of the inescapably mundane, the little daily voice that insists and insists: *right now, not now, too late, too soon, why not, better not, turn it on, turn it off, notice this, notice that, be sure to take care of, remember not to.* The nonstop chatter that gossips, worries, envies, invokes, yearns, condemns, self-condemns.

But innerness—this persistent internal hum—is more than lamentation and desire. It is the quiver of intuition that catches experience and draws it close, to be examined, interpreted, judged. Innerness is discernment; penetration; imagination; self-knowledge. The inner life is the enemy of crowds, because the life of crowds snuffs the mind's murmurings. Mind is many-threaded, mazy, meandering, while every crowd turns out to be a machine—a collectivity of parts united as to purpose.

And with the ratcheting up of technology, every machine turns out to be a crowd. All these contemporary story-grinding contrivances and appliances that purport to capture, sometimes to mimic, the inner life— what are they, really, if not the brute extrusions of the principle of Crowd? Films, with their scores of collaborators, belong to crowds. Films are addressed to crowds (even if you are alone in front of your TV screen). As for those other machine-generated probings—television confessionals, radio psychologists, telephone marketing quizzers, the retrograde e-mail contagion that reduces letter-writing to stunted nineteenth-century telegraphese, electronic "chat rooms" and "blogs" and "magazines" that debase discourse through hollow breeziness and the incessant scramble for the cutting edge—what are they, really, if not the dwarfing gyrations of crowds? Superhero cybernetics, but lacking flight. Picture Clark Kent entering a handy telephone booth not to rise up as a universal god, but to sidle out diminished and stuttering, still wearing his glasses and hat. The very disappearance of telephone booths—those private cells for the whis-perings of lovers and conspirators—serves the mentality of crowds, where ubiquitously public cell phones announce confidential assignations to the teeming streets.

Tête-à-tête gone flagrante delicto.

Yet there remains a countervailing power. Its sign blazes from the title of Thomas Hardy's depiction of the English countryside, with its lost old phrase: *Far from the Madding Crowd.* How, in this madding American hour, to put a distance between the frenzy of crowds and the mind's whispered necessities? Get thee to the novel!—the novel, that word-woven submarine, piloted by intimation and intuition, that will dive you to the deeps of the heart's maelstrom.

The electronic revolution, with its accelerating development of this or that apparatus, is frequently compared to the invention of movable type—but the digital is antithetical to the inward life of letters. Print first made possible the individual's solitary engagement with an intimate text; the Gutenberg era moved human awareness from the collective to the reflective. Electronic devices promote the collective, the much-touted "global community"—again the crowd. Microchip chat employs a ghostly simulacrum of print, but chat is not an essay. Film reels out plots, but a movie is not a novel. The inner life dwells elsewhere, occasionally depositing its conscious vibrations in what we think of as the "personal" essay. Though journalism floods us with masses of articles—verbal packets of information suitable to crowds—there are, nowadays, few essays of the meditative kind.

And what of the utterly free precincts of the novel? Is the literary novel, like the personal essay, in danger of obsolescence? An academic alarm goes up every so often, and I suppose the novel may fall out of luck or fashion, at least in the long run. Where, after all, are the sovereign forms of yesteryear—the epic, the sage, the Byronic narrative poem, the autobiographical Wordsworthian ode? Literary grandeur is out of style. If Melville lived among us, would he dare to grapple with the mammoth rhapsody that is *Moby-Dick*? Forms and genres, like all breathing things, have their natural life spans. They are born into a set of societal conditions and become moribund when those conditions attenuate. But if the novel were to wither—if, say, it metamorphosed altogether into a species of journalism or movies, as many popular novels already have—then the last trustworthy vessel of the inner life (aside from our heads) would crumble away.

The novel has not withered; it holds on, held in the warmth of the hand. "It can do simply everything," Henry James wrote a century ago, "and that is its strength and its life. Its plasticity, its elasticity is infinite." These words appeared under the head "The Future of the Novel." There are advanced minds who may wish to apply them to the Internet—with predictive truth, no doubt, on their side. Communications technology may indeed widen and widen, and in ways beyond even our current fantasies. But the novel commands a realm far more perceptive than the "exchange of ideas" that, in familiar lingo, is heralded as communication, and means only what the crowd knows. Talk-show hosts who stimulate the public outpourings of the injured are themselves hedged behind the inquisitive sympathy of crowds, which is no sympathy at all. Downloading specialized knowledge—one of the encyclopedic triumphs of communications technology—is an act equal in practicality to a wooden leg; it will support your standing in the world, but there is no blood in it.

What does the novel know? It has no practical or educational aim; yet it knows what ordinary knowledge cannot seize. The novel's intricate tangle of character-and-incident alights on the senses with a hundred cobwebby knowings fanning their tiny threads, stirring up nuances and disclosures. The arcane designs and driftings of metaphor—what James called the figure in the carpet, what Keats called negative capability, what Kafka called explaining the inexplicable—are what the novel knows. It can make sentient even the furniture in a room:

> Pavel Petrovich meanwhile had gone back to his elegant study. Its walls were covered with grayish wallpaper and hung with an assortment of weapons on a many-hued Persian tapestry. The walnut furniture was upholstered in dark green velvet. There was a Renaissance bookcase of old black oak, bronze statuettes on the magnificent writing-table, an open hearth. He threw himself on the sofa, clasped his hands behind his head and remained motionless, staring at the ceiling with an expression verging on despair. Perhaps because he wanted to hide from the very walls what was reflected in his face, or for some other reason—anyway, he got up, unfastened the heavy window curtains and threw himself back on the sofa.

That is Turgenev. A modernist would have omitted that "expression verging on despair." The despair is in the wallpaper, as Turgenev hinted; it was the literary habits of the nineteenth century that made him say the word outright. Virginia Woolf's wallpaper is sentient, too—though, because she is a modernist, she never explicitly names its mood:

> Only through the rusty hinges and swollen sea-moistened woodwork certain airs, detached from the body of the wind (the house was ramshackle after all) crept round corners and ventured indoors. Almost one might imagine them, as they entered the drawing-room questioning and wondering, toying with the flaps of the wallpaper, asking, would it hang much longer, when will it fall? Then smoothly brushing the walls, they passed on musingly as if asking the red and yellow roses on the wallpaper whether they would fade, questioning (gently, for there was time at their disposal) the torn letters in the waste-paper basket, the flowers, the books, all of which were open to them and asking, Were they allies? Were they enemies? How long would they endure?

Two small portraits, each of a room—but the subject of both (if such wavering tendrils of sensation can be termed a subject) is incorporeal, intuitional, deeply interior. A weight of sorrow inheres in Turgenev's heavy black bookcase; the feather-tap of the ephemeral touches Woolf's torn letters. And both scenes breathe out the one primordial cry: Life! Life!

Life—the inner life—is not in the production of story lines alone, or movies would suffice. The micro-universe of the modem? Never mind. The secret voices in the marrow elude these multiplying high-tech implements that facilitate the spread of information. (High tech! Facilitate the spread of information! The jargon of the wooden leg, the wooden tongue.) The din in our heads, that relentless inward hum of fragility and hope and transcendence and dread—where, in an age of machines addressing crowds, and crowds mad for machines, can it be found? In the art of the novel; in the novel's infinity of plasticity and elasticity; in a flap of imaginary wallpaper. And nowhere else.

Possibilities for Writing

1. What is the "din in the head" that Ozick highlights in her essay, and why does she value it? To what extent do you agree with Ozick that this internal mental monologue should be cherished and nurtured?

2. Why does Ozick consider the novel to be so important? According to Ozick, what does the novel "know"? To what extent are you persuaded that the novel is as important as Ozick suggests? To what extent do you share her sense of the dangers of technology in affecting our interior lives of thought and reflection?

3. Write an essay in which you support, modify, or contest what Ozick says in this essay about technology and about the novel. Or write an essay in which you propose another form of art or entertainment valuable for sustaining and developing the interior life of the imagination.

> **Neil Postman** *(1931–2003) was born in New York City, where he spent most of*
> *his life. In 1953 he graduated from the State University of New York at*
> *Fredonia. He received a Master's Degree in 1955 and a Doctorate in Education*
> *in 1958, both from Teachers College, Columbia University. He began teaching*
> *at New York University in 1959 and was affiliated with NYU for forty years.*
> *In 1971 he founded the program in Media Ecology at NYU's Steinhardt School*
> *of Education. Appointed a University Professor in 1993, he was chairman of the*
> *Department of Culture and Communication until 2002. Postman published*
> *more than two hundred newspaper and magazine articles for such periodicals*
> *as the* New York Times Magazine, The Atlantic Monthly, Harper's, Time
> Magazine, The Washington Post, *the* Los Angeles Times, *and* Le Monde. *For ten*
> *years, from 1976 to 1986, he was the editor of the quarterly journal* ETC.,
> *a Review of General Semantics. Among his eighteen books are* Teaching as a
> Subversive Activity *(1969)*, Technopoly *(1992)*, The End of Education *(1995)*,
> *and* Amusing Ourselves to Death *(1985), from which "The Medium Is the*
> *Metaphor" has been taken.*

Neil Postman

The Medium Is the Metaphor

In "The Medium Is the Metaphor," Neil Postman takes his cue from Marshall
McLuhan, whose book *Understanding Media* (1964), which popularized the
saying "the medium is the message" and which introduced the concept of media
ecology, is central to both Postman's essay and the book from which it has been
excerpted. For McLuhan and later for Postman, the medium, or the means
through which communication occurs, is part of the message or meaning of that
communication.

Postman invites us to consider how a particular medium, such as a book, as
compared with another medium, such as radio or television, changes the way
we perceive and understand ourselves and our world. Postman makes
abundantly clear that he laments the technological and cultural shift that
occurred in the middle of the twentieth century when television replaced
reading with a consequent change in the content and meaning of public
discourse.

At different times in our history, different cities have been the focal
point of a radiating American spirit. In the late eighteenth century, for
example, Boston was the center of a political radicalism that ignited a
shot heard round the world—a shot that could not have been fired any
other place but the suburbs of Boston. At its report, all Americans,

including Virginians, became Bostonians at heart. In the mid-nineteenth century, New York became the symbol of the idea of a melting-pot America—or at least a non-English one—as the wretched refuse from all over the world disembarked at Ellis Island and spread over the land their strange languages and even stranger ways. In the early twentieth century, Chicago, the city of big shoulders and heavy winds, came to symbolize the industrial energy and dynamism of America. If there is a statue of a hog butcher somewhere in Chicago, then it stands as a reminder of the time when America was railroads, cattle, steel mills and entrepreneurial adventures. If there is no such statue, there ought to be, just as there is a statue of a Minute Man to recall the Age of Boston, as the Statue of Liberty recalls the Age of New York.

Today, we must look to the city of Las Vegas, Nevada, as a metaphor of our national character and aspiration, its symbol a thirty-foot-high cardboard picture of a slot machine and a chorus girl. For Las Vegas is a city entirely devoted to the idea of entertainment, and as such proclaims the spirit of a culture in which all public discourse increasingly takes the form of entertainment. Our politics, religion, news, athletics, education and commerce have been transformed into congenial adjuncts of show business, largely without protest or even much popular notice. The result is that we are a people on the verge of amusing ourselves to death.

As I write, the President of the United States is a former Hollywood movie actor. One of his principal challengers in 1984 was once a featured player on television's most glamorous show of the 1960's, that is to say, an astronaut. Naturally, a movie has been made about his extraterrestrial adventure. Former nominee George McGovern has hosted the popular television show "Saturday Night Live." So has a candidate of more recent vintage, the Reverend Jesse Jackson.

Meanwhile, former President Richard Nixon, who once claimed he lost an election because he was sabotaged by make-up men, has offered Senator Edward Kennedy advice on how to make a serious run for the presidency: lose twenty pounds. Although the Constitution makes no mention of it, it would appear that fat people are now effectively excluded from running for high political office. Probably bald people as well. Almost certainly those whose looks are not significantly enhanced by the cosmetician's art. Indeed, we may have reached the point where cosmetics has replaced ideology as the field of expertise over which a politician must have competent control.

America's journalists, i.e., television newscasters, have not missed the point. Most spend more time with their hair dryers than with their scripts, with the result that they comprise the most glamorous group of people this side of Las Vegas. Although the Federal Communications Act makes no mention of it, those without camera appeal are excluded from addressing the public about what is called "the news of the day." Those with camera appeal can command salaries exceeding one million dollars a year.

American businessmen discovered, long before the rest of us, that the quality and usefulness of their goods are subordinate to the artifice of their display; that, in fact, half the principles of capitalism as praised by Adam Smith or condemned by Karl Marx are irrelevant. Even the Japanese, who are said to make better cars than the Americans, know that economics is less a science than a performing art, as Toyota's yearly advertising budget confirms.

Not long ago, I saw Billy Graham join with Shecky Green, Red Buttons, Dionne Warwick, Milton Berle and other theologians in a tribute to George Burns, who was celebrating himself for surviving eighty years in show business. The Reverend Graham exchanged one-liners with Burns about making preparations for Eternity. Although the Bible makes no mention of it, the Reverend Graham assured the audience that God loves those who make people laugh. It was an honest mistake. He merely mistook NBC for God.

Dr. Ruth Westheimer is a psychologist who has a popular radio program and a nightclub act in which she informs her audiences about sex in all of its infinite variety and in language once reserved for the bedroom and street corners. She is almost as entertaining as the Reverend Billy Graham, and has been quoted as saying, "I don't start out to be funny. But if it comes out that way, I use it. If they call me an entertainer, I say that's great. When a professor teaches with a sense of humor, people walk away remembering." She did not say what they remember or of what use their remembering is. But she has a point: It's great to be an entertainer. Indeed, in America God favors all those who possess both a talent and a format to amuse, whether they be preachers, athletes, entrepreneurs, politicians, teachers or journalists. In America, the least amusing people are its professional entertainers.

Culture watchers and worriers—those of the type who read books like this one—will know that the examples above are not aberrations but, in fact, clichés. There is no shortage of critics who have observed and recorded the dissolution of public discourse in America and its conversion into the arts of show business. But most of them, I believe, have barely begun to tell the story of the origin and meaning of this descent into a vast triviality. Those who have written vigorously on the matter tell us, for example, that what is happening is the residue of an exhausted capitalism; or, on the contrary, that it is the tasteless fruit of the maturing of capitalism; or that it is the neurotic aftermath of the Age of Freud; or the retribution of our allowing God to perish; or that it all comes from the old stand-bys, greed and ambition.

I have attended carefully to these explanations, and I do not say there is nothing to learn from them. Marxists, Freudians, Lévi-Straussians, even Creation Scientists are not to be taken lightly. And, in any case, I should be very surprised if the story I have to tell is anywhere near the whole truth. We are all, as Huxley says someplace, Great Abbreviators, meaning that none of us has the wit to know the whole truth, the time to tell it if we believed we did, or an audience so gullible as to accept it. But you *will* find an argument here that presumes a clearer grasp of the matter than many that have come before. Its value, such as it is, resides in the directness of its perspective, which has its origins in observations made 2,300 years ago by Plato. It is an argument that fixes its attention on the forms of human conversation, and postulates that how we are obliged to conduct such conversations will have the strongest possible influence on what ideas we can conveniently express. And what ideas are convenient to express inevitably become the important content of a culture.

I use the word "conversation" metaphorically to refer not only to speech but to all techniques and technologies that permit people of a particular culture to exchange messages. In this sense, all culture is a conversation or, more precisely, a corporation of conversations, conducted in a variety of symbolic modes. Our attention here is on how forms of public discourse regulate and even dictate what kind of content can issue from such forms.

To take a simple example of what this means, consider the primitive technology of smoke signals. While I do not know exactly what content was once carried in the smoke signals of American Indians, I can safely guess that it did not include philosophical argument. Puffs of smoke are insufficiently complex to express ideas on the nature of existence, and even if they were not, a Cherokee philosopher would run short of either wood or blankets long before he reached his second axiom. You cannot use smoke to do philosophy. Its form excludes the content.

To take an example closer to home: As I suggested earlier, it is implausible to imagine that anyone like our twenty-seventh President, the multi-chinned, three-hundred-pound William Howard Taft, could be put forward as a presidential candidate in today's world. The shape of a man's body is largely irrelevant to the shape of his ideas when he is addressing a public in writing or on the radio or, for that matter, in smoke signals. But it is quite relevant on television. The grossness of a three-hundred-pound image, even a talking one, would easily over-whelm any logical or spiritual subtleties conveyed by speech. For on television, discourse is conducted largely through visual imagery, which is to say that television gives us a conversation in images, not words. The emergence of the image-manager in the political arena and the concomitant decline of the speech writer attest to the fact that television demands a different kind of content from other media. You cannot do political philosophy on television. Its form works against the content.

To give still another example, one of more complexity: The information, the content, or, if you will, the "stuff" that makes up what is called "the news of the day" did not exist—could not exist—in a world that lacked the media to give it expression. I do not mean that things like fires, wars, murders and love affairs did not, ever and always, happen in places all over the world. I mean that lacking a technology to advertise them, people could not attend to them, could not include them in their daily business. Such information simply could not exist as part of the content of culture. This idea—that there is a content called "the news of the day"—was entirely created by the telegraph (and since amplified by newer media), which made it possible to move decontextualized infor-mation over vast spaces at incredible speed. The news of the day is a fig-ment of our technological imagination. It is, quite precisely, a media event. We attend to fragments of events from all over the world because we have multiple media whose forms are well suited to fragmented con-versation. Cultures without speed-of-light media—let us say, cultures in which smoke signals are the most efficient space-conquering tool avail-able—do not have news of the day. Without a medium to create its form, the news of the day does not exist.

To say it, then, as plainly as I can, this book is an inquiry into and a lamentation about the most significant American cultural fact of the second half of the twentieth century: the decline of the Age of Typography and the ascendancy of the Age of Television. This change-over has dramatically and irreversibly shifted the content and meaning of public discourse, since two media so vastly different cannot accommodate the same ideas. As the influence of print wanes, the content of politics, religion, education, and anything else that comprises public business must change and be recast in terms that are most suitable to television.

If all of this sounds suspiciously like Marshall McLuhan's aphorism, the medium is the message, I will not disavow the association (although it is fashionable to do so among respectable scholars who, were it not for McLuhan, would today be mute). I met McLuhan thirty years ago when I was a graduate student and he an unknown English professor. I believed then, as I believe now, that he spoke in the tradition of Orwell and Huxley—that is, as a prophesier, and I have remained steadfast to his teaching that the clearest way to see through a culture is to attend to its tools for conversation. I might add that my interest in this point of view was first stirred by a prophet far more formidable than McLuhan, more ancient than Plato. In studying the Bible as a young man, I found intimations of the idea that forms of media favor particular kinds of content and therefore are capable of taking command of a culture. I refer specifically to the Decalogue, the Second Commandment of which prohibits the Israelites from making concrete images of anything. "Thou shalt not make unto thee any graven image, any likeness of any thing that is in heaven above, or that is in the earth beneath, or that is in the water beneath the earth." I wondered then, as so many others have, as to why the God of these people would have included instructions on how they were to symbolize, or not symbolize, their experience. It is a strange injunction to include as part of an ethical system *unless its author assumed a connection between forms of human communication and the quality of a culture*. We may hazard a guess that a people who are being asked to embrace an abstract, universal deity would be rendered unfit to do so by the habit of drawing pictures or making statues or depicting their ideas in any concrete, iconographic forms. The God of the Jews was to exist in the Word and through the Word, an unprecedented conception requiring the highest order of abstract thinking. Iconography thus became blasphemy so that a new kind of God could enter a culture. People like ourselves who are in the process of converting their culture from word-centered to image-centered might profit by reflecting on this Mosaic injunction. But even if I am wrong in these conjectures, it is, I believe, a wise and particularly relevant supposition that the media of communication available to a culture are a dominant influence on the formation of the culture's intellectual and social preoccupations.

Speech, of course, is the primal and indispensable medium. It made us human, keeps us human, and in fact defines what human means. This is not to say that if there were no other means of communication all humans would find it equally convenient to speak about the same things in the same way. We know enough about language to understand that variations in the structures of languages will result in variations in what may be called "world view." How people think about time and space, and about things and processes, will be greatly influenced by the grammatical features of their language. We dare not suppose therefore that all human minds are unanimous in understanding how the world is put together. But how much more divergence there is in world view among different cultures can be imagined when we consider the great number and variety of tools for conversation that go beyond speech. For although culture is a creation of speech, it is recreated anew by every medium of communication—from painting to hieroglyphs to the alphabet to television. Each medium, like language itself, makes possible a unique mode of discourse by providing a new orientation for thought, for expression, for sensibility. Which, of course, is what McLuhan meant in saying the medium is the message. His aphorism, however, is in need of amendment because, as it stands, it may lead one to confuse a message with a metaphor. A message denotes a specific, concrete statement about the world. But the forms of our media, including the symbols through which they permit conversation, do not make such statements. They are rather like metaphors, working by unobtrusive but powerful implication to enforce their special definitions of reality. Whether we are experiencing the world through the lens of speech or the printed word or the television camera, our media-metaphors classify the world for us, sequence it, frame it, enlarge it, reduce it, color it, argue a case for what the world is like. As Ernst Cassirer remarked:

Physical reality seems to recede in proportion as man's symbolic activity advances. Instead of dealing with the things themselves man is in a sense constantly conversing with himself. He has so enveloped himself in linguistic forms, in artistic images, in mythical symbols or religious rites that he cannot see or know anything except by the interposition of [an] artificial medium.

What is peculiar about such interpositions of media is that their role in directing what we will see or know is so rarely noticed. A person who reads a book or who watches television or who glances at his watch is not usually interested in how his mind is organized and controlled by these events, still less in what idea of the world is suggested by a book, television, or a watch. But there are men and women who have noticed these things, especially in our own times. Lewis Mumford, for example, has been one of our great noticers. He is not the sort of a man who looks at a clock merely to see what time it is. Not that he lacks interest in the content of clocks, which is of concern to everyone from moment to moment, but he is far more interested in how a clock creates the idea of "moment to moment." He attends to the philosophy of clocks, to clocks as metaphor, about which our education has had little to say and clock makers nothing at all. "The clock," Mumford has concluded, "is a piece of power machinery whose 'product' is seconds and minutes." In manu-facturing such a product, the clock has the effect of disassociating time from human events and thus nourishes the belief in an independent world of mathematically measurable sequences. Moment to moment, it turns out, is not God's conception, or nature's. It is man conversing with himself about and through a piece of machinery he created.

In Mumford's great book *Technics and Civilization*, he shows how, beginning in the fourteenth century, the clock made us into time-keepers, and then time-savers, and now time-servers. In the process, we have learned irreverence toward the sun and the seasons, for in a world made up of seconds and minutes, the authority of nature is superseded. Indeed, as Mumford points out, with the invention of the clock, Eternity ceased to serve as the measure and focus of human events. And thus, though few would have imagined the connection, the inexorable ticking of the clock may have had more to do with the weakening of God's supremacy than all the treatises produced by the philosophers of the Enlightenment; that is to say, the clock introduced a new form of conversation between man and God, in which God appears to have been the loser. Perhaps Moses should have included another Commandment: Thou shalt not make mechanical representations of time.

That the alphabet introduced a new form of conversation between man and man is by now a commonplace among scholars. To be able to *see* one's utterances rather than only to hear them is no small matter, though our education, once again, has had little to say about this. Nonetheless, it is clear that phonetic writing created a new conception of knowledge, as well as a new sense of intelligence, of audience and of posterity, all of which Plato recognized at an early stage in the development of texts. "No man of intelligence," he wrote in his Seventh Letter, "will venture to express his philosophical views in language, especially not in language that is unchangeable, which is true of that which is set down in written characters." This notwithstanding, he wrote voluminously and understood better than anyone else that the setting down of views in written characters would be the beginning of philosophy, not its end. Philosophy cannot exist without criticism, and writing makes it possible and convenient to subject thought to a continuous and concentrated scrutiny. Writing freezes speech and in so doing gives birth to the grammarian, the logician, the rhetorician, the historian, the scientist— all those who must hold language before them so that they can see what it means, where it errs, and where it is leading.

Plato knew all of this, which means that he knew that writing would bring about a perceptual revolution: a shift from the ear to the eye as an organ of language processing. Indeed, there is a legend that to encourage such a shift Plato insisted that his students study geometry before entering his Academy. If true, it was a sound idea, for as the great literary critic Northrop Frye has remarked, "the written word is far more powerful than simply a reminder; it re-creates the past in the present, and gives us, not the familiar remembered thing, but the glittering intensity of the summoned-up hallucination."

All that Plato surmised about the consequences of writing is now well understood by anthropologists, especially those who have studied cultures in which speech is the only source of complex conversation. Anthropologists know that the written word, as Northrop Frye meant to suggest, is not merely an echo of a speaking voice. It is another kind of voice altogether, a conjurer's trick of the first order. It must certainly have appeared that way to those who invented it, and that is why we should not be surprised that the Egyptian god Thoth, who is alleged to have brought writing to the King Thamus, was also the god of magic. People like ourselves may see nothing wondrous in writing, but our anthropologists know how strange and magical it appears to a purely oral people—a conversation with no one and yet with everyone. What could be stranger than the silence one encounters when addressing a question to a text? What could be more metaphysically puzzling than addressing an unseen audience, as every writer of books must do? And correcting oneself because one knows that an unknown reader will disapprove or misunderstand?

I bring all of this up because what my book is about is how our own tribe is undergoing a vast and trembling shift from the magic of writing to the magic of electronics. What I mean to point out here is that the introduction into a culture of a technique such as writing or a clock is not merely an extension of man's power to bind time but a transformation of his way of thinking—and, of course, of the content of his culture. And that is what I mean to say by calling a medium a metaphor. We are told in school, quite correctly, that a metaphor suggests what a thing is like by comparing it to something else. And by the power of its suggestion, it so fixes a conception in our minds that we cannot imagine the one thing without the other: Light is a wave; language, a tree; God, a wise and venerable man; the mind, a dark cavern illuminated by knowledge. And if these metaphors no longer serve us, we must, in the nature of the matter, find others that will. Light is a particle; language, a river; God (as Bertrand Russell proclaimed), a differential equation; the mind, a garden that yearns to be cultivated.

But our media-metaphors are not so explicit or so vivid as these, and they are far more complex. In understanding their metaphorical function, we must take into account the symbolic forms of their information, the source of their information, the quantity and speed of their information, the context in which their information is experienced. Thus, it takes some digging to get at them, to grasp, for example, that a clock recreates time as an independent, mathematically precise sequence; that writing recreates the mind as a tablet on which experience is written; that the telegraph recreates news as a commodity. And yet, such digging becomes easier if we start from the assumption that in every tool we create, an idea is embedded that goes beyond the function of the thing itself. It has been pointed out, for example, that the invention of eyeglasses in the twelfth century not only made it possible to improve defective vision but suggested the idea that human beings need not accept as final either the endowments of nature or the ravages of time. Eyeglasses refuted the belief that anatomy is destiny by putting forward the idea that our bodies as well as our minds are improvable. I do not think it goes too far to say that there is a link between the invention of eyeglasses in the twelfth century and gene-splitting research in the twentieth.

Even such an instrument as the microscope, hardly a tool of everyday use, had embedded within it a quite astonishing idea, not about biology but about psychology. By revealing a world hitherto hidden from view, the microscope suggested a possibility about the structure of the mind.

If things are not what they seem, if microbes lurk, unseen, on and under our skin, if the invisible controls the visible, then is it not possible that ids and egos and superegos also lurk somewhere unseen? What else is psychoanalysis but a microscope of the mind? Where do our notions of mind come from if not from metaphors generated by our tools? What does it mean to say that someone has an IQ of 126? There are no numbers in people's heads. Intelligence does not have quantity or magnitude, except as we believe that it does. And why do we believe that it does? Because we have tools that imply that this is what the mind is like. Indeed, our tools for thought suggest to us what our bodies are like, as when someone refers to her "biological clock," or when we talk of our "genetic codes," or when we read someone's face like a book, or when our facial expressions telegraph our intentions.

When Galileo remarked that the language of nature is written in mathematics, he meant it only as a metaphor. Nature itself does not speak. Neither do our minds or our bodies or, more to the point of this book, our bodies politic. Our conversations about nature and about ourselves are conducted in whatever "languages" we find it possible and convenient to employ. We do not see nature or intelligence or human motivation or ideology as "it" is but only as our languages are. And our languages are our media. Our media are our metaphors. Our metaphors create the content of our culture.

Possibilities for Writing

1. Summmarize the gist of Postman's argument in this essay, the opening chapter of his book, *Amusing Ourselves to Death: Public Discourse in the Age of Show Business*. Consider the

implications of the title of both the book and the chapter in explaining Postman's main idea and the examples he provides in its support.

2. Discuss the extent to which television has altered people's habits—the effects it has had on their leisure activities, on how they learn, and on family life. Explain your view of the benefits and drawbacks of television as a medium of communiction. You may wish to focus on something as specific as television news.

3. Write an essay in which you explore the benefits and drawbacks of another technological development for communication—the computer, for example, the Internet, or the cell phone. Consider the extent to which your chosen technology has affected both how we communicate and what we communicate. And consider both its benefits and drawbacks, as you explain its effects on public and private life.

Scott Russell Sanders (b. 1945) was born into a working class family in Memphis and received scholarships to Brown and to Cambridge University in England. He has published books in many genres: novels, poetry, children's stories, science fiction, nature writing, and personal essays. These essays, noted for their sincerity and subtle grace, have been collected in The Paradise of Bombs *(1988),* Secrets for the Universe *(1991), and* Writing from the Center *(1995), among others. Among Sanders latest books for adult readers are* The Country of Language *(1999). and* A Private History of Awe *(2006). He is a professor of English and creative writing at Indiana University.*

Scott Russell Sanders
Under the Influence

In "Under the Influence," Scott Russell Sanders explains why he doesn't drink alcohol. Sanders's title refers to the influence that alcohol had on his father, who drank heavily, nearly constantly, and whose drinking not only harmed his family, but also left an indelible impression on his son. Sanders describes the self-deception his father engaged in along with the deception of others, who played along and pretended with him that his drinking was not a serious problem either for him or for them. And Sanders describes unflinchingly what he calls "the corrosive mixture of helplessness, responsibility, and shame" that he felt "as the son of an alcoholic."

Sanders's essay, however, is not only about his father. It is also about himself—about how, in important ways, he remains "under the influence" of his father. Not as a drinker, since he only "sips warily," drinking perhaps a glass of wine or beer a week—nothing more and nothing stronger. Sanders drinks little alcohol and drinks warily out of fear and out of knowledge, a knowledge and a fear that as the child of an alcoholic he is four times more likely than others to become an alcoholic himself.

My father drank. He drank as a gut-punched boxer gasps for breath, as a starving dog gobbles food—compulsively, secretly, in pain and trembling. I use the past tense not because he ever quit drinking but because he quit living. That is how the story ends for my father, age sixty-four, heart bursting, body cooling and forsaken on the linoleum of my brother's trailer. The story continues for my brother, my sister, my mother, and me, and will continue so long as memory holds.

In the perennial present of memory, I slip into the garage or barn to see my father tipping back the flat green bottles of wine, the brown cylinders of whiskey, the cans of beer disguised in paper bags. His Adam's apple bobs, the liquid gurgles, he wipes the sandy-haired back of a hand over his lips, and then, his bloodshot gaze bumping into me, he stashes the bottle or can inside his jacket, under the workbench, between two bales of hay, and we both pretend the moment has not occurred.

"What's up, buddy?" he says, thick-tongued and edgy.

"Sky's up," I answer, playing along.

"And don't forget prices," he grumbles. "Prices are always up. And taxes."

In memory, his white 1951 Pontiac with the stripes down the hood and the Indian head on the snout jounces to a stop in the driveway; or it is the 1956 Ford station wagon, or the 1963 Rambler shaped like a toad, or the sleek 1969 Bonneville that will do 120 miles per hour on straightaways; or it is the robin's-egg blue pickup, new in 1980, battered in 1981, the year of his death. He climbs out, grinning dangerously, unsteady on his legs, and we children interrupt our game of catch, our building of snow forts, our picking of plums, to watch in silence as he weaves past into the house, where he slumps into his overstuffed chair and falls asleep. Shaking her head, our mother stubs out the cigarette he has left smoldering in the ashtray. All evening, until our bedtimes, we tiptoe past him, as past a snoring dragon. Then we curl in our fearful sheets, listening. Eventually he wakes with a grunt, Mother slings accusations at him, he snarls back, she yells, he growls, their voices clashing. Before long, she retreats to their bedroom, sobbing—not from the blows of fists, for he never strikes her, but from the force of words.

Left alone, our father prowls the house, thumping into furniture, rummaging in the kitchen, slamming doors, turning the pages of the newspaper with a savage crackle, muttering back at the late-night drivel from television. The roof might fly off, the walls might buckle from the pressure of his rage. Whatever my brother and sister and mother may be thinking on their own rumpled pillows, I lie there hating him, loving him, fearing him, knowing I have failed him. I tell myself he drinks to ease an ache that gnaws at his belly, an ache I must have caused by disappointing him somehow, a murderous ache I should be able to relieve by doing all my chores, earning A's in school, winning baseball games, fixing the broken washer and the burst pipes, bringing in money to fill his empty wallet. He would not hide the green bottles in his tool box, would not sneak off to the barn with a lump under his coat, would not fall asleep in the daylight, would not roar and fume, would not drink himself to death, if only I were perfect.

I am forty-two as I write these words, and I know full well now that my father was an alcoholic, a man consumed by disease rather than by disappointment. What had seemed to me a private grief is in fact a public scourge. In the United States alone some ten or fifteen million people share his ailment, and behind the doors they slam in fury or disgrace, countless other children tremble. I comfort myself with such knowledge, holding it against the throb of memory like an ice pack against a bruise. There are keener sources of grief: poverty, racism, rape, war. I do not wish to compete for a trophy in suffering. I am only trying to understand the corrosive mixture of helplessness, responsibility, and shame that I learned to feel as the son of an alcoholic. I realize now that I did not cause my father's illness, nor could I have cured it. Yet for all this grown-up knowledge, I am still ten years old, my own son's age, and as that boy I struggle in guilt and confusion to save my father from pain.

Consider a few of our synonyms for *drunk:* tipsy, tight, pickled, soused, and plowed; stoned and stewed, lubricated and inebriated, juiced and sluiced; three sheets to the wind, in your cups, out of your mind, under the table; lit up, tanked up, wiped out; besotted, blotto, bombed, and buzzed; plastered, polluted, putrified; loaded or looped, boozy, woozy, fuddled, or smashed; crocked and shit-faced, corked and pissed, snockered and sloshed.

It is a mostly humorous lexicon, as the lore that deals with drunks—in jokes and cartoons, in plays, films, and television skits—is largely comic. Aunt Matilda nips elderberry wine from the sideboard and burps politely during supper. Uncle Fred slouches to the table glassy-eyed, wearing a lamp shade for a hat and murmuring, "Candy is dandy but liquor is quicker." Inspired by cocktails, Mrs. Somebody recounts the events of her day in a fuzzy dialect, while Mr. Somebody nibbles her ear and croons a bawdy song. On the sofa with Boyfriend, Daughter giggles, licking gin from her lips, and loosens the bows in her hair. Junior knocks back some brews with his chums at the Leopard Lounge and stumbles home to the wrong house, wonders foggily why he cannot locate his pajamas, and crawls naked into bed with the ugliest girl in school. The family dog slurps from a neglected martini and wobbles to the nursery, where he vomits in Baby's shoe.

It is all great fun. But if in the audience you notice a few laughing faces turn grim when the drunk lurches on stage, don't be surprised, for these are the children of alcoholics. Over the grinning mask of Dionysus, the leering mask of Bacchus, these children cannot help seeing the bloated features of their own parents. Instead of laughing, they wince, they mourn. Instead of celebrating the drunk as one freed from constraints, they pity him as one enslaved. They refuse to believe *in vino veritas*, having seen their befuddled parents skid away from truth toward folly and oblivion. And so these children bite their lips until the lush staggers into the wings.

My father, when drunk, was neither funny nor honest; he was pathetic, frightening, deceitful. There seemed to be a leak in him somewhere, and he poured in booze to keep from draining dry. Like a torture victim who refuses to squeal, he would never admit that he had touched a drop, not even in his last year, when he seemed to be dissolving in alcohol before our very eyes. I never knew him to lie about anything, ever, except about this one ruinous fact. Drowsy, clumsy, unable to fix a bicycle tire, throw a baseball, balance a grocery sack, or walk across the room, he was stripped of his true self by drink. In a matter of minutes, the contents of a bottle could transform a brave man into a coward, a buddy into a bully, a gifted athlete and skilled carpenter and shrewd businessman into a bumbler. No dictionary of synonyms for *drunk* would soften the anguish of watching our prince turn into a frog.

Father's drinking became the family secret. While growing up, we children never breathed a word of it beyond the four walls of our house. To this day, my brother and sister rarely mention it, and then only when I press them. I did not confess the ugly, bewildering fact to my wife until his wavering walk and slurred speech forced me to. Recently, on the seventh anniversary of my father's death, I asked my mother if she ever spoke of his drinking to friends. "No, no, never," she replied hastily. "I couldn't bear for anyone to know."

The secret bores under the skin, gets in the blood, into the bone, and stays there. Long after you have supposedly been cured of malaria, the fever can flare up, the tremors can shake you. So it is with the fevers of shame. You swallow the bitter quinine of knowledge, and you learn to feel pity and compassion toward the drinker. Yet the shame lingers in your marrow, and, because of the shame, anger.

For a long stretch of my childhood we lived on a military reservation in Ohio, an arsenal where bombs were stored underground in bunkers, vintage airplanes burst into flames, and unstable artillery shells boomed nightly at the dump. We had the feeling, as children, that we played in a mine field, where a heedless footfall could trigger an explosion. When Father was drinking, the house, too, became a mine field. The least bump could set off either parent.

The more he drank, the more obsessed Mother became with stopping him. She hunted for bottles, counted the cash in his wallet, sniffed at his breath. Without meaning to snoop, we children blundered left and right into damning evidence. On afternoons when he came home from work sober, we flung ourselves at him for hugs, and felt against our ribs the telltale lump in his coat. In the barn we tumbled on the hay and heard beneath our sneakers the crunch of buried glass. We tugged open a drawer in his workbench, looking for screwdrivers or crescent wrenches, and spied a gleaming six-pack among the tools. Playing tag, we darted around the house just in time to see him sway on the rear stoop and heave a finished bottle into the woods. In his good night kiss we smelled the cloying sweetness of Clorets, the mints he chewed to camouflage his dragon's breath.

I can summon up that kiss right now by recalling Theodore Roethke's lines about his own father in "My Papa's Waltz":

> The whiskey on your breath
> Could make a small boy dizzy;
> But I hung on like death:
> Such waltzing was not easy.

Such waltzing was hard, terribly hard, for with a boy's scrawny arms I was trying to hold my tipsy father upright.

For years, the chief source of those incriminating bottles and cans was a grimy store a mile from us, a cinder block place called Sly's, with two gas pumps outside and a moth-eaten dog asleep in the window. A strip of flypaper, speckled the year round with black bodies, coiled in the doorway. Inside, on rusty metal shelves or in wheezing coolers, you could find pop and Popsicles, cigarettes, potato chips, canned soup, raunchy postcards, fishing gear, Twinkies, wine, and beer. When Father drove anywhere on errands, Mother would send us kids along as guards, warning us not to let him out of our sight. And so with one or more of us on board, Father would cruise up to Sly's, pump a dollar's worth of gas or pump the tires with air, and then, telling us to wait in the car, he would head for that fly-spangled doorway.

Dutiful and panicky, we cried, "Let us go in with you!"

"No," he answered. "I'll be back in two shakes."

"Please!"

"No!" he roared. "Don't you budge, or I'll jerk a knot in your tails!"

So we stayed put, kicking the seats, while he ducked inside. Often, when he had parked the car at a careless angle, we gazed in through the window and saw Mr. Sly fetching down from a shelf behind the cash register two green pints of Gallo wine. Father swigged one of them right there at the counter, stuffed the other in his pocket, and then out he came, a bulge in his coat, a flustered look on his red face.

Because the Mom and Pop who ran the dump were neighbors of ours, living just down the tar-blistered road, I hated them all the more for poisoning my father. I wanted to sneak in their store and smash the bottles and set fire to the place. I also hated the Gallo brothers, Ernest and Julio, whose jovial faces shone from the labels of their wine, labels I would find, torn and curled, when I burned the trash. I noted the Gallo brothers' address, in California, and I studied the road atlas to see how far that was from Ohio, because I meant to go out there and tell Ernest and Julio what they were doing to my father, and then, if they showed no mercy, I would kill them.

While growing up on the back roads and in the country schools and cramped Methodist churches of Ohio and Tennessee, I never heard the word *alcoholism*, never happened across it in books or magazines. In the nearby towns, there were no addiction treatment programs, no community mental health centers, no Alcoholics Anonymous chapters, no therapists. Left alone with our grievous secret, we had no way of understanding Father's drinking except as an act of will, a deliberate folly or cruelty, a moral weakness, a sin. He drank because he chose to, pure and simple. Why our father, so playful and competent and kind when sober, would choose to ruin himself and punish his family, we could not fathom.

Our neighborhood was high on the Bible, and the Bible was hard on drunkards. "Woe to those who are heroes at drinking wine, and valiant men in mixing strong drink," wrote Isaiah. "The priest and the prophet reel with strong drink, they are confused with wine, they err in vision, they stumble in giving judgment. For all tables are full of vomit, no place is without filthiness." We children had seen those fouled tables at the local truck stop where the notorious boozers hung out, our father occasionally among them. "Wine and new wine take away the under- standing," declared the prophet Hosea. We had also seen evidence of that in our father, who could multiply seven-digit numbers in his head when sober, but when drunk could not help us with fourth-grade math. Proverbs warned: "Do not look at wine when it is red, when it sparkles in the cup and goes down smoothly. At the last it bites like a serpent, and stings like an adder. Your eyes will see strange things, and your mind utter perverse things." Woe, woe.

Dismayingly often, these biblical drunkards stirred up trouble for their own kids. Noah made fresh wine after the flood, drank too much of it, fell asleep without any clothes on, and was glimpsed in the buff by his son Ham, whom Noah promptly cursed. In one passage—it was so shocking we had to read it under our blankets with flashlights—the patriarch Lot fell down drunk and slept with his daughters. The sins of the fathers set their children's teeth on edge.

Our ministers were fond of quoting St. Paul's pronouncement that drunkards would not inherit the kingdom of God. These grave preach- ers assured us that the wine referred to during the Last Supper was in fact grape juice. Bible and sermons and hymns combined to give us the impression that Moses should have brought down from the mountain another stone tablet, bearing the Eleventh Commandment: Thou shalt not drink.

The scariest and most illuminating Bible story apropos of drunkards was the one about the lunatic and the swine. Matthew, Mark, and Luke each told a version of the tale. We knew it by heart: When Jesus climbed out of his boat one day, this lunatic came charging up from the grave- yard, stark naked and filthy, frothing at the mouth, so violent that he broke the strongest chains. Nobody would go near him. Night and day for years this madman had been wailing among the tombs and bruising himself with stones. Jesus took one look at him and said, "Come out of the man, you unclean spirits!" for he could see that the lunatic was possessed by demons. Meanwhile, some hogs were conveniently rooting nearby. "If we have to come out," begged the demons, "at least let us go into those swine." Jesus agreed. The unclean spirits entered the hogs, and the hogs rushed straight off a cliff and plunged into a lake. Hearing the story in Sunday school, my friends thought mainly of the pigs. (How big a splash did they make? Who paid for the lost pork?) But I thought of the redeemed lunatic, who bathed himself and put on clothes and calmly sat at the feet of Jesus, restored—so the Bible said—to "his right mind."

When drunk, our father was clearly in his wrong mind. He became a stranger, as fearful to us as any graveyard lunatic, not quite frothing at the mouth but fierce enough, quick-tempered, explosive; or else he grew maudlin and weepy, which frightened us nearly as much. In my boyhood despair, I reasoned that maybe he wasn't to blame for turning into an ogre. Maybe, like the lunatic, he was possessed by demons. I found support for my theory when I heard liquor referred to as "spirits," when the newspapers reported that somebody had been arrested for "driving under the influence," and when church ladies railed against that "demon drink."

If my father was indeed possessed, who would exorcise him? If he was a sinner, who would save him? If he was ill, who would cure him? If he suffered, who would ease his pain? Not ministers or doctors, for we could not bring ourselves to confide in them; not the neighbors, for we pretended they had never seen him drunk; not Mother, who fussed and pleaded but could not budge him; not my brother and sister, who were only kids. That left me. It did not matter that I, too, was only a child, and a bewildered one at that. I could not excuse myself.

On first reading a description of delirium tremens—in a book on alcoholism I smuggled from the library—I thought immediately of the frothing lunatic and the frenzied swine. When I read stories or watched films about grisly metamorphoses—Dr. Jekyll becoming Mr. Hyde, the mild husband changing into a werewolf, the kindly neighbor taken over by a brutal alien—I could not help seeing my own father's mutation from sober to drunk. Even today, knowing better, I am attracted by the demonic theory of drink, for when I recall my father's transformation, the emergence of his ugly second self, I find it easy to believe in possession by unclean spirits. We never knew which version of Father would come home from work, the true or the tainted, nor could we guess how far down the slope toward cruelty he would slide.

How far a man *could* slide we gauged by observing our back-road neighbors—the out-of-work miners who had dragged their families to our corner of Ohio from the desolate hollows of Appalachia, the tight-fisted farmers, the surly mechanics, the balked and broken men. There was, for example, whiskey-soaked Mr. Jenkins, who beat his wife and kids so hard we could hear their screams from the road. There was Mr. Lavo the wino, who fell asleep smoking time and again, until one night his disgusted wife bundled up the children and went outside and left him in his easy chair to burn; he awoke on his own, staggered out coughing into the yard, and pounded her flat while the children looked on and the shack turned to ash. There was the truck driver, Mr. Sampson, who tripped over his son's tricycle one night while drunk and got so mad that he jumped into his semi and drove away, shifting through the dozen gears, and never came back. We saw the bruised children of these fathers clump onto our school bus, we saw the abandoned children huddle in the pews at church, we saw the stunned and battered mothers begging for help at our doors.

Our own father never beat us, and I don't think he ever beat Mother, but he threatened often. The Old Testament Yahweh was not more terrible in his wrath. Eyes blazing, voice booming, Father would pull out his belt and swear to give us a whipping, but he never followed through, never needed to, because we could imagine it so vividly. He shoved us, pawed us with the back of his hand, as an irked bear might smack a cub, not to injure, just to clear a space. I can see him grabbing Mother by the hair as she cowers on a chair during a nightly quarrel. He twists her neck back until she gapes up at him, and then he lifts over her skull a glass quart bottle of milk, the milk running down his forearm, and he yells at her, "Say just one more word, one goddamn word, and I'll shut you up!" I fear she will prick him with her sharp tongue, but she is terrified into silence, and so am I, and the leaking bottle quivers in the air, and milk slithers through the red hair of my father's uplifted arm, and the entire scene is there to this moment, the head jerked back, the club raised.

When the drink made him weepy, Father would pack a bag and kiss each of us children on the head, and announce from the front door that he was moving out. "Where to?" we demanded, fearful each time that he would leave for good, as Mr. Sampson had roared away for good in his diesel truck. "Someplace where I won't get hounded every minute," Father would answer, his jaw quivering. He stabbed a look at Mother, who might say, "Don't run into the ditch before you get there," or, "Good riddance," and then he would slink away. Mother watched him go with arms crossed over her chest, her face closed like the lid on a box of snakes. We children bawled. Where could he go? To the truck stop, that den of iniquity? To one of those dark, ratty flophouses in town? Would he wind up sleeping under a railroad bridge or on a park bench or in a cardboard box, mummied in rags, like the bums we had seen on our trips to Cleveland and Chicago? We bawled and bawled, wondering if he would ever come back.

He always did come back, a day or a week later, but each time there was a sliver less of him.

In Kafka's *The Metamorphosis*, which opens famously with Gregor Samsa waking up from uneasy dreams to find himself transformed into an insect, Gregor's family keep reassuring themselves that things will be just fine again, "When he comes back to us." Each time alcohol transformed our father, we held out the same hope, that he would really and truly come back to us, our authentic father, the tender and playful and competent man, and then all things would be fine. We had grounds for such hope. After his weepy departures and chapfallen returns, he would sometimes go weeks, even months without drinking. Those were glad times. Joy banged inside my ribs. Every day without the furtive glint of bottles, every meal without a fight, every bedtime without sobs encouraged us to believe that such bliss might go on forever.

Mother was fooled by just such a hope all during the forty-odd years she knew this Greeley Ray Sanders. Soon after she met him in a Chicago delicatessen on the eve of World War II, and fell for his butter-melting Mississippi drawl and his wavy red hair, she learned that he drank heavily. But then so did a lot of men. She would soon coax or scold him into breaking the nasty habit. She would point out to him how ugly and foolish it was, this bleary drinking, and then he would quit. He refused to quit during their engagement, however, still refused during the first years of marriage, refused until my sister came along. The shock of fatherhood sobered him, and he remained sober through my birth at the end of the war and right on through until we moved in 1951 to the Ohio arsenal, that paradise of bombs. Like all places that make a business of death, the arsenal had more than its share of alcoholics and drug addicts and other varieties of escape artists. There I turned six and started school and woke into a child's flickering awareness, just in time to see my father begin sneaking swigs in the garage.

He sobered up again for most of a year at the height of the Korean War, to celebrate the birth of my brother. But aside from that dry spell, his only breaks from drinking before I graduated from high school were just long enough to raise and then dash our hopes. Then during the fall of my senior year—the time of the Cuban missile crisis, when it seemed that the nightly explosions at the munitions dump and the nightly rages in our household might spread to engulf the globe—Father collapsed. His liver, kidneys, and heart all conked out. The doctors saved him, but only by a hair. He stayed in the hospital for weeks, going through a withdrawal so terrible that Mother would not let us visit him. If he wanted to kill himself, the doctors solemnly warned him, all he had to do was hit the bottle again. One binge would finish him.

Father must have believed them, for he stayed dry the next fifteen years. It was an answer to prayer, Mother said, it was a miracle. I believe it was a reflex of fear, which he sustained over the years through courage and pride. He knew a man could die from drink, for his brother Roscoe had. We children never laid eyes on doomed Uncle Roscoe, but in the stories Mother told us he became a fairy-tale figure, like a boy who took the wrong turning in the woods and was gobbled up by the wolf.

The fifteen-year dry spell came to an end with Father's retirement in the spring of 1978. Like many men, he gave up his identity along with his job. One day he was a boss at the factory, with a brass plate on his door and a reputation to uphold; the next day he was a nobody at home. He and Mother were leaving Ontario, the last of the many places to which his job had carried them, and they were moving to a new house in Mississippi, his childhood stomping grounds. As a boy in Mississippi, Father sold Coca-Cola during dances while the moonshiners peddled their brew in the parking lot; as a young blade, he fought in bars and in the ring, seeking a state Golden Gloves championship; he gambled at poker, hunted pheasants, raced motorcycles and cars, played semiprofessional baseball, and, along with all his buddies—in the Black Cat Saloon, behind the cotton gin, in the wood—he drank. It was a perilous youth to dream of recovering.

After his final day of work, Mother drove on ahead with a car full of begonias and violets, while Father stayed behind to oversee the packing. When the van was loaded, the sweaty movers broke open a six-pack and offered him a beer.

"Let's drink to retirement!" they crowed. "Let's drink to freedom! to fishing! hunting! loafing! Let's drink to a guy who's going home!"

At least I imagine some such words, for that is all I can do, imagine, and I see Father's hand trembling in midair as he thinks about the fifteen sober years and about the doctors' warning, and he tells himself *Goddamnit, I am a free man,* and *Why can't a free man drink one beer after a lifetime of hard work?* and I see his arm reaching, his fingers closing, the can tilting to his lips. I even supply a label for the beer, a swaggering brand that promises on television to deliver the essence of life. I watch the amber liquid pour down his throat, the alcohol steal into his blood, the key turn in his brain.

Soon after my parents moved back to Father's treacherous stomping ground, my wife and I visited them in Mississippi with our five-year-old daughter. Mother had been too distraught to warn me about the return of the demons. So when I climbed out of the car that bright July morning and saw my father napping in the hammock, I felt uneasy, for in all his sober years I had never known him to sleep in daylight. Then he lurched upright, blinked his bloodshot eyes, and greeted us in a syrupy voice. I was hurled back helpless into childhood.

"What's the matter with Papaw?" our daughter asked.

"Nothing," I said. "Nothing!"

Like a child again, I pretended not to see him in his stupor, and behind my phony smile I grieved. On that visit and on the few that remained before his death, once again I found bottles in the workbench, bottles in the woods. Again his hands shook too much for him to run a saw, to make his precious miniature furniture, to drive straight down back roads. Again he wound up in the ditch, in the hospital, in jail, in treatment centers. Again he shouted and wept. Again he lied. "I never touched a drop," he swore. "Your mother's making it up."

I no longer fancied I could reason with the men whose names I found on the bottles—Jim Beam, Jack Daniels—nor did I hope to save my father by burning down a store. I was able now to press the cold statistics about alcoholism against the ache of memory: ten million victims, fifteen million, twenty. And yet, in spite of my age, I reacted in the same blind way as I had in childhood, ignoring biology, forgetting numbers, vainly seeking to erase through my efforts whatever drove him to drink. I worked on their place twelve and sixteen hours a day, in the swelter of Mississippi summers, digging ditches, running electrical wires, planting trees, mowing grass, building sheds, as though what nagged at him was some list of chores, as though by taking his worries on my shoulders

I could redeem him. I was flung back into boyhood, acting as though my father would not drink himself to death if only I were perfect.

I failed of perfection; he succeeded in dying. To the end, he considered himself not sick but sinful. "Do you want to kill yourself?" I asked him. "Why not?" he answered. "Why the hell not? What's there to save?" To the end, he would not speak about his feelings, would not or could not give a name to the beast that was devouring him.

In silence, he went rushing off the cliff. Unlike the biblical swine, however, he left behind a few of the demons to haunt his children. Life with him and the loss of him twisted us into shapes that will be familiar to other sons and daughters of alcoholics. My brother became a rebel, my sister retreated into shyness, I played the stalwart and dutiful son who would hold the family together. If my father was unstable, I would be a rock. If he squandered money on drink, I would pinch every penny. If he wept when drunk—and only when drunk—I would not let myself weep at all. If he roared at the Little League umpire for calling my pitches balls, I would throw nothing but strikes. Watching him flounder and rage, I came to dread the loss of control. I would go through life without making anyone mad. I vowed never to put in my mouth or veins any chemical that would banish my everyday self. I would never make a scene, never lash out at the ones I loved, never hurt a soul. Through hard work, relentless work, I would achieve something dazzling— in the classroom, on the basketball floor, in the science lab, in the pages of books—and my achievement would distract the world's eyes from his humiliation. I would become a worthy sacrifice, and the smoke of my burning would please God.

It is far easier to recognize these twists in my character than to undo them. Work has become an addiction for me, as drink was an addiction for my father. Knowing this, my daughter gave me a placard for the wall: WORKAHOLIC. The labor is endless and futile, for I can no more redeem myself through work than I could redeem my father. I still panic in the face of other people's anger, because his drunken temper was so terrible. I shrink from causing sadness or disappointment even to strangers, as though I were still concealing the family shame. I still notice every twitch of emotion in the faces around me, having learned as a child to read the weather in faces, and I blame myself for their least pang of unhappiness or anger. In certain moods I blame myself for everything. Guilt burns like acid in my veins.

I am moved to write these pages now because my own son, at the age of ten, is taking on himself the griefs of the world, and in particular the griefs of his father. He tells me that when I am gripped by sadness he feels responsible; he feels there must be something he can do to spring me from depression, to fix my life. And that crushing sense of responsibility is exactly what I felt at the age of ten in the face of my father's drinking. My son wonders if I, too, am possessed. I write, therefore, to drag into the light what eats at me—the fear, the guilt, the shame—so that my own children may be spared.

I still shy away from nightclubs, from bars, from parties where the solvent is alcohol. My friends puzzle over this, but it is no more peculiar than for a man to shy away from the lions' den after seeing his father torn apart. I took my own first drink at the age of twenty-one, half a glass of burgundy. I knew the odds of my becoming an alcoholic were four times higher than for the sons of nonalcoholic fathers. So I sipped warily.

I still do—once a week, perhaps, a glass of wine, a can of beer, nothing stronger, nothing more. I listen for the turning of a key in my brain.

Possibilities for Writing

1. Despite his harrowing depiction of his father's drunkenness, do you think Sanders manages to create any sympathy for the man? If so, how does he do this? If not, how do you respond to Sanders's sense of caring for his father?

2. Throughout, the essay is characterized by numerous biblical references. Find as many of these as you can and analyze them, discussing what they contribute to the essay's overall meaning and impact.

3. Write an essay about your own experiences with alcohol, though not necessarily as a drinker yourself; you may focus on how alcohol has affected people you know.

Susan Sontag (1933–2004) was one of America's most prominent intellectuals, having been involved with the world of ideas all her life. After studying at the University of California at Berkeley, she earned a B.A. in philosophy from the University of Chicago at the age of eighteen, after which she studied religion at the Union Theological Seminary in New York, then philosophy and literature at Harvard, receiving master's degrees in both fields. Sontag also studied at Oxford and the Sorbonne. From the other side of the desk, she taught and lectured extensively at universities around the world, but for many years she made her academic home at Columbia and Rutgers universities. Sontag's books range widely, and include a collection of stories, I, etcetera *(1978); a play,* Alice in Bed *(1993); and six volumes of essays, including* Against Interpretation *(1966),* Illness as Metaphor *(1978), and* On Photography *(1977). Among her four novels are* The Volcano Lover *(1992), which was a best-seller, and* In America *(2000), which won the National Book Critics Circle Award. In addition, Sontag wrote and directed four feature-length films and was a human rights activist for more than two decades. She was also a MacArthur Fellow.*

Susan Sontag

A Woman's Beauty: Put-Down or Power Source?

In "A Woman's Beauty: Put-Down or Power Source?" Sontag displays her historical interest as well as her interest in current attitudes toward gender roles. In arguing against the dangerous and limiting ideals to which women have subjected themselves (and been subjected by men), Sontag brings to bear a brisk analysis of Greek and Christian perspectives, implicating both in their consequences for contemporary women's obsessive and compulsive efforts to make themselves beautiful.

Unlike many contemporary essays, Sontag's essays lack a strong autobiographical impulse. One might expect such a personal strain in an essay on women's beauty—it certainly would not be out of place—but Sontag assiduously avoids the personal note. But Sontag is less concerned either with her own experience of beauty or with past perspectives on beauty in and of themselves. She is far more interested in how the past can help us understand the present, and how past perspectives affect modern women's fascination with and desire for personal beauty.

For the Greeks, beauty was a virtue: a kind of excellence. Persons then were assumed to be what we now have to call—lamely, enviously— *whole* persons. If it did occur to the Greeks to distinguish between a person's "inside" and "outside," they still expected that inner beauty would be matched by beauty of the other kind. The well-born young Athenians who gathered around Socrates found it quite paradoxical that their hero was so intelligent, so brave, so honorable, so seductive—and so ugly. One of Socrates' main pedagogical acts was to be ugly—and teach those innocent, no doubt splendid-looking disciples of his how full of paradoxes life really was.

They may have resisted Socrates' lesson. We do not. Several thousand years later, we are more wary of the enchantments of beauty. We not only split off—with the greatest facility—the "inside" (character, intellect) from the "outside" (looks); but we are actually surprised when someone who is beautiful is also intelligent, talented, good.

It was principally the influence of Christianity that deprived beauty of the central place it had in classical ideals of human excellence. By limiting excellence (*virtus* in Latin) to *moral* virtue only, Christianity set beauty adrift—as an alienated, arbitrary, superficial enchantment. And beauty has continued to lose prestige. For close to two centuries it has become a convention to attribute beauty to only one of the two sexes: the sex which, however Fair, is always Second. Associating beauty with women has put beauty even further on the defensive, morally.

A beautiful woman, we say in English. But a handsome man. "Handsome" is the masculine equivalent of—and refusal of—a compliment which has accumulated certain demeaning overtones, by being reserved for women only. That one can call a man "beautiful" in French and in Italian suggests that Catholic countries—unlike those countries shaped by the Protestant version of Christianity—still retain some vestiges of the pagan admiration for beauty. But the difference, if one exists, is of degree only. In every modern country that is Christian or post-Christian, women *are* the beautiful sex—to the detriment of the notion of beauty as well as of women.

To be called beautiful is thought to name something essential to women's character and concerns. (In contrast to men—whose essence is to be strong, or effective, or competent.) It does not take someone in the throes of advanced feminist awareness to perceive that the way women are taught to be involved with beauty encourages narcissism, reinforces dependence and immaturity. Everybody (women and men) knows that. For it is "everybody," a whole society, that has identified being feminine with caring about how one *looks*. (In contrast to being masculine—which is identified with caring about what one *is* and *does* and only secondarily, if at all, about how one looks.) Given these stereotypes, it is no wonder that beauty enjoys, at best, a rather mixed reputation.

It is not, of course, the desire to be beautiful that is wrong but the obligation to be—or to try. What is accepted by most women as a flattering idealization of their sex is a way of making women feel inferior to what they actually are—or normally grow to be. For the ideal of beauty is administered as a form of self-oppression. Women are taught to see their bodies in *parts*, and to evaluate each part separately. Breasts, feet, hips, waistline, neck, eyes, nose, complexion, hair, and so on—each in turn is submitted to an anxious, fretful, often despairing scrutiny. Even if some pass muster, some will always be found wanting. Nothing less than perfection will do.

In men, good looks is a whole, something taken in at a glance. It does not need to be confirmed by giving measurements of different regions of the body; nobody encourages a man to dissect his appearance, feature by feature. As for perfection, that is considered trivial—almost unmanly. Indeed, in the ideally good-looking man a small imperfection or blemish is considered positively desirable. According to one movie critic (a woman) who is a declared Robert Redford fan, it is having that cluster of skin-colored moles on one cheek that saves Redford from being merely a "pretty face." Think of the depreciation of women—as well as of beauty—that is implied in that judgment.

"The privileges of beauty are immense," said Cocteau. To be sure, beauty is a form of power. And deservedly so. What is lamentable is that it is the only form of power that most women are encouraged to seek. This power is always conceived in relation to men; it is not the power to do but the power to attract. It is a power that negates itself. For this power is not one that can be chosen freely—at least, not by women—or renounced without social censure.

To preen, for a woman, can never be just a pleasure. It is also a duty. It is her work. If a woman does real work—and even if she has clambered up to a leading position in politics, law, medicine, business, or whatever—she is always under pressure to confess that she still works at being attractive. But in so far as she is keeping up as one of the Fair Sex, she brings under suspicion her very capacity to be objective, professional, authoritative, thoughtful. Damned if they do—women are. And damned if they don't.

One could hardly ask for more important evidence of the dangers of considering persons as split between what is "inside" and what is "outside" than that interminable half-comic half-tragic tale, the oppression of women. How easy it is to start off by defining women as caretakers of their surfaces, and then to disparage them (or find them adorable) for being "superficial." It is a crude trap, and it has worked for too long. But to get out of the trap requires that women get some critical distance from that excellence and privilege which is beauty, enough distance to see how much beauty itself has been abridged in order to prop up the mythology of the "feminine." There should be a way of saving beauty *from* women—and *for* them.

Possibilities for Writing

1. Consider the extent to which you agree (or disagree) with Sontag regarding what she says about the plight of contemporary women with respect to beauty. To what extent are men responsible for women's obsession with beauty? To what extent are women themselves responsible? Explain.

2. Sontag makes a brief historical excursion to consider the place of beauty in classical Greek culture and in early Christian times. How effective is this excursion into history? How important is it for Sontag's argument? And how persuasive is Sontag's use of these references?

3. Do your own little study of women's attitudes to beauty by surveying women you know in varying age groups. Consider both what they say and what they do with regard to the use of beauty products. Write up your findings and your analysis of the significance of beauty for women today.

Elizabeth Cady Stanton (1815–1902), an important leader of the early women's movement, was born in Johnstown, New York, and received a rigorous education for a woman of her day at the Troy Female Seminary. After attending a congress of abolitionists during which women were barred from participating, she was inspired to promote greater equality for women. She helped organize the first women's rights convention in Seneca Falls, New York, in 1848, and she continued to be a strong leader in the movement to gain women the right to vote, to liberalize divorce laws, and to help women achieve parity with men in terms of education, employment, and legal status. The mother of seven children, she was nevertheless a tireless organizer, lecturer, and writer for the cause, as president of major women's suffrage associations from 1869 until her death.

Elizabeth Cady Stanton
Declaration of Sentiments and Resolutions

Elizabeth Cady Stanton's "Declaration of Sentiments and Resolutions" was created at the Seneca Falls Convention, at which women gathered in Seneca Falls, New York, to assert their rights and demand equal respect as full United States citizens. In the "Declaration," Stanton makes clear and purposeful reference to the United States Declaration of Independence. At certain points, Stanton uses the exact wording of the American Declaration. But she adds "women" to the equation.

Stanton also follows the logical structure of the Declaration of Independence, arguing that men have mistreated women, denied women their "inalienable" rights, and generally established "an absolute tyranny" over them, a tyranny analogous to that which England had established over the American colonies. In addition, Stanton also creates a list of examples she cites as evidence of men's tyrannical treatment of women. From this evidence she draws the conclusion that women be given "immediate admission to all the rights and privileges which belong to them as citizens of the United States."

When, in the course of human events, it becomes necessary for one portion of the family of man to assume among the people of the earth a position different from that which they have hitherto occupied, but one to which the laws of nature and of nature's God entitle them, a decent respect to the opinions of mankind requires that they should declare the causes that impel them to such a course.

We hold these truths to be self-evident: that all men and women are created equal; that they are endowed by their Creator with certain inalienable rights; that among these are life, liberty, and the pursuit of happiness; that to secure these rights governments are instituted, deriving their just powers from the consent of the governed. Whenever any form of government becomes destructive of these ends, it is the right of those who suffer from it to refuse allegiance to it, and to insist upon the institution of a new government, laying its foundation on such principles, and organizing its powers in such form, as to them shall seem most likely to effect their safety and happiness. Prudence indeed, will dictate that governments long established should not be changed for light and transient causes; and accordingly all experience hath shown that mankind are more disposed to suffer, while evils are sufferable, than to right themselves by abolishing the forms to which they were accustomed. But when a long train of abuses and usurpations, pursuing invariably the same object evinces a design to reduce them under absolute despotism, it is their duty to throw off such government, and to provide new guards for their future security. Such has been the patient sufferance of the women under this government, and such is now the necessity which constrains them to demand the equal station to which they are entitled.

The history of mankind is a history of repeated injuries and usurpations on the part of man toward woman, having in direct object the establishment of an absolute tyranny over her. To prove this, let facts be submitted to a candid world.

He has never permitted her to exercise her inalienable right to the elective franchise.

He has compelled her to submit to laws, in the formation of which she had no voice.

He has withheld from her rights which are given to the most ignorant and degraded men—both natives and foreigners.

Having deprived her of this first right of a citizen, the elective franchise, thereby leaving her without representation in the halls of legislation, he has oppressed her on all sides.

He has made her, if married, in the eye of the law, civilly dead.

He has taken from her all right in property, even to the wages she earns.

He has made her, morally, an irresponsible being, as she can commit many crimes with impunity, provided they be done in the presence of her husband. In the covenant of marriage, she is compelled to promise obedience to her husband, he becoming, to all intents and purposes, her master—the law giving him power to deprive her of her liberty, and to administer chastisement.

He has so framed the laws of divorce, as to what shall be the proper causes, and in case of separation, to whom the guardianship of the children shall be given, as to be wholly regardless of the happiness of women—the law, in all cases, going upon a false supposition of the supremacy of man, and giving all power into his hands.

After depriving her of all rights as a married woman, if single, and the owner of property, he has taxed her to support a government which recognizes her only when her property can be made profitable to it.

He has monopolized nearly all the profitable employments, and from those she is permitted to follow, she receives but a scanty remuneration. He closes against her all the avenues to wealth and distinction which he considers most honorable to himself. As a teacher of theology, medicine, or law, she is not known.

He has denied her the facilities for obtaining a thorough education, all colleges being closed against her.

He allows her in Church, as well as State, but a subordinate position, claiming Apostolic authority for her exclusion from the ministry, and, with some exceptions, from any public participation in the affairs of the Church.

He has created a false public sentiment by giving to the world a different code of morals for men and women, by which moral delinquencies which exclude women from society, are not only tolerated, but deemed of little account in man.

He has usurped the prerogative of Jehovah himself, claiming it as his right to assign for her a sphere of action, when that belongs to her conscience and to her God.

He has endeavored, in every way that he could, to destroy her confidence in her own powers, to lessen her self-respect, and to make her willing to lead a dependent and abject life.

Now, in view of this entire disfranchisement of one-half the people of this country, their social and religious degradation—in view of the unjust laws above mentioned, and because women do feel themselves aggrieved, oppressed, and fraudulently deprived of their most sacred rights, we insist that they have immediate admission to all the rights and privileges which belong to them as citizens of the United States.

In entering upon the great work before us, we anticipate no small amount of misconception, misrepresentation, and ridicule; but we shall use every instrumentality within our power to effect our object. We shall employ agents, circulate tracts, petition the State and National legislatures, and endeavor to enlist the pulpit and the press in our behalf. We hope this Convention will be followed by a series of Conventions embracing every part of the country.

Possibilities for Writing

1. Analyze the list of grievances Stanton enumerates. In particular, consider the extent to which these follow a logical sequence, building one upon another. Do you find that they lead successfully to her larger conclusion? Why or why not?

2. Based on your reading of Stanton's Declaration, how were women viewed in 1848, when the document was drafted and delivered—that is, what arguments *against* Stanton's position seem to have prevailed at the time? For example, how might denying women any right to vote, the most controversial grievance listed in the document, have been justified? You might do some research in responding to this question.

3. Draft your own Declaration based on Jefferson's and Stanton's. Cast yourself as a member of an aggrieved party, explain your grievances, and end with a call to action. Your effort may be serious, or you may focus on more light-hearted grievances (those of first-year college students, for example).

Brent Staples *(b. 1951) grew up in the poor neighborhood of Chester, Pennsylvania, and attended Widener University on scholarship, later receiving a doctorate in psychology from the University of Chicago. After a short stint as a teacher, he found a job as a reporter with the* Chicago Sun-Times *and was later hired by the* New York Times, *where he is now a member of the editorial board and contributes opinion pieces under his own by-line. His 1994 memoir* Parallel Time: Growing Up in Black and White *explores his experiences as a black youth trying to escape the poverty and violence that surrounded his family and the tragic inability of his younger brother to do so.*

Brent Staples

Just Walk on By: Black Men and Public Space

The title, "Just Walk on By: Black Men and Public Space," conveys the casual manner of Brent Staples's essay about a black male's power to intimidate white people. Staples tells a series of stories and then reflects on their significance. The first story, which is a paradigm for the others, reveals the fear that he as a large black man induces in others, particularly in white women. He describes people's responses to seeing him—locking their cars, walking on the opposite of the street, holding tightly to their pocketbooks. And he describes the actions he takes to alleviate their unfounded fear of him—whistling melodies from classical music, for example.

Acknowledging that women and men, black and white are victimized disproportionately by young black males through violent crime, Staples offers some reasons why this is so. But he also explains his own very real fear that, as a black male, he may be victimized by other people's mistaken fear of him, since he is basically a timid and unthreatening soul. The precautions he takes are his attempt to minimize that fear and to protect himself from its potentially dangerous consequences.

My first victim was a woman—white, well dressed, probably in her early twenties. I came upon her late one evening on a deserted street in Hyde Park, a relatively affluent neighborhood in an otherwise mean, impoverished section of Chicago. As I swung onto the avenue behind her, there seemed to be a discreet, uninflammatory distance between us. Not so. She cast back a worried glance. To her, the youngish black man—a broad six feet two inches with a beard and billowing hair, both hands shoved into the pockets of a bulky military jacket—seemed menacingly close. After a few more quick glimpses, she picked up her pace and was soon running in earnest. Within seconds she disappeared into a cross street.

That was more than a decade ago, I was twenty-two years old, a graduate student newly arrived at the University of Chicago. It was in the echo of that terrified woman's footfalls that I first began to know the unwieldy inheritance I'd come into—the ability to alter public space in ugly ways. It was clear that she thought herself the quarry of a mugger, a rapist, or worse. Suffering a bout of insomnia, however, I was stalking sleep, not defenseless wayfarers. As a softy who is scarcely able to take a knife to a raw chicken—let alone hold one to a person's throat—I was surprised, embarrassed, and dismayed all at once. Her flight made me feel like an accomplice in tyranny. It also made it clear that I was indistinguishable from the muggers who occasionally seeped into the area from the surrounding ghetto. That first encounter, and those that followed, signified that a vast, unnerving gulf lay between nighttime pedestrians—particularly women—and me. And I soon gathered that being perceived as dangerous is a hazard in itself. I only needed to turn a corner into a dicey situation, or crowd some frightened, armed person in a foyer somewhere, or make an errant move after being pulled over by a policeman. Where fear and weapons meet—and they often do in urban America—there is always the possibility of death.

In that first year, my first away from my hometown, I was to become thoroughly familiar with the language of fear. At dark, shadowy intersections, I could cross in front of a car stopped at a traffic light and elicit the *thunk, thunk, thunk, thunk* of the driver—black, white, male, or female—hammering down the door locks. On less traveled streets after dark, I grew accustomed to but never comfortable with people crossing to the other side of the street rather than pass me. Then there were the standard unpleasantries with policemen, doormen, bouncers, cabdrivers, and others whose business it is to screen out troublesome individuals *before* there is any nastiness.

I moved to New York nearly two years ago and I have remained an avid night walker. In central Manhattan, the near-constant crowd cover minimizes tense one-on-one street encounters. Elsewhere—in SoHo, for example, where sidewalks are narrow and tightly spaced buildings shut out the sky—things can get very taut indeed.

After dark, on the warrenlike streets of Brooklyn where I live, I often see women who fear the worst from me. They seem to have set their faces on neutral, and with their purse straps strung across their chests bandolier-style, they forge ahead as though bracing themselves against being tackled. I understand, of course, that the danger they perceive is not a hallucination. Women are particularly vulnerable to street violence, and young black males are drastically overrepresented among the perpetrators of that violence. Yet these truths are no solace against the kind of alienation that comes of being ever the suspect, a fearsome entity with whom pedestrians avoid making eye contact.

It is not altogether clear to me how I reached the ripe old age of twenty-two without being conscious of the lethality nighttime pedestrians attributed to me. Perhaps it was because in Chester, Pennsylvania, the small, angry industrial town where I came of age in the 1960s, I was scarcely noticeable against a backdrop of gang warfare, street knifings, and murders. I grew up one of the good boys, had perhaps a half-dozen fistfights. In retrospect, my shyness of combat has clear sources.

As a boy, I saw countless tough guys locked away; I have since buried several, too. They were babies, really—a teenage cousin, a brother of twenty-two, a childhood friend in his mid-twenties—all gone down in episodes of bravado played out in the streets. I came to doubt the virtues of intimidation early on. I chose, perhaps unconsciously, to remain a shadow—timid, but a survivor.

The fearsomeness mistakenly attributed to me in public places often has a perilous flavor. The most frightening of these confusions occurred in the late 1970s and early 1980s, when I worked as a journalist in Chicago. One day, rushing into the office of a magazine I was writing for with a deadline story in hand, I was mistaken for a burglar. The office manager called security and, with an ad hoc posse, pursued me through the labyrinthine halls, nearly to my editor's door. I had no way of proving who I was. I could only move briskly toward the company of someone who knew me.

Another time I was on assignment for a local paper and killing time before an interview. I entered a jewelry store on the city's affluent Near North Side. The proprietor excused herself and returned with an enormous red Doberman pinscher straining at the end of a leash. She stood, the dog extended toward me, silent to my questions, her eyes bulging nearly out of her head. I took a cursory look around, nodded, and bade her good night.

Relatively speaking, however, I never fared as badly as another black male journalist. He went to nearby Waukegan, Illinois, a couple of summers ago to work on a story about a murderer who was born there. Mistaking the reporter for the killer, police officers hauled him from his car at gunpoint and but for his press credentials would probably have tried to book him. Such episodes are not uncommon. Black men trade tales like this all the time.

Over the years, I learned to smother the rage I felt at so often being taken for a criminal. Not to do so would surely have led to madness. I now take precautions to make myself less threatening. I move about with care, particularly late in the evening. I give a wide berth to nervous people on subway platforms during the wee hours, particularly when I have exchanged business clothes for jeans. If I happen to be entering a building behind some people who appear skittish, I may walk by, letting them clear the lobby before I return, so as not to seem to be following them. I have been calm and extremely congenial on those rare occasions when I've been pulled over by the police.

And on late-evening constitutionals I employ what has proved to be an excellent tension-reducing measure: I whistle melodies from Beethoven and Vivaldi and the more popular classical composers. Even steely New Yorkers hunching toward nighttime destinations seem to relax, and occasionally they even join in the tune. Virtually everybody seems to sense that a mugger wouldn't be warbling bright, sunny selections from Vivaldi's *Four Seasons.* It is my equivalent of the cowbell that hikers wear when they know they are in bear country.

Possibilities for Writing

1. Staples's essay was published in the mid-1980s and has since been widely anthologized. How do you account for its popularity? In responding, consider both the way it is written, the points Staples has to make, and the essay's relevance today. Do you think this popularity is justified? Why or why not?

2. Rather than confront the fears and prejudice of the strangers he encounters, Staples explains that he goes out of his way to

accommodate them. How does he do so? *Why* does he do so? How do you respond to his actions and motives?

3. Write about any times you have made strangers uncomfortable because of the way you "alter public space." How did you respond? Alternatively, write about any times you have judged others as threatening solely because of their appearance. Were your responses justified? Do you think people tend to mistrust one another based too much on appearances?

Jonathan Swift (1667–1745) was born to English parents in Dublin, Ireland, and received a degree from Trinity College there. Unable to obtain a living in Ireland, he worked for some years as a secretary to a nobleman in Surrey, England, during which time he became acquainted with some of the most important literary figures of his day. He eventually returned to Ireland to assume a clerical post but still spent much of his time among the literary set in London. Swift published several volumes of romantic poetry and a wide variety of literary lampoons and political broadsides, but he is best known today for Gulliver's Travels *(1726), a sharp satire of human foibles. Appointed Dean of Dublin's St. Patrick's Cathedral in 1713, Swift was a tireless defender of the Irish in their struggle against England's harsh, sometimes unbearable rule.*

Jonathan Swift
A Modest Proposal

Jonathan Swift's "A Modest Proposal" is among the most famous satires in English. In it Swift—or rather the persona or speaker he creates to make the modest proposal—recommends killing Irish babies at one year of age. The speaker makes this proposal as a way to solve a severe economic problem that occasions great human suffering: the overpopulation of the Irish people, particularly among Irish Catholics.

The essay's power resides partly in Swift's never lifting the mask he wears, portraying his speaker as a man with a serious public service proposal. It resides, too, in the tone of consummate seriousness and scientific objectivity with which it is offered. And it also derives from Swift's use of irony and digression, from his leaving unspoken the proposal's violation of morality. The consummate reasonableness of the speaker and the wonderful summary of benefits his enacted proposal would provide show Swift wearing his mask to the very end of the essay.

It is a melancholy object to those who walk through this great town or travel in the country, when they see the streets, the roads, and cabin doors, crowded with beggars of the female-sex, followed by three, four, or six children, all in rags and importuning every passenger for an alms. These mothers, instead of being able to work for their honest livelihood, are forced to employ all their time in strolling to beg sustenance for their helpless infants, who, as they grow up, either turn thieves for want of work, or leave their dear native country to fight for the Pretender in Spain, or sell themselves to the Barbadoes.

I think it is agreed by all parties that this prodigious number of children in the arms, or on the backs, or at the heels of their mothers, and frequently of their fathers, is in the present deplorable state of the kingdom a very great additional grievance; and therefore whoever could find out a fair, cheap, and easy method of making these children sound, useful members of the commonwealth would deserve so well of the public as to have his statue set up for a preserver of the nation.

But my intention is very far from being confined to provide only for the children of professed beggars; it is of a much greater extent, and shall take in the whole number of infants at a certain age who are born of parents in effect as little able to support them as those who demand our charity in the streets.

As to my own part, having turned my thoughts for many years upon this important subject, and maturely weighed the several schemes of other projectors, I have always found them grossly mistaken in their computation. It is true, a child just dropped from its dam may be supported by her milk for a solar year, with little other nourishment; at most not above the value of two shillings, which the mother may certainly get, or the value in scraps, by her lawful occupation of begging; and it is exactly at one year old that I propose to provide for them in such a manner as instead of being a charge upon their parents or the parish, or wanting food and raiment for the rest of their lives, they shall on the contrary contribute to the feeding, and partly to the clothing, of many thousands.

There is likewise another great advantage in my scheme, that it will prevent those voluntary abortions, and that horrid practice of women murdering their bastard children, alas, too frequent among us, sacrificing the poor innocent babes, I doubt, more to avoid the expense than the shame, which would move tears and pity in the most savage and inhuman breast.

The number of souls in this kingdom being usually reckoned one million and a half, of these I calculate there may be about two hundred thousand couples whose wives are breeders; from which number I subtract thirty thousand couples who are able to maintain their own children, although I apprehend there cannot be so many under the present distresses of the kingdom; but this being granted, there will remain an hundred and seventy thousand breeders. I again subtract fifty thousand for those women who miscarry, or whose children die by accident or disease within the year. There only remain an hundred and twenty thousand children of poor parents annually born. The question therefore is, how this number shall be reared and provided for, which, as I have already said, under the present situation of affairs, is utterly impossible by all the methods hitherto proposed. For we can neither employ them in handicraft or agriculture; we neither build houses (I mean in the country) nor cultivate land. They can very seldom pick up a livelihood by stealing till they arrive at six years old, except where they are of towardly parts; although I confess they learn the rudiments much earlier, during which time they can however be looked upon only as probationers, as I have been informed by a principal gentleman in the county of Cavan, who protested to me that he never knew above one or two instances under the age of six, even in a part of the kingdom so renowned for the quickest proficiency in that art.

I am assured by our merchants that a boy or a girl before twelve years old is no salable commodity; and even when they come to this age they will not yield above three pounds, or three pounds and half a crown at most on the Exchange; which cannot turn to account either to the parents or the kingdom, the charge of nutriment and rags having been at least four times that value.

I shall now therefore humbly propose my own thoughts, which I hope will not be liable to the least objection.

I have been assured by a very knowing American of my acquaintance in London, that a young healthy child well nursed is at a year old a most delicious, nourishing, and wholesome food, whether stewed, roasted, baked, or boiled; and I make no doubt that it will equally serve in a fricassee or a ragout.

I do therefore humbly offer it to public consideration that of the hundred and twenty thousand children, already computed, twenty thousand may be reserved for breed, whereof only one fourth part to be males, which is more than we allow to sheep, black cattle, or swine; and my reason is that these children are seldom the fruits of marriage, a circumstance not much regarded by our savages, therefore one male will be sufficient to serve four females. That the remaining hundred thousand may at a year old be offered in sale to the persons of quality and fortune through the kingdom, always advising the mother to let them suck plentifully in the last month, so as to render them plump and fat for a good table. A child will make two dishes at an entertainment for friends; and when the family dines alone, the fore or hind quarter will make a reasonable dish, and seasoned with a little pepper or salt will be very good boiled on the fourth day, especially in winter.

I have reckoned upon a medium that a child just born will weigh twelve pounds, and in a solar year if tolerably nursed increaseth to twenty-eight pounds.

I grant this food will be somewhat dear, and therefore very proper for landlords, who, as they have already devoured most of the parents, seem to have the best title to the children.

Infant's flesh will be in season throughout the year, but more plentiful in March, and a little before and after. For we are told by a grave author, an eminent French physician, that fish being a prolific diet, there are more children born in Roman Catholic countries about nine months after Lent than at any other season; therefore, reckoning a year after Lent, the markets will be more glutted than usual, because the number of popish infants is at least three to one in this kingdom; and therefore it will have one other collateral advantage, by lessening the number of Papists among us.

I have already computed the charge of nursing a beggar's child (in which list I reckon all cottagers, laborers, and four fifths of the farmers) to be about two shillings per annum, rags included; and I believe no gentleman would repine to give ten shillings for the carcass of a good fat child, which, as I have said, will make four dishes of excellent nutritive meat, when he hath only some particular friend or his own family to dine with him. Thus the squire will learn to be a good landlord, and grow popular among the tenants; the mother will have eight shillings net profit, and be fit for work till she produces another child.

Those who are more thrifty (as I must confess the times require) may flay the carcass; the skin of which artificially dressed will make admirable gloves for ladies, and summer boots for fine gentlemen.

As to our city of Dublin, shambles may be appointed for this purpose in the most convenient parts of it, and butchers we may be assured will not be wanting; although I rather recommend buying the children alive, and dressing them hot from the knife as we do roasting pigs.

A very worthy person, a true lover of his country, and whose virtues I highly esteem, was lately pleased in discoursing on this matter to offer a refinement upon my scheme. He said that many gentlemen of this kingdom, having of late destroyed their deer, he conceived that the want of venison might be well supplied by the bodies of young lads and maidens, not exceeding fourteen years of age nor under twelve, so great a number of both sexes in every county being now ready to starve for want of work and service; and these to be disposed of by their parents, if alive, or otherwise by their nearest relations. But with due deference to so excellent a friend and so deserving a patriot, I cannot be altogether in his sentiments; for as to the males, my American acquaintance assured me from frequent experience that their flesh was generally tough and lean, like that of our schoolboys, by continual exercise, and their taste disagreeable; and to fatten them would not answer the charge. Then as to the females, it would, I think with humble submission, be a loss to the public, because they soon would become breeders themselves: and besides, it is not improbable that some scrupulous people might be apt to censure such a practice (although indeed very unjustly) as a little bordering upon cruelty; which, I confess, hath always been with me the strongest objection against any project, how well soever intended.

But in order to justify my friend, he confessed that this expedient was put into his head by the famous Psalmanazar, a native of the island Formosa, who came from thence to London above twenty years ago, and in conversation told my friend that in his country when any young person happened to be put to death, the executioner sold the carcass to persons of quality as a prime dainty; and that in his time the body of a plump girl of fifteen, who was crucified for an attempt to poison the emperor, was sold to his Imperial Majesty's prime minister of state, and other great mandarins of the court, in joints from the gibbet, at four hundred crowns. Neither indeed can I deny that if the same use were made of several plump young girls in this town, who without one single groat to their fortunes cannot stir abroad without a chair, and appear at the playhouse and assemblies in foreign fineries which they never will pay for, the kingdom would not be the worse.

Some persons of a desponding spirit are in great concern about that vast number of poor people who are aged, diseased, or maimed, and I have been desired to employ my thoughts what course may be taken to ease the nation of so grievous an encumbrance. But I am not in the least pain upon that matter, because it is very well known that they are every day dying and rotting by cold and famine, and filth and vermin, as fast as can be reasonably expected. And as to the younger laborers, they are now in almost as hopeful a condition. They cannot get work, and consequently pine away for want of nourishment to a degree that if at any time they are accidentally hired to common labor, they have not strength to perform it; and thus the country and themselves are happily delivered from the evils to come.

I have too long digressed, and therefore shall return to my subject. I think the advantages by the proposal which I have made are obvious and many, as well as of the highest importance.

For first, as I have already observed, it would greatly lessen the number of Papists, with whom we are yearly overrun, being the principal breeders of the nation as well as our most dangerous enemies; and who stay at home on purpose to deliver the kingdom to the Pretender, hoping to take their advantage by the absence of so many good Protestants, who have chosen rather to leave their country than to stay at home and pay tithes against their conscience to an Episcopal curate.

Secondly, the poorer tenants will have something valuable of their own, which by law may be made liable to distress, and help to pay their landlord's rent, their corn and cattle being already seized and money a thing unknown.

Thirdly, whereas the maintenance of an hundred thousand children, from two years old and upwards, cannot be computed at less than ten shillings a piece per annum, the nation's stock will be thereby increased fifty thousand pounds per annum, besides the profit of a new dish introduced to the tables of all gentlemen of fortune in the kingdom who have any refinement in taste. And the money will circulate among ourselves, the goods being entirely of our own growth and manufacture.

Fourthly, the constant breeders, besides the gain of eight shillings sterling per annum by the sale of their children, will be rid of the charge of maintaining them after the first year.

Fifthly, this food would likewise bring great custom to taverns, where the vintners will certainly be so prudent as to procure the best receipts for dressing it to perfection, and consequently have their houses frequented by all the fine gentlemen, who justly value themselves upon their knowledge in good eating; and a skillful cook, who understands how to oblige his guests, will contrive to make it as expensive as they please.

Sixthly, this would be a great inducement to marriage, which all wise nations have either encouraged by rewards or enforced by laws and penalties. It would increase the care and tenderness of mothers toward their children, when they were sure of a settlement for life to the poor babes, provided in some sort by the public, to their annual profit instead of expense. We should see an honest emulation among the married women, which of them could bring the fattest child to the market. Men would become as fond of their wives during the time of their pregnancy as they are now of their mares in foal, their cows in calf, or sows when they are ready to farrow; nor offer to beat or kick them (as is too frequent a practice) for fear of a miscarriage.

Many other advantages might be enumerated. For instance, the addition of some thousand carcasses in our exportation of barreled beef, the propagation of swine's flesh, and improvement in the art of making good bacon, so much wanted among us by the great destruction of pigs, too frequent at our tables, which are no way comparable in taste or magnificence to a well-grown, fat, yearling child, which roasted whole will make a considerable figure at a lord mayor's feast or any other public entertainment. But this and many others I omit, being studious of brevity.

Supposing that one thousand families in this city would be constant customers for infants' flesh, besides others who might have it at merry meetings, particularly weddings and christenings, I compute that Dublin would take off annually about twenty thousand carcasses, and the rest of the kingdom (where probably they will be sold somewhat cheaper) the remaining eighty thousand.

I can think of no one objection that will possibly be raised against this proposal, unless it should be urged that the number of people will be thereby much lessened in the kingdom. This I freely own, and it was indeed one principal design in offering it to the world. I desire the reader will observe, that I calculate my remedy for this one individual kingdom of Ireland and for no other that ever was, is, or I think ever can be upon earth. Therefore let no man talk to me of other expedients: of taxing our absentees at five shillings a pound: of using neither clothes nor household furniture except what is of our own growth and manufacture: of utterly rejecting the materials and instruments that promote foreign luxury: of curing the expensiveness of pride, vanity, idleness, and gaming in our women: of introducing a vein of parsimony, prudence, and temperance: of learning to love our country, in the want of which we differ even from Laplanders and the inhabitants of Topinamboo: of quitting our animosities and factions, nor acting any longer like the Jews, who were murdering one another at the very moment their city was taken: of being a little cautious not to sell our country and conscience for nothing: of teaching landlords to have at least one degree of mercy toward their tenants: lastly, of putting a spirit of honesty, industry, and skill into our shopkeepers; who, if a resolution could now be taken to buy only our native goods, would immediately unite to cheat and exact upon us in the price, the measure, and the goodness, nor could ever yet be brought to make one fair proposal of just dealing, though often and earnestly invited to it.

Therefore I repeat, let no man talk to me of these and the like expedients, till he hath at least some glimpse of hope that there will ever be some hearty and sincere attempt to put them in practice.

But as to myself, having been wearied out for many years with offering vain, idle, visionary thoughts, and at length utterly despairing of success, I fortunately fell upon this proposal, which, as it is wholly new, so it hath something solid and real, of no expense and little trouble, full in our own power, and whereby we can incur no danger in disobliging England. For this kind of commodity will not bear exportation, the flesh being of too tender a consistence to admit a long continuance in salt, although perhaps I could name a country which would be glad to eat up our whole nation without it.

After all, I am not so violently bent upon my own opinion as to reject any offer proposed by wise men, which shall be found equally innocent, cheap, easy, and effectual. But before something of that kind shall be advanced in contradiction to my scheme, and offering a better, I desire the author or authors will be pleased maturely to consider two points. First, as things now stand, how they will be able to find food and raiment for an hundred thousand useless mouths and backs. And secondly, there being a round million of creatures in human figure throughout this kingdom, whose sole subsistence put into a common stock would leave them in debt two millions of pounds sterling, adding those who are beggars by profession to the bulk of farmers, cottagers, and laborers, with their wives and children who are beggars in effect; I desire those politicians who dislike my overture, and may perhaps be so bold to attempt an answer, that they will first ask the parents of these mortals whether they would not at this day think it a great happiness to have been sold for food at a year old in the manner I prescribe, and thereby have avoided such a perpetual scene of misfortunes as they have since gone through by the oppression of landlords, the impossibility of paying rent without money or trade, the want of common sustenance, with neither house nor clothes to cover them from the inclemencies of the weather, and the most inevitable prospect of entailing the like or greater miseries upon their breed forever.

I profess, in the sincerity of my heart, that I have not the least personal interest in endeavoring to promote this necessary work, having no other motive than the public good of my country, by advancing our trade, providing for infants, relieving the poor, and giving some pleasure to the rich. I have no children by which I can propose to get a single penny; the youngest being nine years old, and my wife past childbearing.

Possibilities for Writing

1. Throughout "A Modest Proposal," Swift uses language that dehumanizes the Irish people. Point out examples of such language, and explain their effect both in terms of Swift's satire and his underlying purpose.

2. Though Swift never fully drops his mask, he does make a number of veiled appeals toward sympathy for the Irish and legitimate suggestions for alleviating their predicament. Citing the text, examine when and where he does so. How can you recognize his seriousness?

3. Write a "modest proposal" of your own in which you offer an outrageous solution to alleviate some social problem. Make sure that readers understand that your proposal is satirical and that they recognize your real purpose in writing.

Amy Tan (b. 1952) grew up in Oakland, California, her parents having immigrated from China only shortly before her birth. She graduated from San Francisco State University with degrees in English and linguistics and began her writing career in the business world, drafting presentations, marketing materials, and producing various corporate publications. Tan began pursuing fiction writing as a break from the stress of her job, and in 1987, after years of literary workshops, she produced The Joy Luck Club, *a group of interrelated stories about four Chinese immigrant mothers and their assimilated, second-generation daughters. It was an immediate success both with critics and readers and was followed by* The Kitchen's God's Wife *(1991),* The Hundred Secret Senses *(1995),* The Bonesetter's Daughter *(2001), and* Saving Fish from Drowning *(2005) all dealing with similar themes of family and culture.*

Amy Tan
Mother Tongue

In "Mother Tongue," Amy Tan describes the various kinds of English she uses—from the "broken" English she uses in speaking with her mother, to the formal and sophisticated English she employs in public settings. Tan plays upon the meaning of the term "mother tongue," referring both to English as one's native language and to the English her own mother uses, that is, her mother's English, which is not her mother's "mother tongue."

For Amy Tan herself, English is a variety of tongues. English is more than a single and monolithic way of using the language. Tan finds in her mother's "broken" English, for example, a powerful self-presence, even though the mother's use of English is riddled with grammatical errors and idiomatic incongruities. Part of the pleasure of Tan's essay is the way the writer plays off various kinds of English against one another. Part of the essay's power lies in its invitation to see how English provides multiple possibilities for conveying ideas and expressing oneself. An additional but related aspect of Tan's essay is its revelation of culturally conflicting perspectives—and how language, in this case English, both reflects and exacerbates them.

I am not a scholar of English or literature. I cannot give you much more than personal opinions on the English language and its variations in this country or others.

I am a writer. And by that definition, I am someone who has always loved language. I am fascinated by language in daily life. I spend a great deal of my time thinking about the power of language—the way it can evoke an emotion, a visual image, a complex idea, or a simple truth. Language is the tool of my trade. And I use them all—all the Englishes I grew up with.

Recently, I was made keenly aware of the different Englishes I do use. I was giving a talk to a large group of people, the same talk I had already given to half a dozen other groups. The nature of the talk was about my writing, my life, and my book, *The Joy Luck Club*. The talk was going along well enough, until I remembered one major difference that made the whole talk sound wrong. My mother was in the room. And it was perhaps the first time she had heard me give a lengthy speech, using the kind of English I have never used with her. I was saying things like "The intersection of memory upon imagination" and "There is an aspect of my fiction that relates to thus-and-thus"—a speech filled with carefully wrought grammatical phrases, burdened, it suddenly seemed to me, with nominalized forms, past perfect tenses, conditional phrases, all the forms of standard English that I had learned in school and through books, the forms of English I did not use at home with my mother.

Just last week, I was walking down the street with my mother, and I again found myself conscious of the English I was using, the English I do use with her. We were talking about the price of new and used furniture and I heard myself saying this: "Not waste money that way." My husband was with us as well, and he didn't notice any switch in my English. And then I realized why. It's because over the twenty years we've been together I've often used that same kind of English with him, and sometimes he even uses it with me. It has become our language of intimacy, a different sort of English that relates to family talk, the language I grew up with.

So you'll have some idea of what this family talk I heard sounds like, I'll quote what my mother said during a recent conversation which I videotaped and then transcribed. During this conversation, my mother was talking about a political gangster in Shanghai who had the same last name as her family's, Du, and how the gangster in his early years wanted to be adopted by her family, which was rich by comparison. Later, the gangster became more powerful, far richer than my mother's family, and one day showed up at my mother's wedding to pay his respects. Here's what she said in part:

"Du Yusong having business like fruit stand. Like off the street kind. He is Du like Du Zong—but not Tsung-ming Island people. The local people call putong, the river east side, he belong to that side local people. That man want to ask Du Zong father take him in like become own family. Du Zong father wasn't look down on him, but didn't take seriously, until that man big like become a mafia. Now important person, very hard to inviting him. Chinese way, came only to show respect, don't stay for dinner. Respect for making big celebration, he shows up. Mean gives lots of respect. Chinese custom. Chinese social life that way. If too important won't have to stay too long. He come to my wedding. I didn't see, I heard it. I gone to boy's side, they have YMCA dinner. Chinese age I was nineteen."

You should know that my mother's expressive command of English belies how much she actually understands. She reads the *Forbes* report, listens to *Wall Street Week*, converses daily with her stockbroker, reads all of Shirley MacLaine's books with ease—all kinds of things I can't begin to understand. Yet some of my friends tell me they understand 50 percent of what my mother says. Some say they understand 80 to 90 percent. Some say they understand none of it, as if she were speaking pure Chinese. But to me, my mother's English is perfectly clear, perfectly natural. It's my mother tongue. Her language, as I hear it, is vivid, direct, full of observation and imagery. That was the language that helped shape the way I saw things, expressed things, made sense of the world.

Lately, I've been giving more thought to the kind of English my mother speaks. Like others, I have described it to people as "broken" or "fractured" English. But I wince when I say that. It has always bothered me that I can think of no other way to describe it other than "broken," as if it were damaged and needed to be fixed, as if it lacked a certain wholeness and soundness. I've heard other terms used, "limited English," for example. But they seem just as bad, as if everything is limited, including people's perceptions of the limited English speaker.

I know this for a fact, because when I was growing up, my mother's "limited" English limited *my* perception of her. I was ashamed of her English. I believed that her English reflected the quality of what she had to say. That is, because she expressed them imperfectly her thoughts were imperfect. And I had plenty of empirical evidence to support me: the fact that people in department stores, at banks, and at restaurants did not take her seriously, did not give her good service, pretended not to understand her, or even acted as if they did not hear her.

My mother has long realized the limitations of her English as well. When I was fifteen, she used to have me call people on the phone to pretend I was she. In this guise, I was forced to ask for information or even to complain and yell at people who had been rude to her. One time it was a call to her stockbroker in New York. She had cashed out her small portfolio and it just so happened we were going to go to New York the next week, our very first trip outside California. I had to get on the phone and say in an adolescent voice that was not very convincing, "This is Mrs. Tan."

And my mother was standing in the back whispering loudly, "Why he don't send me check, already two weeks late. So mad he lie to me, losing me money."

And then I said in perfect English, "Yes, I'm getting rather concerned. You had agreed to send the check two weeks ago, but it hasn't arrived."

Then she began to talk more loudly. "What he want, I come to New York tell him front of his boss, you cheating me?" And I was trying to calm her down, make her be quiet, while telling the stockbroker, "I can't tolerate any more excuses. If I don't receive the check immediately, I am going to have to speak to your manager when I'm in New York next week." And sure enough, the following week there we were in front of this astonished stockbroker, and I was sitting there red-faced and quiet, and my mother, the real Mrs. Tan, was shouting at his boss in her impeccable broken English.

We used a similar routine just five days ago, for a situation that was far less humorous. My mother had gone to the hospital for an appointment, to find out about a benign brain tumor a CAT scan had revealed a month ago. She said she had spoken very good English, her best English, no mistakes. Still, she said, the hospital did not apologize when they said they had lost the CAT scan and she had come for nothing. She said they did not seem to have any sympathy when she told them she was anxious to know the exact diagnosis, since her husband and son had both died of brain tumors. She said they would not give her any more information until the next time and she would have to make another appointment for that. So she said she would not leave until the doctor called her daughter. She wouldn't budge. And when the doctor finally called her daughter, me, who spoke in perfect English—lo and behold—we had assurances the CAT scan would be found, promises that a conference call on Monday would be held, and apologies for any suffering my mother had gone through for a most regrettable mistake.

I think my mother's English almost had an effect on limiting my possibilities in life as well. Sociologists and linguists probably will tell you that a person's developing language skills are more influenced by peers. But I do think that the language spoken in the family, especially in immigrant families which are more insular, plays a large role in shaping the language of the child. And I believe that it affected my results on achievement tests, IQ tests, and the SAT. While my English skills were never judged as poor, compared to math, English could not be considered my strong suit. In grade school I did moderately well, getting perhaps B's, sometimes B-pluses, in English and scoring perhaps in the sixtieth or seventieth percentile on achievement tests. But those scores were not good enough to override the opinion that my true abilities lay in math and science, because in those areas I achieved A's and scored in the ninetieth percentile or higher.

This was understandable. Math is precise; there is only one correct answer. Whereas, for me at least, the answers on English tests were always a judgment call, a matter of opinion and personal experience. Those tests were constructed around items like fill-in-the-blank sentence completion, such as "Even though Tom was ____, Mary thought he was ____." And the correct answer always seemed to be the most bland combinations of thoughts, for example, "Even though Tom was shy, Mary thought he was charming," with the grammatical structure "even though" limiting the correct answer to some sort of semantic opposites, so you wouldn't get answers like, "Even though Tom was foolish, Mary thought he was ridiculous." Well, according to my mother, there were very few limitations as to what Tom could have been and what Mary might have thought of him. So I never did well on tests like that.

The same was true with word analogies, pairs of words in which you were supposed to find some sort of logical, semantic relationship—for example, "*Sunset* is to *nightfall* as ____ is to ____." And here you would be presented with a list of four possible pairs, one of which showed the same kind of relationship: *red* is to *stoplight, bus* is to *arrival, chills* is to *fever, yawn* is to *boring*. Well, I could never think that way. I knew what the tests were asking, but I could not block out of my mind the images already created by the first pair, "*sunset* is to *nightfall*"—and I would see a burst of colors against a darkening sky, the moon rising, the lowering of a curtain of stars. And all the other pairs of words—red, bus, stoplight, boring—just threw up a mass of confusing images, making it impossible for me to sort out something as logical as saying: "A sunset precedes nightfall" is the same as "a chill precedes a fever." The only way I would have gotten that answer right would have been to imagine an associative situation, for example, my being disobedient and staying out past sunset, catching a chill at night, which turns into feverish pneumonia as punishment, which indeed did happen to me.

I have been thinking about all this lately, about my mother's English, about achievement tests. Because lately I've been asked, as a writer, why there are not more Asian Americans represented in American literature. Why are there few Asian Americans enrolled in creative writing programs? Why do so many Chinese students go into engineering? Well, these are broad sociological questions I can't begin to answer. But I have noticed in surveys—in fact, just last week—that Asian students, as a whole, always do significantly better on math achievement tests than in English. And this makes me think that there are other Asian-American students whose English spoken in the home might also be described as "broken" or "limited." And perhaps they also have teachers who are steering them away from writing and into math and science, which is what happened to me.

Fortunately, I happen to be rebellious in nature and enjoy the challenge of disproving assumptions made about me. I became an English major my first year in college, after being enrolled as pre-med. I started writing nonfiction as a freelancer the week after I was told by my former boss that writing was my worst skill and I should hone my talents toward account management.

But it wasn't until 1985 that I finally began to write fiction. And at first I wrote using what I thought to be wittily crafted sentences, sentences that would finally prove I had mastery over the English language. Here's an example from the first draft of a story that later made its way into *The Joy Luck Club*, but without this line: "That was my mental quandary in its nascent state." A terrible line, which I can barely pronounce.

Fortunately, for reasons I won't get into today, I later decided I should envision a reader for the stories I would write. And the reader I decided upon was my mother, because these were stories about mothers. So with this reader in mind—and in fact she did read my early drafts—I began to write stories using all the Englishes I grew up with: the English I spoke to my mother, which for lack of a better term might be described as "simple"; the English she used with me, which for lack of a better term might be described as "broken"; my translation of her Chinese, which could certainly be described as "watered down"; and what I imagined to be her translation of her Chinese if she could speak in perfect English, her internal language, and for that I sought to preserve the essence, but neither an English nor a Chinese structure. I wanted to capture what language ability tests can never reveal: her intent, her passion, her imagery, the rhythms of her speech, and the nature of her thoughts.

Apart from what any critic had to say about my writing, I knew I had succeeded where it counted when my mother finished reading my book and gave me her verdict: "So easy to read."

Possibilities for Writing

1. Tan's focus here is on the "different Englishes" she uses. What are these, and what occasions her shift from one to another? Consider, as well, her feelings about these various "Englishes" and about her mother's fractured English. In what ways are these both limiting and liberating for communication?

2. Tan is pleased when her mother's verdict on her first novel was that it was "So easy to read." Do you find Tan's style in this essay "easy to read"? In an essay, evaluate her style, quoting from the text to support your viewpoint.

3. How does your language and that of your peers differ from that of a different generation of speakers—your parents, say, or your children? How does the language you use in formal situations differ from that you use in less formal ones? In an essay, describe the different sorts of "Englishes" you encounter in your life.

Henry David Thoreau (1817–1862) was born in Concord, Massachusetts, where he spent most of his life. A graduate of Harvard, he was an early protégé of Ralph Waldo Emerson, whom he served for several years as an assistant and under whose tutelage he began to write for publication. Thoreau was philosophically a strict individualist and antimaterialist, and in 1845 he retired for two years to an isolated cabin on Walden Pond, near Concord, where he lived in comparative solitude, studying the natural world, reading, and keeping a journal that would become the basis for Walden *(1854), a lyrical but deeply reasoned account of his experiences there and what they meant to him, as well as four later volumes. His work has influenced generations of writers, thinkers, and even political movements in terms of determining what constitutes true human and natural value.*

Henry David Thoreau
Why I Went to the Woods

In this excerpt from the second chapter of *Walden*, Thoreau explains why he "went to the woods," that is, why he took a sabbatical from civilization to get away from it all for a while. (Thoreau spent two years and two weeks at Walden pond, where he built himself a cabin, grew his own food, and subsisted simply, as an experiment to see how little he would really need to live.) Essentially, Thoreau wanted time to read, write, and think. He wanted to make time for nature. And he wanted to test himself, to see just how much he could simplify his life, to determine how much time he could save to do what he really wanted to do with every minute of every day.

The appeal of Thoreau's central idea and fundamental ideal is especially acute for twenty-first century America, where people strive to accomplish as much as they can as fast as they can so as to accumulate everything they think they need. Thoreau postulates an opposite ideal: to see how little we really require to live our lives, with an appreciation for what is truly essential and a respect for the rhythms of the natural world.

I went to the woods because I wished to live deliberately, to front only the essential facts of life, and see if I could not learn what it had to teach, and not, when I came to die, discover that I had not lived. I did not wish to live what was not life, living is so dear; nor did I wish to practice resignation, unless it was quite necessary. I wanted to live deep and suck out all the marrow of life, to live so sturdily and Spartan-like as to put to rout all that was not life, to cut a broad swath and shave close, to drive life into a corner, and reduce it to its lowest terms, and, if it proved to be mean, why then to get the whole and genuine meanness of it, and publish its meanness to the world; or if it were sublime, to know it by experience, and be able to give a true account of it in my next excursion. For most men, it appears to me, are in a strange uncertainty about it, whether it is of the devil or of God, and have *somewhat hastily* concluded that it is the chief end of man here to "glorify God and enjoy him forever."

Still we live meanly, like ants; though the fable tells us that we were long ago changed into men; like pygmies we fight with cranes; it is error upon error, and clout upon clout, and our best virtue has for its occasion a superfluous and evitable wretchedness. Our life is frittered away by detail. An honest man has hardly need to count more than his ten fingers, or in extreme cases he may add his ten toes, and lump the rest. Simplicity, simplicity, simplicity! I say, let your affairs be as two or three, and not a hundred or a thousand; instead of a million count half a dozen, and keep your accounts on your thumb-nail. In the midst of this chopping sea of civilized life, such are the clouds and storms and quicksands and thousand-and-one items to be allowed for, that a man has to live, if he would not founder and go to the bottom and not make his port at all, by dead reckoning, and he must be a great calculator indeed who succeeds. Simplify, simplify. Instead of three meals a day, if it be necessary eat but one; instead of a hundred dishes, five; and reduce other things in proportion. Our life is like a German Confederacy, made of up petty states, with its boundary forever fluctuating, so that even a German cannot tell you how it is bounded at any moment. The nation itself, with all its so-called internal improvements, which, by the way are all external and superficial, is just such an unwieldy and overgrown establishment, cluttered with furniture and tripped up by its own traps, ruined by luxury and heedless expense, by want of calculation and a worthy aim, as the million households in the lands; and the only cure for it, as for them, is in a rigid economy, a stern and more than Spartan simplicity of life and elevation of purpose. It lives too fast. Men think that it is essential that the *Nation* have commerce, and export ice, and talk through a telegraph, and ride thirty miles an hour, without a doubt, whether *they* do or not; but whether we should live like baboons or like men, is a little uncertain. If we do not get our sleepers, and forge rails, and devote days and nights to the work, but go to tinkering upon our *lives* to improve *them*, who will build railroads? And if railroads are not built, how shall we get to heaven in season? But if we stay at home and mind our business, who will want railroads? We do not ride on the railroad; it rides upon us. Did you ever think what those sleepers are that underlie the railroad? Each one is a man, an Irishman, or a Yankee man. The rails are laid on them, and they are covered with sand, and the cars run smoothly over them. They are sound sleepers, I assure you. And every few years a new lot is laid down and run over; so that, if some have the pleasure of riding on a rail, others have the misfortune to be ridden upon. And when they run over a man that is walking in his sleep, a supernumerary sleeper in the wrong position, and wake him up, they suddenly stop the cars, and make a hue and cry about it, as if this were an exception. I am glad to know that it takes a gang of men for every five miles to keep the sleepers down and level in their beds as it is, for this is a sign that they may sometimes get up again.

Why should we live with such hurry and waste of life? We are determined to be starved before we are hungry. Men say that a stitch in time saves nine, and so they take a thousand stitches to-day to save nine tomorrow. As for *work*, we haven't any of any consequence. We have the Saint Vitus' dance, and cannot possibly keep our heads still. If I should only give a few pulls at the parish bell-rope, as for a fire, that is, without setting the bell, there is hardly a man on his farm in the outskirts of Concord, notwithstanding that press of engagements which was his excuse so many times this morning, nor a boy, nor a woman, I might almost say, but would foresake all and follow that sound, not mainly to save property from the flames, but, if we will confess the truth, much more to see it burn, since burn it must, and we, be it known, did not set it on fire—or to see it put out, and have a hand in it, if that is done as handsomely; yes, even if it were the parish church itself. Hardly a man takes a half-hour's nap after dinner, but when he wakes he holds up his head and asks, "What's the news?" as if the rest of mankind had stood his sentinels. Some give directions to be waked every half-hour, doubtless for no other purpose; and then, to pay for it, they tell what they have dreamed. After a night's sleep the news is as indispensable as the breakfast. "Pray tell me anything new that has happened to a man anywhere on this globe"—and he reads it over his coffee and rolls, that a man has had his eyes gouged out this morning on the Wachito River; never dreaming the while that he lives in the dark unfathomed mammoth cave of this world, and has but the rudiment of an eye himself.

For my part, I could easily do without the post-office. I think that there are very few important communications made through it. To speak critically, I never received more than one or two letters in my life—I wrote this some years ago—that were worth the postage. The penny-post is, commonly, an institution through which you seriously offer a man that penny for his thoughts which is so often safely offered in jest. And I am sure that I never read any memorable news in a newspaper. If we read of one man robbed, or murdered, or killed by accident, or one house burned, or one vessel wrecked, or one steamboat blown up, or one cow run over on the Western Railroad, or one mad dog killed, or one lot of grasshoppers in the winter—we never need read of another. One is enough. If you are acquainted with the principle, what do you care for a myriad instances and applications? To a philosopher all *news*, as it is called, is gossip, and they who edit and read it are old women over their tea. Yet not a few are greedy after this gossip. There was such a rush, as I hear, the other day at one of the offices to learn the foreign news by the last arrival, that several large squares of plate glass belonging to the establishment were broken by the pressure—news which I seriously think a ready wit might write a twelvemonth, or twelve years, beforehand with sufficient accuracy. As for Spain, for instance, if you know how to throw in Don Carlos and the Infanta, and Don Pedro and Seville and Granada, from time to time in the right proportions—they may have changed the names a little since I saw the papers—and serve up a bullfight when other entertainments fail, it will be true to the letter, and give us as good an idea of the exact state or ruin of things in Spain as the most succinct and lucid reports under this head in the newspapers; and as for England, almost the last significant scrap of news from that quarter was the revolution of 1649; and if you have learned the history of her crops for an average year, you never need attend to that thing again, unless your speculations are of a merely pecuniary character. If one may judge who rarely looks into the newspapers, nothing new does ever happen in foreign parts, a French revolution not excepted.

What news! how much more important to know what that is which was never old! "Kieou-he-yu (great dignitary of the state of Wei) sent a man to Khoung-tseu to know his news. Khoung-tseu caused the messenger to be seated near him, and questioned him in these terms: What is your master doing? The messenger answered with respect: My master desires to diminish the number of his faults, but he cannot come to the end of them. The messenger being gone, the philosopher remarked: What a worthy messenger! What a worthy messenger!" The preacher, instead of vexing the ears of drowsy farmers on their day of rest at the end of the week—for Sunday is the fit conclusion of an ill-spent week, and not the fresh and brave beginning of a new one—with this one other draggle-tail of a sermon, should shout with thundering voice, "Pause! Avast! Why so seeming fast, but deadly slow?"

Shams and delusions are esteemed for soundless truths, while reality is fabulous. If men would steadily observe realities only, and not allow themselves to be deluded, life, to compare it with such things as we know, would be like a fairy tale and the Arabian Nights' Entertainments. If we respected only what is inevitable and has a right to be, music and poetry would resound along the streets. When we are unhurried and wise, we perceive that only great and worthy things have any permanent and absolute existence, that petty fears and petty pleasures are but the shadow of the reality. This is always exhilarating and sublime. By closing the eyes and slumbering, and consenting to be deceived by shows, men establish and confirm their daily life of routine and habit everywhere, which still is built on purely illusory foundations. Children, who play life, discern its true law and relations more clearly than men, who fail to live it worthily, but who think that they are wiser by experience, that is, by failure. I have read in a Hindoo book, that "there was a king's son, who, being expelled in infancy from his native city, was brought up by a forester, and, growing up to maturity in that state, imagined himself to belong to the barbarous race with which he lived. One of his father's ministers having discovered him, revealed to him what he was, and the misconception of his character was removed, and he knew himself to be a prince. So soul," continues the Hindoo philosopher, "from the circumstances in which it is placed, mistakes its own character, until the truth is revealed to it by some holy teacher and then it knows itself to be *Brahme.*" I perceive that we inhabitants of New England live this mean life that we do because our vision does not penetrate the surface of things. We think that that *is* which *appears* to be. If a man should walk through this town and see only the reality, where, think you, would the "Milldam" go to? If he should give us an account of the realities he beheld there, we should not recognize the place in his description. Look at the meetinghouse, or a courthouse, or a jail, or a shop, or a dwelling-house, and say what that thing really is before a true gaze, and they would all go to pieces in your account of them. Men esteem truth remote, in the outskirts of the system, behind the farthest star, before Adam and after the last man. In eternity there is indeed something true and sublime. But all these times and places and occasions are now and here. God himself culminates in the present moment, and will never be more divine in the lapse of all the ages. And we are enabled to apprehend at all what is sublime and noble only by the perpetual instilling and drenching of the reality that surrounds us. The universe constantly and obediently answers to our conceptions; whether we travel fast or slow, the track is laid for us. Let us spend our lives in conceiving then. The poet or the artist never yet had so fair and noble a design but some of his posterity at least could accomplish it.

Let us spend one day as deliberately as Nature, and not be thrown off the track by every nutshell and mosquito's wing that falls on the rails. Let us rise early and fast, or breakfast, gently and without perturbation; let company come and let company go, let the bells ring and the children cry—determined to make a day of it. Why should we knock under and go with the stream? Let us not be upset and overwhelmed in that terrible rapid and whirlpool called a dinner, situated in the meridian shallows. Weather this danger and you are safe, for the rest of the way is downhill. With unrelaxed nerves, with morning vigor, sail by it, looking another way, tied to the mast like Ulysses. If the engine whistles, let it whistle till it is hoarse for its pains. If the bell rings, why should we run? We will consider what kind of music they are like. Let us settle ourselves and work and wedge our feet downward through the mud and slush of opinion, and prejudice, and tradition, and delusion, and appearance, that alluvion which covers the globe, through Paris and London, through New York and Boston and Concord, through Church and State, through poetry and philosophy and religion, till we come to a hard bottom and rocks in place, which we can call *reality*, and say, This is, and no mistake; and then begin, having a *point d'appui*, below freshet and frost and fire, a place where you might found a wall or a state, or set a lamp-post safely, or perhaps a gauge, not a Nilometer, but a Realometer, that future ages might know how deep a freshet of shams and appearances had gathered from time to time. If you stand right fronting and face to face to a fact, you will see the sun glimmer on both its surfaces, as if it were a cimeter, and feel its sweet edge dividing you through the heart and marrow, and so you will happily conclude your mortal career. Be it life or death, we crave only reality. If we are really dying, let us hear the rattle in our throats and feel cold in the extremities; if we are alive, let us go about our business.

Time is but the stream I go afishing in. I drink at it; but while I drink I see the sandy bottom and detect how shallow it is. Its thin current slides away but eternity remains. I would drink deeper; fish in the sky, whose bottom is pebbly with stars. I cannot count one. I know not the first letter of the alphabet. I have always been regretting that I was not as wise as the day I was born. The intellect is a cleaver; it discerns and rifts its way into the secret of things. I do not wish to be any more busy with my hands than is necessary. My head is hands and feet. I feel all my best faculties concentrated in it. My instinct tells me that my head is an organ for burrowing, as some creatures use their snout and fore paws, and with it I would mine and burrow my way through these hills. I think that the richest vein is somewhere hereabouts; so by the divining-rod and thin rising vapors, I judge; and here I will begin to mine.

Possibilities for Writing

1. Analyze the recommendations that Thoreau is making here. What are his general recommendations? What are his specific recommendations? How might these recommendations be applied to life as it is lived in the twenty-first century?
2. Thoreau's writing is characterized by extensive use of metaphor. Choose several of these to analyze in detail. How well does metaphor contribute to clarifying Thoreau's ideas?
3. Throughout the essay, Thoreau includes what are for him statements of observed truth—for example, "Our life is frittered away by detail" and "I perceive that we . . . live this mean life that we do because our vision does not penetrate the surface of things." Choose one of these ideas that you find interesting as the basis for an essay of your own.

James Thurber (1894–1961), one the country's premiere humorists, was born in Columbus, Ohio, and educated at Ohio State University, where he wrote for the school newspaper. After working as a reporter for the Columbus Dispatch *and later a Paris-based correspondent for the* Chicago Tribune, *in 1927 he joined the staff of the* New Yorker, *a magazine with which he would be associated for the rest of his life (as a freelancer from 1936). His stylish wit marked by psychological insight, Thurber produced droll short stories, a comic play about college life, and a number of works of gentle satire on various subjects. He is probably best remembered today for his cartoons and drawings, of which there are many collections. These often depict hapless middle-aged men besieged by the demands of domineering wives and beset by the petty irritations of everyday life.*

James Thurber

University Days

In "University Days," the American humorist James Thurber writes comically about his college experience at Ohio State University. Thurber entertains and amuses while conveying his sense of frustration and bemusement at what he experienced and observed there.

Thurber arranges this excerpt from his autobiography, *My Life and Hard Times*, as a series of linked stories. In an anecdote about his botany class, Thurber describes his frustration at not being able to see what he is supposed to see through a microscope, and what, presumably, his fellow classmates see. He structures the botany anecdote to allow for the hope of success, only to dash that hope with comic deflation. Through stories about gym and journalism and military drill, Thurber creates a comic persona that is, paradoxically, both blind and insightful. In showing readers what Thurber the character didn't see, Thurber the writer shows us some things we can smile about.

His anecdote about economics class shifts the focus from Thurber himself to another hapless student—a Polish football player, Bolenciecwz, who serves as a comic stereotype of the intellectually challenged but lovable oversized athlete. His professors and fellow students together help Bolenciecwz to just scrape by academically so as to retain his athletic eligibility. A large part of the humor of this anecdote lies in the variety of ways students and professor hint at the answer to a question Bolenciecwz is asked in class—what goes "choo-choo"; "toot-toot"; "chuffa, chuffa"—and the delay in Bolenciecwz's finally realizing that the answer is "a train."

I passed all the other courses that I took at my university, but I could never pass botany. This was because all botany students had to spend several hours a week in a laboratory looking through a microscope at plant cells, and I could never see through a microscope. I never once saw a cell through

a microscope. This used to enrage my instructor. He would wander around
the laboratory pleased with the progress all the students were making in
drawing the involved and, so I am told, interesting structure of flower cells,
until he came to me. I would just be standing there. "I can't see anything,"
I would say. He would begin patiently enough, explaining how anybody
can see through a microscope, but he would always end up in a fury, claiming that I could *too* see through a microscope but just pretended that I
couldn't. "It takes away from the beauty of flowers anyway," I used to tell
him. "We are not concerned with beauty in this course," he would say. "We
are concerned solely with what I may call the *mechanics* of flowers."
"Well," I'd say, "I can't see anything." "Try it just once again," he'd say,
and I would put my eye to the microscope and see nothing at all, except
now and again a nebulous milky substance—a phenomenon of maladjust-
ment. You were supposed to see a vivid, restless clockwork of sharply
defined plant cells. "I see what looks like a lot of milk," I would tell him.
This, he claimed, was the result of my not having adjusted the microscope
properly, so he would readjust it for me, or rather, for himself. And I would
look again and see milk.

I finally took a deferred pass, as they called it, and waited a year
and tried again. (You had to pass one of the biological sciences or
you couldn't graduate.) The professor had come back from vacation
brown as a berry, bright-eyed, and eager to explain cell-structure again
to his classes. "Well," he said to me, cheerily, when we met in the first
laboratory hour of the semester, "we're going to see cells this time,
aren't we?" "Yes, sir," I said. Students to right of me and to left of me
and in front of me were seeing cells; what's more, they were quietly
drawing pictures of them in their notebooks. Of course, I didn't see
anything.

"We'll try it," the professor said to me, grimly, "with every adjustment of the microscope known to man. As God is my witness, I'll
arrange this glass so that you see cells through it or I'll give up teaching.
In twenty-two years of botany, I—" He cut off abruptly for he was
beginning to quiver all over, like Lionel Barrymore, and he genuinely
wished to hold onto his temper; his scenes with me had taken a great
deal out of him.

So we tried it with every adjustment of the microscope known to man.
With only one of them did I see anything but blackness or the familiar
lacteal opacity, and that time I saw, to my pleasure and amazement,

a variegated constellation of flecks, specks, and dots. These I hastily drew. The instructor, noting my activity, came back from an adjoining desk, a smile on his lips and his eyebrows high in hope. He looked at my cell drawing. "What's that?" he demanded, with a hint of a squeal in his voice. "That's what I saw" I said. "You didn't, you didn't, you *didn't!*" he screamed, losing control of his temper instantly, and he bent over and squinted into the microscope. His head snapped up. "That's your eye!" he shouted. "You've fixed the lens so that it reflects! You've drawn your eye!"

Another course that I didn't like, but somehow managed to pass, was economics. I went to that class straight from the botany class, which didn't help me any in understanding either subject. I used to get them mixed up. But not as mixed up as another student in my economics class who came there direct from a physics laboratory. He was a tackle on the football team, named Bolenciecwcz. At that time Ohio State University had one of the best football teams in the country, and Bolenciecwcz was one of its outstanding stars. In order to be eligible to play it was necessary for him to keep up in his studies, a very difficult matter, for while he was not dumber than an ox he was not any smarter. Most of his professors were lenient and helped him along. None gave him more hints in answering questions or asked him simpler ones than the economics professor, a thin, timid man named Bassum. One day when we were on the subject of transportation and distribution, it came Bolenciecwcz's turn to answer a question. "Name one means of transportation," the professor said to him. No light came into the big tackle's eyes. "Just any means of transportation," said the professor. Bolenciecwcz sat staring at him. "That is," pursued the professor, "any medium, agency, or method of going from one place to another." Bolenciecwcz had the look of a man who is being led into a trap. "You may choose among steam, horse-drawn, or electrically propelled vehicles," said the instructor. "I might suggest the one which we commonly take in making long journeys across land." There was a profound silence in which everybody stirred uneasily, including Bolenciecwcz and Mr. Bassum. Mr. Bassum abruptly broke this silence in an amazing manner. "Choo-choo-choo," he said, in a low voice, and turned instantly scarlet. He glanced appealingly around the room. All of us, of course, shared Mr. Bassum's desire that Bolenciecwcz should stay abreast of the class in economics, for the Illinois game, one of the hardest and most important of the season, was only a week off. "Toot, toot, too-tooooooot!" some student with a deep voice moaned, and we all looked encouragingly at Bolenciecwcz. Somebody else gave a fine imitation of a locomotive letting off steam. Mr. Bassum himself rounded off the little show. "Ding, dong, ding, dong," he said, hopefully. Bolenciecwcz was staring at the floor now, trying to think, his great brow furrowed, his huge hands rubbing together, his face red.

"How did you come to college this year, Mr. Bolenciecwcz?" asked the professor. "*Chuffa* chuffa, *chuffa* chuffa."

"M'father sent me," said the football player.

"What on?" asked Bassum.

"I git an 'lowance," said the tackle, in a low, husky voice, obviously embarrassed.

"No, no," said Bassum. "Name a means of transportation. What did you *ride* here on?"

"Train," said Bolenciecwcz.

"Quite right," said the professor. "Now, Mr. Nugent, will you tell us—"

If I went through anguish in botany and economics—for different reasons—gymnasium work was even worse. I don't even like to think about it. They wouldn't let you play games or join in the exercises with your glasses on and I couldn't see with mine off. I bumped into professors, horizontal bars, agricultural students, and swinging iron rings. Not being able to see, I could take it but I couldn't dish it out. Also, in order to pass gymnasium (and you had to pass it to graduate) you had to learn to swim if you didn't know how. I didn't like the swimming pool, I didn't like swimming, and I didn't like the swimming instructor, and after all these years I still don't. I never swam but I passed my gym work anyway, by having another student give my gymnasium number (978) and swim across the pool in my place. He was a quiet, amiable blond youth, number 473, and he would have seen through a microscope for me if we could have got away with it, but we couldn't get away with it. Another thing I didn't like about gymnasium work was that they made you strip the day you registered. It is impossible for me to be happy when I am stripped and being asked a lot of questions. Still, I did better than a lanky agricultural student who was cross-examined just before I was. They asked each student what college he was in—that is, whether Arts, Engineering, Commerce, or Agriculture. "What college are you in?" the instructor snapped at the youth in front of me. "Ohio State University," he said promptly.

It wasn't that agricultural student but it was another a whole lot like him who decided to take up journalism, possibly on the ground that when farming went to hell he could fall back on newspaper work. He didn't realize, of course, that that would be very much like falling back full-length on a kit of carpenter's tools. Haskins didn't seem cut out for journalism, being too embarrassed to talk to anybody and unable to use a typewriter, but the editor of the college paper assigned him to the cow barns, the sheep house, the horse pavilion, and the animal husbandry department generally. This was a genuinely big "beat," for it took up five times as much ground and got ten times as great a legislative appropriation as the College of Liberal Arts. The agricultural student knew animals, but nevertheless his stories were dull and colorlessly written. He took all afternoon on each of them, on account of having to hunt for each letter on the typewriter. Once in a while he had to ask somebody to help him hunt. "C" and "L," in particular, were hard letters for him to find. His editor finally got pretty much annoyed at the farmer-journalist because his pieces were so uninteresting. "See here, Haskins," he snapped at him one day, "why is it we never have anything hot from you on the horse pavilion? Here we have two hundred head of horses on this campus—more than any other university in the Western Conference except Purdue—and yet you never get any real lowdown on them. Now shoot over to the horse barns and dig up something lively." Haskins shambled out and came back in about an hour; he said he had something. "Well, start it off snappily," said the editor. "Something people will read." Haskins set to work and in a couple of hours brought a sheet of typewritten paper to the desk; it was a two-hundred-word story about some disease that had broken out among the horses. Its opening sentence was simple but arresting. It read: "Who has noticed the sores on the tops of the horses in the animal husbandry building?"

Ohio State was a land grant university and therefore two years of military drill was compulsory. We drilled with old Springfield rifles and studied the tactics of the Civil War even though the World War was going on at the time. At 11 o'clock each morning thousands of freshmen and sophomores used to deploy over the campus, moodily creeping up on the old chemistry building. It was good training for the kind of warfare that was waged at Shiloh but it had no connection with what was going on in Europe. Some people used to think there was German money behind it, but they didn't dare say so or they would have been thrown in jail as German spies. It was a period of muddy thought and marked, I believe, the decline of higher education in the Middle West.

As a soldier I was never any good at all. Most of the cadets were glumly indifferent soldiers, but I was no good at all. Once General Littlefield, who was commandant of the cadet corps, popped up in front of me during regimental drill and snapped, "You are the main trouble with this university!" I think he meant that my type was the main trouble with the university but he may have meant me individually. I was mediocre at drill, certainly—that is, until my senior year. By that time I had drilled longer than anybody else in the Western Conference, having failed at military at the end of each preceding year so that I had to do it all over again. I was the only senior still in uniform. The uniform which, when new, had made me look like an interurban railway conductor, now that it had become faded and too tight made me look like Bert Williams in his bellboy act. This had a definitely bad effect on my morale. Even so, I had become by sheer practice little short of wonderful at squad maneuvers.

One day General Littlefield picked our company out of the whole regiment and tried to get it mixed up by putting it through one movement after another as fast as we could execute them: squads right, squads left, squads on right into line, squads right about, squads left front into line, etc. In about three minutes one hundred and nine men were marching in one direction and I was marching away from them at an angle of forty degrees, all alone. "Company, halt!" shouted General Littlefield. "That man is the only man who has it right!" I was made a corporal for my achievement.

The next day General Littlefield summoned me to his office. He was swatting flies when I went in. I was silent and he was silent too, for a long time; I don't think he remembered me or why he had sent for me, but he didn't want to admit it. He swatted some more flies, keeping his eyes on them narrowly before he let go with the swatter. "Button up your coat!" he snapped. Looking back on it now I can see that he meant me although he was looking at a fly, but I just stood there. Another fly came to rest on a paper in front of the general and began rubbing its hind legs together. The general lifted the swatter cautiously. I moved restlessly and the fly flew away. "You startled him!" barked General Littlefield, looking at me severely. I said I was sorry. "That won't help the situation!" snapped the General, with cold military logic. I didn't see what I could do except offer to chase some more flies toward his desk, but I didn't say anything. He stared out the window at the faraway figures of co-eds crossing the campus toward the library. Finally, he told me I could go. So I went. He either didn't know which cadet I was or else he forgot what he wanted to see me about. It may have been that he wished to apologize for having called me the main trouble with the university; or maybe he had decided to compliment me on my brilliant drilling of the day before and then at the last minute decided not to. I don't know. I don't think about it much any more.

Possibilities for Writing

1. Thurber here describes several different incidents from his college days. Consider each as a separate anecdote, and analyze the source of its humor individually. Who—or what—is the "butt" of each story, and how, in your opinion, does this determine the success of its comic effect?

2. Analyze the comic persona Thurber creates here. Is he always in on the joke? How does Thurber achieve this effect?

3. Relate some of your own comic experiences in high school, college, or both to suggest some of the absurdity found in any educational environment. Change names as you see fit, and don't be afraid to exaggerate a bit.

Sojourner Truth (c.1797–1883) was born a slave in Ulster County, New York, with the given name Isabella. When slavery was abolished in the state, she worked for a time with a Quaker family and was caught up in the religious fervor then sweeping American Protestantism. In 1843, announcing that she had received messages from heaven, she took on the name Sojourner Truth and began a career as an itinerant preacher, advocating the abolishment of slavery and the advancement of women's rights. While basically illiterate, she was nevertheless a highly effective speaker and a powerful physical presence, and she had an intense following. After the Civil War, she counseled newly freed slaves and petitioned for a "Negro state" on public lands in the West. Her memoirs, dictated to Olive Gilbert, were published as Narratives of Sojourner Truth *(1878).*

Sojourner Truth
And Ain't I a Woman?

The following speech was made by Sojourner Truth, a black female slave, when she attended a women's rights convention held in Akron, Ohio in May of 1851. Sojourner Truth was the only black woman in attendance. On the second day of the convention she approached the podium, and addressed the audience in a deep and powerful voice. The speech was recorded by Frances D. Gage, who presided at the convention, and was later transcribed.

Part of the power of Sojourner Truth's short speech is its spontaneous refutation of those who spoke before her. Part of the pleasure for readers of the speech is listening to her rebuttal of implied arguments made by the speakers who preceded her. Readers can infer the type of arguments they made about why women were inferior to men from how Sojourner Truth addresses those implied arguments.

Well children, where there is so much racket there must be somethin' out o'kilter. I think that 'twixt the Negroes of the North and the South and the women at the North, all talkin' 'bout rights, the white men will be in a fix pretty soon. But what's all this here talkin' 'bout?

That man over there say that women needs to be helped into carriages, and lifted over ditches, and to have the best place everywhere. Nobody ever helps me into carriages, or over mud-puddles, or give me any best place! And ain't I a woman? Look at me! Look at my arm! I have ploughed, and planted, and gathered into barns, and no man could head me! And ain't I a woman? I could work as much and eat as much as a man—when I could get it—and bear the lash as well! And ain't I a woman? I have borne thirteen children, and seen 'em mos' all sold off to slavery, and when I cried out with my mother's grief, none but Jesus heard me! And ain't I a woman?

Then they talk about this thing in the head; what's this they call it? ["Intellect," whispered some one near.] That's it honey. What's that got to do with women's rights or Negro's rights? If my cup won't hold but a pint and yours holds a quart, wouldn't you be mean not to let me have my little measure full?

Then that little man in black there, he says women can't have as much rights as men, 'cause Christ wasn't a woman! Where did your Christ come from? Where did your Christ come from? From God and a woman! Man had nothin' to do with Him.

If the first woman God ever made was strong enough to turn the world upside down all alone, these women together ought to be able to turn it back and get it right side up again; and now they is asking to do it, they better let 'em. 'Bliged to you for hearin' me, and now ole Sojourner hasn't got nothin' more to say.

Possibilities for Writing

1. There are a number of striking points packed into this very brief argument—about both slavery and women's rights. Analyze each of the assertions Sojourner Truth makes, whether explicit or implied, and how she supports each assertion.

2. Read "And Ain't I a Woman?" along with Elizabeth Cady Stanton's "Declaration of Sentiments and Resolutions" (pages 329–332). Although the two speeches are very different, consider in particular what they have in common. Then think about how the two women go about achieving their point.

3. "Translate" Sojourner Truth's speech into standard, more formal English. Then analyze the differences between the two texts, taking into account differences when the two are read aloud.

E. B. White (1899–1985) was born to wealthy parents in Mount Vernon, New York, a suburb of Manhattan. At Cornell University, he was editor of the campus newspaper, and he early settled on a career in journalism. In 1927 he joined the staff of the newly formed New Yorker *magazine and contributed greatly to the sophisticated, sharply ironic tone of the publication. He relocated his family to rural Maine in 1933 and left the* New Yorker *in 1937 to write a monthly column for* Harper's. *These more serious and emotionally felt essays were collected in* One Man's Meat *(1942), and White published two more major essay collections in 1954 and 1962. He is also the author of several popular children's books, including* Stuart Little *(1945) and* Charlotte's Web *(1952). Considered a peerless stylist, White also edited and expanded* The Elements of Style *by Willard Strunk, Jr.*

E. B. White

Once More to the Lake

E. B. White's "Once More to the Lake" describes a visit to a Maine Lake that White makes with his family, which evokes memories of the annual trip he made there when he was a young boy. Reflecting on his recent trip in the context of the time he spent at the lake as a youth, White creates a lyrical remembrance of the place and a speculative essay about the passage of time, about change and changlessness, and about mortality.

One of the most striking features of the essay is the way White describes himself, his father, and his son. White explains, for example, how, as he watched his son doing the things he did when he was a boy at the lake— preparing the fishing tackle box, running the boat's outboard motor, casting his fishing line—White felt that he was "living a dual existence." Inhabiting the essay's present as the adult father of his son, White sees himself in his son as the boy he had been when his father occupied the paternal role that White himself later occupies. "It gave me," he writes "a creepy sensation." Just how creepy we only understand with White's culminating realization at the end of the essay.

One summer, along about 1904, my father rented a camp on a lake in Maine and took us all there for the month of August. We all got ring-worm from some kittens and had to rub Pond's Extract on our arms and legs night and morning, and my father rolled over in a canoe with all his clothes on; but outside of that the vacation was a success and from then on none of us ever thought there was any place in the world like that lake in Maine. We returned summer after summer—always on August 1 for one month. I have since become a salt-water man, but sometimes in summer there are days when the restlessness of the tides and the fearful

cold of the sea water and the incessant wind that blows across the afternoon and into the evening make me wish for the placidity of a lake in
the woods. A few weeks ago this feeling got so strong I bought myself a
couple of bass hooks and a spinner and returned to the lake where we
used to go, for a week's fishing and to revisit old haunts.

I took along my son, who had never had any fresh water up his nose
and who had seen lily pads only from train windows. On the journey
over to the lake I began to wonder what it would be like. I wondered
how time would have marred this unique, this holy spot—the coves and
streams, the hills that the sun set behind, the camps and the paths
behind the camps. I was sure that the tarred road would have found it
out, and I wondered in what other ways it would be desolated. It is
strange how much you can remember about places like that once you
allow your mind to return into the grooves that lead back. You remember one thing, and that suddenly reminds you of another thing. I guess
I remembered clearest of all the early mornings, when the lake was cool
and motionless, remembered how the bedroom smelled of the lumber it
was made of and of the wet woods whose scent entered through the
screen. The partitions in the camp were thin and did not extend clear to
the top of the rooms, and as I was always the first up I would dress
softly so as not to wake the others, and sneak out into the sweet out-
doors and start out in the canoe, keeping close along the shore in the
long shadows of the pines. I remembered being very careful never to rub
my paddle against the gunwale for fear of disturbing the stillness of the
cathedral.

The lake had never been what you would call a wild lake. There were
cottages sprinkled around the shores, and it was in farming country
although the shores of the lake were quite heavily wooded. Some of the
cottages were owned by nearby farmers, and you would live at the shore
and eat your meals at the farmhouse. That's what our family did. But
although it wasn't wild, it was a fairly large and undisturbed lake and
there were places in it that, to a child at least, seemed infinitely remote and
primeval.

I was right about the tar: it led to within half a mile of the shore. But
when I got back there, with my boy, and we settled into a camp near a
farmhouse and into the kind of summertime I had known, I could tell that
it was going to be pretty much the same as it had been before—I knew it,
lying in bed the first morning, smelling the bedroom and hearing the boy

sneak quietly out and go off along the shore in a boat. I began to sustain the illusion that he was I, and therefore, by simple transposition, that I was my father. This sensation persisted, kept cropping up all the time we were there. It was not an entirely new feeling, but in this setting it grew much stronger. I seemed to be living a dual existence. I would be in the middle of some simple act, I would be picking up a bait box or laying down a table fork, or I would be saying something, and suddenly it would be not I but my father who was saying the words or making the gesture. It gave me a creepy sensation.

We went fishing the next morning. I felt the same damp moss covering the worms in the bait can, and saw the dragonfly alight on the tip of my rod as it hovered a few inches from the surface of the water. It was the arrival of this fly that convinced me beyond any doubt that everything was as it always had been, that the years were a mirage and that there had been no years. The small waves were the same, chucking the rowboat under the chin as we fished at anchor, and the boat was the same boat, the same color green and the ribs broken in the same places, and under the floorboards the same fresh-water leavings and débris—the dead helgramite, the wisps of moss, the rusty discarded fishhook, the dried blood from yesterday's catch. We stared silently at the tips of our rods, at the dragonflies that came and went. I lowered the tip of mine into the water, tentatively, pensively dislodging the fly, which darted two feet away, poised, darted two feet back, and came to rest again a little farther up the rod. There had been no years between the ducking of this dragonfly and the other one—the one that was part of memory. I looked at the boy, who was silently watching his fly, and it was my hands that held his rod, my eyes watching. I felt dizzy and didn't know which rod I was at the end of.

We caught two bass, hauling them in briskly as though they were mackerel, pulling them over the side of the boat in a businesslike manner without any landing net, and stunning them with a blow on the back of the head. When we got back for a swim before lunch, the lake was exactly where we had left it, the same number of inches from the dock, and there was only the merest suggestion of a breeze. This seemed an utterly enchanted sea, this lake you could leave to its own devices for a few hours and come back to, and find that it had not stirred, this constant and trustworthy body of water. In the shallows, the dark, water-soaked sticks and twigs, smooth and old, were undulating in clusters on the bottom against the clean ribbed sand, and the track of the mussel was plain. A school of minnows swam by, each minnow with its small individual shadow, doubling the attendance, so clear and sharp in the sunlight. Some of the other campers were in swimming, along the shore, one of them with a cake of soap, and the water felt thin and clear and unsubstantial. Over the years there had been this person with the cake of soap, this cultist, and here he was. There had been no years.

Up to the farmhouse to dinner through the teeming, dusty field, the road under our sneakers was only a two-track road. The middle track was missing, the one with the marks of the hooves and the splotches of dried, flaky manure. There had always been three tracks to choose from in choosing which track to walk in; now the choice was narrowed down to two. For a moment I missed terribly the middle alternative. But the way led past the tennis court, and something about the way it lay there in the sun reassured me; the tape had loosened along the backline, the alleys were green with plantains and other weeds, and the net (installed in June and removed in September) sagged in the dry noon, and the whole place steamed with midday heat and hunger and emptiness. There was a choice of pie for dessert, and one was blueberry and one was apple, and the waitresses were the same country girls, there having been no passage of time, only the illusion of it as in a dropped curtain— the waitresses were still fifteen; their hair had been washed, that was the only difference—they had been to the movies and seen the pretty girls with the clean hair.

Summertime, oh, summertime, pattern of life indelible, the fade-proof lake, the woods unshatterable, the pasture with the sweetfern and the juniper forever and ever, summer without end; this was the background, and the life along the shore was the design, the cottagers with their innocent and tranquil design, their tiny docks with the flagpole and the American flag floating against the white clouds in the blue sky, the little paths over the roots of the trees leading from camp to camp and the paths leading back to the outhouses and the can of lime for sprinkling, and at the souvenir counters at the store the miniature birchbark canoes and the postcards that showed things looking a little better than they looked. This was the American family at play, escaping the city heat, wondering whether the newcomers in the camp at the head of the cove were "common" or "nice," wondering whether it was true that the people who drove up for Sunday dinner at the farmhouse were turned away because there wasn't enough chicken.

It seemed to me, as I kept remembering all this, that those times and those summers had been infinitely precious and worth saving. There had been jollity and peace and goodness. The arriving (at the beginning of August) had been so big a business in itself, at the railway station the farm wagon drawn up, the first smell of the pine-laden air, the first glimpse of the smiling farmer, and the great importance of the trunks and your father's enormous authority in such matters, and the feel of the wagon under you for the long ten-mile haul, and at the top of the last long hill catching the first view of the lake after eleven months of not seeing this cherished body of water. The shouts and cries of the other campers when they saw you, and the trunks to be unpacked, to give up their rich burden. (Arriving was less exciting nowadays, when you sneaked up in your car and parked it under a tree near the camp and took out the bags and in five minutes it was all over, no fuss, no loud wonderful fuss about trunks.)

Peace and goodness and jollity. The only thing that was wrong now, really, was the sound of the place, an unfamiliar nervous sound of the outboard motors. This was the note that jarred, the one thing that would sometimes break the illusion and set the years moving. In those other summertimes all motors were inboard; and when they were at a little distance, the noise they made was a sedative, an ingredient of summer sleep. They were one-cylinder and two-cylinder engines, and some were make-and-break and some were jump-spark, but they all made a sleepy sound across the lake. The one-lungers throbbed and fluttered, and the twin-cylinder ones purred and purred, and that was a quiet sound, too. But now the campers all had outboards. In the daytime, in the hot mornings, these motors made a petulant, irritable sound; at night, in the still evening when the afterglow lit the water, they whined about one's ears like mosquitoes. My boy loved our rented outboard, and his great desire was to achieve single-handed mastery over it, and authority, and he soon learned the trick of choking it a little (but not too much), and the adjustment of the needle valve. Watching him I would remember the things you could do with the old one-cylinder engine with the heavy flywheel, how you could have it eating out of your hand if you got really close to it spiritually. Motorboats in those days didn't have clutches, and you would make a landing by shutting off the motor at the proper time and coasting in with a dead rudder. But there was a way of reversing them, if you learned the trick, by cutting the switch and putting it on again exactly on the final dying revolution of the flywheel, so that it would kick back against compression and begin reversing. Approaching a dock in a strong following breeze, it was difficult to slow up sufficiently by the ordinary coasting method, and if a boy felt he had complete mastery over his motor, he was tempted to keep it running beyond its time and then reverse it a few feet from the dock. It took a cool nerve, because if you threw the switch a twentieth of a second too soon you would catch the flywheel when it still had speed enough to go up past center, and the boat would leap ahead, charging bull-fashion at the dock.

We had a good week at the camp. The bass were biting well and the sun shone endlessly, day after day. We would be tired at night and lie down in the accumulated heat of the little bedrooms after the long hot day and the breeze would stir almost imperceptibly outside and the smell of the swamp drift in through the rusty screens. Sleep would come easily and in the morning the red squirrel would be on the roof, tapping out his gay routine. I kept remembering everything, lying in bed in the mornings—the small steamboat that had a long rounded stern like the lip of a Ubangi, and how quietly she ran on the moonlight sails, when the older boys played their mandolins and the girls sang and we ate doughnuts dipped in sugar, and how sweet the music was on the water in the shining night, and what it had felt like to think about girls then. After breakfast we would go up to the store and the things were in the same place—the minnows in a bottle, the plugs and spinners disarranged and pawed over by the youngsters from the boys' camp, the Fig Newtons and the Beeman's gum. Outside, the road was tarred and cars stood in front of the store. Inside, all was just as it had always been, except there was more Coca-Cola and not so much Moxie and root beer and birch beer and sarsaparilla. We would walk out with the bottle of pop apiece and sometimes the pop would backfire up our noses and hurt. We explored the streams, quietly, where the turtles slid off the sunny logs and dug their way into the soft bottom; and we lay on the town wharf and fed worms to the tame bass. Everywhere we went I had trouble making out which was I, the one walking at my side, the one walking in my pants.

One afternoon while we were there at that lake a thunderstorm came up. It was like the revival of an old melodrama that I had seen long ago with childish awe. The second-act climax of the drama of the electrical disturbance over a lake in America had not changed in any important respect. This was the big scene, still the big scene. The whole thing was so familiar, the first feeling of oppression and heat and a general air around camp of not wanting to go very far away. In midafternoon (it was all the same) a curious darkening of the sky, and a lull in everything that had made life tick; and then the way the boats suddenly swung the other way at their moorings with the coming of a breeze out of the new quarter, and the premonitory rumble. Then the kettle drum, then the snare, then the bass drum and cymbals, then crackling light against the dark, and the gods grinning and licking their chops in the hills. Afterward the calm, the rain steadily rustling in the calm lake, the return of light and hope and spirits, and the campers running out in joy and relief to go swimming in the rain, their bright cries perpetuating the deathless joke about how they were getting simply drenched, and the children screaming with delight at the new sensation of bathing in the rain, and the joke about getting drenched linking the generations in a strong indestructible chain. And the comedian who waded in carrying an umbrella.

When the others went swimming, my son said he was going in, too. He pulled his dripping trunks from the line where they had hung all through the shower and wrung them out. Languidly, and with no thought of going in, I watched him, his hard little body, skinny and bare, saw him wince slightly as he pulled up around his vitals the small, soggy, icy garment. As he buckled the swollen belt, suddenly my groin felt the chill of death.

Possibilities for Writing

1. Analyze White's essay to focus on its themes of change and changelessness. To what extent, might White say, is change itself changeless?

2. White is justly noted for his writing style, particularly his attention to concrete yet evocative descriptive detail. Choose several passages that appeal to you, and examine White's use of language in them. How would you characterize White's style?

3. Describe a place that holds a personal sense of history for you. It may be a place you have returned to after a long absence, as the lake is for White, or a place that simply holds many memories. Focus on your responses to and feelings about the place both in the past and from your present perspective.

Mary Wollstonecraft (1759–1797), a radical feminist centuries before the term had been coined, was born in London to a well-off family whose fortune was squandered by her dissolute father. Forced to earn a living, she took on the only jobs open to an educated woman of the time: schoolmistress, companion, and governess. In her mid-twenties, Wollstonecraft became part of a circle of radical English thinkers and artists, and in 1790 she published A Vindication of the Rights of Man, *an impassioned defense of the French Revolution which earned her great attention both positive and negative. Even more controversial was her* A Vindication of the Rights of Woman *(1792), a revolutionary examination of the status of women in eighteenth-century society that earned her the epithet "hyena in petticoats." She died of complications related to the birth of her second child, Mary Shelley.*

Mary Wollstonecraft

A Vindication of the Rights of Woman

Mary Wollstonecraft wrote her eighteenth-century *A Vindication of the Rights of Woman* as a defense of women's rights and as an encouragement for women to believe in their strength of mind and spirit. In this excerpt, she provides a bracing antidote to the conventional image of women as frail and fragile, delicate and demure. Wollstonecraft will have none of that, as she urges women to abandon the "soft phrases," "delicacy of sentiment," and "refinement of taste," with which they are presumably comfortable and to which they are presumed to have been accustomed. Wollstonecraft dismisses that characterization of her sex as a dangerous way to subordinate women to the control of men. She presents an image of woman, not as a weaker vessel but as an equal vessel, one who should develop her character as a human being on an equal footing with a man.

Wollstonecraft's language throughout is strong and unapologetic, and her arguments direct and forceful. Wollstonecraft's rhetoric is unrelenting, as she argues that if women possess inferior intelligence and wisdom to men, why do men give them the responsibility of raising children and governing a family? Why, indeed?

My own sex, I hope, will excuse me, if I treat them like rational creatures, instead of flattering their *fascinating* graces, and viewing them as if they were in a state of perpetual childhood, unable to stand alone. I earnestly wish to point out in what true dignity and human happiness consists—I wish to persuade women to endeavor to acquire strength, both of mind and body, and to convince them that the soft phrases, susceptibility of heart, delicacy of sentiment, and refinement of taste, are almost synonymous with epithets of weakness, and that those beings who are only the objects of pity and that kind of love, which has been termed its sister, will soon become objects of contempt.

Dismissing, then, those pretty feminine phrases, which the men condescendingly use to soften our slavish dependence, and despising that weak elegancy of mind, exquisite sensibility, and sweet docility of manners, supposed to be the sexual characteristics of the weaker vessel, I wish to show that elegance is inferior to virtue, that the first object of laudable ambition is to obtain a character as a human being, regardless of the distinction of sex; and that secondary views should be brought to this simple touchstone.

This is a rough sketch of my plan; and should I express my conviction with the energetic emotions that I fed whenever I think of the subject, the dictates of experience and reflection will be felt by some of my readers. Animated by this important object, I shall disdain to cull my phrases or polish my style; I aim at being useful, and sincerity will render me unaffected; for, wishing rather to persuade by the force of my arguments, than dazzle by the elegance of my language, I shall not waste my time in rounding periods, or in fabricating the turgid bombast of artificial feelings, which, coming from the head, never reach the heart. I shall be employed about things, not words! and, anxious to render my sex more respectable members of society, I shall try to avoid that flowery diction which has slided from essays into novels, and from novels into familiar letters and conversation.

These pretty superlatives, dropping glibly from the tongue, vitiate the taste, and create a kind of sickly delicacy that runs away from simple unadorned truth; and a deluge of false sentiments and overstretched feelings, stifling the natural emotions of the heart, render the domestic pleasures insipid, that ought to sweeten the exercise of those severe duties, which educate a rational and immortal being for a nobler field of action.

The education of women has, of late, been more attended to than formerly; yet they are still reckoned a frivolous sex, and ridiculed or pitied by the writers who endeavor by satire or instruction to improve them. It is acknowledged that they spend many of the first years of their lives in acquiring a smattering of accomplishments; meanwhile strength of body and mind are sacrificed to libertine notions of beauty, to the desire of establishing themselves—the only way women can rise in the world—by marriage. And this desire making mere animals of them, when they marry they act as such children may be expected to act— they dress; they paint, and nickname God's creatures. Surely these weak beings are only fit for a seraglio!—Can they be expected to govern a family with judgment, or take care of the poor babes whom they bring into the world?

If then it can be fairly deduced from the present conduct of the sex, from the prevalent fondness for pleasure which takes place of ambition, and those nobler passions that open and enlarge the soul; that the instruction which women have hitherto received has only tended, with the constitution of civil society, to render them insignificant objects of desire—mere propagators of fools!—if it can be proved that in aiming to accomplish them, without cultivating their understandings, they are taken out of their sphere of duties, and made ridiculous and useless when the short-lived bloom of beauty is over,* I presume that *rational* men will excuse me for endeavoring to persuade them to become more masculine and respectable.

Indeed the word masculine is only a bugbear: there is little reason to fear that women will acquire too much courage or fortitude; for their apparent inferiority with respect to bodily strength, must render them, in some degree, dependent on men in the various relations of life; but why should it be increased by prejudices that give a sex to virtue, and confound simple truths with sensual reveries?

Women are, in fact, so much degraded by mistaken notions of female excellence, that I do not mean to add a paradox when I assert, that this artificial weakness produces a propensity to tyrannize, and gives birth to cunning, the natural opponent of strength, which leads them to play off those contemptible infantine airs that undermine esteem even whilst they excite desire. Let men become more chaste and modest, and if women do not grow wiser in the same ratio, it will be clear that they have weaker understandings. It seems scarcely necessary to say, that I now speak of the sex in general. Many individuals have more sense than their male relatives; and, as nothing preponderates where there is a constant struggle for an equilibrium, without it has

---

*A lively writer, I cannot recollect his name, asks what business women turned of forty have to do in the world?

naturally more gravity, some women govern their husbands without degrading themselves, because intellect will always govern.

Possibilities for Writing

1. Wollstonecraft argues here that what in her day was regarded as proper conduct for women allowed men to define them as weak and frivolous. What conduct does she refer to, and what would she substitute in its place? What advice does she have for men?

2. In paragraph 7, Wollstonecraft writes that, although she is encouraging women to become more masculine, "their apparent inferiority with respect to bodily strength must render them, in some degree, dependent on men in the various relations of life." In the context of her whole argument, what point is she making here? To what extent do you think this attitude still exists today? Why?

3. Would you say that women at the beginning of the twenty-first century have achieved equality with men? You may base your essay on personal observations as well as research if you wish.

Virginia Woolf (1882–1941) was born Virginia Stephen into one of London's most prominent literary families. Essentially self-educated in her father's vast library, by her early twenties Woolf was publishing reviews and critical essays in literary journals. Her first novel appeared in 1915, but it was the publication of Mrs. Dalloway *in 1925 and* To the Lighthouse *in 1927 that established her reputation as an important artistic innovator. Four more novels followed, and her criticism and essays were collected in* The Common Reader *(1925, 1932),* Three Guineas *(1938), and* The Death of the Moth and Other Essays *(1942), edited posthumously by her husband after her tragic suicide. Her* Collected Essays *(1967) numbers four volumes. Woolf is also remembered for* A Room of One's Own *(1929), an early feminist consideration of the difficulties facing women writers.*

Virginia Woolf
The Death of the Moth

In her classic essay "The Death of the Moth," Virginia Woolf writes memorably about a moth she chances to see while gazing out her window on a sunny September morning. Watching the moth fly within a small square of window pane, Woolf speculates about the life force that animates the moth and about the myriad forms of life she notices in the fields. With his seemingly unflagging energy, the moth represents for Woolf, the pure energy of "life itself."

Woolf begins with seeing, with careful description of the moth based on attentive observation. The essay moves quickly, however, to speculation, as Woolf reflects on the moth's significance. At first Woof pities the pathetic little moth with its severely circumscribed and limited life. But as she watches it longer, she begins to analogize the life of the moth with human life. Her attitude shifts toward respect for the moth's attempts to live its brief life as exuberantly as it can.

Moths that fly by day are not properly to be called moths; they do not excite that pleasant sense of dark autumn nights and ivy-blossom which the commonest yellow-underwing asleep in the shadow of the curtain never fails to rouse in us. They are hybrid creatures, neither gay like butterflies nor sombre like their own species. Nevertheless the present specimen, with his narrow hay-coloured wings, fringed with a tassel of the same colour, seemed to be content with life. It was a pleasant morning, mid-September, mild, benignant, yet with a keener breath than that of the summer months. The plough was already scoring the field opposite the window, and where the share had been, the earth was pressed flat and gleamed with moisture. Such vigour came rolling in from the fields and the down beyond that it was difficult to keep the eyes strictly turned upon the book. The rooks too were keeping one of their annual festivities; soaring round the tree tops until it looked as if a vast net with thousands of black knots in it had been cast up into the air; which, after a few moments sank slowly down upon the trees until every twig seemed to have a knot at the end of it. Then, suddenly, the net would be thrown into the air again in a wider circle this time, with the utmost clamour and vociferation, as though to be thrown into the air and settle slowly down upon the tree tops were a tremendously exciting experience.

The same energy which inspired the rooks, the ploughmen, the horses, and even, it seemed, the lean bare-backed downs, sent the moth fluttering from side to side of his square of the window-pane. One could not help watching him. One was, indeed, conscious of a queer feeling of pity for him. The possibilities of pleasure seemed that morning so enormous and so various that to have only a moth's part in life, and a day moth's at that, appeared a hard fate, and his zest in enjoying his meagre opportunities to the full, pathetic. He flew vigorously to one corner of his compartment, and, after waiting there a second, flew across to the other. What remained for him but to fly to a third corner and then to a fourth? That was all he could do, in spite of the size of the downs, the width of the sky, the far-off smoke of houses, and the romantic voice, now and then, of a steamer out at sea. What he could do he did. Watching him, it seemed as if a fibre, very thin but pure, of the enormous energy of the world had been thrust into his frail and diminutive body. As often as he crossed the pane, I could fancy that a thread of vital light became visible. He was little or nothing but life.

Yet, because he was so small, and so simple a form of the energy that was rolling in at the open window and driving its way through so many narrow and intricate corridors in my own brain and in those of other human beings, there was something marvellous as well as pathetic about him. It was as if someone had taken a tiny bead of pure life and decking it as lightly as possible with down and feathers, had set it dancing and zig-zagging to show us the true nature of life. Thus displayed one could not get over the strangeness of it. One is apt to forget all about life, seeing it humped and bossed and garnished and cumbered so that it has to move with the greatest circumspection and dignity. Again, the thought of all that life might have been had he been born in any other shape caused one to view his simple activities with a kind of pity.

After a time, tired by his dancing apparently, he settled on the window ledge in the sun, and, the queer spectacle being at an end, I forgot about him. Then, looking up, my eye was caught by him. He was trying to resume his dancing, but seemed either so stiff or so awkward that he could only flutter to the bottom of the window-pane; and when he tried to fly across it he failed. Being intent on other matters I watched these futile attempts for a time without thinking, unconsciously waiting for him to resume his flight, as one waits for a machine, that has stopped momentarily, to start again without considering the reason of its failure. After perhaps a seventh attempt he slipped from the wooden ledge and fell, fluttering his wings, on to his back on the window sill. The helplessness of his attitude roused me. It flashed upon me that he was in difficulties; he could no longer raise himself; his legs struggled vainly. But, as I stretched out a pencil, meaning to help him to right himself, it came over me that the failure and awkwardness were the approach of death. I laid the pencil down again.

The legs agitated themselves once more. I looked as if for the enemy against which he struggled. I looked out of doors. What had happened there? Presumably it was midday, and work in the fields had stopped. Stillness and quiet had replaced the previous animation. The birds had taken themselves off to feed in the brooks. The horses stood still. Yet the power was there all the same, massed outside indifferent, impersonal, not attending to anything in particular. Somehow it was opposed to the little hay-coloured moth. It was useless to try to do anything. One could only watch the extraordinary efforts made by those tiny legs against an oncoming doom which could, had it chosen, have submerged an entire city, not merely a city, but masses of human beings; nothing, I knew, had any chance against death. Nevertheless after a pause of exhaustion the legs fluttered again. It was superb this last protest, and so frantic that he succeeded at last in righting himself. One's sympathies, of course, were all on the side of life. Also, when there was nobody to care or to know, this gigantic effort on the part of an insignificant little moth, against a power of such magnitude, to retain what no one else valued or desired to keep, moved one strangely. Again, somehow, one saw life, a pure bead. I lifted the pencil again, useless though I knew it to be. But even as I did so, the unmistakable tokens of death showed themselves. The body relaxed, and instantly grew stiff. The struggle was over. The insignificant little creature now knew death. As I looked at the dead moth, this minute wayside triumph of so great a force over so mean an antagonist filled me with wonder. Just as life had been strange a few minutes before, so death was now as strange. The moth having righted himself now lay most decently and uncomplainingly composed. O yes, he seemed to say, death is stronger than I am.

Possibilities for Writing

1. The moth in Woolf's essay becomes a potent symbol for life and then also for death more generally. How does Woolf manage to do this? Point to specific passages in the essay that directly or by implication tie the moth to the world beyond itself.

2. For all its concreteness, this essay is quite philosophical. How would you characterize Woolf's conception of the universe, based on the ideas that this essay provokes?

3. In order to explore your feelings about an abstract concept— love, courage, greed, humility, loss, or another of your choice— construct an essay, as Woolf does, around a central symbol. Describe your symbol in primarily concrete terms so that the concept itself becomes concrete.

Credits

388 * Credits

Index

"About Men" (Ehrlich), 132–135

Anzaldúa, Gloria, 31

  "How to Tame a Wild Tongue," 31–43

"Are You Somebody?" (O'Faolain), 282–285

"Aint I a Woman?" (Truth), 368–369

"Arriving at Perfection" (Franklin), 154–158

Bacon, Francis, 1–2, 44

  "Of Studies," 44–46

"Bachelor's Complaint, A" (Lamb), 3, 227–233

Barry, Dave, 47

  "Road Warrior," 47–50

Barthes, Roland, 51

  "Toys," 51–53

Brownmiller, Susan, 54

  "Femininity," 54–59

"Burl's" (Cooper), 77–87

"Calculated Risks" (Cole), 67–76

"Casa: A Partial Remembrance of a Puerto Rican Childhood" (Cofer), 60–66

Cofer, Judith Ortiz, 6, 60

  "Casa: A Partial Remembrance of a Puerto Rican Childhood," 60–66

Cole, K. C., 67

  "Calculated Risks," 67–76

"Colonel, The" (Hogan), 193–198

"Coming Home Again" (Lee), 193–198

"Company Man, The" (Goodman), 173–175

Cooper, Bernard, 77

  "Burl's," 77–87

Darwin, Charles, 88

  "Natural Selection," 88–100

"Death of the Moth, The" (Woolf), 4,6, 381–384

"Declaration of Sentiments and Resolutions" (Stanton), 329–332

Didion, Joan, 101

  "Marrying Absurd," 6, 101–105

Dillard, Annie, 6, 106

  "Living Like Weasels," 6, 10–15, 106–111

"Din in the Head, The" (Oziek), 294–298

Douglass, Frederick, 6, 112

  "Learning to Read and Write," 112–118

Doyle, Brian, 119

  "Joyas Voladoras", 119–122

Du Bois, W. E. B., 123

  "Of Our Spiritual Striving," 123–131

Ehrlich, Gretel, 7, 132

  "About Men," 132–135

Ellison, Ralph, 136

  "Living with Music," 136–145

"Femininity" (Brownmiller), 54–59
Feynman, Richard, 146
    "The Value of Science," 146–153
Franklin, Benjamin, 2, 154
    "Arriving at Perfection," 154–158

Gaddis, John Lewis, 159
    "The Landscape of History,"
        159–172
"Gettysburg Address, The"
    (Lincoln), 245–246
Goodman, Ellen, 173
    "The Company Man," 173–175
Gordon, Mary, 176
    "More than Just a Shrine—Ellis
        Island," 176–181

Hazlitt, William, 3, 182
    "On the Pleasure of Hating," 3,
        182–192
Hogan, Michael, 193
    "The Colonel," 193–198
"How to Tame a Wild Tongue"
    (Anzaldúa), 31–43
Hughes, Langston, 7, 199
    "Salvation," 7, 199–202

Iyer, Pico, 203
    "Nowhere Man," 6, 203–206

"Just Walk on By: Black Men and
    Public Space" (Staples), 333–337
"Joyas Voladoras" (Doyle), 119–122

King, Martin Luther, Jr., 4, 6, 207
    "Letter from Birmingham Jail,"
        207–223
Kingston, Maxine Hong, 7, 224
    "On Discovery," 224–226

Lamb, Charles, 3, 227
    "A Bachelor's Complaint," 3,
        227–233
"Landscape of History, The"
    (Gaddis), 159–172

"Learning to Read and Write"
    (Douglass), 112–118
Lee, Chang-Rae, 234
    "Coming Home Again," 234–244
"Letter from Birmingham Jail"
    (King), 207–223
Lincoln, Abraham, 245
    "The Gettysburg Address,"
        245–246
"Living Like Weasels" (Dillard), 6,
    10–15, 106–111
"Living with Music" (Ellison),
    136–145

Machiavelli, Niccolò, 247
    "The Morals of the Prince,"
        247–255
"Marrying Absurd" (Didion), 6,
    101–105
Mc Bride, James 256
    "Shul," 256–271
"Medium Is the Metaphor"
    (Postman), 299–310
"Modest Proposal, A" (Swift), 3,
    338–346
Momaday, N. Scott, 6, 7, 272
    "The Way to Rainy Mountain," 6,
        272–278
Montaigne, Michel de, 1–2, 6, 279
    "Of Smells," 6, 279–281
"Morals of the Prince, The"
    (Machiavelli), 247–255
"More than Just a Shrine—Ellis
    Island" (Gordon), 176–181
"Mother Tongue" (Tan), 7, 347–353

"Natural Selection" (Darwin), 88–100
"Nowhere Man" (Iyer), 6, 203–206

O' Faolain, 282
    "Are You Somebody?" 282–285
"Of Our Spiritual Striving"
    (Du Bois), 123–131
"Of Smells" (Montaigne), 6, 279–281
"Of Studies" (Bacon), 44–46

"On Discovery" (Kingston),
224–226

"On the Pleasure of Hating"
(Hazlitt), 3, 182–192

"Once More to the Lake" (White), 4,
7, 370–376

Orwell, George, 4, 286
"Shooting an Elephant," 4, 7,
286–293

Ozick, Cynthia, 294
"Din in the Head, The,"
294–298

Postman, Neil, 299
"Medium Is the Metaphor,
The," 299–310

"Road Warrior" (Barry), 47–50

"Salvation" (Hughes), 7, 199–202

Sanders, Scott Russell, 311
"Under the Influence," 311–324

"Shooting an Elephant" (Orwell), 4,
7, 286–293

"Shul" (Mc Bride), 256–271

Sontag, Susan, 325
"A Woman's Beauty: Put-Down
or Power Source?,"
325–328

Stanton, Elizabeth Cady, 329
"Declaration of Sentiments and
Resolutions," 329–332

Staples, Brent, 333
"Just Walk on By: Black Men and
Public Space," 333–337

Swift, Jonathan, 3, 338
"A Modest Proposal," 3,
338–346

Tan, Amy, 347
"Mother Tongue," 7, 347–353

Thoreau, Henry David, 3–4, 354
"Why I Went to the Woods,"
354–360

Thurber, James, 5, 361
"University Days," 6, 361–367

"Toys" (Barthes), 51–53

Truth, Sojourner, 368
"Ain't I a Woman?," 368–369

"Under the Influence" (Sanders),
311–324

"University Days" (Thurber), 6,
361–367

"Value of Science, The" (Feynman),
146–153

"Vindication of the Rights of
Woman, A" (Wollstonecraft),
377–380

"Way to Rainy Mountain, The"
(Momaday), 6, 272–278

White, E. B., 4, 370
"Once More to the Lake," 4, 7,
370–376

"Why I Went to the Woods"
(Thoreau), 354–360

Wollstonecraft, Mary, 377
"A Vindication of the Rights of
Woman," 377–380

"Woman's Beauty: Put-Down or
Power Source, A?" (Sontag),
20–31, 325–328

Woolf, Virginia, 4, 6, 381
"The Death of the Moth," 4, 6,
381–384

Additional Titles of Interest

Allison, Dorothy, *Bastard Out of Carolina*

Alvarez, Julia, *How the Garcia Girls Lost Their Accent*

Austen, Jane, *Persuasion*

Austen, Jane, *Pride and Prejudice*

Austen, Jane, *Sense and Sensibility*

Bloom, Harold, *Shakespeare: The Invention of the Human*

Brontë, Charlotte, *Jane Eyre*

Brontë, Emily, *Wuthering Heights*

Burke, Edmund, *Reflections on the Revolution in France*

Cather, Willa, *My Antonia*

Cather, Willa, *O Pioneers!*

Cellini, Benvenuto, *The Autobiography of Benvenuto Cellini*

Chapman, Abraham, *Black Voices*

Chesnutt, Charles W., *The Marrow of Tradition*

Chopin, Kate, *The Awakening and Selected Stories*

Conrad, Joseph, *Heart of Darkness*

Conrad, Joseph, *Nostromo: A Tale of the Seaboard*

Coraghessan Boyle, T., *The Tortilla Curtain*

Defoe, Daniel, *The Life and Adventures of Robinson Crusoe*

Descartes, René, *Discourse on Method and Meditations*

Descartes, René, *Meditations and Other Metaphysical Writings*

Detocqueville, *Democracy in America*

Dickens, Charles, *Hard Times*

Douglass, Frederick, *Narrative of the Life of Frederick Douglass: An American Slave*

DuBois, W. E. B., *Souls of Black Folk*

Equiano, Olaudah, *The Interesting Narrative and Other Writings*

Gore, Al, *Earth in the Balance: Ecology and the Human Spirit*

Grossman, Lawrence K., *Electronic Republic*

Hawthorne, Nathaniel, *The Scarlet Letter: A Romance*

Hutner, Gordon, *Immigrant Voices: Twenty-Four Narratives on Becoming an American*

Jacobs, Harriet, *Incidents in the Life of a Slave Girl*

Jen, Gish, *Typical American*

King, Martin Luther, Jr., *Why We Can't Wait*

Lewis, Sinclair, *Babbit*

Machiavelli, *The Prince*

Marx, Karl, *The Communist Manifesto*

Mill, Stuart John, *On Liberty*

More, Sir Thomas, *Utopia and Other Essential Writings*

Orwell, George, *1984*

Paine, Thomas, *Common Sense*

Plato, *The Republic*

Postman, Neil, *Amusing Ourselves to Death*

Rose, Mike, *Lives on the Boundary*

Rossiter, *The Federalist Papers*

Rousseau, Jean-Jaques, *The Social Contract*

Shelley, Mary, *Frankenstein*

Sinclair, Upton, *The Jungle*

St. Augustine, *The Confessions of St. Augustine*

Steinbeck, John, *Of Mice and Men*

Stevenson, Robert Louis, *The Strange Case of Dr. Jekyll and Mr. Hyde*

Stoker, Bram, *Dracula*

Stowe, Harriet Beecher, *Uncle Tom's Cabin*

Swift, Jonathan, *Gulliver's Travels*

Taulbert, Clifton L., *Once Upon a Time When We Were Colored*

Thoreau, Henry David, *Walden: Or, Life in the Woods* and *On the Duty of Civil Disobedience*

Truth, Sojourner, *The Narrative of Sojourner Truth*

Woolf, Virginia, *Jacob's Room*

Zola, Emile, *Germinal*